THE RESILIENT CITY

THE RESILIENT CITY

HOW MODERN CITIES RECOVER FROM DISASTER

LAWRENCE J. VALE AND THOMAS J. CAMPANELLA

EDITORS

OXFORD
UNIVERSITY PRESS

2005

OXFORD
UNIVERSITY PRESS

Oxford   New York
Auckland   Bangkok   Buenos Aires   Cape Town   Chennai
Dar es Salaam   Delhi   Hong Kong   Istanbul   Karachi   Kolkata
Kuala Lumpur   Madrid   Melbourne   Mexico City   Mumbai   Nairobi
São Paulo   Shanghai   Taipei   Tokyo   Toronto

Published by Oxford University Press, Inc.
198 Madison Avenue, New York, New York 10016

www.oup.com

Oxford is a registered trademark of Oxford University Press

Library of Congress Cataloging-in-Publication Data
The resilient city : how modern cities recover from disaster /
edited by Lawrence J. Vale and Thomas J. Campanella.
   p. cm.
Includes bibliographical references.
ISBN-13 978-0-19-517584-4; 978-0-19-517583-7 (pbk.)
ISBN 0-19-517584-0; 0-19-517583-2 (pbk.)
1. Urban renewal—History.   2. Disasters—History.   I. Vale, Lawrence J., 1959–
II. Campanella, Thomas J.
HT170.R46 2005
307.3'416'09—dc22   2004049246

9 8 7 6 5 4 3 2

Printed in the United States of America
on acid-free paper

Preface

■ There has already been a surfeit of books about September 11, 2001; this is not another one. But it is nonetheless a product of that fateful day, if only indirectly. As the enormity of that morning's tragedies unfolded, the two editors of this volume wandered incredulously between adjacent offices at the Massachusetts Institute of Technology (MIT), scrambling to gather new information about what was transpiring. In the days and weeks that followed, along with millions of Americans and people around the world, we struggled to make sense of what had taken place. One of us lost a childhood playmate, a former neighbor, fellow alumni from high school, a friend of a friend; the other lost an acquaintance and the relative of a friend, and we found that nearly all of our students were connected in some way to a victim of the terrorist attacks.

As urbanists and planners we were particularly shocked by the destruction of the World Trade Center. Yes, it was the ill-loved colossus that Wolf von Eckhardt decried (even before it was built) as "an instrument of urbicide,"[1] but the extreme violence of 9/11 muted even the harshest critics. Whatever we once thought about the buildings, we now mourned them and joined in the wide-ranging speculation about what they represented. For many, the terrorist attacks were an assault on the ideals of progress and modernity, the values of liberal democracy, the sanctity of human life, and the commitment to an open society that has made the United States the most free and culturally diverse nation in history. But they were also attacks on the city and all that cities represent.

We were particularly perturbed to learn that Mohammed Atta, reputed organizer of the hijacker gang that crashed the planes into the WTC and the Pentagon, had studied architecture and city planning in Germany. His advisor at the Technical University of Hamburg-Harburg claimed that Atta possessed a particularly keen interest in the history of cities and town planning.[2] He had spent several months in Cairo in 1995 documenting urban renewal efforts near the Old City's gates, and was angered by new commercial development that, he believed, "involved little more than knocking down a poor neighborhood to improve the views for tourists."[3] He feared that global capitalism was trivializing or obliterating historic landscapes in the Islamic world, a subject he explored in his master's thesis: "The Conflict between Islam and Modernization in Aleppo."

Atta's thesis subject was, ironically, one of the most resilient cities in history. The 4,000-year-old settlement, located in present-day Syria, has survived a bewildering array of disasters through the ages. A crossroads of trade routes since the second millennium B.C., the city was successively ruled by the Hittites, Assyrians, Arabs, Mongols, Mamelukes, and Ottomans. The Persians destroyed much of Aleppo in 540 A.D. It was besieged by the Crusaders in 1124 A.D. and invaded by the Mongols in 1260 A.D. Ninety percent of its population was killed in yet another attack in 1400 A.D. It was constantly plagued by the plague, destroyed by an earthquake in the 1820s, and even invaded by mice. Yet ancient Aleppo regenerated itself again and again, and flourishes still.[4]

It is this spirit of resilience that inspired the present book. We wanted to know what sorts of questions others had asked in the past when confronted with disaster, and how they had managed to persevere. By October 2001, we began planning for a colloquium, with a book to follow. The colloquium—"The Resilient City: Trauma, Recovery, and Remembrance"—was held weekly during the spring of 2002 at MIT, and drew a large and enthusiastic audience. Some of this attendance was virtual and global, thanks to the staff of the MIT World initiative, who filmed and digitized the content for download on the Resilient City Web site (http://web.mit.edu/dusp/resilientcity) and also linked it to the worldwide architectural community of ArchNet. We then solicited additional chapters to round out the contents of this anthology. The process of organizing and producing this book was, in the end, both a scholarly and a therapeutic exercise.

Many people deserve thanks for helping make this book possible. We are particularly grateful for the initial enthusiasm of William Mitchell, Anne Whiston Spirn, and Bish Sanyal, and for the generous financial support from the dean's office of the School of Architecture and Planning at MIT and the MIT chancellor's office. We are also grateful for fellowship funds provided by the Helena Rubinstein Foundation, which supported the travel and research for the book's chapters on Gernika and Tangshan.

We benefited enormously from the fifteen MIT students who participated in our parallel seminar on the urban design politics of resilient cities: Zabe Bent, Hope Fang, Jasper Goldman, Jessica Katz, Julie Kirschbaum, Aaron Koffman, Justine Minnis, Greg Morrow, Karl Munkelwitz, Keon-Soo Nam, Sonia Parisca, Jason Schupbach, Desirée Sideroff, Shinu Singh, and Florian Urban.

Our colleagues in the Departments of Architecture and Urban Studies and Planning at MIT and City and Regional Planning at the University of North Carolina, Chapel Hill, have offered perceptive criticism and advice throughout this project—especially Julian Beinart, Eran Ben-Joseph, Phil Berke, Ray Burby, Phil Clay, Diane Davis, Bob Fogelson, Dennis Frenchman, Dave Godschalk, Mark Jarzombek, Bill Mitchell, Bish Sanyal, and Anne Whiston Spirn.

Laurie Everett, project manager at MIT World, helped make our colloquium presentations available on the Internet, as did Alexis Sanal, who designed and built the Resilient City Web site. Gaurav Srivastava and Melissa McMahon assisted with literature reviews, and Janice O'Brien's organizational skills helped to keep both the editors and the contributors on track. Duncan Kincaid and John Cook helped with the processing of many illustrations, and Karen Yegian assisted with numerous financial matters. Susan Ferber, our editor at Oxford University Press, deserves our special gratitude for championing this book early on and for her superb editorial attention to the many voices of this manuscript. We are also grateful for additional editorial assistance from Stacey Hamilton and Merryl Sloane. Finally, our own resilience has been carefully nurtured by the love, support, and encouragement of our families and friends.

Notes

1. Quoted in Michael Tomasky, "The World Trade Center: Before, During, and After," *New York Review of Books*, 28 March 2002, 18.
2. Liz Jackson, "A Mission to Die For: Interview with Dittmar Machule, 18 October, 2001," *ABC Four Corners*, 12 November 2001.
3. Jim Yardley, "A Portrait of the Terrorist," *New York Times*, 10 October 2001.
4. Alexander Russell, *The Natural History of Aleppo*, vol. 2 (London: Robinson, 1794), 335–361.

Contents

Contents

Contributors

Julian Beinart is professor of architecture at MIT, where he teaches classes on the theory of city form as well as urban design studios. He holds a BArch from the University of Cape Town, an MArch from MIT, and an M.C.P. from Yale University.

Thomas J. Campanella is assistant professor in the Department of City and Regional Planning at the University of North Carolina, Chapel Hill. He was previously a lecturer at the Massachusetts Institute of Technology and a Fulbright fellow at the Chinese University of Hong Kong. Campanella received his Ph.D. from MIT and M.L.A. from Cornell University. He has consulted on urban design and planning projects in China, South Korea, Thailand, and Hong Kong and is a frequent contributor to *Wired*, *Architectural Record*, *Salon*, *Metropolis*, and other periodicals. His books include *Republic of Shade: New England and the American Elm* and *Cities from the Sky: An Aerial Portrait of America*.

Beatrice Chen is curator of education at the Museum of Chinese in the Americas in New York City. She received a B.A. in history and international studies from Yale University, an Ed.M. from Harvard Graduate School of Education, and an M.C.P. from MIT.

Diane E. Davis is professor of political sociology in the Department of Urban Studies and Planning at MIT. She is the author of *Urban Leviathan: Mexico City in the Twentieth Century* and *Discipline and Development*. In addition to her extensive writings on the history and politics of urbanization and urban social movements in Mexico, Davis has published articles on local governance, leftist mayors, and democratic transition in Latin America.

William Fulton is a journalist, urban planner, researcher, pundit, and author. He is president of Solimar Research Group, a public policy research firm. He is the author of *The Reluctant Metropolis: The Politics of Urban Growth in Los Angeles* and one of the principal authors of *Sprawl Hits the Wall*, a report on the future of Los Angeles. He holds a B.A. in mass communications from St. Bonaventure University, an M.A. in journalism and public affairs from American University, and an M.A. in urban planning from UCLA.

Jasper Goldman, an urbanist and filmmaker, was born and raised in London, England, and studied history at Oxford University and city planning at MIT, where he produced a documentary film on the physical transformation of Beijing. His other film productions include *Reflex* and *The Truck*, an adaptation of a short story by Polish author Ryszard Kapuscinski.

Carola Hein is assistant professor at Bryn Mawr College in the Growth and Structure of Cities Program. She trained in Hamburg (Diplom-Ingenieurin) and Brussels (Architecte) and obtained her doctorate at the Hochschule für bildende Künste in Hamburg in 1995. She is co-editor of *Rebuilding Urban Japan after 1945*.

Julie B. Kirschbaum studied art and architectural history and international relations at Brown University and holds master's degrees in city planning and in transportation from MIT, where she was an Eisenhower fellow. She is a senior transportation planner for the San Francisco County Transportation Authority.

Brian Ladd is a historian and former fellow of the American Academy in Berlin. He holds a Ph.D. from Yale University and is the author of *The Ghosts of Berlin: Confronting German History in the Urban Landscape* and *Urban Planning and Civic Order in Germany, 1860–1914*, as well as several recent articles on East German urban planning. He has also completed a documentary film on Berlin.

Edward T. Linenthal is the Edward M. Penson Professor of Religion and American Culture and the Chancellor's Public Scholar at the University of Wisconsin, Oshkosh. His books include *Sacred Ground: Americans and their Battlefields, Preserving Memory: The Struggle to Create America's Holocaust Museum, History Wars: The Enola Gay and Other Battles for the American Past*, co-edited with Tom Engelhardt, and *The Unfinished Bombing: Oklahoma City in American Memory*.

William J. Mitchell is director of the Program on Media Arts and Sciences at MIT, where he formerly served as dean of the School of Architecture and Planning. He holds a BArch from the University of Melbourne, an M.Ed. from Yale University, and an M.A. from Cambridge University. His books include *City of Bits: Space, Place, and the Infobahn, e-topia: Urban Life, Jim—But Not as We Know It*, and *ME++: The Cyborg Self and the Network City*.

Max Page is associate professor of architecture and history at the University of Massachusetts, Amherst, where he teaches urban, architectural, and public history. He is the author of *The Creative Destruction of Manhattan, 1900–1940*, which won the Spiro Kostof Award of the Society of Architectural Historians. He is the co-editor (with Steven Conn) of *Building the Nation: Americans Write Their Architecture, Their Cities, and Their Environment* and co-author (with Randall Mason) of *Giving Preserving a History: Histories of Historic Preservation in the United States*.

Anthony S. Pitch is the author of *The Burning of Washington: The British Invasion of 1814*. He was a journalist in England, Africa, and Israel before becoming Associated Press broadcast editor in Philadelphia and a senior writer in the books division of *U.S. News & World Report* in Washington. He holds a B.A. from Rhodes University, South Africa.

Kevin Rozario is assistant professor in the American Studies Program at Smith College. He holds a Ph.D. in history from Yale University and has previously taught at Oberlin and Wellesley colleges. He is the author of "What Comes Down Must Go Up: Why Disasters Have Been Good for American Capitalism" (which appeared in Steven Biel, ed., *American Disasters*) and is completing a book entitled *Nature's Evil Dreams: Disaster and the Making of Modern America*.

Hashim Sarkis is Aga Khan Professor of Landscape Architecture and Urbanism in Muslim Societies at the Harvard Design School and a practicing architect in Lebanon. He is executive editor of *CASE*, a publication series of case studies in architecture and urbanism, author of *Circa 1958: Lebanon in the Plans and Photographs of Constantinos Doxiadis*, and co-editor, with Peter G. Rowe, of *Projecting Beirut*. He received his BArch and B.F.A. from the Rhode Island School of Design, his MArch from the Harvard Graduate School of Design, and his Ph.D. in architecture from Harvard University.

Desirée Sideroff is an urban designer with Moore Iacofano Goltsman, in Berkeley, California. She holds a master's degree in city planning from MIT and an undergraduate degree from the University of California, Berkeley.

Anthony M. Townsend is a research scientist at the Taub Urban Research Center at New York University's Robert F. Wagner Graduate School of Public Service. He is the author of more than a dozen scholarly articles and book chapters on the impacts of new information and communications technologies on urban and regional development. He holds a Ph.D. from the Department of Urban Studies and Planning at MIT.

Lawrence J. Vale is professor and head of the Department of Urban Studies and Planning at MIT. He holds an undergraduate degree from Amherst College, the SMArchS degree from MIT, and a DPhil from the University of Oxford. His books include *The Limits of Civil Defence*, *Architecture, Power, and National Identity*, *From the Puritans to the Projects: Public Housing and Public Neighbors*, *Imaging the City*, co-edited with Sam Bass Warner, Jr., and *Reclaiming Public Housing*. He has been a Rhodes scholar and a Guggenheim fellow, a recipient of the Chester Rapkin Award from the Association of Collegiate Schools of Planning, and winner of a Place Research Award from the Environmental Design Research Association.

Contributors

THE RESILIENT CITY

Introduction
The Cities Rise Again

■ Whoever penned the Latin maxim *Sic transit gloria mundi* (thus passes the glory of the world) was likely not an urbanist. Although cities have been destroyed throughout history—sacked, shaken, burned, bombed, flooded, starved, irradiated, and poisoned—they have, in almost every case, risen again like the mythic phoenix. As one painstakingly thorough statistical survey determined, only forty-two cities worldwide were permanently abandoned following destruction between the years 1100 and 1800.[1] By contrast, cities such as Baghdad, Moscow, Aleppo, Mexico City, and Budapest lost between 60 and 90 percent of their populations due to wars during this period, yet they were rebuilt and eventually rebounded. After about 1800, such resilience became a nearly universal fact of urban settlement around the globe. The tenacity of the urban life force inspired one of Rudyard Kipling's most famous poems:

Cities and Thrones and Powers
   Stand in Time's eye,
Almost as long as flowers,
   Which daily die:
But, as new buds put forth
   To glad new men,
Out of the spent and unconsidered Earth,
   The Cities rise again.[2]

LAWRENCE J. VALE

THOMAS J. CAMPANELLA

3

There have been some exceptions, Kipling notwithstanding. One of these is St. Pierre, Martinique—once known as "the Paris of the Antilles." On May 8, 1902, the eruption of Mount Pelée buried the city under pyroclastic lava flows. Nearly 30,000 residents and visitors perished; only one man survived, a prisoner in solitary confinement.[3] St. Pierre was not a resilient city. Yet one is hard-pressed to think of other cities that have not recovered. Atlanta, Columbia, and Richmond all survived the devastation wrought by the American Civil War and remain state capitals today. Chicago emerged stronger than ever following the 1871 fire, as did San Francisco from the earthquake and fires of 1906. We still have Hiroshima and Nagasaki, despite the horrors of nuclear attack. Both Dresden and Coventry have been rebuilt. Warsaw lost 61 percent of its 1.3 million residents during World War II, yet surpassed its prewar population by 1967. Even as the war still raged, farsighted planners and designers surreptitiously assembled voluminous documentation of the city that the Nazis were systematically dismembering. After the war, they painstakingly (if creatively) replicated the exteriors of hundreds of buildings in the Old Town and New Town, while modernizing the interiors. They retained the old surface street pattern, while routing a major expressway under the city center.[4]

Most dramatic of all, perhaps, is the story of Tangshan, China. Here, northeast of Beijing, a massive earthquake in 1976 killed at least 240,000 people—maybe more than twice this number—in a city of 1 million. Within a decade, Chinese officials rebuilt the city in a maze of six-story concrete housing projects.[5] In January 2002, while the world was watching battles over Afghanistan, half of the Congolese city of Goma (population 400,000) disappeared under lava, yet few suggest that the city will relocate.[6] Does anyone doubt that Kabul and Kandahar—or Baghdad and Basra—will also reemerge, once protracted fighting finally comes to a close?

There are other facets to the resilience phenomenon. Even as contemporary places rebuild following devastation, many of the places destroyed in more distant eras—Roman cities such as Pompeii or Algeria's Timgad or the pre-Columbian settlements of the Americas—persist in a different mode. Such "lost cities" are recovered as sites for tourism, education, remembrance, or even myth. Even St. Pierre survives as a town of 5,000 persons, a tourable set of ruins, and a volcano museum.

Introduction

Less innocently, building and rebuilding have often been tied to attempts to control and manipulate meanings. Mussolini excavated ancient monuments and ripped new axial roads through the heart of Rome in an explicit effort to rival ancient glories; Hitler and Speer plotted to replace Berlin with a Germania scaled to dwarf past empires; Saddam Hussein even recreated Babylon, undeterred by scant archaeological remains.[7]

Subjected to everything from earthquakes to smart bombs, cities are among humankind's most durable artifacts. Whether they are reconstructed to accommodate and restore ongoing urban life or rebuilt to serve as sites for periodic visitation and commemoration, it has become exceedingly rare for a major city to be truly or permanently lost.

Just why this should be so—and why the rate of resilience seems to have increased since 1800 even though the mechanisms for destruction have multiplied—is not entirely obvious. Is there a link to the rise of the nation-state or to the spread of capitalism? How central is the growth of the insurance industry? What is the role of international aid organizations or globally disseminated media? Why, precisely, do cities get rebuilt? The purpose of this book is to begin a process of broad comparative inquiry on these and other questions. Our central intellectual challenge is to develop a framework for understanding both the commonalities and the significant differences inherent in the vast array of post-disaster urbanism. In what follows, we explore the question engaged by this book's subtitle: How do modern cities recover from disaster?

Urban disaster, like urban resilience, takes many forms, and can be categorized in many ways. First, there is the scale of destruction, which may range from a small single precinct to an entire city (or, potentially, an even larger area). Second, these disasters can be viewed in terms of their human toll, as measured by deaths and disruption of lives. Third, these destructive acts can be conceptualized according to their presumed cause—some result from largely uncontrollable forces of nature, such as earthquakes and tsunamis; others from combinations of natural forces and human action, such as fires; still others result from deliberate human will, whether executed by conquering armies, a flight of enemy bombers, or a lone terrorist. Sometimes, social and political disasters are even self-inflicted, usually by regimes seeking drastic over-

Chart I-1. A Typology of Disaster

Type of Disaster	Cause of Damage/Death	Example
Natural Disasters		
Fire	Burning	Chicago, 1871
		London, 1666
Earthquake	Structural Collapse/Fire	S.F., 1906
		Tangshan, 1976
Flood/Tidal Wave	Drowning	Lisbon, 1755
Drought	Starvation	Nyala, Sudan, 2000
Volcano	Lava Flows	St. Pierre, 1902
		Pompeii, 79 A.D.
Hurricane/Typhoon	Illness/Collapse	Chittagong, 1970
Epidemic Disease	Illness	Plague, Mid-14th Century
Human Disasters		
Accidental		
Industrial Accidents/Sabotage	Poisoning	Bhopal, 1984
Nuclear Accidents	Radiation	Chernobyl, 1986
Deliberate, Place-Targeted		
Civil War	Bombing/Gunfire	Beirut, 1980s
	Arson	Atlanta, 1864
	Biological Weapons	
	Chemical Weapons	
International War	Bombing/Gunfire	World War I/World War II
	Nuclear Weapons	Hiroshima, 1945
	Biological Weapons	
	Chemical Weapons	
International Terrorism	Explosives	
	Hijacked Planes	WTC Attack, 2001
	Biological Weapons	
	Chemical Weapons	
	Nuclear Weapons	
Domestic Terrorist Campaign	Explosives	Okla. City, 1995
	Biological Weapons	
	Chemical Weapons	Halabja, Iraq, 1988
	Nuclear Weapons	
Riots/Civil Disturbances	Gunfire/Arson	U.S. Cities, 1960s
		L.A., 1992
Urban Renewal/Clearance	Displacement	U.S. Cities, 1950s/1960s

haul as a means to promote massive, rapid modernization. Finally, there are economic disasters—triggered by demographic change, a major accident, or an industrial or commercial crisis—that may contribute to massive population flight, diminishing investment in infrastructure and buildings, perhaps even large-scale abandonment. This latter variety of disaster—epitomized by the significant post-1950 population declines endured by many American Rust Belt cities, such as Detroit—often results from a cluster of traumatic episodes, rather than a single disaster. Protracted socioeconomic decay makes urban resilience exceptionally difficult to sustain. This book, focused as it is on more sudden or episodic forms of disruption, therefore stops short of considering this sort of attenuated trauma. Still, socioeconomic consequences pervade any discussion of post-disaster recovery, so such matters remain a salient feature in every chapter in this volume.

Disasters vary greatly by scale and by source, and there are significant differences within these categories. Some large-scale disasters have inflicted widespread and massive damage to buildings, but resulted in relatively little loss of life—examples include the Great Fire of London in 1666, the sacking of previously evacuated cities, the rioting in and burning of neighborhoods over civil rights issues, and even the controlled neighborhood destruction carried out under the auspices of urban renewal programs. Although this last sort of intentional disruption to the urban fabric does not usually result in deaths, its psychic injuries are often profound, as illustrated by Marc Fried's classic essay, "Grieving for a Lost Home," which examined the losses suffered by those displaced from Boston's West End.[8] At the other extreme, large-scale urban destruction has, suddenly and simultaneously, killed tens or even hundreds of thousands of humans. Alternatively, relatively concentrated destruction—if deliberately chosen to target densely inhabited areas—can produce massive casualties, while leaving surrounding built areas physically intact. Finally, there is the possibility of destruction by biological or chemical agents or nuclear fallout—mechanisms that may kill urban civilian populations without directly affecting the built environment at all, not unlike the Black Death of earlier eras.

In any of these broad scenarios, the impact of urban destruction is not necessarily proportional to the scale of attack. Rather, impact is largely a function of the meaning a disaster holds for survivors—even those who live at some distance from the epicenter of the physical destruction. In this sense, trauma persists long after the physical impacts of a disaster have been repaired. Certainly, many individual citizens suffer long-term emotional effects from disasters, but it is also possible to regard cities, themselves, as traumatized. A traumatized city endures not only physical injury and economic hardship but also damage to its image. In the case of the September 11, 2001, terrorist attacks on the United States—an event that unified the nation, however briefly—the symbolic resonance was nearly as strong 2,000 miles from Ground Zero as in lower Manhattan. To some extent, the broader impact of a disaster is rendered in economic terms—the ripple effects of disruption to commerce and investment in surrounding areas or, increasingly, to global markets. Beyond this, in cases where destruction has been brought to bear on places of particularly resonant symbolism, a disaster exposes and unleashes the contested politics of local power struggles and global interconnections.

The perceived source of a given disaster also profoundly affects urban resilience. In cases where the sources of destruction are largely natural forces ("acts of God"), urban populations receive both sympathy and humanitarian assistance, often accompanied by warnings (usually unheeded) against rebuilding in locations deemed vulnerable to repeat instances of similar destruction. Such cycles are epitomized by the portrait of Los Angeles rendered by Mike Davis in *Ecology of Fear*.[9] Even though particular urban patterns and building practices are often deeply implicated in the causes of destruction, we often *perceive* these kinds of urban calamities to result from nonhuman agency. At the opposite extreme, history is replete with examples of cities literally overrun by human forces. The destruction of cities is seen as the means to effect political change and to demonstrate conclusively that it has been carried out. From the mosque/cathedral of Cordoba to Jerusalem's Temple Mount, the skylines of cities reveal the processes of symbolic succession. We can observe who is in power—and who is not—by examining closely what gets built. For many long-inhabited cities, this succession is layered into the landscape.

Over the course of the last century, it has become increasingly possible to inflict major destruction on cities without actually conquering them. War-at-a-distance moved beyond long-distance artillery to encompass aerial bombardment and missile attacks, unleashing massive firestorms and weapons of mass destruction. After hundreds of years of wars in which military forces usually suffered the brunt of casualties, in the last several decades, civilian populations have often become both the principal targets and the principal victims of warfare and attacks. With this increased spatial discontinuity between attacker and attacked, it becomes possible for destruction to occur without warning and even without identification of its perpetrator. At the opposite extreme, however, cities continue to be battlegrounds. Urban warfare is one of the hottest areas of military science today, in which a range of "engagement options" are studied, from raids and embassy evacuations, to "sustained urban combat."[10]

This book investigates diverse examples of urban disaster and recovery, but it is also a search for unexpected commonalities. By studying historical examples, we can learn the pressing questions that have been asked in the past as cities and their residents struggled to rebuild. This enables us to explore the full richness of the design politics entailed by reconstruction. Such a design politics takes two intertwined forms: a politics of symbolic succession and a politics of institutional processes. How has the symbolic power of the built environment been used as both a magnet for attack and as a signal of recovery? What does each particular process of recovery reveal about the balance of power in the society seeking to rebuild? Whose vision for the future gets built, and why?

Although there are many case studies of post-disaster reconstruction in individual cities, until very recently few scholars have attempted cross-cultural comparisons, and even fewer have attempted to compare urban resilience in the face of natural disasters with resilience following human-inflicted catastrophes, such as wars or terrorist attacks.[11]

Comparing a diverse sample of traumatized cities on a single chart presents a somewhat daunting challenge. Chart I.2 plots responses to two commonly asked questions about disasters: How many people died? and How much was destroyed? Both questions yield crude and incomplete measures of trauma, but they do reveal striking differences in the scale and nature of major world tragedies. In its horizontal dimension, the chart necessarily makes use of a logarithmic scale to measure loss of life. The results—however depressing—reveal a wealth of information. We can see that only a handful of people died in the Great

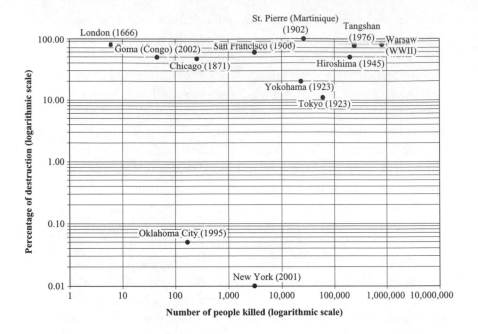

Chart I.2.
Traumatized Cities

Fire of London, even though 80 percent of the City was destroyed. By contrast, when an earthquake leveled a similar portion of Tangshan, the death toll reached at least a quarter of a million, and the city of Warsaw, also 80 percent destroyed, lost 800,000 of its 1.3 million residents during the course of World War II. Seen in this broader context, terrorist attacks in Oklahoma City (1995) and New York (2001) appear as a strikingly different sort of phenomenon, since their horrific destruction and loss of life were so concentrated into small portions of large cities. Even though we continue to speak of these events in relation to cities, they were of course attacks on buildings. This is not meant to minimize their impact, but serves as a reminder that American cities—at least the post-Columbian ones—have thankfully never faced the scale of trauma implied by the upper-right reaches of this chart.

Such a chart, while undeniably provocative, raises many questions of method and metrics. Seemingly straightforward questions of How many people died? and How much was destroyed? fail to elicit simple answers. In many cases, death tolls are disputed or never fully calculated—often for politically motivated reasons. Moreover, a focus on

Introduction

death misses the broader range of injury and illness that is traumatic but not fatal, including the persistent ripples of psychological devastation faced by survivors and all those who are physically removed from the disaster, yet nonetheless consider themselves to be victims. Similarly, it is difficult to account for destruction. One can count buildings, but this does no justice to the complexities of urban form and begs the question of when a given structure counts as wholly destroyed. Alternatively, one can speak of the percentage of a built-up area that has been damaged. Here, too, it is difficult to obtain reputable and consistent data, since there is again no consensus on what constitutes a threshold of destruction. Moreover, to speak in percentage terms demands clarity as to a proper context for measuring destruction: percentage of what? or, more precisely, percentage of where?

Is Manhattan the relevant urban denominator of the World Trade Center destruction, or is it New York City as a whole, or is it the broader tristate region? Such questions may matter little: in any case we are talking about less than a thousandth of the area in question. In a world city of high rents and global interconnectedness, destruction is measured in dollars (and euros) rather than acres. The trauma of September 11, 2001, was inflicted on the viability of local businesses, on the lower Manhattan class-A office supply, on the New York City tourist trade, on the infrastructure of regional transportation, on the insurance industry, and on countless other directly and indirectly connected aspects of life in the New York region and beyond. In short, even if the numbers on this chart are reasonably accurate, they only begin to hint at the nature and scale of devastation that their shorthand connotes. A world war, by definition, is forced upon a global audience but, increasingly, even smaller disasters attract worldwide attention because of where they take place and what they symbolize. Many tragic events have exceeded the destruction and death tolls inflicted on 9/11, but the impact of these attacks brought near-instantaneous visibility in global media. From television screens to the front pages of newspapers, locally and worldwide, the searing images were disseminated everywhere. The World Trade Center housed workers and hosted visitors from all corners of the world. Destroying them not only eviscerated a key symbol of New York but hit at—and highlighted—the global economy itself.

Assessing Recovery

■ It is also important to consider the vexed question of recovery. What does it mean for a city to recover? It all depends on what and who we mean when we say "city," and on what we mean by "recovery." Can "the city" be defined by its buildings and its infrastructure? Clearly, this is part of the answer, but hardly sufficient. Cities, intrinsically, are distinguished by the relative density of residents, cultural institutions, and opportunities for commerce, so recovery must also entail some sort of return to normalcy in the human terms of social and economic relations, even if that so-called normalcy merely replicates and extends the inequities of the pre-disaster past. Is it sufficient to say that a city has recovered when its aggregate population returns to pre-disaster levels? In some cases, where the toll of death and displacement has been high, the numerical resilience of the population may be a reasonable proxy for recovery. For cities that have lost huge percentages of their populations, the restoration of the city as a place of habitation is itself a signal achievement. Others will judge recovery through different sorts of mindsets, conditioned by both professional training and by personal attachment to places and people. Economists will look toward restoration of economic activity; transportation planners will seek measures of local and regional traffic flows; designers will look for the healing of streetscapes and the advent of new buildings and memorials; psychologists, clergy, and schoolteachers will make assessments of emotional well-being. Those who can resist such professional frames will view recovery as an ongoing search for a "new normal."

The process of post-disaster recovery is a window into the power structure of the society that has been stricken. Understanding the meaning of urban disasters therefore entails more than examining the various institutions every society sets up to manage recovery. These institutions—such as civil defense organizations, law enforcement agencies, charities, insurance brokers, and victims compensation funds—are certainly vital aspects of urban resilience. Yet the broad cultural question of recovery is more than a problem of "disaster management," however daunting and important that may be. What we call "recovery" is also driven by value-laden questions about equity. Who sets the priorities for the recovering communities? How are the needs of low-income residents valued in relation to the pressing claims of disrupted businesses? Who decides what will be rebuilt where, and which voices carry forth the dominant narratives that interpret what transpires? Who gets displaced when new facilities are constructed in the name of recovery? What roles do nonlocal agencies, national disaster-assistance policies, and international relief organizations have in setting guidelines for reconstruction? How can urban leaders overcome the lingering stigma inflicted by their city's victimization? What place is there for visionary architecture and long-range planning? In trying to answer these questions, this book searches out and assesses the full range of forces that work to rebuild the post-disaster city and its institutions.

Memorializing Disaster

■ Architects, artists, and urban designers tend to regard themselves as having some special jurisdiction over another key aspect of recovery from disaster: the question of how a disaster should be interpreted and commemorated. To analyze remembrance is to look at how what is remembered gets selected, when, and by whom. Clearly, there is some process by which direct recall is supplanted by memorialization, abstraction, and metaphor. There is a large and growing literature on the clinical psychology of trauma and post-traumatic stress but such issues are not a major focus of this book. Nor do we focus in any depth on the struggles faced by designers of memorials, who must cope with these questions in their work. Although this book certainly engages the internal processes of coping with major loss and explores the aesthetic challenges faced by artists and architects working in emotionally charged environments, its focus is on the social, political, and design processes that play out at the scales of neighborhoods, cities, and regions.

Still, the planning process is thoroughly infused with questions of remembrance. Formal memorials may take years to come to fruition, but the process of remembrance begins almost instantly. Published in the fall of 2001, American cultural historian Edward Linenthal's *The Unfinished Bombing: Oklahoma City in American Memory* narrates the aftermath of the April 19, 1995, terrorist attack on the Murrah Federal Building and proposes three parallel modes for coming to terms with such a traumatic event. First is what Linenthal calls the *progressive narrative*, in which emphasis is placed on the heroic efforts of recovery. This spirit animates many dominant messages: multiple forms of patriotic display, adulation of rescue workers, and calls for accelerated schedules of rebuilding. In faith-centered Oklahoma, Linenthal also identified a second mode, the *redemptive narrative*, in which survivors and their clergy view massive public trauma in explicitly religious terms, regarding themselves as a "remnant community" in search of renewal and redemption. Finally, Linenthal pays special attention to what he calls the *toxic narrative*, the stories of those who have found no solace in either progress or faith. As Linenthal puts it: "Discordant but related stories continue to be lived out: a song celebrating the heroic saga of rescue and response, a prayer for transcendence amid the rubble, and a lament from those for whom April 19 is always today."[12]

The term *resilient city* implies finality, but it is always coupled with an ongoing recovery process that, for many people, will never quite end. It seems a mistake to view the resilience of cities in terms of any such search for "closure." Rather, the goal should be productive openness, an ability to structure and confront the contradictory impulses inherent in the contested processes of recovery and remembrance. The challenge for planners and designers is to navigate between the extremes of triumphalism and despair. We don't always get over traumatic events, but we do get through them. This, too, is a form of resilience, and it is the spirit in which this book was conceived and written.

Structure of the Book

■ The book is organized around three interrelated principal themes: the narratives of resilience, the symbolic dimensions of disaster and recovery, and the politics of reconstruction. To understand urban resilience is to understand the ways that narratives are constructed to interpret the meanings of urban reconstruction. Such narratives, often contested, link the physical reconstruction of buildings—as places and as symbols—to the politically charged restoration of devastated social communities.

Part I, "Narratives of Resilience," explores the ways that humans assemble stories to explain or inspire processes of recovery. Resilience narratives are constructed collective voices that expose a longing to render tragedy in uplifting terms or to append a spiritual or faith-based element to the suffering at hand. Or, as in some American cases, these narratives evoke themes of forbearance and discipline in the face of adversity. The chapters in part I examine the ways that sudden devastating events can become reframed as opportunities for progress and positive change. Even though many affected individuals and groups cling to alternative accounts of events that do not permit such forward-looking interpretations, the resilience of cities has depended on a progressive-oriented dominant narrative, one that views the devastation and rebuilding of cities as no more than an extreme version of capitalism's usual processes of "creative destruction." It is not enough to recognize resilience narratives; they must also be scrutinized: whose story is being told, and who is being left out of the picture?

In chapter 1, "Making Progress: Disaster Narratives and the Art of Optimism in Modern America," cultural historian Kevin Rozario looks closely at the era bracketed by the Great Chicago Fire of 1871 and the San Francisco earthquake and fires of 1906. His careful attention to the progress-oriented narratives constructed to interpret the meaning of disasters demonstrates how such stories form an essential part of any attempt to interpret the nature of urban resilience. Rozario stresses the cultural emergence of new ways to view calamity as a disguised blessing. Formulaic disaster narratives promulgated an "official culture of optimism," reassuring Americans that each upheaval would have a happy ending, while inspiring hard work and capital commitment toward a new urban environment. But these narratives also tended to serve a narrowly bourgeois vision of order and stimulated a morbid preoccupation with spectacle, a fascination that found renewed parallels in the initial American responses to the events of 9/11.

In chapter 2, " 'The Predicament of Aftermath': Oklahoma City and September 11," Edward Linenthal explores the parallels—and disjunctures—between the 1995 terrorist bombing and those traumas unleashed on Manhattan, Washington, D.C., and Pennsylvania six years later. In each case, Linenthal argues, a narrative of civic renewal served as a comforting way to frame mass atrocity. Many commentators adopted familiar religious themes of death and rebirth or argued for rebuilding as an act of protest. Linenthal also engages the issue of re-membrance, analyzing the immediate urge to memorialize. This takes several forms: spontaneously generated memorials at the sites of trauma, commodification of memorabilia, veneration of debris, and elaborate processes of deliberation over the design and siting of me-morials that reveal a hierarchy of privileged voices and unleash pre-dictable resentments among various bereaved communities. In this way, despite the dominant progressive narrative of resilience, questions of recovery and remembrance remain contested.

In chapter 3, "The City's End: Past and Present Narratives of New York's Destruction," urban historian Max Page situates the 9/11 attack on the World Trade Center in the context of New York's history as a place seemingly destined to be destroyed and rebuilt with striking reg-ularity. He discusses the city's resilience in the face of more than two centuries of wide-ranging sudden disasters and compares those de-structive episodes to the equally frequent fictional efforts by artists, writers, and filmmakers to imagine still more outrageous forms of dev-astation. Many works that seemingly revel in invented disaster none-theless contain a final coda of optimism. Page concludes by examining the early efforts to rebuild on the World Trade Center site and questions what form resilience will take in New York.

Seen together, the three chapters of part I demonstrate both the power and the seeming ubiquity of resilience narratives, as well as the importance of narratives that run counter to dominant beliefs. But cities are far more than the words used to describe them. Any full account of urban resilience must come to terms with the ways that the actual physical substance of places remains central to the stories we create to interpret recovery. Those buildings and infrastructure that have been destroyed and get rebuilt are both targets of disaster and rallying points for recovery.

Part II of this book, "The Symbolic Dimensions of Disaster and Recovery," examines the extent to which urban disaster and recovery are driven and signaled by a succession of highly symbolic actions. At least in cases where humans—rather than forces of nature—have per-petrated destructive acts, they often choose targets for their symbolic value, deliberately destroying places of greatest cultural impact. Simi-larly, in the course of rebuilding, city leaders also emphasize particular high-profile projects, designed to show their fellow citizens—as well as a wider world—that their city has come back stronger than ever. This reliance on urban design as an index of resurrected power is one part of the broader political agenda of urban resilience.

In chapter 4, historian Anthony Pitch takes us back to the only city in the United States ever attacked by the forces of a foreign nation: Washington, D.C., in 1814. His essay, "Patriotism and the Reconstruction of Washington, D.C., after the British Invasion of 1814," demonstrates the clear appeal of symbolic targets to would-be attackers. Pitch reveals how the British invaders carefully chose to plunder precisely those buildings that bore the greatest symbolic importance to the upstart republic: the White House, Capitol, State and War departments, and the Treasury. In the wake of the attack, Washington nearly lost its raison d'être, as Philadelphia, New York, Lancaster, and other cities vied for the honor of becoming the national capital. Pitch's chapter traces the confluence of patriotism and politics that enabled the city's proponents to reconstruct the destroyed symbols of Washington and ensure its survival as the seat of government.

In chapter 5, "Double Restoration: Rebuilding Berlin after 1945," historian Brian Ladd takes up the complicated story of German reconstruction following World War II. Ladd focuses on the understandable desire for historical continuity and reconstruction, coupled with the urgent need for a clearly visible break from the immediate Nazi past. Moreover, the city was soon divided between two ideologically opposed regimes in the East and West, each determined to claim the legacy of pre-Nazi Berlin, to display the clearer break with Hitler, and to prove its cultural and political superiority. Under these thorny circumstances, the rebuilding of Berlin became one of the most visible venues of the early Cold War. From the Hansa quarter of the West to the Stalinallee of the East, each major architectural project was clad in ideology.

In chapter 6, "Warsaw: Reconstruction as Propaganda," urban planner and filmmaker Jasper Goldman explores the design politics of the Polish capital's rebirth from the massive devastation of World War II. He focuses on the efforts to construct new symbolic structures and to recast old symbols in ideologically appropriate ways. From the methods of "architectural censorship" employed in the selective reconstruction of the Old Town to the controversies over the restoration of the royal castle; from vast new housing estates and industrial development on nationalized land to the hulking Soviet-style Palace of Culture and

Science, Goldman assesses the array of efforts by the Polish regime (and its Russian overseers) to reestablish Polish identity in a manner consistent with socialist principles. The design politics of a reconstructed Warsaw thereby pursued a triple objective: exalting the achievements of workers and modernist housing estates; deriding the inadequacies and inequities of prewar capitalist residential quarters; and celebrating the nationalist aspirations of the Polish people. Although the tale of Polish resilience is a classic of the genre, Goldman's chapter adds additional dimensions to the story by examining the ways that more recent Polish political freedoms have prompted new interpretations of the buildings and memorials from the Soviet-dominated past.

In chapter 7, "A Delayed Healing: Understanding the Fragmented Resilience of Gernika," city planners Julie B. Kirschbaum and Desirée Sideroff take up a much less well-known story of urban resilience—the protracted struggle by citizens of a Basque town to recover from the devastation of aerial bombardment during the Spanish Civil War. Famous as the inspiration for Picasso's landmark painting about the horrors of war, the town held no military or tactical significance, yet was destroyed on market day by the German Luftwaffe on April 26, 1937, with Franco's assent. By demolishing this symbolic center of Basque culture, Franco sought to destroy morale as well as buildings. Although the Spanish substantially rebuilt the town soon afterward (for which Franco took full credit), political repression continued for decades, imposing clear limits on recovery. For Kirschbaum and Sideroff, the saga of Gernika highlights the separation between the physical resilience of reconstruction and the more attenuated efforts to attain emotional and cultural recovery.

In chapter 8, architect Julian Beinart considers the case of Jerusalem, arguably the most destroyed and rebuilt city in history. "Resurrecting Jerusalem" traces ideas about resilience in the stories and laws of Jewish, Christian, and Muslim texts, and uses these to interpret four of the city's major shrines: the built and imagined temples of the Jews, destroyed and never rebuilt; the Christian Church of the Holy Sepulchre, frequently destroyed but constantly rebuilt; the Muslim buildings on the Haram al-Sharif, threatened but never destroyed by human hands; and the Hurva synagogue, twice destroyed, and not yet rebuilt, despite proposals by distinguished architects. Beinart concludes with a series of general principles about the resilience of buildings, derived from both the religious and architectural evidence of Jerusalem.

Taken collectively, the five chapters of part II make clear that the symbolic dimensions of disaster and recovery cannot be separated from political history. Even as buildings and memorials become the touchstones of memory and identity, they are also implicated in larger social, cultural, and political processes. Resilience, whether in Gernika or Warsaw, Berlin or Jerusalem, Washington or New York, is always contested.

Part III, "The Politics of Reconstruction," views urban recovery through a broader lens of urban development. Through examining the processes of urban reconstruction—the choices made about who recovers which parts of cities for whose benefit—these chapters reveal the conflict-riddled nature of resilience. Sometimes resilience is carefully cultivated by dominant public authorities seeking renewed legitimacy; at other times an urban disaster serves as an occasion to demonstrate the resilience of ordinary citizens, determined to use traumatic events as a means to redirect the balance of power in their society. No two cities have recovered in precisely the same way, as a variety of social, economic, and cultural factors determine the path and timing of the recovery process. Resilience is always a function of political power.

In chapter 9, "Resilient Tokyo: Disaster and Transformation in the Japanese City," urbanist Carola Hein focuses on a city that has suffered not only a major earthquake (in 1923), but also a much longer pattern of destructive fires, as well as the cataclysmic devastation wrought by World War II air raids. These vast transformations of the urban landscape occurred in the context of more than a century of significant modernization and wrenching political change. In all of this, however, Hein finds remarkable continuity in the underlying traditional urban patterns of Tokyo and other Japanese cities. She demonstrates that the Japanese generally left the reconstruction of cities to private initiative; Japanese planners effected significant transformations only when destruction coincided with some other political or economic change in tune with the necessities of Japanese society, and in areas deemed necessary for the country's modernization.

Chapter 10, a study of China's Tangshan earthquake, shows what happens when post-quake recovery coincides exactly with a major political transformation. In " 'Resist the Earthquake and Rescue Our-selves': The Reconstruction of Tangshan after the 1976 Earthquake," urban planner Beatrice Chen situates the unparalleled destruction of this earthquake in the context of a similar sea-change in Chinese pol-itics, occasioned by the death of Mao Zedong just six weeks after the quake. Mao's ideologically grounded ideas about self-reliant citizens dominated the immediate aftermath; assumptions about such resil-ience led him to refuse foreign aid and attempt to keep secret the magnitude of the disaster. With Mao's death, other priorities came to the fore. The dramatic rebuilding of Tangshan as a series of modernist housing blocks, launched under the economic liberalization of the Deng Xiaoping regime, yielded a vastly different city, albeit one that rapidly regained an important position in the industrial economy of a modernizing China.

In chapter 11, "Reverberations: Mexico City's 1985 Earthquake and the Transformation of the Capital," political sociologist Diane Davis views the quake as inducing political shake-ups, not just seismic ones. Davis examines the earthquake's impact on the organization of social movements, the character of land use and property ownership, and the legitimacy of the city's political leaders. In so doing, she finds evidence of a resilient citizenry, but also explores ways that resilience can some-times entail a return to disreputable practices that preceded the disaster. Still, Davis views the earthquake as an important catalyst for political change: empowered citizens challenged a corrupt local government (whose illicit practices were sometimes exposed quite literally in the ruins of damaged buildings) and accelerated democratic transition. Meanwhile, downtown Mexico City (where most of the damage oc-curred) benefited from new low-income housing and regained its social and symbolic centrality.

In chapter 12, architect Hashim Sarkis investigates the urban design politics involved in rebuilding Beirut since 1990, viewed as one window into Lebanon's attempt to recover from fifteen years of war. "A Vital Void: Reconstruction of Downtown Beirut" assesses the cultural strug-gle over the heart of the capital, as expressed through both literature and urban design. In assessing the prospects for Martyrs' Square—the primary open space of the old center—Sarkis contrasts the glossy pro-motional brochures of SOLIDERE (the private real estate holding com-pany charged with directing redevelopment) with the actual contested claims over who will be welcome to partake of urban life in the city's center. Caught between Beirut's "myth of self-consumption" (its alleged excesses) and its "myth of self-renewal" (its resilience), its citizens struggle with both nostalgia and conflicting images for the future.

In chapter 13, urbanist William Fulton addresses the aftermath of the most destructive urban riot in American history, unleashed by indignation over the acquittal of Los Angeles police officers accused of beating black motorist Rodney King. "After the Unrest: Ten Years of Rebuilding Los Angeles following the Trauma of 1992" examines the political struggle to revive the economy and communities of South Central Los Angeles. Fulton faults the official Rebuild L.A. effort for failing to launch substantial new real estate development, but praises the less quantifiable resilience of the local citizenry, buoyed by an influx of immigrants. In Los Angeles, as in Mexico City after its earthquake, any attempt to define the resilience of "the city" merely in terms of its restored buildings misses the complex interplay of demographic energy that nurtures new urban development.

In chapter 14, urban theorists William J. Mitchell and Anthony M. Townsend look toward future threats to the resilience of cities. In "Cyborg Agonistes: Disaster and Reconstruction in the Digital Electronic Era," they assess the vulnerability of urban infrastructure, in which digital communication networks now play an increasingly vital role. Twenty-first-century cities are susceptible not only to overt attacks on buildings, but also to the covert disruption of cyber attacks on the nodes and links of critical networks. Mitchell and Townsend also warn of the dangers that could result from turning networks back against themselves, especially given "the miniaturization of destructive power," which could be occasioned by some deadly marriage of biotechnology and nanotechnology. Given such dire potential consequences, their analysis of the immediate and medium-term impacts of the September 11 attacks on the infrastructure of Manhattan is gratifyingly upbeat; most critical networks (except for the subway) had the built-in redundancy to recover quickly. Even so, larger questions raised by the 9/11 attacks continue to resonate: how will (or should) future urban-based businesses balance the risk of life in a landmark office tower with the advantages of agglomeration economies and face-to-face contact? Will more organizations seek to spread risk (and reduce insurance costs) through decentralization? Mitchell and Townsend do not attempt to find generalizable answers to such questions, but clearly demonstrate that future urban resilience depends on increasingly far-flung patterns of connectivity.

In the concluding chapter, the editors, Lawrence Vale and Thomas Campanella, propose a prototheory of urban resilience. The goal here is to extract from a broad selection of historical examples a set of common themes and elements that help explain how and why urban settlements have rebounded throughout history and to shed light on the processes by which cities recover and rebuild.

This book provides windows into many different resilient cities in many different times, places, and cultures, but we seek more than simply a compendium of sagas separated by significant differences. This volume is entitled *The Resilient City* rather than *Resilient Cities* because we want to uncover what all humans share when they cope with sudden traumatic changes to their environment.

Notes

1. Tertius Chandler and Gerald Fox, *3000 Years of Urban Growth* (New York: Academic, 1974).
2. Rudyard Kipling, "A Centurion of the Thirtieth," in *Puck of Pook's Hill* (1906), reprinted in *Rudyard Kipling: Complete Verse* (New York: Anchor Doubleday, 1989), p. 484.
3. Ernest Zebroski, Jr., *The Last Days of St. Pierre: The Volcanic Disaster That Claimed Thirty Thousand Lives* (New Brunswick, N.J.: Rutgers University Press, 2002), p. 39.
4. Anthony M. Tung, *Preserving the World's Great Cities* (New York: Clarkson Potter, 2001), pp. 73–95.
5. Chen Yong et al., eds., *The Great Tangshan Earthquake of 1976: An Anatomy of Disaster* (Oxford: Pergamon, 1988).
6. Marc Lacey, "Under Congo Volcano, a Rebel City Trembles but Learns to Make the Most of Lava," *New York Times*, 10 November 2002.
7. Lawrence J. Vale, "Mediated Monuments and National Identity," *Journal of Architecture* 4 (Winter 1999): 391–408.
8. Marc Fried, "Grieving for a Lost Home: Psychological Costs of Relocation," in *Urban Renewal: The Record and the Controversy*, ed. James Q. Wilson (Cambridge, Mass.: MIT Press, 1966), pp. 359–379.
9. Mike Davis, *Ecology of Fear: Los Angeles and the Imagination of Disaster* (New York: Vintage, 1999).
10. See, for example, Daryl G. Press, "Urban Warfare: Options, Problems and

the Future" (January 1999). Summary of a conference sponsored by the MIT Security Studies Program at the Officers' Club, Hanscom Air Force Base, Bedford, Massachusetts, 20 May 1998. Ironically, even the U.S. Army's 10th Mountain Division has undergone intensive training for possible urban combat, something even the top brass admits would be a costly undertaking (one training manual cut to the chase, advising, "Avoid cities if you can"). See Vernon Loeb, "Bracing for 'Primordial Combat,'" *Washington Post*, 31 October 2002.

11. Recent attempts to address this striking omission include Joan Ockman, ed., *Out of Ground Zero: Case Studies in Urban Reinvention* (Munich: Prestel, 2002); Raymond W. Gastil and Zoë Ryan, eds., *Information Exchange: How Cities Renew, Rebuild, and Remember* (New York: Van Alen Institute, 2002); Geneviève Massard-Guilbaud, Harold L. Platt, and Dieter Schott, eds., *Cities and Catastrophes: Coping with Emergency in European History* (Frankfurt am Main: Lang, 2002); and a three-volume collection of essays edited by Martin Körner, *Destruction and Reconstruction of Towns* (Bern: Haupt, 2000). These books are catalogs of cases, however, and do not attempt a comparative framework for assessing the design politics of urban recovery and remembrance.

12. Edward T. Linenthal, *The Unfinished Bombing: Oklahoma City in American Memory* (New York: Oxford University Press, 2001), pp. 41–80.

PART I

Making Progress
Disaster Narratives and the Art of Optimism in Modern America

1

KEVIN ROZARIO

■ As the philosopher Martin Heidegger once revealed, there are etymological affinities linking the words *building*, *dwelling*, and *thinking*.[1] The history of language, in this instance, teaches a profound lesson: that building is never simply a technical exercise, never solely a question of shelter, but also inevitably a forum for dwelling on life; it is nothing less, in many respects, than a form of thinking. Louis Sullivan famously described the architect as "a poet who uses not words but building materials as a medium of expression."[2] Certainly, when we build we are telling stories about the world, sculpting the cultural landscape even as we remold the physical one. But if buildings tell stories, it is also true that stories make buildings. When offices, stores, and homes are suddenly and unexpectedly annihilated, it is necessary not only to manufacture new material structures but also to repair torn cultural fabrics and damaged psyches. With this in mind, I propose to explore the relationship between the rebuilding of cities with mortar and bricks and the rebuilding of cultural environments with words and images in the aftermath of great urban disasters—a double process neatly caught in the twin meanings of the word *reconstruction* as "remaking" and as "retelling."

The reconstruction of events in our minds, the stories we hear and tell about disasters, the way we see and imagine destruction—all of these things have a decisive bearing on how we reconstruct damaged buildings, neighborhoods, or cities. Construction, in this sense, is always cultural. We cannot build what we cannot imagine. We create worlds with words. We build stories with stories. Certainly we cannot build with any confidence or ambition without some faith in the future. So when we consider the extraordinary endurance of American cities over the past couple of centuries when confronting fires, floods, earthquakes, and wars, one of our tasks must be to ask how people have perceived and described the disasters that have befallen them.

In this chapter, I will examine the role of disaster writings and what I am calling a "narrative imagination" in helping Americans to conceive of disasters as instruments of progress, and I will argue that this expectation has contributed greatly to this nation's renowned resilience in the face of natural disasters. Through an analysis of the writings generated by the Chicago fire of 1871 and the San Francisco earthquake and fire of 1906, I will argue for the significance of disaster zones as cultural construction sites, as locations affirming dominant ideologies of progress and expansion for an industrial age beset by urban conflagrations, economic recessions, and escalating social conflicts. I conclude with some speculative observations about the lessons of this history for our understanding of the destruction of New York's World Trade Center on September 11, 2001.

The Chicago fire of 1871 and the San Francisco earthquake of 1906 are still the two most devastating urban catastrophes in American history in terms of sheer property destruction. Chicago burned down over two October days in 1871, when fierce and gusting winds whipped a small barn-house blaze into a raging conflagration that blew through the heart of the city. Tens of thousands fled amid scenes of chaos as flames tore through one tinderbox district after another. When drizzling rain put out the last of the fire, 300 people were dead. More stunning yet was the material devastation: nearly 18,000 buildings leveled and as many as 100,000 people, nearly one-third of the population, suddenly homeless.[3] The San Francisco earthquake took place thirty-five years later on a balmy April morning in 1906. Seismic shocks shattered rows of chimneys and pulled down some of the city's frailer structures, but most of the damage was wrought by a series of fires that blazed through the city for three days. Several occupants trapped in wrecked homes and hotels were burned alive by the advancing flames while fire fighters and spectators looked on helplessly. Some 5,000 people died, and the destruction exceeded even that at Chicago. When statisticians tallied the destruction they discovered that 28,000 build-

Figure 1.1.
"The Rush for Life over Randolph Street Bridge," by John R. Chapin in *Harper's Weekly*, October 28, 1871.

ings had been obliterated and that half of the city's 400,000 residents were without shelter.[4]

The extraordinary recovery of each city from sudden ruination remains compelling and inspiring. Stores, hotels, factories, residential neighborhoods, and streets were speedily repaired in San Francisco, and "a new and improved city" stood atop the ruins in just four years. Chicago's restoration was even more astounding. Within a week, more than 5,000 new makeshift buildings were ready for occupation, and work had begun on 200 more permanent structures.[5] In spite of the comprehensive destruction, the city was substantially rebuilt in just two years; even a deep depression between 1873 and 1879 presented only a temporary impediment to an extraordinary wave of expansion that transformed Chicago into the nation's second-largest metropolis, after New York City, by 1890. Remarkably, Chicago's economy grew even faster in the year after the fire than it had in the year before, and land values actually outstripped pre-fire rates in some downtown districts amid a post-disaster construction boom.[6] Chicago, in fact, would become the fastest growing city in the Western Hemisphere in the two decades after the Great Fire.[7]

The foundations for the restoration of both Chicago and San Francisco were undoubtedly laid by an expansive industrial economy. The

CORNER
STATE & MADISON ST
AFTER CHICAGO FIRE

Figure 1.2.
"Corner [of] State and Madison St[reets] after Chicago Fire."
Photographer unknown.

communications advances, technological innovations, economic re-organizations, and migrations of the post–Civil War period ensured the availability not only of essential resources like lumber, steel, and labor, but also of insurance money and investment capital to cover the costs of reconstruction.[8] Moreover, both cities enjoyed favorable geographical locations, strategically placed at the center of rich hinterlands as well as at the hub of trade and transportation networks.[9] Chicago, for example, lost its business district but the stockyards and packing plants, along with most of the lumberyards and mills upon which the city's wealth rested, were spared.[10] It was upon these institutions, structures, and money circuits that recovery ultimately depended.

But crucial also, I believe, were the cultural expectations that shaped the ways that the calamities were seen and interpreted, the hopes and

Narratives of Resilience

aspirations that dictated how money would flow and where buildings would grow, and, above all, the faith that reassured citizens that their future prospects were bright even as they endured misfortune on an epic scale.[11] The sociologist Kai Erikson has written:

> One of the crucial tasks of culture . . . is to help people cam-
> ouflage the actual risks of the world around them—to help
> them edit reality in such a way that it seems manageable, to
> help them edit it in such a way that the dangers pressing in on
> them from all sides are screened out of their line of vision as
> they go about their everyday rounds.[12]

Accordingly, one of the most urgent tasks of reconstruction has been to try to make sense of the disaster, to discover (or establish) meanings that help people to recover a sense of mastery over their natural and social surroundings, and in both 1871 and 1906 this was accomplished with striking success. In fact, observers and survivors of both calamities tended to agree that these particular disasters were "blessings."

When George Harvey, the editor of *Harper's*, sat down to write a commentary on the San Francisco earthquake and fire, it was utterly conventional for him to assure subscribers that the city was "certain to arise quickly from its ashes, greater and more beautiful than ever." Few faulted the stirring sentiments or disputed Harvey's prediction "that for those who five years hence shall behold the brand-new splendor of the resuscitated capital, the earthquake of 1906, with all its unparalleled destructiveness, will serve only to point a moral and adorn a tale."[13] Yet such confidence surely warrants further analysis. What induced this man, this esteemed voice of American civilization, to assume that vast destruction would inevitably pave the way for progress? This optimistic outlook was certainly appropriate for a modern industrial society that was pulled forward and apart by tides of creative destruction, a (business) culture in which ruination was a necessary means of renewal and in which the demolition of obsolete products was understood to be necessary for the innovation and streamlining that supposedly stimulated economic growth and promoted urban development. In such a dynamic economic system, the decimation of a major metropolis presented itself as an opportunity for growth and expansion.[14]

While economic, environmental, and political factors played primary roles in determining the reconstruction of Chicago and San Francisco, the narrative imagination also made an essential contribution to the rebuilding. There is something singularly apt in Harvey's choice of words: "the earthquake . . . will serve only to point a moral and adorn a tale." Harvey was typical in treating the San Francisco disaster as an episode in a story rather than as a random event or as a fleeting spectacle. It was not just any story but one with a dependably happy ending. This is significant on several counts. To begin with, Harvey, like most other commentators and witnesses, wrote and thought in an idiom that inexorably swept his concern forward. Possessed of a narrative imagination, it was impossible for him—as it was impossible even for those fleeing the flames—to live entirely in the present, heedless of future outcomes. And, given the prevailing narrative conventions of the day, this meant anticipating a happy ending. Throwing words at the chaos, spreading a narrative grid over the bewildering mayhem, was thus a therapeutic act, helping victims to cope with trauma by reassuring them that any devastation was certain to be fleeting. This steadied many survivors to meet the material challenges that lay ahead, though most disaster narratives were also plainly ideological, serving a narrowly bourgeois vision of order, encouraging forms of physical reconstruction that plainly discriminated against the poor, immigrants, and nonwhites.[15]

Culture matters, then, but I wish to make it absolutely clear here that I am not trying to pass off narrative as an autonomous and unchanging force, floating free of history and context, imposing interpretations and outlooks on disaster's witnesses. The conditions of life in 1906 San Francisco, for example, were such that a narrative understanding of disaster worked differently, and with different effects, than at Chicago in 1871. In any case, the narrative imagination has hardly been singular and unchanging. To take one obvious example, the advent of movies and an image-based mass media over the past century has introduced a new "cinematic" or "televisual" mode of perception, or grammar of seeing, that has decisively transformed how people apprehend, feel, and process—that is to say, "narrate"—calamities.[16] These variations deserve much more detailed attention than I have space for here. But even so, there are enough consistencies, or persistencies, over the past century or so to suggest that (internalized) narrative conventions continue to organize emotional and conceptual responses to disaster.

Narratives of Resilience

The Poetics of Disaster

■ To grasp the appeal of fire narratives in the modern era, we would do well to follow recent critical and psychoanalytical literature into what Susan Sontag once naughtily dubbed the "erotics" of art—exploring the way texts respond to and organize fears and desires.[17] It is a commonplace of narrative theory that humans are storytelling animals, that we are driven to tell stories to make sense of the chaos and flux of experience, to make life meaningful and purposeful, to cope with adversity, and to learn how to feel and act in the world. Stories are always important for orienting us toward the world, but at no time are they more important than in the midst of crisis and uncertainty. Part of the attraction of disaster narratives surely lies in their power to settle those who have experienced the unsettling of their worlds, to make sense of that which seems most senseless. Although postmodern literary critics of this last generation have properly sought to dismantle the idea that narratives, or the events they seek to describe, have any real unity or orderliness (demonstrating instead how narratives unsettle meanings and disrupt apparent unities), narratives continue to appeal to the extent that they supply comforting illusions of order. This aspect of narrative helps us to understand why so many people are drawn to stories to express and represent their feelings about disasters: to make sense of nonsense.[18] Stories, in short, can domesticate disasters.

If disasters need narratives to become meaningful, narratives also, in a sense, depend on disasters. Since Aristotle, narratives in Western culture have had certain intrinsic and defining properties. Most basic is the plot structure of beginning, middle, and end, but a key ingredient of any plot is what Aristotle called the *peripeteia*, the turning point or reversal that moves a story forward.[19] In most plots, there is a reversal of fortune or a moment of adversity that throws the hero or protagonist into turmoil. In "comic" plots, a crisis or disruption of some sort presents an obstacle that must be overcome, a propulsive force that enables the development, growth, and insight that eventually produces an emotionally satisfying happy ending. A peripeteia is required to move the narrative forward. Without it, we have stasis. We have no story. This is significant. The configuration of narrative tends to pull disaster toward the middle of a story, encoding it as a principle of transformation.

This helps to explain not only the appeal of narratives for finding meaning in real calamities, but also why calamities tend to figure as beginnings or middles of such narratives, and why they encourage an expectation of favorable outcomes.

A quick glance at American history shows that narrative has long been the magic that makes blessings out of calamities. Sermons and private writings attest that calamities were among the most enthralling topics in colonial America. Disasters had to be explained but there was little doubt they were meaningful. They were part of God's greater designs. Misfortunes were not exactly welcome, of course, but a religious framework for understanding them was by and large consoling. Possessing a strong conviction that God was especially close in calamity and that God was good, Puritans, like most other European settlers, simply had to believe that disasters possessed some benevolent purpose.[20] Hence they found themselves plotting their disasters according to "comic," as opposed, in the Aristotelian scheme, to "tragic" conventions. The narrative sequence usually went something like this: some wretch or group of wretches commits a sin; God sends a disaster to punish and test the individual or the community; people heed the warning and mend their ways; they rededicate themselves to God and ultimately earn salvation.

Dominant colonial traditions encouraged a remarkably constructive approach to calamity, leading settlers on a constant search for silver linings. Disaster narratives became self-fulfilling prophecies, inspiring a faith in betterment and generating the energy, will, and capital commitment that made material reconstruction viable—ultimately turning calamities into opportunities and thereby, as the title of this chapter claims, making progress. Indeed, an argument can be made that this expectation of reformation and growth via adversity would become the sustaining force behind that most powerful of myths: America as the land of infinite possibility and renewal.[21] By 1871, many Americans were practically conditioned to view disasters as peripeteias. Indeed, the narrative conventions of the dominant Western literary tradition supplied a perfect vehicle for navigating and normalizing the world that creative destruction made. Narrative and economic logics merged, with extraordinary consequences for the politics of disaster.

Narratives of Resilience

Cradles and Graves: Chicago, 1871

■ Both the Chicago fire and the San Francisco earthquake unleashed (or provoked) a torrent of words. And these words did not fall into random patterns. Significantly, nearly every piece of writing about the two disasters (memoirs, newspaper stories, magazine articles, historical accounts, letters, diary entries, poems) assumed a narrative form—that is to say, they presented each disaster as a sequential story with a beginning, a middle, and an end.[22] This is not, perhaps, so remarkable. It may well be instinctive for people to turn calamities into stories— they have been doing so at least since the flood of the Gilgamesh epic— but nineteenth-century men and women turned to narrative on such occasions with a new urgency, as if convinced that only in such historical tales (rather than in the stars or the Bible) would they find answers to the deepest mysteries of nature, society, and suffering. Over and over again, those who wrote about the Chicago fire acknowledged the impossibility of ever really grasping its meaning, resolving instead to describe incidents in the hope that this would enable readers to "arrive at some little comprehension of the catastrophe."[23] These writings helped survivors and readers across the nation to cope with the calamity. In effect, Americans were enfolding this disaster into stories to soothe anxieties raised by such a confounding event, domesticating the conflagration by describing it in the terms most familiar to their society. The cultural theorist Hayden White has argued suggestively:

> Understanding is a process of rendering the unfamiliar, or the "uncanny" in Freud's sense of that term, familiar; of removing it from the domain of things felt to be "exotic" and unclassified into one or another domain of experience encoded adequately enough to be felt to be humanly useful, non-threatening, or simply known by association.[24]

Part of the attraction of disaster narratives lay in their power to settle those who had experienced the unsettling of their lives.

By 1871, the conviction that stories revealed the meaning of events had become deeply ingrained in the American consciousness. Attempting to understand the Chicago fire, a *New York Tribune* correspondent found the desire to locate origins and ends irresistible, though he was willing to concede that such an endeavor might be little more than a "folly." As he explained in "The Cradle and the Grave of the Fire," it was as if human nature itself impelled him to trace a path from Mrs. O'Leary's barn (the cradle: where the fire broke out) to the last house burned at Chicago (the fire's grave). He followed this route in the expectation that a chronological trail would lead him most directly to an understanding of the fire, its lessons, and its message of hope.[25] As it turns out, he was on a crowded path. Indeed, one of the most noteworthy features of fire narratives is their similarity and conventionality, their cleaving to a redemptive script with one inevitable outcome: prosperity. One witness did dare to argue that the fire had "written the untimely epitaph of the highest worldly hopes and loftiest ambitions of men of enterprise and worth, in the several departments of human endeavor, in the ashes of their achievements!"[26] But few survivors or commentators really believed that the Chicago fire was an ending.

The rapid restoration of the Windy City graphically demonstrated, and every story about the fire testified, that the death of Chicago was actually the prerequisite for its more glorious rebirth. One detailed history of the disaster, *Chicago and the Great Conflagration*, was utterly typical in its three-part structure, beginning with the prehistory of the city (charting the development of Chicago from frontier fort to metropolis), settling into the exciting middle section describing the disaster, and concluding with expansive assurances about Chicago's fabulous future. To gauge the weight of this narrative expectation—and the commingling of belief and material opportunities—we can take as an example the private journey from despair to confidence of Robert Collyer, the city's most influential clergyman. He was profoundly distressed after the fire, spinning into deep depression, finding it hard to stir himself to action. And yet as he began to seek the meaning of the horrifying events he had witnessed, as he looked for the moral and the tale, his gloom began to lift. He just knew there had to be a happy ending here, some benevolent purpose. His religious training compelled him to believe that God had sent the conflagration to do good, but more than this, no story of the fire finally felt right unless it ended well. He recast and recombined the events of the fire and its aftermath until they fit the reassuring progressive pattern. In Boston, a month later, he recorded his struggle for comprehension:

Narratives of Resilience

When that great calamity settled down upon us I thought I ought to try and find some view of the better *meaning* of it. . . . But I couldn't find it. I said this whole thing is just as bad as it can be. . . . Now I take it all back just as Job did. I said it because I couldn't say anything better. . . . I thought the devil had overthrown God, and had wrought the destruction of our beautiful city. But I have altered my mind since then; I have begun to talk more like "Brother Collyer."[27]

His determined search for uplifting outcomes led him to fabricate (and actually believe in) happy endings, and the effect was instant and therapeutic. He was soon hard at work rebuilding his church and encouraging others to throw themselves into the task of reconstruction, earning him international fame as a symbol of the plucky Chicago spirit.[28] To be sure, not everyone was able to find the better meaning of the fire. Insurance agent Gurdon Hubbard, for example, was defeated by the "catastrophe," unable to respond energetically because,

Figure 1.3.
"Map Showing the Burnt District in Chicago," by R. P. Studley Company.

as a friend of his explained, his "resilience was gone."[29] But this fragility made Hubbard more exceptional than typical. For most affluent Chicagoans, at least, the disaster was, indeed had to be, a blessing.

But there was still more to the therapeutic work of disaster narratives. If the dominant narrative form encouraged the expectation that good would come of calamity, the content of actual narratives helped Americans to work through abiding and socially specific anxieties about the disorderly and dangerous times in which they lived. Sensational accounts offered an opportunity to dwell on the darker moments of the fire (and of the era). Unsurprisingly, most writings about the conflagration were authored by middle- and upper-class men and women who had access to the print media or who were brought up to express their feelings in letters and diaries. These individuals were particularly unsettled by fears that the calamity would unleash social disorder. Even as they mouthed liberal platitudes about the blessings of disaster and the perfectibility of man, most commentators and diarists projected personal and social apprehensions onto the fire, returning compulsively to tales and scenes of looting, lynching, incendiarism, and the depredations of alcohol-sopped rioters. It is not immediately obvious why they should have done so. There is no reason to dispute Mayor Roswell Mason's claim that "not the slightest indication of a lawless, riotous disposition had ever been manifested, and that all the rumors of incendiaries, murder and lynching existed only in the imagination of the frightened population," an assessment confirmed by police officers, soldiers, and some of the more judicious civilian observers.[30] Nevertheless, "the imagination of the frightened population" alerts us to abiding perils in this dynamic age that the fire threatened to unleash.

Try as they might to accept modernization as a benevolent process, as a manifestation of progress, even the most optimistic of Americans were unable to wish away the very real anxieties and terrors produced by rapid change in the last decades of the nineteenth century. The Chicago fire provided an outlet for a whole gamut of fears about immigration, mechanization, the perils of urban vice and crime, the emergence of class hostilities, and the uncertainties of an unpredictable future. Fire narratives brought these anxieties to the surface. In one account, a writer wrote vividly about the sufferings of men and women who had been prey to the "invisible hand" of pickpockets and thieves during the chaos of the fire.[31] This invisible hand was clearly much more palpable to affluent Chicagoans during the fire than that other invisible hand, which devotees of Adam Smith maintained was lifting them toward peace and prosperity.[32]

Subtly equating the poor with elemental and chaotic forces that threatened civilization, sensationalized stories about the fire had political effects, establishing the emotional environment for a brutal restoration of order. Prominent Chicagoans invited soldiers into their city during and after the fire to harass and monitor a supposedly dangerous (but actually mostly quiescent) working class. This action is a forceful reminder that disaster narratives, despite the claims of their authors, do not speak to universal human concerns about death and rebirth but to the specific hopes and fears of white upper- and middle-class men and women.[33] Accounts of the disaster turned the fire into a parable for the virtue of the respectable and for the creeping menace of the dangerous poor. In so doing, these writings provided a language for fears and anxieties that progress narratives barely acknowledged, supplying emotional reinforcement for a relief agenda focused on the needs of the middle class, suspicious of the demands of the poor, and openly discriminatory—favoring the claims of the genteel over those of the working poor.[34]

Images of villains rampaging through the streets of Chicago did more than cultivate an atmosphere of authoritarianism and suspicion. These depictions also helped middle-class Americans come to terms with broader concerns about the industrial age. Fire narratives produced a cathartic reaction. Since Aristotle, *catharsis* has been understood as a double movement, involving the satisfaction of both pity and fear. Sentimental identification with sufferers of the fire undoubtedly supplied an outlet for the salts of pity. Stories about carnage and chaos provided a similar release for fears. Dark tales of the fire helped men and women find words and images for the inchoate worries generated by modernity. Catharsis, of course, works by naming (and thus taming) fears, by replaying the inevitable defeat of evil. In short, narratives of the fire allayed some of the anxieties they raised by routinely concluding with happy endings that replayed (and naturalized) the conquest of chaos and the restoration of (a thoroughly bourgeois) order. By dwelling on the overcoming of harm and danger, Chicago fire writings helped middle-class men and women to connect emotionally

Figure 1.4.
"Chicago in Ruins:
Laying the Corner-stone
of the First Building after
the Fire." *Harper's
Weekly*, November 6,
1871.

with an official culture of optimism. A narrative imagination enabled Americans to figure chaos as an imprint of progress.

As self-fulfilling prophecies, disaster narratives inspired a faith in betterment that generated the energy and will—not to mention the capital commitment—that made material reconstruction viable, encouraging the actions that ensured that catastrophes would become blessings. Of course, this had as much to do with capitalist logics as with narrative logics. This is a crucial point to emphasize. Narrative theorists have a tendency to argue that narratives impose on us certain ways of seeing the world. But what is remarkable is how well suited classical narrative forms were to describing the world that industrial capitalism made, and in ways that suited the interests of its commercial and professional elites. Persuaded that the future was secure, Chicagoans roused themselves to the task of rebuilding, and rebuilding with haste in order to capitalize on the profits that were sure to be made in the new and improved metropolis. Assured that restoration was written into the order of things, leading citizens strenuously opposed any attempts to interfere with free market mechanisms or to violate laissez-faire practices, refusing to countenance state or government relief. In a significant sense, then, disaster narratives were romances of capitalism, though some might prefer to describe them as capitalist plots. Who got to tell the story of the fire went a long way toward determining who was entitled to shape the reconstruction of Chicago, who would benefit, and who would not.

Capitalist plots certainly left an imprint on the great rebuilding.

What one journal described as the city's "reckless go-aheaditiveness" ensured that the "New Chicago" would be quite as shoddy as the old one.[35] In the meantime, this unseemly haste encouraged a shocking disregard for the welfare of laboring people, compelling even the conservative *Chicago Tribune* to warn that unless reforms were introduced, more lives would be "sacrificed to the New Chicago than were engulfed in the fiery end of the nearly-forgotten city."[36] One of the more grotesque statistics to emerge from the whole affair is that the great rebuilding took more lives than the fire itself, with as many as twelve construction workers dying each day because of the need for speed and inattention to safety. The mad rush toward a happy ending would not produce happiness for all. And yet, this lesson would be largely forgotten. It was the resilience of Chicago that would enter American lore.

Figure 1.5. "Bird's-Eye View of the Business District of Chicago, 1893." Artist unknown.

BIRD'S-EYE VIEW OF THE BUSINESS DISTRICT OF CHICAGO

San Francisco, 1906

■ As with the Chicago conflagration, the 1906 San Francisco earth quake and fire inspired survivors and commentators to turn to narratives to make sense of the devastation and carnage before them. Once again their stories plotted the fall and rise of their city. Account after account concluded with descriptions of the splendid city that was sure to emerge out of the ruins of San Francisco. "Never mind the unpleasant things of this terrific episode in our history," the *Oakland Herald* cheered from across the bay. "Think of the good times coming."[37] But some things had changed since 1871, and this subtly transformed the style and function of these narratives. Although both disasters generated hundreds of written accounts deploying almost identical plot devices, these narratives offered contrasting consolations. Whereas Chicago fire narratives supplied welcome illusions of order for a middle class beset by anxieties of disorder, San Francisco earthquake narratives provided equally welcome illusions of *disorder* for a comfortable class that was beginning to revolt against the tiresome predictabilities of convention and social order in an emerging corporate bureaucratic age. Part of the appeal of the narrative form was that it was flexible enough to cater to both of these desires.

As eagerly as middle-class San Franciscans grasped the opportunity to make their city more rational and orderly in the wake of the disaster,

Figure 1.6.
View of San Francisco's business district after the earthquake and fire, 1906.

many were smitten by a strong sense of nostalgia for the "city that was."[38] "The old San Francisco is dead," one writer reflected. "It may rebuild; it probably will; but those who have known that peculiar city by the Golden Gate and have caught its flavor of the Arabian Nights feel that it can never be the same. When it rises out of its ashes it will probably resemble other modern cities and have lost its old strange flavor."[39]

The anticipated ending to the earthquake, in other words, was not unambiguously agreeable. This is perhaps unsurprising. After all, this was an age in which closure had a bad name. The most famous essay of the age, Frederick Jackson Turner's frontier thesis, presented the "closing of the frontier" as an occasion for regret (auguring the loss of a certain propulsive energy and regenerative possibility).[40] Many earthquake narratives similarly expressed regret at the passing of San Francisco's disorderly past. To understand why, it is helpful to recall that the San Francisco earthquake and fire occurred at a time when many well-to-do Americans were actively recoiling from a society governed by an apparent excess of order—what they called "overcivilization." President Theodore Roosevelt was only the most prominent of a whole class of citizens who were much more interested in adventure and danger—"the strenuous life"—than in orderly living. The establishment of corporate order, the passing of the pioneering age, abiding

Figure 1.7.
The restored business district three years later. The view is shifted a little to the east.

concerns about the women's movement, and the apparent feminization of American culture all provoked something close to a cult of chaos at the turn of the century, particularly among the middle classes.

It is important, however, not to mistake these discontents with resistance to progress. On the contrary, this display of nostalgia is probably best conceptualized as a form of what literary critics Peter Stallybrass and Allon White have called "constitutive ambivalence"—the emotion that registers change and enables accommodation to it. In their account of the civilizing process, these scholars have argued that the modern bourgeois world view, with its imperatives of efficiency and order, was constructed and enforced through a repudiation of unruly and chaotic behaviors.[41] As they point out, however, there is a twist: any such "labor of exclusion" seems to generate desires for that which has been lost. We cannot, it seems, remove chaos from the world without longing for its return, even if only in a sanitized form. By 1906, many comfortable Americans were so confident about the march of progress that they were beginning to regret the passing of old ways.

What distinguishes the disaster narratives of 1906 is a new appreciation for the (presumably fleeting) disorder introduced into modern life by calamities. Whereas Chicago fire writings had percolated with anxieties about the depredations of the lower orders, earthquake writings tended to focus on the excitement of living through a great calamity. To be sure, the collapse of institutional authority did provoke some fears of masterless men rampaging through the streets as a result of "the loosening of the bands of law in the burning city," and a good number of earthquake narratives did focus on scenes of looting and general lawlessness.[42] But few accounts expressed genuine concerns about chaos. This was no doubt partly due to the speedy deployment of federal troops on the streets of the city, but it was also an index of a broader expectation that things would turn out well. Assured of the restoration of order, comfortable Americans could enjoy the suspension of routines. And it was in their narratives that they most freely indulged their appetite for vicarious encounters with danger. As the writer Gertrude Atherton observed soon after the earthquake:

> Everybody looks back upon the era "before the earthquake"
> as a period of insipidity, and wonders how he managed to exist.
> If they are appalled at the sight of a civilization arrested and

millions of property and still more to be lamented treasure[s] gone up in smoke, they are usually aquiver with a renewed sense of individuality, . . . they feel all the half-terrified delight of the adventurer stepping upon unknown shores and into a problematic future.[43]

In the final analysis, these writings did provide assurance that the earthquake would facilitate the improvement of San Francisco. Disaster narratives made the recovery of the Bay City seem inevitable. George Harvey was correct. The earthquake, with all its unparalleled destructiveness, did serve to point a moral and adorn a tale. But, contrary to his prediction, this story did not take five years to seize the American imagination. Disaster narratives ensured that the 1906 calamity instantly featured as the sort of reversal that inspired and enabled progress. Moreover, by allowing Americans to work through modern yearnings for color and excitement, these narratives provided an outlet for passions that might otherwise have fueled resistance to an ascendant bureaucratic conception of "progress" that extolled discipline, efficiency, productivity, and orderliness. Not only did these twentieth-century disaster narratives help to make progress believable, but they also helped to make progress bearable by providing a harmless outlet for recidivistic cravings. Of course, different social groups and organizations—from urban designers to businesspeople to social workers to labor unions—would contest, and thereby try to define, the "improvements" that reconstruction was supposed to achieve. By and large, satisfied that a better future could be realized, San Franciscans applied themselves to the labor of rebuilding a new and improved city that they were sure would do them proud.[44]

A Distinctly American Embrace: New York, 2001

Despite the apocalyptic nature of the scene, the response was unhesitant and almost childishly optimistic: it was simply understood that you would find survivors, and then that you would find the dead, and that this would help their families to get on with their lives, and that your resources were unlimited, and that you would work day and night to clean up the mess, and that this would allow the world's greatest city to rebuild quickly, and maybe even to make itself into something better than before.[45]

This is William Langewiesche describing the attitude of rescue workers as they plunged into the wreckage of the World Trade Center soon after the terrorist attacks of September 11, 2001, a disaster which was thereby, in his appraisal, "smothered in an exuberant and distinctly American embrace."

Several observations might be offered here. One is that an optimistic narrative script has endured in some manner. According to Langewiesche, this enthusiastic future-mindedness remains the impulsive American response, a modern analogue of the buoyant spirit observed at Chicago in 1871. We are also still clearly driven to enfold our disasters in stories. The above words, from an article in *Atlantic Monthly*, are among millions expended on describing and interpreting the attacks in newspapers, magazines, letters, the Internet, broadcast news, and so on.

Indeed, this very book on the resilient city surely testifies to our ongoing yearning for stories to help us come to terms with major disasters. We pick through the past quite as much for comfort as for instruction, and to this end it is undoubtedly reassuring to discover how well American cities have recovered from the terrible calamities that have befallen them, even as we must surely be aware that a terrorist attack presents challenges quite different from those of a natural disaster. At the same time, this history teaches us to be wary and critical of the stories that are circulating about this recent calamity. There are important questions that any responsible critic must ask: Whose stories are getting heard? Whose emotional and psychic needs do they address? Whose interests do they serve? Who are the heroes? Who are the scapegoats? Given our apparently undiminished appetite for heroes, the celebration of blue-collar fire fighters and police officers is surely worth pondering. But how do we respond, say, to the graffiti in the Banker's Trust building, allegedly left by one of those same courageous fire fighters, that reads, "Kill All Muslims, 9-11-01"?[46]

We have already seen narratives of the attack become vehicles for articulating buried cultural anxieties and for expressing social agendas, for defining, contesting, and policing proper American values and behaviors. Just as accounts of the Chicago fire can be read as displaced discourses on the turbulent experience of industrial capitalism and as exercises in social control, so too can these latter tales be read as allegories of our own time, as attempts to come to terms with the wider destructiveness of a world that is still governed by the capitalist logics of creative destruction but in which fewer people are sustained by expectations of unending material progress. Rather than take the attacks in stride, early commentators and ordinary citizens alike insisted that September 11 had changed everything, that the United States had finally lost its innocence, and that things would never be the same again. This gloom has left a powerful impression on our stories. Take, as just one prominent example, Bruce Springsteen's song "Countin' on a Miracle" from the chart-topping album *The Rising*—an artistic meditation on the state of the union in the aftermath of 9/11:

> There ain't no storybook story
> There's no never-ending song
> Our happily ever after Darlin'
> Forever come and gone . . .
> We've got no fairytale ending.[47]

This outlook (fatalistic, hard-bitten) is characteristic of working-class responses to calamity, highlighting the class-bound nature of official progress narratives. But the disillusionment is also symptomatic of a cautious and skeptical (perhaps postmodern) mood, in which many Americans seem to be losing the plot, no longer convinced that reversals are instruments of progress. This note of introspection certainly shaped the reconstruction debates. New York governor George E. Pataki, for example, went on record vowing that no buildings would be permitted on the "footprints," the "hallowed land," of the twin towers.[48] The sentiment behind this restriction, and the political climate sustaining it, offers a striking contrast to the "reckless go-aheaditiveness" displayed at Chicago 130 years before. In 1872, plans for a monument to memorialize the Great Fire petered out in the face of resounding public indifference. That had been no time for looking backward, or for dwelling on losses, but rather an occasion for looking ahead and building for the future.[49]

An unpredictable mix of commercial demands, legal decisions, and political compromises will no doubt loom largest in the plans to replace the World Trade Center, but disaster narratives will surely leave some

Figure 1.8.
Daniel Libeskind's winning design for rebuilding the World Trade Center, 2003. © studio daniel libeskind.

impression on the restoration of lower Manhattan. Although some dissenting voices have endeavored to reconstruct the destruction of the twin towers as a tale of the violence incited and invited by the ravages of global capitalism, a "beautiful suicide," in Jean Baudrillard's provocative verdict, it is clear that most Americans have continued to embrace narratives that present this calamity as an occasion for revealing and affirming "characteristic" American values of "strength," "decency," "courage," and "faith."[50] The moral and the tale, in George Harvey's formulation, will likely yet demand a forward-looking outcome. The restored site will tell a story, and, if letters to the *New York Times* (written in response to early redevelopment plans) are any indication, the public wants new buildings that will be both "healing" and uplifting. While some imagined Ground Zero covered with gardens of repose, most seemed to favor, in the words of one correspondent,

Narratives of Resilience

"something soaring to fill the void, something that says we are stronger than ever." "It may not be practical to rebuild grandly," this New Yorker concludes, "but maybe that isn't the most important consideration. Whatever we put there will say who we are for generations to come."[51]

In this context, Daniel Libeskind's winning design for a "Freedom Tower" to replace the twin towers takes on fresh significance. Like Louis Sullivan, Libeskind imagines architecture as "a communicative art." His message, however, is an ambivalent one. He sounds almost like Springsteen when he pronounces: "conflict is not simply a story with a happy or unhappy ending, but an ongoing momentum which structures one's understanding of the future in relation to the past."[52] At the same time, Libeskind's initial vision for the Freedom Tower suggested a determination to build a structure that soars. To be sure, this is not a matter of mere idealism. There is a strong commercial incentive to restore a spectacular New York skyline that can continue to attract businesses and tourists to this hub of global capitalism.[53] Libeskind's aspiring spire has already been altered by collaboration with David Childs, the developer's chosen architect; volatile capital flows and complex legal rulings may yet favor those tenants who want a more "practical" building, one that gives primacy to profitable office space rather than to the making of grand gestures. Whatever the exact outcome, this much is surely true: the new structure will make a statement, reminding us that our stories make us builders still.

Notes

1. Martin Heidegger, "Building Dwelling Thinking," in *Basic Writings*, ed. David Farrell Krell (New York: Harper Collins, 1976), 343–363. Special thanks to Ambreen Hai, Lane Hall-Witt, Larry Vale, and Tom Campanella for ideas and counsel during the writing of this essay. Thanks also to the audiences of the 2002 Resilient City lecture series at MIT and the 1997 International Narrative Conference at the University of Florida for responses to earlier versions of this material.
2. Louis H. Sullivan, "What Is an Architect?" in his *Kindergarten Notes and Other Writings* (New York: Wittenborn Art Books, 1947), 140.
3. Elias Colbert and Everett Chamberlin, *Chicago and the Great Conflagration* (1871; reprint, New York: Viking, 1971), 285–305.
4. *Report of the Sub-Committee on Statistics* (San Francisco, Calif.: 24 April 1907); Russell Sage Foundation, *San Francisco Relief Survey* (New York:

Survey Associates, 1913), 5. The exact numbers of casualties will never be known because so many carcasses were entirely consumed by the tremendous heat and because the city had such a large and undocumented transient population in 1906. Officially estimated at 674 at the time of the disaster, the suspected figure has been growing ever since, largely as a result of the careful tabulations of Gladys Hansen, the curator of the Museum of the City of San Francisco. The most recent chronicle by Dan Kurzman puts the death toll closer to 10,000. *Disaster! The Great San Francisco Earthquake and Fire* (New York: Morrow, 2002).

5. Harold M. Mayer, *Chicago: Growth of a Metropolis* (Chicago: University of Chicago Press, 1969), 117.

6. Andrew Sherman, "One Year After," *Lakeside Monthly* 8 (October 1871): 241–243, 246; Homer Hoyt, *One Hundred Years of Land Values in Chicago: The Relationship of the Growth of Chicago to the Rise of Its Land Values, 1830–1933* (Chicago: University of Chicago Press, 1933), 101–104, 116. Also see Christine Meisner Rosen, *The Limits of Power: Great Fires and the Process of City Growth in America* (New York: Cambridge University Press, 1986).

7. Donald L. Miller, *The City of the Century: The Epic of Chicago and the Making of America* (New York: Simon and Schuster, 1996), 17, 177; Karen Sawislak, *Smoldering City: Chicagoans and the Great Fire, 1871–1874* (Chicago: University of Chicago Press, 1995), 283, n. 21.

8. Admittedly, most insurance companies covering Chicago were unable to meet their obligations and policyholders would receive only $35 million of the $100 million they were owed. "The Burning of Chicago," *Science Record for 1872–1876: A Compendium of Scientific Progress and Discovery* (New York: Munn, 1976), 307. According to the *Report of the Illinois Auditor*, sixty-nine American companies went into liquidation as a result of losses at Chicago. See Richard Warren Shepro, "The Reconstruction of Chicago after the Great Fire of 1871" (B.A. senior thesis, Harvard University, 1975), 47. See also *Chicago Fire and the Fire Insurance Companies: An Exhibit of the Capital, Assets, and Losses of the Companies, Together with a Graphic Account of the Great Disaster* (Chicago: Goodsell, 1871). The insurance industry performed much better at San Francisco, eventually paying out about $200 million of $235 million claimed by property holders. Archibald Mac Phail, *Of Men and Fire: A Story of Fire Insurance in the Far West* (San Francisco, Calif.: Fire Underwriters Association of the Pacific, 1948), 101–102, 111. Despite awesome losses, only five companies went bankrupt and seven retired from business. "The Fire Insurance History of the World's Greatest Conflagration," *Emanu-El* 22, no. 19 (21 September 1906): 12–17; Christopher Morris Douty, "The Economics of Localized Disasters: An Empirical Analysis of the 1906 Earthquake and Fire in San Francisco" (Ph.D. diss., Stanford University, 1970), 281–298.

9. As William Cronon has forcefully argued, all of the boosting in the world

Narratives of Resilience

would have amounted to little in Chicago were it not for the city's favorable geographic site at the core of a rich hinterland of lumber, grain, and meat as well as ready access to waterways and a transcontinental railroad network along which to convey products to national and world markets. *Nature's Metropolis: Chicago and the Great West* (New York: Norton, 1991).

10. Colbert and Chamberlin, *Chicago and the Great Conflagration*, 315–318.

11. For two exemplary treatments of the fire as an event shaped by literature and myths see Ross Miller, *American Apocalypse: The Great Fire and the Myth of Chicago* (Chicago: University of Chicago Press, 1990); and Carl S. Smith, *Urban Disorder and the Shape of Belief* (Chicago: University of Chicago Press, 1995).

12. Kai Erikson, "Notes on Trauma and Community," in *Trauma: Explorations in Memory*, ed. Cathy Caruth (Baltimore, Md.: Johns Hopkins University Press, 1995), 194.

13. George Harvey, "Comment," *Harper's Weekly*, 5 May 1906, 616.

14. Kevin Rozario, "What Comes Down Must Go Up: Why Disasters Have Been Good for American Capitalism," in *American Disasters*, ed. Steven Biel (New York: New York University Press, 2001), 72–102. See also Max Page, *The Creative Destruction of Manhattan, 1900–1940* (Chicago: University of Chicago Press, 1999).

15. For an excellent analysis of the ways elites exploited fears of urban disorder to construct a bourgeois vision of order in the late nineteenth century, see Carl Smith, *Urban Disorder and the Shape of Belief: The Great Chicago Fire, the Haymarket Bomb, and the Model Town of Pullman* (Chicago: University of Chicago Press, 1995).

16. A sample of key texts from a vast number of sources on this subject are Mary Ann Diane, "Information, Crisis, Catastrophe," in *The Logics of Television: Essays in Cultural Criticism*, ed. Patricia Mellencamp (Bloomington: Indiana University Press, 1990), 222–239; Gilles Deleuze, *Cinema 1: The Movement-Image*, trans. Hugh Tomlinson and Barbara Habberjam (Minneapolis: University of Minnesota Press, 1986), and *Cinema 2: The Time-Image*, trans. Hugh Tomlinson and Robert Galeta (Minneapolis: University of Minnesota Press, 1989); and Brian Massumi, *Parables of the Virtual: Movement, Affect, Sensation* (Durham, N.C.: Duke University Press, 2002).

17. Susan Sontag, *Against Interpretation and Other Essays* (New York: Farrar, Straus, and Giroux, 1964), 14.

18. Few scholars disagree with Peter Brooks's observation that the narrative form appeals because it "demarcates, encloses, establishes limits, orders." *Reading for the Plot: Design and Intention in Narrative* (Cambridge, Mass.: Harvard University Press, 1984), 6.

19. J. Hillis Miller maintains that reversal is a defining component of the narrative form. "Narrative," in *Critical Terms for Literary Study*, ed. Frank Lentricchia and Thomas McLaughlin (Chicago: University of Chicago

Press, 1990), 75. According to Frank Kermode, the narrative form exploits and fulfills a deeply rooted human longing for endings, for the closure that makes sense of events and invests lives with meaning. In this economy of desire few elements of narrative are as important as the peripeteias, which are valued by readers for deferring expected and desired endings, thereby making them more satisfying and realistic when they finally come. *The Sense of an Ending: Studies in the Theory of Fiction* (New York: Oxford University Press, 1968).

20. David D. Hall, *Worlds of Wonder, Days of Judgment: Popular Religious Belief in Early New England* (New York: Knopf, 1989).

21. The classic scholarly treatment of this outlook is Sacvan Bercovitch, *The American Jeremiad* (Madison: University of Wisconsin Press, 1978).

22. My analysis in this chapter rests upon exhaustive archival research of the published and unpublished disaster narratives collected at the Chicago Historical Society, the Newberry Library, the San Francisco Public Library, the Bancroft Library, and the California Historical Society.

23. A. T. Andreas, *History of Chicago* (Chicago: Andreas, 1884–1886), 2:754.

24. Hayden White, *Tropics of Discourse: Essays in Cultural Criticism* (Baltimore, Md.: Johns Hopkins University Press, 1985), 5.

25. "The Cradle and the Grave of the Fire," *New York Tribune*, 17 October 1871, 1.

26. Frank Luzerne, *The Lost City! Drama of the Fire-Fiend* (New York: Wells, 1872), 119.

27. My italics. Sermon delivered at the Reverend E. E. Hale's church in Boston, 12 November 1871. Quoted in James Washington Sheahan and George P. Upton, *The Great Conflagration* (Philadelphia: Union, 1872), 314.

28. As Karen Sawislak pointedly notes, he was helped in his recovery by his privileged class position, especially his ability to earn money lecturing about the fire and as the recipient of thousands of dollars sent to him for his personal use by well-wishers. *Smoldering City*, 72–73.

29. Lloyd Wendt, *"Swift Walker": An Informal Biography of Gurdon Saltonstall Hubbard* (Chicago: Regnery, 1986), 470.

30. H. Dilger, "Report of Adjutant-General Dilger, October 15, 1871, to His Excellency John M. Palmer, Governor of Illinois." Newberry Library, 2. As the president of the Board of Police later testified, despite "an unusual amount of larcenies" on the night of the fire, "From any other species of crime or misdemeanor, the city was then, and continued to remain, remarkably exempt." Illinois General Assembly, *Report of the House Select Committee on the Governor's Messages of Nov. 15 & Dec. 9, 1871* (Springfield, Ill.: State Journal Print, 1872), 17. See also H. W. S. Cleveland, "Recollections of the Fire," 10 November 1871, 5–6, Fire Narratives Collection, Chicago Historical Society.

31. *Chicago Evening Post*, 18 October 1871, 2.

32. Luzerne, *The Lost City!* 70.

Narratives of Resilience

33. Although it is harder to find documentation for the opinions and feelings of Chicago's largely Catholic and immigrant working population, Karen Sawislak provides plenty of evidence to suggest that laborers favored a more collectivist response to the crisis even as they resisted "improvements" (for example, fire codes) that threatened to put home ownership out of their reach in the post-conflagration period. Less protected by money, reliable insurance, servants, and the like, these groups were less susceptible, though not immune, to optimistic readings of the great fire. *Smoldering City*, 23–24, 35–36, 76.

34. The Relief and Aid Society charged with relieving the burned-out population actively sought out those whose "previous condition in life unfitted them to endure the exposure and suffering incident to such modes of receiving relief"—the genteel. The committee, which soon thoroughly earned its reputation for driving away poorer supplicants, asked its officials to be especially kind and sympathetic to the persons who had fallen from comfortable circumstances, arguing that they were "the keenest sufferers of all": "They were not accustomed to exposures and hardships which were easily borne by the laboring people. . . . They were borne in a single night from homes of comfort and plenty into absolute destitution. Nothing could exceed the misery which they were compelled to undergo." *First Report of the Committee on Special Relief to the Executive Committee of the Chicago Relief and Aid Society* (Chicago: Horton and Leonard, 1872), 3, 5.

35. "The Lesson of Chicago," *Frank Leslie's Illustrated Newspaper*, 28 October 1871, 98. It was not until the depression brought construction to a virtual stop between 1873 and 1879, leaving time for reflection, that a truly "new school" of Chicago architects led by Burnham and Root and Sullivan and Wright would denounce the great rebuilding and introduce the modern designs and techniques that made Chicago into a byword for design innovation. Miller, *American Apocalypse*, 63.

36. *Chicago Tribune*, 23 June 1872.

37. *Oakland Herald*, 26 April 1906, 4.

38. Will Irwin, *The City That Was: A Requiem of Old San Francisco* (New York: Huebsch, 1906).

39. Charles Morris, *The San Francisco Calamity by Earthquake and Fire* (1906; reprint, Secaucus, N.J.: Citadel, 1986), 159. Gertrude Atherton, writing in George Harvey's *Harper's Weekly*, concurred: "while we are all excited over the prospect of a new and 'most beautiful city in America,' there are few of us that were born and brought up here that will not regret the old San Francisco." "San Francisco's Tragic Dawn," *Harper's Weekly*, 12 May 1906, 660.

40. Frederick Jackson Turner, "The Significance of the Frontier in American History," in *Rereading Frederick Jackson Turner* (New York: Holt, 1994), 31–60.

41. Peter Stallybrass and Allon White, *The Politics and Poetics of Transgression* (Ithaca, N.Y.: Cornell University Press, 1986).

42. Sara Dean, *Travers: A Story of the San Francisco Earthquake* (New York: Stokes, 1907), 78–79. One delirious example: "When law and order were strained a crew of hell rats crept out of their holes and in the flamelight plundered and reveled in bacchanalian orgies like the infamous inmates of Javert in 'Les Miserables.'" Richard Linthicum, *Complete Story of the San Francisco Horror* (Russell, 1906), 107. Tales of criminal activity were not entirely without substance. San Francisco was a major seaport with a large drifting population of single men and, as the anarchist and self-styled "hobo king" Ben Reitman attested, tramps and criminals did prowl through the burning city in search of booty. Ben L. Reitman, "Following the Monkey," ms., n.d., 181, Folder 1, Ben L. Reitman Papers, Manuscripts Collection, University of Illinois, Chicago. See also Frederick Funston, "The Work of the Regulars," *New San Francisco Magazine* 1, no. 1 (May 1906): 33. But there was no murderous frenzy during or after the fire.

43. Gertrude Atherton, "San Francisco's Tragic Dawn," *Harper's Weekly*, 12 May 1906, 660, 675.

44. For a comprehensive account of the politics and mechanics of relief and reconstruction, see Russell Sage Foundation, *San Francisco Relief Survey* (New York: Survey Associates, 1913). For two scholarly accounts, see Christopher Morris Douty, *The Economics of Localized Disasters: An Empirical Analysis of the 1906 Earthquake and Fire in San Francisco* (New York: Arno, 1977); and Judd Kahn, *Imperial San Francisco: Politics and Planning in an American City, 1897–1906* (Lincoln: University of Nebraska Press, 1979).

45. William Langewiesche, "American Ground: Unbuilding the World Trade Center," *Atlantic Monthly*, July–August 2002, 47. See also his book *American Ground: Unbuilding the World Trade Center* (New York: North Point, 2002).

46. Langewiesche, "American Ground," 50.

47. Bruce Springsteen, "Countin' on a Miracle," *The Rising* (Sony, 2002).

48. "No Buildings Where Towers Once Stood, Pataki Vows," *New York Times*, 30 June 2002, 23.

49. Miller, *American Apocalypse*, 146–149. It was not until 1956 that the city finally built a memorial to the fire, a small and unremarkable flame sculpture on the site where Mrs. O'Leary's barn once stood.

50. Jean Baudrillard, *The Spirit of Terrorism and Requiem for the Twin Towers* (New York: Verso, 2002); see also Alexander Stille, "French Philosophy and the Spirit of Terrorism," *Correspondence: An International Review of Culture & Society* 9 (Spring 2002). For more mainstream American responses see Alison Gilbert et al., *Covering Catastrophe: Broadcast Journalists Report September 11* (Chicago: Bonus Books, 2002).

51. Letters to the Editor, *New York Times*, 19 July 2002.

52. Daniel Libeskind, "Conflict Resolution," *New Statesman*, 24 June 2002.

53. On the link between spectacular buildings and the demands of international capitalism, see David Harvey, *The Condition of Postmodernity* (Cambridge: Blackwell, 1990), 92.

Narratives of Resilience

"The Predicament of Aftermath"
Oklahoma City and September 11

2

EDWARD T. LINENTHAL

■ Memorial response in the wake of violence is an expression of re-silience—whether marking "everyday" acts of murder, or more dra-matic outbreaks of terrorism or war. Particularly in an age of mass death, when individuals become statistics signifying the anonymous death of millions, such response is about more than providing a tran-quil sacred space for rituals of mourning. It is a protest, a way of saying, "We will not let these dead become faceless and forgotten. This me-morial exists to keep their names, faces, stories in our memories." In-creasingly, memorial expression has become an immediate language of engagement, not just a language of commemoration. This is clearly evident in the rise of a new generation of activist memorial environ-ments, in particular the U.S. Holocaust Memorial Museum and the Oklahoma City National Memorial, consciously modeled after the Ho-locaust Museum. Both include memorial space, museum exhibition space, archival space, educational space, and outreach programs, pro-moting activist agendas designed to spark civic energies to combat anti-Semitism, terrorism, and other ills of modernity. Ideally, these insti-tutions are sites of conscience on the civic landscape. Their role is to immerse visitors in a compelling and often horrific story, and trans-form them into actively engaged citizens.

The terrorist attacks in Oklahoma City on April 19, 1995, and in New York on September 11, 2001, brought communities together and at the same time tore them apart. Whether represented in thousands of letters suggesting appropriate memorial forms, in the creation of so-called spontaneous memorials—so popular now that they represent "planned spontaneity" and perhaps even memorial cliché—or in the formation of formal memorial processes, memorial expression helps people to transform bereavement, anger, fear, and resolve into an active communal grief that mournfully celebrates ongoing life, albeit transformed.

There is instability in memorial expression, however. The fragility of memory is never more apparent than when memorials are envisioned. Memorial expression tasks creators to ensure remembrance through significant memorial forms, since the danger of forgetfulness, even oblivion, is enduring. There is instability as well in the rhetoric of civic resilience, which bravely proclaims that just as those murdered will be intensely remembered through memorials, the cityscape will be intensely remembered through acts of civic renewal. And yet can a beloved civic community be built on an edifice of mass death? Once the collective effervescence of "we're all in this together" or "people were all the same color on that day" wears off, is civic resilience more enduring than an intense celebration of the heroism of the moment and a formulaic rhetoric of defiance? Over time, does the chronic impact of violence on the minds, souls, and bodies of so many corrode the consolatory properties of civic renewal? Is the rhetoric of resilience, so appropriate when thinking about the courage of individuals, simply not as persuasive when struggling with the gaping social wounds brought about by mass murder?

This chapter is an engagement with these questions, a comparison of some similarities and differences in the ways in which Oklahoma City and New York City responded to acts of mass murder. It is about the allure of memorialization, the uses of the rhetoric of renewal, and the inevitable instability inherent in these responses.

Several months before the atrocity of September 11, 2001, I was preparing to write the conclusion for *The Unfinished Bombing: Oklahoma City in American Memory*, and a colleague asked me, "What will be the staying power of the memorial? Will it continue to occupy a prominent place on the landscape?" These were timely questions, reminding me that memorials rarely stay situated in public memory in predictable ways. Even the most seemingly secure—the Lincoln Memorial, for example—are multivocal. Many memorials, of course, are not enduring lodestars of public attention. Would not members of the Civil War generation—particularly members of the Grand Army of the Republic—have been shocked at the recent neglect of Grant's Tomb? Even the shattering impact of the Great War in Europe has not ensured that all World War I memorials remain secure in public memory. Historian Jay Winter reminds us that they are subject to a "trajectory of decomposition, a passage from the active to the inert. . . . Seventy-five years after the Armistice, war memorials have become the artifacts of a vanished age, remnants of the unlucky generation that had to endure the carnage of the Great War."[1]

My colleague's question and Winter's insightful comment reminded me that it would be some time before the status of the Oklahoma City National Memorial was settled. So, in the book's conclusion, I asked the following:

Figure 2.1.
The shattered remains of the Alfred P. Murrah Federal Building in Oklahoma City became a grimly familiar image. Courtesy of David Allen, Oklahoma City.

Will the prominence of the Oklahoma City bombing be ensured by its location in the nation's official memory? Will it become an enduring part of the national landscape, a site as important as Monticello, Gettysburg, or the Vietnam Veterans Memorial? Will a future terrorist act that inflicts even more death consign Oklahoma City to a less prestigious location on the landscape of violence? Or might such an act increase its prestige as the first event in a continuing body count of domestic terrorism?[2]

These questions became terribly, horrifically relevant after September 11, 2001. The bombing of the Murrah Federal Building was no longer the worst single act of terrorism in the nation's history. In so many ways, it seemed, the events of 9/11 trumped April 19, 1995, offering support for those few who had argued that the Oklahoma City National Memorial had taken shape too quickly, been rushed into being before the event had found a stable place in the nation's memory. It was, some critics said, an example of a problematic aspect of the popularity of contemporary memorial expression: events are memorialized before they are assimilated into historical consciousness.

It seemed to me, however, that while the rich cultural afterlife of the Oklahoma City bombing offered not an exact template of the struggles awaiting those directly affected by terrorism in New York City and at the Pentagon, as well as the residents of Shanksville and Somerset County, Pennsylvania, it was an appropriate road map to the dark and alien landscape that awaited, a "microcosm of hindsight in advance."[3]

Often, I heard people in Oklahoma City speak of life after the bombing as the "new normal." I didn't appreciate well enough the appropriateness of that phrase until September 11. Oklahoma City offered some warnings and some encouragement, and the people of Oklahoma City became valuable resources as the embryonic shape of the post–September 11 new normal began to be formed. In particular, Oklahoma City shed light on cultural processes by which we engage such horrific and subversive events, particularly the narratives through which we frame them and the immediacy of memorial expression to contain them.

Is this a fruitful or appropriate comparison? Is it like comparing apples and oranges? After all, domestic terrorists apparently operating

Narratives of Resilience

alone, though certainly immersed in the conspiratorial world view that energizes the extremist fringe of domestic militia groups, carried out the attack in Oklahoma City. Timothy McVeigh and Terry Nichols were soon captured, tried, and sentenced. And the civic ritual of purification that is the death penalty removed the defiling presence of McVeigh from the body politic, a fate that nearly befell Nichols after state trial in Oklahoma. The events of September 11, however, had an immense international impact that the bombing in Oklahoma City did not. And while domestic terrorist threats remained—and still remain—after Oklahoma City, there was in 1995 nowhere near the post–September 11 level of public fear of an increasing crescendo of biological, chemical, or nuclear terrorist attacks. Oklahoma City did not bring in its wake fears of an enduring, palpable terrorist threat. It seemed a single, contained event.

Of course the scale of death was quite different, as was the coordinated attack on several places. The nature of the two cities was also different: the attack in Oklahoma City was widely seen as an attack on the nation's heartland, proving that even a daycare center in a federal building in a moderate-sized city was not safe. (As this so-called lesson was being proclaimed, there were of course other Americans who had long known there were no zones of safety from terrorism. How painful it must have been for the families of the girls blown up by white supremacist terrorists in the Sixteenth Street Baptist Church in Birmingham, Alabama, in 1963 to hear that "now" we know.) The attack on New York City was not only an attack on perhaps the most prominent city in the world, but an attack on an icon of American capitalism, the World Trade Center. Except for those who worked in the Murrah Building, saw it as an intimate part of their lives, and mourned its implosion some five weeks after the bombing, it was not a public symbol of any import in Oklahoma City. Its destruction did not engender the apocalyptic imagery as did that of the World Trade Center, including use of the term *Ground Zero*, an image of total destruction taken directly from Manhattan Project rhetoric describing the dead zone in New Mexico where the first atomic test took place in July 1945. The unforgettable images of the towers crumbling sparked commentary on not only the death of a particular icon, but also the death of the very idea of the skyscraper.

The nature of the sites themselves was also different. Three sets of human remains rested in the Murrah Building for five weeks, until the building was imploded. After that, the site was no longer an "open grave." It became possible to envision a memorial environment, no longer charged by human remains, but certainly transformed by the horrific event that had forever changed the site. In New York City, however, there will perhaps never be a time when some family members of those murdered will consider the site anything but an open grave. The cremated remains of thousands (including the defiling presence of the perpetrators) were scattered throughout the area, making even more complex any memorial discussion.

In Oklahoma City, custodianship of the site was not an enduring issue, as a consensus soon emerged that a new federal building would not be built there, that it would be reserved as a memorial site, and that leadership in a memorial process would come from the city. In New York City, there were complex issues of ownership and stewardship, immense economic and social reverberations from damage done to neighborhoods, subway lines, hundreds of small businesses, and tourism.

In both cities, the term *sacred ground* was used often. In Oklahoma City, it referred to the Murrah "footprint" and, for some, Fifth Street—now transformed into an eloquent reflecting pool within the memorial environment—where many grievously wounded people were carried. One of the major issues with which the Oklahoma City National Memorial Foundation successfully dealt was the desire to close permanently this street so that a memorial complex could stretch from the Murrah footprint to the Journal-Record Building across Fifth Street. Some argued that closing the street would permanently alter the cityscape and provide the terrorists with a symbolic victory. Others successfully argued that reopening the street was not an appropriate way to honor the memory of the few people who died in buildings across from the Murrah Building, and if the street were reopened, one family member observed, the city would be burdened with the dubious distinction of having the nation's first "drive-thru" memorial.

The issue of sacred ground in New York City, however, proved more troublesome. Christy Ferer, Mayor Michael Bloomberg's liaison between the city and families (who later joined the Lower Manhattan Development Corporation board), observed in May 2002 that families were

Narratives of Resilience

struggling with the question of just what part of the 16-acre site should be treated as sacred ground. Does it extend down 70 feet from ground level, the depth of the buildings' implosion? Does it extend 110 stories into the sky? Does sacred ground include the areas half a mile away where human remains were found atop neighboring buildings? Is it the part of the Fresh Kills landfill where forensic detectives painstakingly filtered 1.6 million tons of twisted wreckage and pulverized debris?[4]

The international impact of September 11, the scales of death, the nature of the cities, the complexity of the sites are some of the ways that the events of April 19, 1995, and September 11, 2001, are quite different. And yet in so many ways, cultural responses after September 11 reminded me of the aftermath of the bombing in Oklahoma City and reveal striking similarities in how these cities struggled to make meaning out of murderous events.

In both locations, a narrative of civic renewal—"yes, it was horrible, but . . ."—signaled the defiance of these wounded cities. This narrative celebrated many types of heroism. In Oklahoma City, it honored nurse Rebecca Anderson, who rushed into the Murrah Building to help, was struck by falling debris, and died a few days later. It paid tribute to wounded workers who escaped the building and immediately returned to help friends and coworkers. It is a narrative that celebrates the response of thousands of people who gave blood and helped in so many different ways. It is a narrative that celebrates new life emerging out of death, for many hoped that the city would be energized by the disaster to invest enthusiastically in civic renewal projects. A revitalized city, it was thought, would be a most appropriate response to an act of mass murder. The disaster, many hoped, showed how strong were the bonds of community, demonstrated how good were the hearts of most people.

Some people in Oklahoma City thought a crucial sign of a resilient city would be a new federal building on the same site. There were even a few, including one of the building's architects, who hoped that the damaged building itself could be repaired, but it was clearly a fatally wounded structure. "Rebuild," many said, "so that a skyline transformed by the presence of the absence of the Murrah Building does not memorialize the act of mass murder." Fairly soon, however, enthusiasm for a new building faded and the conviction that this was sacred ground took hold, engendering memorial suggestions, not visions of reconstruction.

In New York City, a rhetoric of civic renewal emerged immediately, focusing on the heroism of hundreds who died trying to save those trapped in the World Trade Center and on the urgent need to rebuild. Shortly after the bombing, Mayor Rudolph Giuliani declared that the "skyline will be made whole again," and there was widespread discussion of a new World Trade Center that would be even taller, thus declaring the city's defiance. Historian Kenneth Jackson, president of the New-York Historical Society, said, "I hope they rebuild, whether they rebuild that exact structure or not." New York, he observed, is about "density and bustling sidewalks, and that's the nature of the city." *New York Times* reporter John Tierney informed readers that "the skyline is our psychic equivalent of the cathedrals and temples and mosques that other cities rushed to rebuild after other attacks."[5] And surely, the selection of Daniel Libeskind's competition-winning design for the rebuilt site—following overt public rejection of the more quotidian schemes initially proposed by the Lower Manhattan Development Corporation—confirmed this longing for psychic restoration.

As in Oklahoma City, the disaster was seen as an opportunity, in this case to restore a vibrant sense of local community that had been destroyed when the World Trade Center towers were built. Given the status of New York City, the *New York Times*'s Herbert Muschamp understood the attack as more than a strike at an economic icon but an attack on a "great city and its relationship to the world." "We have not found ways," he wrote, "to integrate into policy the global civilization that technology is creating. This task should be performed by cities, starting with New York."[6]

Within hours of the terrorist attacks in each city, memorial suggestions—mostly from within the United States, but a significant number from around the world—flooded the offices of mayors and other city and state officials. Certainly, the intense media attention to these disasters sparked some of these responses, as people felt enfranchised by their vicarious participation in the horrific spectacle of destruction, in the pathos and drama of the lives of survivors, and in the public eulogies of those murdered. The line between private and intimate mourning and public shared mourning was effectively erased by intense media coverage. This led people who would never think to intrude into the funeral service of a stranger in their own communities to take an active interest in memorial planning, and even occasionally to intrude into the lives of family members and survivors.

Memorial ideas in Oklahoma City revealed a richly varied American memorial vocabulary. It should be, people said, like the Vietnam Veterans Memorial, the U.S. Holocaust Memorial Museum, Mount Rushmore, the eternal flame of John F. Kennedy. Or it should be a memorial garden, reflecting pool, a center for peace or international studies, a place for concerts and poetry readings, or a statue of the iconic image of Oklahoma City: the fireman and the baby. Spontaneous commemorations arose on the site of destruction itself, as rescue workers created small memorials in the rubble as they worked, and soon, the fence that surrounded the site became a "people's memorial," a place where visitors left both planned and spontaneous offerings, and a site where family members created public and personal memorial spaces for their murdered loved ones.[7]

Some suggested that rubble from the Murrah Building be used as or in a memorial. Such rubble—immediately both a sacred relic and a commercial commodity—was understood to be a material way for

Figure 2.2. A number of spontaneous memorials sprang up in downtown Oklahoma City shortly after the bombing. Courtesy of David Allen, Oklahoma City.

"The Predicament of Aftermath"

visitors to "touch" the event, in the same way that material evidence of the Holocaust in the national museum—a railcar from Poland, shoes from those gassed at Maidanek, a portion of a women's barrack from Auschwitz, for example—was understood to convey the reality of this event to visitors in the nation's capital. There were elaborate memorial Web sites, and in addition to the thousands of unsolicited ideas for a physical memorial in Oklahoma City, there was a vast array of memorial programs and other activities, from quilt making and tree planting to athletic events, publications, concerts, and a wide variety of artistic creations.

In Oklahoma City, Mayor Ron Norick initiated a formal memorial process within several months of the bombing, and a memorial task force, which eventually became the Oklahoma City National Memorial Foundation, was formed by July 1995. Unsolicited memorial suggestions continued to pour in for several years, but soon after the bombing it became clear that the task force was the official voice through which a memorial process would emerge. In New York City, the events of September 11 sparked an even greater outpouring of unsolicited memorial expression, with more emphasis on the intricacies of specific architectural designs.

Some thought the immediate attention—almost eagerness—of some architectural firms to envision a World Trade Center memorial troubling. Herbert Muschamp cautioned that "there is no need to rush. . . . It takes time to achieve transparency where meaning is concerned." And Hans Butzer, who with his wife, Torrey, designed the Oklahoma City National Memorial, informed readers of the *New York Times* that "working together to achieve a consensus will be just as much a memorial as any construct that is built."[8]

Only rarely did anyone suggest that these events should *not* be recalled on the landscape, that forgetting, not remembering, was the appropriate way to treat such volatile places of memory, an attitude that had been the norm until recently. As cultural geographer Kenneth Foote observes, most sites of mass murder—"sites of shame," he calls them—have traditionally been destroyed or returned to previous uses. Only recently have such sites become potential memorial environments.[9]

Certainly, there are many reasons for this new attitude. Among them is the aforementioned conviction that such memorials are acts of protest as much as acts of remembrance, and there is also the seeming inability to stop the terrorist acts, hence the need to compensate by memorializing the dead as a form of apology. Perhaps also there is the illusory but comforting conviction that by memorializing such events, we proclaim them to be over, recalled as a horrific instance, assigned cultural meaning and location through memorialization, then placed on the memorial bookshelf so as to not trouble our meaning systems any further. In the case of Oklahoma City, this was plausible, as it *did* seem a single act, unlike the attacks on September 11. And perhaps since those attacks seemed to open a new and much darker vision of the future, in which national vulnerability would now be brought home in even more bloody ways, the desire to contain the conceptual wreckage of September 11 through memorial expression was even more intense.

As in Oklahoma City, spontaneous memorials erupted in New York City and throughout the nation. Manhattan firehouses and police stations, for example, became sites of mourning and shrines for those murdered, as did fences that surrounded the site. The *New York Times* offered its own form of remembrance through memorial biographies, and under way within a few months were programs to collect oral histories, well-attended public exhibitions of memorial designs, and photographic exhibitions. There were also more unusual forms of memorial expression, sometimes centered on the visceral presence of rubble. A small department store near the site, for example, enclosed in glass one section of the store as it was immediately after the attack. "The ash sits thick on the jeans. . . . It forms a crust on the shoulders of the sweaters, and put[s] a gray-white stripe on red tank tops."[10]

The tremendous memorial energies in both cities are a powerful statement of resilience, protest, resolve. The narrative of civic renewal is a very real one, not merely a rhetorical strategy to domesticate the horror of these events. Those killed while rescuing others, the heartfelt kindness of tens of thousands in the cities and beyond offer graphic testimony to the bonds of affection that link people together when disaster strikes. Perhaps imagined membership in a media-shaped bereaved community is itself a stance of resilience. Bereavement is, I believe, one of the only ways that Americans can imagine themselves as one. It trumps that which separates, including race, class, gender, and political ideology. Bereavement, then, is not simply a personal stance toward loss, but a powerful vision of an imagined community, the source of resilience.

The narrative of civic renewal contains and transforms the impact of what might be seen as meaningless mass murder into a heroic saga of redemption. The murdered become the sacrificed, as a new, stronger community emerges from their deaths. And yet just as these horrific events sparked acts of resilience that brought people together, they also tore communities apart.

In both cities, the events immediately became commodities used in ongoing ideological battles. There were bitter divisions over the causes of the Oklahoma City bombing. Was it brought about by the militia threat, or the toxic effect of right-wing talk radio? Did the immediate stereotyping of Muslims thought to have carried out the act suggest a higher level of racism than was generally acknowledged? Was the death penalty appropriate for the perpetrators, and would the delicate balance of civil liberties and security be upset by reaction to the bombing? A good deal of public discussion turned to issues of American identity. Was this an act of outsiders, those "in" but not "of" the nation? Or was such an act graphic evidence of a nation deformed from its origins by populist violence?

In New York City—and beyond—public venom focused on those who sought to divide, most particularly on the obscene words of the Reverend Jerry Falwell, who, appearing on Pat Robertson's "700 Club," blamed "the pagans and the abortionists and the feminists and the gays and the lesbians." Also seeking to make ideological hay was Anne Graham Lotz, the daughter of evangelist Billy Graham, who, appearing on the CBS "Early Show" on September 13, said, "For years now Americans in a sense have shaken their fist at God and said, 'God, we want you out of our schools, our government, our businesses, we want you out of the marketplace.' " Interpreting disaster as an expression of divine displeasure is nothing new. To many people, however, the divisive rhetoric of scapegoating seemed beyond the pale of the publicly appropriate. It threatened the narrative of civic renewal.[11]

How angry at Falwell's disgraceful condemnation of gays might have been New York City fire fighters, for example, who demonstrated their love for Father Mychal Judge, a gay priest and chaplain for the New York City fire department, who died while ministering to fire fighters at the site?

Narratives of Resilience

The firefighters . . . carried him up to St. Peter's Church and they laid out his body on the altar, and they put his rosaries in his hand, and they pinned his Fire Department badge [on him], and they prayed over him. Later that night, they wouldn't let his body go to the morgue. They brought him back to their firehouse, and they laid him in the back room. And all the friars came from across the street at St. Francis Assisi, lit candles and said a vigil.[12]

Both cities faced the difficulty of dealing with memorial hierarchies, which by their very nature divide rather than bring together. Such hierarchies

strive for exactitude in what is being remembered, who is being remembered, and the forms through which remembrance is expressed. . . . To mischaracterize the significance of an event, to blur lines between different groups, or to commemorate in inappropriate ways is often perceived as an act of defilement, a polluting of memory.[13]

In Oklahoma City there were tensions between family members and survivors, resentments among family members over some people who seemed to receive intense media attention, resentment by some family members of adult murdered "children" over the attention paid to the families of younger children.

One of the most difficult issues in the making of the memorial was how to decide who was a survivor. When it was decided that survivors' names would appear on the Murrah site, definition became a necessity, and for a year and a half a survivor definition subcommittee agonized over this issue. What about those who were not at work that day, but lost so many friends and coworkers? How should the lines of inclusion in and exclusion from the prestige of survivordom be drawn?

Tensions emerging out of hierarchical consciousness also emerged in New York City, particularly in the contentious issues of who is entitled to what portion of federal funds. And this, of course, angered some in Oklahoma City, who quickly pointed out that there was no special fund set up for them. The *Washington Post* summarized the tensions: "Is the life of a firefighter worth more than that of a bond trader? A military officer more than a civilian contractor? Should the janitor who fed his family in El Salvador get no aid because he was in this country illegally? Should relief funds pay to install window bars for a new widow?" There was some resentment at the attention given to those murdered in New York, as if their deaths mattered more in some public way than those murdered at the Pentagon or in Pennsylvania. There was resentment among some families of "victims" at the attention paid to the "heroes." *Newsday* reported, for example, that family members were angered when they "gathered at the memorial service at Ground Zero, often pushed back to the edge of the crowd where they were barely able to hear anything, and then watched as firefighters' wives were escorted to seats." And there was even anger among groups of rescuers as, for example, families and union representatives of World Trade Center security guards killed while helping people to escape received far less monetary compensation than other rescuers. Union president Mike Fishman declared, "Our members . . . are heroes in their own right. . . . They knew the building. You can save 1,000 people by knowing which door to go through and how to get down."[14]

In both cities there was concern over other forms of defilement. There was anger about commercialization, statues for sale of the fireman and baby, for example, or, in New York City, images of the World Trade Center on various tourist items "from key rings to coffee mugs." The Web site eBay for a time sold "recordings of fire and police transmissions, pirated photos, office keys and patches." Many were angered that the site became a spectacle with tour companies doing a lively business. There was anger among family members that hundreds of tons of steel scrap from WTC ruins were sold to companies overseas "where it will be turned into everything from appliances and bridges to car parts and even new skyscrapers." And, resembling very much the aesthetic/moral discussions that followed NBC's airing of a nine-and-a-half-hour miniseries, "The Holocaust," in April 1978, when Auschwitz survivor and Nobel Laureate Elie Wiesel and others angrily objected to the trivialization of Holocaust memory in popular culture, impassioned discussions took place about the appropriateness of certain "unspeakable" scenes appearing on television, particularly burning bodies falling from the towers.[15]

And there were, of course, a seemingly infinite number of imperceptible tensions that tore at the rhetoric of resilience: the continuing

Narratives of Resilience

toll of such atrocity on people, including suicide, drug abuse, and divorce. In both cities, conspiracy theories attracted some, and the rhetoric of psychobabble—words like *closure* and *healing process*—did its own insidious violence to those enmeshed in profound grief by telling them that if they grieved too long, they were "ill," and that there was a "process" by which they could chart their so-called progress.

The aftermath of the bombing in Oklahoma City is indeed a rich road map through this terrain. While different from New York City in so many ways, it is a stark example of how a city responds to an act of mass atrocity. It clearly reveals the consolatory value of the narrative of civic renewal, and it also reveals how the toxic impacts of such events are divisive, not healing. It should give those enamored of memorialization of September 11 both hope and caution. The memorial process in Oklahoma City eloquently demonstrated that family members and survivors are not "too close" to the event to play a meaningful role in the process. For many, memorial work became a form of active grief. For some, their participation has led them to further civic involvement. For all who stayed the course, they practiced the arts of democracy as they worked together to shape a process that resulted in a moving memorial that reflects their conviction that it is important to recall faces, names, and stories.

Whatever memorial gets built in New York City, there is no guarantee that it, or the event it recollects, will remain enduringly prominent in the nation's memory. Writer Michael Miscione cautions, "The planners, survivors and philosophers who contemplate the monument that will certainly be built . . . would do well to realize that not a single memorial has successfully held the attention and affection of New Yorkers for more than a generation or two." There have been several horrific events in New York, he observes, that do not register at all in contemporary memory, including the 1904 fire on the excursion boat *General Slocum* in the East River, which resulted in the deaths of more than 1,000 people, and the deaths of more than 11,000 people on British prison ships anchored near the current Brooklyn Navy Yard during the Revolutionary War. "Bones washed up for decades," Miscione writes, and eventually the Prison Ship Martyrs' Monument was erected in Fort Greene Park. It is, he observes, a forgotten and often vandalized monument. "Survivors will die or move away, neighborhoods will sour, sensibilities will change and modern events will eclipse

Figure 2.3.
A view of the Oklahoma
City National Memorial
from the Journal-Record
Building, which houses
the memorial center.
Courtesy of David Allen,
Oklahoma City.

Figure 2.4.
Those murdered are
memorialized in 168
empty chairs on the
"footprint" of the
Murrah Building.
Courtesy of David Allen,
Oklahoma City.

Figure 2.5.
Individually lit memorial chairs transform the site into a stunning and compelling memorial space. Courtesy of David Allen, Oklahoma City.

bygone ones. These social forces work faster in New York than anyplace else."[16]

The questions I asked in the conclusion to *The Unfinished Bombing* are as appropriate for New York City as they are for Oklahoma City: Will a World Trade Center memorial become an enduring part of the nation's memorial landscape? Will a future terrorist attack that claims even more lives diminish its significance, or will it become even more prominent as a memorial to the first, but not last, major foreign terrorist attack in our time? Already, there is subtle posturing emerging in the hierarchy of the constellation of September 11 sites. The courage of those aboard who brought down United Flight 93 near Shanksville, Pennsylvania, apparently saving either the White House or the Capitol from destruction, is widely celebrated as the first salvo in the American war against terrorism: the "battle over Shanksville." It alone on that dark day was a battle, not an act of mass murder.

People in Oklahoma City have reached out to those in New York City in many ways. Some Oklahoma City family members and first-responder teams have visited their counterparts in New York City, on occasion visiting the World Trade Center site with them. The Oklahoma City National Memorial has shared information on the long-term impact of such events, archival collection processes, programs for commemorative events, and development of educational materials. It has also opened a temporary exhibition, "A Shared Experience," with sections on shared terror, courage, responses, experiences, and lessons. Poignantly, it remembers the New York City fire fighters who took part in rescue and recovery operations in Oklahoma City and who later died in the World Trade Center. It also remembers the rescue team from Fairfax, Virginia, that worked in Oklahoma City and at the Pentagon.[17]

I also have a personal memory about the significance of Oklahoma City for the events of September 11, although from Shanksville, Pennsylvania, not New York City. In early December 2001, I traveled to Shanksville to join Robert Johnson, who as chairperson of the foundation guided the memorial process in Oklahoma City, and Philip Thompson, whose mother's remains could not be recovered from the Murrah Building until it was imploded after the bombing. Thompson became the first co-chair of the family member committee that was so crucial to the success of the memorial process. We participated in an extraordinary town meeting in Shanksville High School on a Sunday evening. Approximately 250 people gathered to think about what this event meant to their lives, to consider how they would be worthy stewards of the site—particularly a beautiful grove of trees in which most of the virtually atomized human remains will endure—and to think about memorialization. As Robert Johnson and Philip Thompson spoke about Oklahoma City, and responded to so many anguished questions, I felt tremendous respect for them and for those in Shanksville willing to struggle with the enduring impact of this atrocity. There was no lofty rhetoric, no evidence of cheap grace, just people moving carefully through a dark time together. Perhaps this modest yet powerful form of resilience is the most honest. Perhaps this, the sober mapping of the struggle ahead, is what Oklahoma City has to tell us about the new normal that awaits.

Narratives of Resilience

Notes

The phrase in the title is from an essay by the late Terrence Des Pres, professor of English at Colgate University and author of *The Survivor: Anatomy of Life in the Death Camps.* The whole sentence reads, "The predicament of aftermath defines us, and not merely as individuals but as creatures of an age that has never been able to assimilate the implications of the event we call the Holocaust." It appears in his essay "The Dreaming Back," *Centerpoint* 4, no. 1 (Fall 1980): 14. I am not making any simplistic equation between these terrorist attacks and the Holocaust, but there is at least a family resemblance in the predicament of shaping cultural reactions.

1. Jay Winter, *Sites of Memory, Sites of Mourning: The Great War in European Cultural History* (Cambridge: Cambridge University Press, 1995), p. 98; see as well Christopher A. Thomas, *The Lincoln Memorial & American Life* (Princeton, N.J.: Princeton University Press, 2002).
2. Edward T. Linenthal, *The Unfinished Bombing: Oklahoma City in American Memory* (New York: Oxford University Press, 2001), pp. 233–234.
3. Lauren Sandler made this comment about my book in her review, "Terrorism in the Heartland," *Newsday*, 16 December 2001.
4. Christy Ferer, "Lives Lost and the Renewal of Downtown," *New York Times*, 18 May 2002.
5. Kenneth Jackson, "Rebuild the WTC Towers? Death of the Skyscraper? Architects and Engineers Weigh In," *Architectural Record* 189, no. 10 (October 2001): 25; John Tierney, "The Big City: Restore the Skyline, but Do It the New York Way," *New York Times*, 14 September 2001.
6. Herbert Muschamp, "Leaping from One Void into Others," *New York Times*, 23 December 2001.
7. I cover the range of memorial expression in some detail in Linenthal, *The Unfinished Bombing.*
8. Herbert Muschamp, "With Viewing Platforms, a Dignified Approach to Ground Zero," *New York Times*, 22 December 2001; Hans Butzer, "Deciding What Our Loss Means," *New York Times*, 10 October 2001.
9. Kenneth E. Foote, *Shadowed Ground: America's Landscapes of Violence and Tragedy* (Austin: University of Texas Press, 1997).
10. Jimmy Breslin, "Simple Sight Is Most Moving," *Newsday*, 21 May 2002.
11. Michael E. Naparstek, "Falwell and Robertson Stumble," *Religion in the News* 4, no. 3 (Fall 2001): 5.
12. Andrew Walsh, "Good for What Ails Us," *Religion in the News* 4, no. 3 (Fall 2001): 4. See also Michael Ford, *Father Mychal Judge: An Authentic American Hero* (New York: Paulist Press, 2002). Ford observes, "In many respects he lived a very open life as a gay Catholic priest, attending meetings of Dignity, regularly joining gay gatherings of A.A., and supporting

gay friends publicly. But he never trumpeted the fact he was gay or politicized it" (p. 118).

13. See Linenthal, *The Unfinished Bombing*, pp. 195ff.

14. Lena H. Sun and Jacqueline L. Salmon, "Disparities Pit Survivor Groups against Each Other," *Washington Post*, 10 December 2001; Roni Rabin, "Families of Civilian Victims Battle for Recognition, Benefits," *Newsday*, 17 December 2001; Steven Greenhouse, "Survivors See Inequity in Aid to Families of Guards Who Died," *New York Times*, 16 December 2001.

15. Andy Newman, "Ground Zero: The Merchandise," *New York Times*, 12 January 2002; Graham Rayman, "It's a Disgrace," *Newsday*, 20 February 2002; Rama Lakshmi, "Shipments of Scrap and Stress: Indian Groups Say Steel from Twin Towers Is Contaminated," *Washington Post*, 18 February 2002. There was, of course, a storm of protest after the publication of William Langewiesche's *American Ground: Unbuilding the World Trade Center* (New York: North Point, 2002), in which he spoke of the "tribal" tensions between groups of rescue and recovery workers, and made accusations of looting at the site by some workers as well.

16. Michael Miscione, "The Forgotten," *New York Times*, 23 December 2001.

17. I thank the Oklahoma City National Memorial's Joanne Riley and Jane Thomas for this information.

Narratives of Resilience

The City's End
Past and Present Narratives
of New York's Destruction

As usual in New York, everything is torn down
before you have had time to care for it.
—James Merrill, "An Urban Convalescence," from *Water Street*

3

MAX PAGE

■ There were two phrases spoken over and over again on September 11, 2001, and in the weeks and months following: "It was unimaginable" and, in an apparent contradiction, "It was just like a movie." The sight of the twin towers falling was, in fact, both: utterly incomprehensible for New Yorkers and Americans of today and, at the same time, wholly recognizable to our well-trained popular-culture imaginations. If the first phrase was an accurate accounting of our daily experience, the second was an accurate statement of what we see when we turn on the television or go to a movie. Americans have been imagining New York's destruction for two centuries. America's writers and image makers have visualized New York's annihilation in a stunning range of ways. Imagining New York's destruction has not been the purview only of artists and novelists, but also a common narrative, inscribed in the daily world of newspapers and television shows, computer programs, and music albums. The images are pervasive and disturbing, but largely unstudied. Looking back, into New York's history, we need to understand how and why American culture has so readily and so creatively narrated the city's end, before 9/11 and after.

Figure 3.1.
A sketch by an Italian teenager, c. 1936, in a private notebook. Imagining New York's destruction was not only the purview of professional artists and writers, but a theme in the casual sketches of people around the world, especially in the midst of war. Collection of Max Page.

Realities: Natural Disasters and Creative Destruction in the Capital of Capitalism

■ Cultural forms express and reproduce social experience. It might not be surprising, then, that a leitmotif of American popular culture of the last 200 years has been the imagining of New York's destruction. The United States is a deeply religious nation; students of American history need constantly to be reminded that the United States remains the most religious of Western industrialized nations. The country has exhibited a strong apocalyptic strain that has not been hard to translate into popular culture. But these visions of the city's destruction stem in part from the real, lived experience of New Yorkers—their lives and the life of the city have been powerfully and permanently shaped by very real destruction and rebuilding. The specific fantasies and premonitions of New York's destruction have followed the fears of the city's people. Some of those fears were built on real experiences—a series of natural disasters, as well as what I have called the city's relentless creative destruction—that have led New Yorkers to believe that, despite the dominance of their city in the nineteenth and twentieth centuries, the mighty city is fragile.

José Martí, a Cuban revolutionary who lived in New York at the

Narratives of Resilience

end of the nineteenth century, spoke admiringly of the city's resilience in the wake of the crippling blizzard of 1888. New York, "like the victim of an outrage, goes about freeing itself of its shroud." The democracy of snowfall, covering Fifth Avenue as heavily as it did Mulberry Bend on the Lower East Side, had brought out a "sense of great humility and a sudden rush of kindness, as though the dread hand had touched the shoulders of all men."[1] Martí's written account was accompanied by thousands upon thousands of photographs taken by members of the nascent profession of photojournalism to document a defining natural calamity in the city's history.

Ironically, the city has not had the single destructive natural disaster that other cities can claim. Chicago had its fire, San Francisco its earthquake, Galveston and Johnstown their floods, but New York has never had the defining natural event that would divide the city's history in two. This fact should not blind historians to the many bouts with catastrophe in the city's history. The list is long. In 1776, the city was burned. A full third of it was destroyed during the battle of New York, which almost devastated George Washington and his army. When Washington returned in 1789 to be inaugurated as the first president of the new nation, he walked by the charred embers of some of what the British had burned more than a decade earlier. The 1835 fire was even more devastating, with 674 buildings in lower Manhattan destroyed in a blaze begun in a warehouse. In 1863, riots erupted over the Civil War draft and claimed the lives of more than 100 people. On June 15, 1904, in the *General Slocum* disaster, 1,021 people were killed aboard a steamboat that caught fire in the East River. The milestones continued into the twentieth century: the Triangle Shirtwaist Factory fire of March 25, 1911, in which 146 workers died; the anarchist bombing on Wall Street in 1920; the plane that struck the Empire State Building in 1945. New York has had its share of disasters.[2] September 11 did not bring about a wholly new city, as some have alleged, but brought New Yorkers back to an older New York, where it was understood that the city was extremely fragile.

Fertilizing the soil of imagination has been the sense, as the poet James Merrill wrote so simply: "as usual in New York, everything is torn down." When Henry James returned from Europe to his home city of New York in 1904, he declared that New York is, and always has been a "provisional city," defined by a "dreadful chill of change."[3]

Figure 3.2.
Berenice Abbott, *Wall Street, South and DePeyster Streets,* November 26, 1935. Abbott's image, from her *Changing New York* project of the 1930s, is a classic statement of what had by then become a common artistic trope: old New York being displaced by the new. Museum of the City of New York.

Thirty years later, in 1935, a long-awaited visitor came from Europe to inspect Manhattan. Like Henry James, who had journeyed back to his hometown, the Swiss architect Le Corbusier came to see how well the most modern of cities measured up. In Manhattan he found a perfect soapbox for pontificating about his vision of the modern city, a "radiant city" of residential and office towers, submerged highways, and wide-open park spaces. Accompanied by reporters and architects, Le Corbusier toured New York, walked the narrow streets of lower Manhattan, and glided to the top of the Empire State Building.[4] Summarizing the essence of the island, he echoed James, declaring ephemerality to be the city's most defining feature. "New York," wrote Le Corbusier, "is nothing more than a provisional city. A city which will be replaced by another city."[5]

Though they used the same words, there was little similarity between these two men. For Henry James, the "restless renewals" of Manhattan were a nightmare. The city's mad, money-hungry speculation had brought down his boyhood home and replaced it with a loft factory, and his genteel Fifth Avenue was filled with garish mansions of the nouveau riche. But what James had put forward as an indictment, Le Corbusier now offered as high praise. New York was "a city in the process of becoming." He celebrated the city for being "overwhelming, amazing, exciting, violently alive—a wilderness of stupendous experiment toward the new order that is to replace the current tumult."[6]

Those two identical comments, made thirty years apart, remind us of the central tension in New York life between celebrating and lamenting the city's propensity to destroy and rebuild constantly and its desire to hold onto parts of the past. Transposed into the cultural life of the city, the constant transformation of the physical landscape is mimicked in its social and cultural life. Conversely, the city's cultural vitality has been inspired by the city's physical resilience in the wake of New York's unique hurricane—the wrecking ball.

The economist Joseph Schumpeter captured the essential process of capitalism—the never-ending cycle of destroying and inventing new products and methods of production—with his phrase *creative destruc-*

Narratives of Resilience

tion. "Capitalism," wrote Schumpeter in 1942, "is by nature a form or method of economic change and not only never is but never can be stationary. This process of Creative Destruction is the essential fact about capitalism. . . . To ignore this central fact is like *Hamlet* without the Danish prince."[7] Schumpeter was interested in economic creative destruction, but what critical cultural geographers have shown is that this economic process inscribed itself onto the landscape of cities and into the minds of city people.

Fantasies and Premonitions

■ Visions of the city's end arise out of this set of economic, physical, and natural forces. The sense that the city's economic engine would destroy what the previous generation had created, and that natural disaster was lurking around the corner, spawned a genre of New York destruction. At each stage of New York's development over the past two centuries, visions of how the city would be demolished, blown up, swallowed by the sea, or toppled by monsters have proliferated in films and science fiction novels, photography, painting, graphic arts, television advertisements, postcards, cartoons, and computer software. Visions of New York's destruction have resonated with some of the most long-standing themes in American history: the ambivalence toward cities, the troubled reaction to immigrants and racial diversity, the fear of technology's impact, and the apocalyptic strain in American religious life. But furthermore, visions of the city's end have paralleled the city's economic, political, racial, and physical transformations for nearly two centuries. Projections of the city's end reflected and refracted the dominant social issues. Each era of transition has produced its own apocalyptic imagery that explores, exploits, and seeks to resolve contemporary cultural tensions and fears.

In 1835, Italian painter Nicolino V. Calyo portrayed New York's most calamitous fire, which destroyed some twenty square blocks along New York's bustling harbor on a freezing December night, and launched the New York destruction genre. As the city rebuilt in the wake of that fire, New York became a city of Irish, German, and, later, Italian and Jewish immigrants. Among "natives"—descendants of Dutch and English settlers—the fear of ethnic and racial clashes came to dominate apocalyptic imagery. The Civil War draft riots of 1863 and the many imaginings of immigrant revolt in the late nineteenth century highlighted fears among the upper class that New York would descend into a catastrophic war between classes and races. In Joaquin Miller's widely read 1886 book, *The Destruction of Gotham*, a great fire engulfed the city as lower-class mobs violently attacked the homes and stores of the wealthy. Only when Manhattan had "burned and burned and burned to the very bed-rock" was the apocalypse complete.[8] *The Last American* (1889) offered a parable about the death of a great civilization—the Mehrikans—which had destroyed itself through material excess. The remnants of this once-great civilization are visited by an explorer party from Persia in 2951; they intend to bring back the choicest artifacts of this civilization to their museum in Tehran.[9]

These are just two of dozens of books in the late nineteenth and early twentieth centuries that imagined the destruction of the city, usually by some form of alien invasion. *The Destruction of Gotham* and *The Last American* were joined by Ignatius Donnelly's *Caesar's Column* (1889), which imagined the rebellion of Jews and Italians leading to a massive column of the dead assembled on Union Square. The next year, Arthur Vinton, in *Looking Further Backward* (1890), a parody of Edward Bellamy's influential *Looking Backward* (1888), imagined a failed government run by women falling to a bombing attack by the Chinese from without and rebellion from within. Fantasies of New York's future downfall pervaded not only novels, but writing of all types. On a visit to one of New York's beaches, the housing reformer Jacob Riis worried about the "resistless flood" of immigrants, whom he feared would overwhelm New York. At Coney Island, a few years later, he would have found a different type of fantasy or nightmare of New York's destruction: the images of tenement fires shown hourly at Coney Island's amusement parks.[10]

The obsession with working-class revolt in *The Destruction of Gotham* and its contemporaries gave way in the early twentieth century to apocalyptic visions of invaders from beyond New York (from Europe and Asia, as well as from beyond the earth). H. G. Wells's 1908 portrayal of a German air attack in *The War in the Air* is but one example. Wells drew a portrait that could have been transported to the morning of September 11, 2001, without a single change of word:

Lower Manhattan was soon a furnace of crimson flames, from which there was no escape. Cars, railways, ferries, all had ceased, and never a light lit the way of the distracted fugitives in that dusky confusion but the light of burning. . . . Dust and black smoke came pouring into the street, and were presently shot with red flame.[11]

A number of novels were didactic tales designed to highlight America's lack of preparedness for an attack. In *America Fallen!* (1915), the German navy manages, just days after surrendering in World War I, to slip into New York harbor and bombard the city into submission. Carefully choosing its targets—especially the Woolworth Tower, then the tallest skyscraper in the world, the Germans destroy the confidence of New Yorkers: "The roar of the bombardment had ceased, and save for a few shell holes in the taller buildings, there was nothing to indicate that, for one fell hour, Hell had vented its fury upon their noble city."[12] Fear of invasion from abroad and weakness within (that is, lack of military preparedness) had supplanted the fears of immigrant and labor revolt that had dominated the fictive imaginings of New York's end in the late nineteenth and early twentieth centuries.

By the 1920s, nightmarish visions born of the fear of exploding skyscrapers led to scores of pulp fiction novels that ended with those suspect skyscrapers toppled in a landscape of ruins.[13] This phase of the New York destruction genre was in turn swept away by the pervasive fear of a nuclear attack in the 1940s and 1950s. In 1950, the Hollywood science fiction movie illustrator Chesley Bonestell was asked by *Collier's* magazine to illustrate its disturbingly and provocatively entitled issue, "Hiroshima USA: Can Anything Be Done about It?" [Fig 3.4] Bonestell, who had studied architecture at Columbia University and had worked in San Francisco as a designer, had made the switch to special effects painting. To his credit were the powerful images in *War of the Worlds* and the *Hunchback of Notre Dame*, as well as more docile movies such as *Mr. Deeds Goes to Town* and *How Green Was My Valley*.[14]

For *Collier's*, Bonestell produced a stunningly detailed portrait of Manhattan in the aftermath of an atomic bomb detonated in midtown. The following year, he would reprise this effort for *Collier's* 1951 issue "World War III: Preview of the War We Do Not Want" with a hydrogen

Figure 3.3.
Harrison Walter Cady,
The Unready Nation/The Grave of Liberty, 1917,
ink on paper, 24 × 19 inches. A central theme of readiness campaigns in World War I was the imagining of New York's destruction at the hands of the enemy. Alexander Gallery, New York.

bomb dropping on lower Manhattan (with effects looking remarkably like what many saw on television on September 11, 2001). He also portrayed what would happen if similar bombs were dropped on Moscow and Washington, D.C. Virtually every major newspaper and news magazine offered its own provocative—some might say titillating—illustrated stories about American cities' fate in the new type of war.

Bonestell's career as a nuclear-disaster illustrator was fueled by Cold War fears made much worse by the "losses" of 1949—the fall of China to the communists, the detonation by the Soviet Union of the atomic bomb—as well as the lingering horror of Hiroshima and Nagasaki.

Narratives of Resilience

After this immediate rush of nuclear-disaster what-ifs subsided (although they were never far below the surface), Bonestell moved on to illustrating many of the most important science fiction novels, such as those of Arthur C. Clarke, and speculative books about space travel.

In numerous movies, apocalyptic novels, federal disaster scenarios, and planning documents, Americans feared that New York's destruction was an inevitable part of perhaps an unstoppable nuclear war. Just a year before Bonestell's *Collier's* illustrations, E. B. White, in his 1949 essay "Here Is New York," wrote one of the most lasting (and often recalled in the wake of 9/11) literary nightmares of an atom bomb dropping on New York: "If it were to go, all would go—this city, this mischievous and marvelous monument which not to look upon would be like death."[15] Nuclear fears remained central to American popular culture through the 1960s.

Figure 3.4.
Cover of *Collier's*, August 5, 1950, which served as an illustration to Jonathan Lear's article "Hiroshima USA."

Those scenarios did not come true, but New York's economic and physical decline in the 1960s and 1970s, which created what many called "war zones," proved to be fertile ground for American popular-culture makers. Artists imagined the end of American civilization by portraying New York's future as a huge prison or a crime-infested jungle in such movies as *Fort Apache the Bronx* and *Escape from New York*. Articles in New York and national newspapers and magazines highlighted images of the burning Bronx and of looting during the 1977 blackout, among other images of the urban crisis. In ways not portrayed with such directness since the early twentieth century and its racial "invasion" stories, popular culture of the 1960s and 1970s linked New York's imagined destruction with the growing concentration of minorities in the impoverished city. As the city experienced a renewed influx of immigrants (from the American South, Mexico, Puerto Rico, and Asia) after the reopening of immigration gates in 1965, visions of the city's end once again centered around the threat of racial and ethnic violence. The signature image of this era's post-apocalyptic scenarios remains the original, 1968 version of *Planet of the Apes*, which combined fears of nuclear holocaust and overtones of race wars. It is the last image—of a nearly buried Statue of Liberty that remains etched in the viewer's memory as a symbol of New York's demise, even as the city's worst years of economic and social decline were still a few years ahead.

As the millennium approached, American culture became fascinated with violence and disaster scenarios of all types, from police-chase television programs, to animal-attack exposés, to nuclear-apocalypse movies. As always, New York galvanized culture makers. The obsession with destroying New York continued to pervade every aspect of our culture. The cover of the hip-hop group Busta Rhyme's 1998 album *E.L.E.*, which stands for "Extinction Level Event," for example, consists of an image of a massive ball of fire engulfing all of lower Manhattan. SimCity software allows computer users to choose what disaster will strike New York, or just watch as programmed disasters play out before their eyes. Microsoft's Flight Simulator software made it possible to fly between the World Trade Center towers, or, if one weren't skilled enough, to crash into them. (In the software, however, only the plane crashes, leaving the buildings undisturbed.) In the 1998 *Godzilla* movie, the Chrysler Building crashes to the ground, hit by a stray missile seeking to stop the monster on its march through the city. In *Deep Impact*, released the same year as *Godzilla*, huge waves rose over the World Trade Center, obliterating all in their path. And in the months before 9/11, American image makers portrayed disasters that were remarkably similar to what happened on 9/11. In the summer just before September 11, New York and its World Trade Center were repeatedly destroyed. The Japanese-animation movie *Final Fantasy* portrayed a devastated lower Manhattan beneath a dome, which was supposed to protect it from the assaults of viruslike aliens. In *A.I.*, the child robot finds himself drawn to a forbidden zone, called "Man-Hattan," overflowing with water. He makes his way, a child searching for home, past the almost submerged Statue of Liberty, past the lonely World Trade Center towers peeking out above the water, and back to the laboratory where he was "born." Up to the very moment of the attacks on September 11, these fantasies seemed to be irresistible to writers and filmmakers.

Figure 3.5.
Still image from *Final
Fantasy* (Sony Pictures,
2001). This film, from
the summer of 2001,
opens with a scene of
Times Square in ruins,
beyond the confines of a
protected "Barrier City"
in Lower Manhattan.

Explaining Fictional Disaster

■ What do these fantasies tell us? The precise connection over time
between the daily destruction that defined New York life and the fan-
tastical imaginings of the city's demise remains elusive. It would certainly be a far stretch to suggest that New Yorkers—and especially the
thousands of culture producers (writers and artists) who were born or
lived their lives in New York—were somehow inspired to dream up
the city's terrible destruction because of a numbness caused by the city's
relentless cycles of destruction and rebuilding. (A parallel and detest-
able notion—that the terrorist attacks had been brought on by the
moral debasement of American life, centered in New York—was floated
in the days after September 11.)[16]

But one answer is clear: New York has been the preeminent city of
the United States for more than a century. Despite its economic travails
in the 1970s and the rise of Los Angeles (which has, not surprisingly,
seen a growth in its own brand of destruction movies and novels), New
York remains the city to beat in all arenas. To destroy New York is to
strike symbolically at the heart of the United States.

Beyond New York's preeminence lies New York's form and the aesthetics of destruction. We have seen, especially in recent years, a genre
of film and television that we might term "disaster porn"—a salacious

obsession with graphically portraying death, mayhem, and destruction, whether via alligators, extreme cops, or alien spaceships.[17] With this cultural ferment, no place looks better destroyed than does New York. Godzilla pounding through Phoenix instead of the canyons of Manhattan would not have the same visual impact. Some of those who watched the disaster on television from afar—and who will admit it—found the site of the World Trade Centers falling to be horrifying and also frighteningly beautiful on an aesthetic level. It was a remarkable sight, in all senses of that term. Millions of us have watched these movies and played these games—all to get a charge from watching the skyscrapers of Manhattan toppling over.

We have continued to destroy New York in books, on canvas, and on movie screens and computer monitors for many reasons. But we should not ignore the psychological and the sociological, the more abstract benefits this society has gained from watching New York be destroyed repeatedly. New York remains a place apart, to many an island thankfully on the edge of the continent. To Americans beyond the city's boundaries, New York City has been and remains a touchstone, the symbol of the best and worst of everything, the barometer of the nation's health and sickness, poverty and wealth. Americans are married, not always happily but always intensely and profoundly, to New York.

Finally, one reason American culture has destroyed New York is that it is so unimaginable for Americans not to have this city. It is, in a Freudian way, a healthy playing-out of our fears on the screen. As E. B. White wrote, "New York is to the nation what the white church spire is to the village—the visible symbol of aspiration and faith, the white plume saying the way is up!"[18] The white plume we saw on Tuesday, September 11, 2001, was the billowing debris of two massive towers falling down, taking with them thousands of lives. This seemed a conscious choice—to make our fantasies and our nightmares horrible reality, to turn gleaming symbols of the city into burning sites of terror.

In the United States, the early prediction that American culture would thereafter stay away from imagining New York's destruction (and, indeed, from violence in general) was quickly proved wrong. Post-9/11 films such as *Spiderman* and *Gangs of New York*, to cite just two examples, reveled in the physical destruction of New York, even as many other movies and television shows sought to edit out the World

Narratives of Resilience

Trade Center from scenes shot before 9/11.[19] Future summer block-buster action movies will undoubtedly feature creative new ways of destroying the city, despite the pious claims that our culture would never deign to make light of New York's tragedy on the silver screen. Some artists have chosen to avoid criticism of destroying New York while feeding audiences the disaster imagery they apparently still crave, by shifting the locus of disaster to other cities. Los Angeles has competed with New York in the disaster genre for the past few decades, and has found new life, or death, in the last couple of years (such as in the television series "24," which has subjected the city to an atomic bomb and bioterrorism). Baltimore was destroyed in the *Sum of All Fears* in 2002. San Francisco fell in the *Hulk* in 2003.

Whether September 11 shifts the trajectory of New York City's portrayals remains to be seen. But with the continued war on terrorism and the ongoing interpretation of 9/11, there is no doubt that American culture and world culture will continue to spin real and imagined stories of New York's end. On Memorial Day 2004, the makers of *Independence Day* (1996), one of the more visually arresting films that portrayed the end of New York, released *The Day after Tomorrow*, a movie calculated to play on the fears of global warming. In this scenario, New York is overcome by water and then threatened with an ice age. The signature image in the marketing campaign for the film in the months before its release showed a frozen city, the buildings intact, but not a person alive.

Narratives of Resilience in Stone and Steel

■ Each type of destructive event in New York's history has provided an opportunity for the city's imaginers—its writers and journalists, painters and filmmakers—to offer narratives of the city's future. While at times—such as during the violent class tensions of the late nineteenth century or the depths of New York's economic despair of the 1970s—the stories New Yorkers told about themselves emphasized the apocalyptic, the more powerful narrative has been one of renewal, where destruction is followed by robust growth and rebuilding. From the birth of the republic up through the end of World War II, New York has grown, not always steadily but—over the long run—larger and larger in all ways. Narratives of New York's destruction—real or imagined—have generally paralleled this trajectory. Whatever disasters are imagined, readers and viewers are usually offered a coda of renewal. Many of the most dramatic films of New York's destruction, for example, end with the city saved from utter annihilation. Godzilla, in fact, does relatively little damage to the city; most of the destruction is self-inflicted (much to the chagrin of some *Godzilla* fans). *Deep Impact* ends with the clear sense that New York (and Washington) will be rebuilt by a new generation. Others, less relenting in their vision (such as *Caesar's Column*), are jeremiads invoking the Puritan era—harsh warnings of impending doom, if the community does not return to its purer, original ideals, or saner environmental habits. In this way, fantasies and premonitions of New York's destruction have often mimicked the narrative of resilience believed and perpetuated by the city's elite: that New York would always rebound from disaster, whether perpetrated from within or without. Fantasies of New York's destruction have often ended with an expectation that the "city resilient" would rebound again.[20]

This narrative mode has permeated the debate over rebuilding at Ground Zero. From September 12, a narrative has been slowly, fitfully unfolding through the debates over the reconstruction of the towers and the design of a memorial to the events of September 11. The outgoing mayor of the city, Rudolph Giuliani, left office urging that the entire sixteen-acre site be left open, from the depths of the site to the sky. Others immediately urged using the moment to reknit the fabric of Manhattan, by reconnecting streets that had been dead-ended when the multiblock World Trade Center was built in the early 1970s. The Lower Manhattan Development Commission launched a design study that produced, in August 2002, a series of monumentally uninteresting plans. The city and nation responded with a Bronx cheer (partly because they mistook conceptual massing models as actual building designs), and the commission went back to the drawing board. It sponsored a new master-plan competition that led, in December 2002, to the selection of Daniel Libeskind's *Memorial Foundations* plan. A tower would mark the northwest corner of the site, with a series of smaller towers spiraling down to encircle and reveal the exposed slurry wall that had been built to hold back the Hudson River when the foundations for the World Trade Center were built. The four acres facing this

Narratives of Resilience

wall, including the two one-acre foundations of the twin towers, would be left open, for use in a memorial.

Just before Christmas 2003, the architects David Childs and Daniel Libeskind, who were thrown together in a shotgun marriage by the developer Larry Silverstein and the Lower Manhattan Development Commission, announced that they had agreed upon a design for Freedom Tower, which would make it the tallest skyscraper in the world. And on January 6, 2004, Michael Arad's design, *Reflecting Absence*, was selected as the winner of the memorial competition that had attracted 5,201 entries from 63 nations and 49 states. His design features a solemn pair of pools of water on the foundations of the two towers that empty into a void at their centers.[21]

As with *Reflecting Absence*, none of the finalists in the memorial competition incorporated any of the thousands of pieces of the World Trade Center that lay quietly waiting in the Fresh Kills landfill and in a hangar at Kennedy airport. Few could forget the sight of those steel beams, that stood long enough to save thousands of lives, being carted in a solemn funeral cortege down the streets of Manhattan, onto waiting barges, to their resting place in Fresh Kills. Many wished that Americans could assemble on the streets to watch a reverse journey—as these steel heroes returned to help us remember and rebuild. Just two weeks after 9/11, on September 25, 2001, the director of the Metropolitan Museum of Art, Philippe de Montebello, expressed what many were thinking: the still-standing three-story facade of one of the towers would be the most eloquent memorial imaginable. Many assumed that this would happen, especially since the memorial commission had specifically urged that entrants consider reusing "surviving original elements" as a way to "convey historical authenticity." In response to criticism from victims' families and architectural critics, the jury insisted that Arad (by then joined by landscape architect Peter Walker) incorporate an underground space where artifacts from the disaster could be viewed. It remains to be seen if this new element is built and becomes integral to the memorial design.[22]

Negotiations over Freedom Tower continued as this book went to press, and the design for the memorial will also inevitably be transformed. Nonetheless, at the beginning of 2004, the dominant players in the city believed that they had reached closure on this stage of the city's rebuilding of the World Trade Center site. Meanwhile, a story of

9/11 was being crafted in models displayed at Federal Hall on Wall Street and in the Winter Garden, across from the site. That narrative paralleled some of the simplistic movie-script endings found in popular culture portrayals of the city's end, and rebirth.

At Ground Zero, a movie-script narrative of resilience—an overwhelming attack from beyond, a heroic response, and a patriotic rebirth—is supplanting a real willingness to wrestle with the pain, agony, and loss of life. Libeskind's master plan for the site brilliantly incorporated the exposed slurry wall of the western part of the site. But patriotic kitsch soon eclipsed the design's elegance: the tower was to be named "Freedom" and would rise to 1,776 feet tall—a singularly evocative number for Americans, to be sure, but a wholly imperceptible visual gesture. The slurry wall was designed to be a visible symbol of the Constitution, the foundation of the nation. Predictably, the groundbreaking ceremony for the Freedom Tower took place on the Fourth of July. These rhetorical efforts to make patriotism take architectural form were, in turn, given partisan appeal, when the Republican party marched into town in late August 2004 to crown George W. Bush as their candidate for reelection, thereby linking him to the accelerated timetable for rebuilding. Indeed, to many, everything about the rebuilding process seems rushed, as if speed were a substitute for true rebirth and renewal.

As rebuilding commences, it remains to be seen whether the nation can move beyond the sense that 9/11 was "just like a movie"—especially one with an ending that appeals to the most simplistic and nationalistic narratives. The cool, abstract elegance of the designs for the Freedom Tower and the memorial deliberately seeks to transcend the awful images of destruction. Although Libeskind's master plan for the site cerebrally evokes aspects of the tragedy in its geometries, the overall redesign effort—and the staged hype surrounding it—seeks to deflect any residual remains of Linenthal's "toxic narrative."

Instead, the response to loss in New York remains poised between two kinds of resilience. On the one hand, resilience connotes renewed vitality, with the implication that disaster leads to more exuberant growth and progress. This is the resilience that honored the efforts of fire fighters and aid workers. It is this sense of resilience that permitted Rudy Giuliani to extol 9/11 as "the most successful rescue operation in our history," since "twenty-five thousand lives were saved that day,"

Narratives of Resilience

both before and after the towers fell.[23] It is this sort of resilience that compels designers and developers to consider rebuilding bigger than ever and that led the Port Authority to capitalize on the opportunity by rethinking and dramatically enhancing the ability of the site to serve as a memorable and much-needed hub for public transit. And it is this definition of resilience that led, in the months after 9/11, to an unprecedented outpouring of radical ideas for rebuilding commercial hubs, public housing, and parks across the entire city.

But resilience also can simply mean elasticity—that is, like a rubber band, things return back to normal, to life before the event. With the closing of the first phase of rebuilding—the clearing of the site, the choosing of an overall design, and the selection of a memorial designer—it seems clear that so far, resilience has meant the latter: a return to where New York was before 9/11. Everything, we were told, would change. With office towers ringing a beautiful, clean park and an elegant, clean memorial, we have returned to a vision of New York—including its political and economic state—before 9/11. If all that the rebuilding comes to is a memorial garden with some reconnected streets, a thicket of office towers, and a million-plus square feet for a hotel and shopping mall, then we will have failed to invest in a more vibrant, more just New York, our national jewel, what E. B. White called "the greatest human concentrate on earth, the poem whose magic is comprehensible to millions."[24]

Notes

1. José Martí, "New York under the Snow," in *Writing New York: A Literary Anthology*, ed. Phillip Lopate (New York: Library of America, 1998), p. 277.

2. Some of these earlier disasters have even warranted book-length treatment; see, for example, David von Drehle, *Triangle: The Fire That Changed America* (Boston: Atlantic Monthly Press, 2003); and Edward T. O'Donnell, *Ship Ablaze: The Tragedy of the Steamboat General Slocum* (New York: Broadway Books, 2003).

3. Henry James, *New York Revisited* (New York: Franklin Square Press, 1994; originally published 1906 in *Harper's Monthly Magazine*), p. 34. This section is derived from Max Page, *The Creative Destruction of Manhattan, 1900–1940* (Chicago: University of Chicago Press, 1999).

4. See "Le Corbusier Scans Gotham's Towers," *New York Times Magazine*, 3 November 1935.

5. Le Corbusier, *When the Cathedrals Were White* (New York: Reynal & Hitchcock, 1947), p. 45. Also see Nathan Silver, *Lost New York*, rev. ed. (Boston: Houghton Mifflin, 2000), p. 11.

6. Le Corbusier, *When the Cathedrals Were White*, p. 45.

7. See Joseph A. Schumpeter, "The Process of Creative Destruction," in *Capitalism, Socialism and Democracy* (1942; reprint, New York: Harper and Row, 1976), chap. 7.

8. Joaquin Miller, *The Destruction of Gotham* (New York: Funk & Wagnalls, 1886).

9. J. A. Mitchell, *The Last American: A Fragment from the Journal of Khan-li* (New York: Stokes, 1889).

10. Jacob Riis, *How the Other Half Lives* (New York: Scribner's, 1890), p. 229.

11. H. G. Wells, *The War in the Air* (Lincoln: University of Nebraska Press, 2002 [1908, orig.]), p. 136. See Mike Davis, "The Flames of New York," *New Left Review* 12 (Nov.–Dec. 2001): 34–50, for a discussion of Wells.

12. J. Bernard Walker, *America Fallen! The Sequel to the European War* (New York: Dodd, Mead, 1915), p. 119.

13. The first and most popular of these was George Allan England, *Darkness and Dawn* (Boston: Maynard, 1914), frequently reprinted.

14. For information on Bonestell, see Ron Miller and Frederick C. Durant III, *The Art of Chesley Bonestell* (New York: Sterling, 2001).

15. E. B. White, "Here Is New York," in *Essays of E. B. White* (New York: Harper & Row, 1977), p. 132.

16. Conservative Christian religious leader Jerry Falwell suggested a version of this on September 12, 2001. Calling on long-standing conservative views of New York's debased moral milieu, Falwell declared, "I really believe that the pagans, and the abortionists, and the feminists, and the gays and the lesbians who are actively trying to make that an alternative lifestyle, the ACLU, People For the American Way, all of them who have tried to secularize America. I point the finger in their face and say 'you helped this happen.' " For a discussion of this, see Gustav Niebuhr, "After the Attacks: Finding Fault; U.S. 'Secular' Groups Set Tone for Terror Attacks, Falwell Says," *New York Times*, 14 September 2001.

17. Historians have explored this recent tendency and its roots. See, for example, Mike Davis, *The Ecology of Fear: Los Angeles and the Imagination of Disaster* (New York: Metropolitan Books, 1998); and Paul Boyer, *When Time Shall Be No More: Prophecy Belief in Modern American Culture* (Cambridge, Mass.: Harvard University Press, 1992).

18. White, "Here Is New York," p. 123.

19. Ironically, Martin Scorsese, in *Gangs of New York*, chose to leave the World Trade Center in the final view of the movie, where the heroes look over Manhattan from Brooklyn and see the city of 1863 transforming before their eyes into the city of 2002.

20. Mike Wallace uses this phrase in *A New Deal for New York* (New York: Bell and Weiland, 2002).

21. David W. Dunlap, "After Year of Push and Pull, 2 Visions Meet at 1,776 Feet," *New York Times*, 26 December 2003; Glenn Collins, "Memorial to 9/11 Victims Is Selected," *New York Times*, 6 January 2004.

22. Philippe de Montebello, "The Iconic Power of an Artifact," *New York Times*, 25 September 2001; David W. Dunlap and Glenn Collins, "How Winning 9/11 Memorial Acquired Its 2nd Designer," *New York Times*, 8 January 2004; David W. Dunlap and Eric Lipton, "Revised 9/11 Memorial to Include Artifact Center," *New York Times*, 14 January 2004.

23. Rudolph Giuliani, comments on 31 December 2001, introducing a Website featuring photographs by Joel Meyerowitz, "After September 11th: Images of Ground Zero," www.911exhibit.com/gallery.

24. White, "Here Is New York," p. 122.

The Symbolic Dimensions of Trauma and Recovery

PART II

Patriotism and the Reconstruction of Washington, D.C., after the British Invasion of 1814

4

ANTHONY S. PITCH

■ Symbols are the choicest targets for those who would make war or instill terror. Destroying the symbolic center of a nation or culture destroys the spirit of its people—or so it would seem. This chapter examines the British invasion of Washington, D.C., during the War of 1812 and reveals how the attackers carefully chose to torch a set of buildings symbolically important for the upstart republic. In the wake of the attack, Washington nearly lost its raison d'être, as Philadelphia, Georgetown, Lancaster, and other cities vied for the honor of becoming the national capital. Invoking the memory of General George Washington himself, the city's proponents finally convinced Congress to stay put. By hastily reconstructing the edifices of government, Congress effectively sealed the decision to remain and assured the recovery of Washington, D.C. The program of surgical destruction calls to mind the events of September 11, 2001, when another set of symbols—the Pentagon and the World Trade Center—was similarly targeted and, in the case of the WTC, destroyed. But rather than wreck the country's spirit, both actions instead galvanized the nation and strengthened its commitment to unity, freedom, and democracy.

Washington in 1814 was a steamy southern backwater with a population of only 8,000 residents, one-sixth of whom were slaves. The attorney general at the time, Richard Rush, described it as "a meager village, with a few bad houses and extensive swamps."[1] Nonetheless, it was the capital of the young republic, and capitals, however meager, have symbolic import.

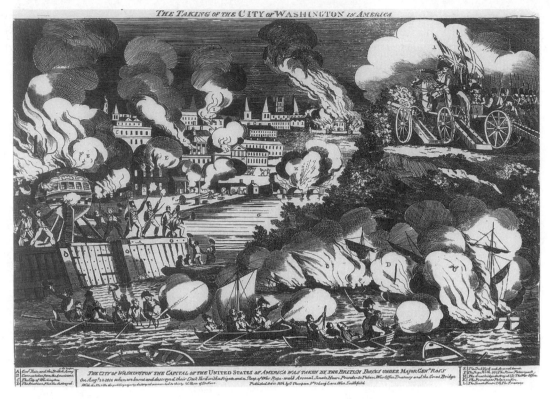

Figure 4.1.
Wood engraving of the capture of Washington, D.C., published by G. Thompson, London, 1814. Courtesy of Library of Congress. Image supplied by U.S. Senate Historical Office.

The British raided Washington in 1814 partly because they wanted to humiliate and demoralize the Americans, and they calculated that razing public buildings in the nascent capital would accomplish this in the most direct way. After all, Americans had done much the same in the Canadian capital of York the year before, when they torched and plundered public buildings before raiding villages on the Niagara frontier the following year.[2] To retaliate, the British admiral George Cockburn pressed for the seizure of Washington, arguing that the fall of a capital was "always so great a blow to the government of a country."[3]

By this time the countries had been at war for two years. The roots of the conflict lay in the British ban of American ships from certain European ports, and the impressment, or forcible abduction, of thousands of British-born sailors from American ships in compliance with a policy that denied the right of any of its citizens to renounce their nationality. Over a six-year period some 1,300 of these 5,000 sailors were later revealed to have been born in the United States.[4] Americans

The Symbolic Dimensions of Trauma and Recovery

could no longer endure such affronts to national sovereignty, and in June 1812, Congress declared war on Britain.

Until the summer of 1814 it had been a remote and distant affair, almost entirely confined to the Canadian frontier. The British, concentrated some 500 miles to the north, seemed unlikely to launch an attack on Washington. So complacent were Americans that the capital lay largely undefended. Even Secretary of War John Armstrong dismissed the threat to Washington, in spite of murmurs in the British press that such an attack was indeed being contemplated.

And then it came. On August 19, 1814, some 5,000 British troops landed at Benedict, Maryland, on the Patuxent River, striking out on a fifty-mile march west toward the vulnerable capital. Word of their approach preceded the troops. Fear turned into pandemonium as thousands of Washingtonians fled to the surrounding countryside. No troops or law enforcement officials remained to defend the city. Nevertheless, a handful of men and women risked their lives to salvage national treasures.

At the State Department a note arrived from Secretary of State James Monroe, then on horseback spying on the British advance east of Washington. It was an order to his staff to save precious national documents and records. In response, Stephen Pleasonton and several other clerks gently removed the Declaration of Independence and the Constitution, together with treaties and George Washington's correspondence, and placed them into linen bags. Pleasonton loaded the documents into carts, crossed the Potomac River, and drove to an abandoned mill two miles north of Georgetown. He did so in bold defiance of Secretary of War Armstrong, who ridiculed him for thinking the British were coming. The mill, it seemed, would be a prime target for the invaders, so Pleasonton secured wagons, loaded them up, and drove hard to Leesburg, Virginia, thirty-five miles to the west. There he locked the founding papers in an empty house. In this humble sanctuary they remained, even as the British torched the State Department's offices. Had Pleasonton not taken such swift and noble action, it is unlikely that the original Declaration of Independence and Constitution would have survived.[5]

President James Madison had already fled across the Potomac into Virginia, planning to rendezvous later with his wife, Dolley. But she delayed fleeing the White House, risking capture to direct another hasty salvage operation—this time to secure Gilbert Stuart's larger-than-life portrait of George Washington. Only when she saw the national treasure loaded into a wagon, to be hauled off through Georgetown into the countryside, did the First Lady consider her own safety and flee the White House.[6]

The British arrived on Capitol Hill only hours later. The troops looked in awe at the architectural splendors of the federal legislature—the great buildings of the Senate in the north and the House in the south, linked by a covered wooden walkway 100 feet in length. The invaders moved past fluted columns, up grand staircases, under archways, into vestibules with vaulted ceilings.

Benjamin Henry Latrobe, architect of the Capitol for a decade, had created a colossus of formidable beauty. He had looked to the land of Michelangelo for gifted artisans, as none could be found in America. He hired Giovanni Andrei to sculpt the columns and Giusseppe Franzoni to model a monumental bald eagle with a twelve-foot wingspan. When the great raptor was complete, Latrobe wrote to Jefferson pronouncing it the finest eagle in the history of sculpture.[7] The bird was placed high above the Speaker's chair in the hall of the House of Representatives. But its life was short.

The British regulars turned to wrecking the splendors that had entranced them moments before. Soldiers and sailors built bonfires with furniture in the House of Representatives. Franzoni's eagle burned and crumbled, along with other works of art. That night, the British set fire to the White House, the Treasury, and the navy yard; the following morning they torched the buildings housing the State and War departments. The inferno was so bright that the glow in the night sky could be seen as far as Baltimore, and even aboard British warships on the Patuxent River, fifty miles east.[8]

The British withdrew from the burning city after only twenty-four hours, concerned they might be cut off on the way back to their ships. With few exceptions, the marauders spared all of the private buildings and did no harm to the few cowering residents who could not flee for lack of transportation. Others, who had escaped the city, slowly filtered back. The president returned two days after the enemy withdrawal, followed by the dejected First Lady. The infant capital still smoldered and smoked.

The scale of the city's degradation was numbing. All seemed life-

The Symbolic Dimensions of Trauma and Recovery

less and sepulchral. Scorched and roofless, the once-glorious Capitol sat alone and conspicuous on the hill that Pierre L'Enfant had described as "a pedestal waiting for a monument."[9] A mile to the west, the White House stood cracked and wobbly, hollowed out by the flames.

The reverberations were equally disquieting. Within a week of the British withdrawal rumors began circulating that Congress would pull up stakes and leave the city. Almost overnight Washington stood to lose its very raison d'être. The consequences could have been dire indeed. Government was the city's heart and soul. Without the president, Congress, and various government agencies, the city would wither and die. It might even revert to farmland and apple orchards, or the malarial swamps from which the city had been raised. An exodus of government employees would lead to tumbling property values, business closures, and bankruptcies; the city would shrivel for want of commerce and people.

The pro-government daily newspaper, the *National Intelligencer*, quickly assumed the offensive, seething that such an eventuality could even be contemplated. It did not matter to the *Intelligencer* whether the move might be temporary or permanent. Both were denounced as cruel blows to residents who had just borne the brunt of an enemy occupation. Setting the tone for what would develop into a highly charged debate, the newspaper characterized removal as "a treacherous breach of the faith of the nation." It would amount to finishing what the invading army began, deserting the city at the dictate of the British.[10] "Where is the firmness of Republicanism? Where the stability of patriotism?" the newspaper thundered, savaging those who would cut and run. The *Intelligencer* invoked the memory of George Washington, speculating on how the legendary leader would have reacted to such mischief. "With what shame and mortification would he hear a debate in Congress about a removal from his capital."[11]

The city's misfortune was met with opportunism elsewhere. Other urban centers moved to snatch the prize from Washington. Georgetown, neighbor to the west, offered to vacate college buildings to accommodate Congress on the heights above the Potomac.[12] In an equally predatory move, the burgesses of Lancaster, Pennsylvania, touted their picturesque city as an admirable place for a new capital.[13] Madison remained unmoved by such self-serving appeals. Instead, he selected

Figure 4.2.
The burned House and Senate wings of the U.S. Capitol as depicted in an 1814 watercolor by George Munger. Courtesy of Kiplinger Washington Collection.

the undamaged Patent Office Building as the venue for the imminent congressional session.[14]

It soon became evident that Washington's fate would depend on the votes of a handful of congressional representatives. Congress would be the sole arbiter of Washington's future, and so the legislators themselves would have to be badgered, coaxed, shamed, or reasoned into staying put.

Civic leaders hurriedly appealed to the patriotism and self-interest of Washingtonians to help sway Congress.[15] An alert went out to anyone with wood or building materials to spare, and all able-bodied carpenters were called upon to help outfit the temporary congressional quarters. Military carpenters, too, were brought in to ready the interior.[16] In the end it was a tight fit: representatives were squeezed up to

The Symbolic Dimensions of Trauma and Recovery

the windows and against the fireplaces, but there was still not enough room to seat everyone.[17]

The president and government departments were forced to relocate to private homes throughout the city. James and Dolley Madison moved into the Octagon, an elegant eighteenth-century mansion two blocks west of the crumbling White House. The Department of State opened for business in a home recently occupied by a judge. The Treasury Department took over a house vacated at the outbreak of the war by the top British diplomat. The War Department headquartered itself in a building two blocks east of the White House, while the Navy Department and the General Post Office crammed into private homes.[18]

Figure 4.3.
Ruined White House with twisted lightning rod on roof, in an 1814 watercolor by George Munger. Courtesy of Kiplinger Washington Collection.

The Reconstruction of Washington, D.C., after 1814

Monday, September 26, 1814, was an ominous day for Washington, as representatives voted by more than 2–1 to discuss whether a committee should be appointed to consider moving the capital to "a place of greater security and less inconvenience."[19] It hardly mattered to Washingtonians that this decision was meant to be only for the current session. Their well-founded fear was that once Congress had cut its cord to Washington, it would be easier to stay away indefinitely.

This was especially clear to Virginian Joseph Lewis, whose state—along with Maryland—had ceded land for the creation of the ten-mile-square federal capital. He warned that, once the government picked up and left, it would never return. Thousands of investors who had been induced to fund a permanent national capital stood to lose everything. Representative Nathaniel Macon of North Carolina imagined a capital on wheels, with nobody knowing where it would stop.[20]

Other representatives fretted over relocation, but for different reasons. Some worried that Europeans might see the shifting capital as a sign of weakness. One patriotic South Carolinian said he would "rather sit under canvass [sic] in the city than remove one mile out of it to a palace."[21] A Kentuckian refused to add to the disgrace by running away when the British had already fled.[22] Even newly elected Alexander Contee Hanson of Maryland, the outspoken Georgetown publisher who had been so fanatically opposed to war with Britain (and who loathed Washingtonians for supporting it), argued that removing the capital would demean national dignity and honor.[23]

But Washington was in ruins, which did little to bolster the national image. The devastation was an eyesore, with no prospect of quick repair. The fledgling capital, so wanting in housing and office space even before the fires, looked doomed and sacrificial. On September 26, Jonathan Fisk, the New Yorker spearheading the drive to quit and head north to his home state, rallied a robust 72–51 majority to set up the committee.[24]

This was perilous news for Washington, for it looked very much like the start of the city's slide into oblivion. The *Intelligencer* denounced the outcome as "revolting to the feelings of nine-tenths of the people of the United States."[25] The verbal tug of war dragged on into October 1814, with the whole House sitting in committee and some members openly expressing discontent with makeshift quarters. Richard Stockton of New Jersey wondered why members would risk their

The Symbolic Dimensions of Trauma and Recovery

health in such inadequate rooms when Philadelphia offered finer alternatives. He also thought that the congressional presence in Washington would tempt the enemy to attack again in hopes of scattering or capturing the legislators.[26]

Willfully or not, proponents of removal were stoking the same regional prejudices that had swirled before the historic compromise to site the capital on the banks of the Potomac. Rankled southerners sprang up to defend the status quo. Fearful that the capital would be pushed even farther north, southerners denied that Congress had the right even to consider the issue, let alone make a ruling. Time and again, Representative Joseph Pearson of North Carolina called attention to the words "permanent seat of government," which had appeared in legislative language creating the federal capital, and described the conveyance of privately held land for the new city.[27] Pearson, and many others, clung stubbornly to the wording of the legislation that had created Washington.

Their activism was not without effect. They parried every thrust, and blunted every offensive. Those who claimed the federal district could be defended from attack only at huge expense were told the area would have to be defended regardless of where Congress convened. Those who suggested that the presence of Congress would tempt the British to come back were told the enemy could just as well drive representatives out of Philadelphia.[28] Washington's defenders suggested that exodus would only sharpen the disgrace and complete the humiliation.[29] Opponents claimed there had never been an intention to chain Congress to the spot, that common sense allowed Congress to depart at will, especially if faced with pestilence, famine, or war.[30] To soften the blow to Washingtonians, those pressing for departure conceded that compensation would have to be paid to a great number of residents, who, they agreed, would undoubtedly suffer financial losses.[31] Attitudes were so entrenched that the deep congressional divide held firm on October 6, with a 72–71 vote to prepare formal legislation authorizing removal.[32]

Mounting an ever more spirited attack, New York representative Fisk even ventured to question the patriotism of Washingtonians: would they place their own interests ahead of the nation's? They were hundreds of miles south of the active war front, making supplies and communications costlier than if the capital were removed to Philadelphia or New York. Surely, he maintained, government creditors would feel a lot better about their securities if Congress itself were safe.[33] Again, the slim majority held, 79-76, with more representatives present for the vote, this time for removal within twenty days of the passage of legislation. And then a large, unrecorded majority voted in favor of Philadelphia if the capital were indeed to relocate.[34]

The House stood poised for a decisive vote. Whatever the outcome, the decision would be a momentous one, not only for its influence on the Senate, but also for the psychological damage it would inflict on Washington if representatives voted to pack their bags and leave. There was a larger than usual turnout for the third and final vote, and when it was over the tally was a complete reversal of all that had gone before. By a margin of 83–74 the House of Representatives killed the bill. The government would stay.[35] The long and bitter fight was over. The city of Washington had won a last-minute stay of execution from the House of Representatives.

With the relocation issue in abeyance, winter moved quietly onto the Hill. Sentiment to move the capital was far more subdued in the more cautious and conservative Senate. There was never a formal motion nor even a scheduled debate on the matter. And even if the Senate had unexpectedly voted to abandon the capital, the *Intelligencer* suggested that Congress would never muster the necessary two-thirds majority to override an expected presidential veto.[36]

Senator Eligius Fromentin of Louisiana spoke for many in decrying the lack of leadership that had led to the British invasion. But even if Washington were little more than a "wilderness, dignified with the name of a city," a mean clutch of edifices that brought to mind "a camp of nomad Arabs," it nevertheless bore the illustrious name of Washington. That alone was reason enough to stay.[37]

Now the House focused on whether to rebuild upon the ruins or to regroup the executive offices elsewhere, preferably closer to Congress. It would, of course, be more expensive to build on new foundations. It had cost $1.2 million to erect the original buildings. Estimates now called for about half that sum simply to repair the ruins where they stood.[38]

Then, on the morning of Monday, February 6, 1815, the *Intelligencer* carried an electrifying headline: "Almost Incredible Victory! From New Orleans." Word had just arrived of General Andrew Jackson's victory

The Symbolic Dimensions of Trauma and Recovery

over the mighty British army, which had taken place four weeks earlier. The scope of the victory was so great that disbelief greeted publication of Jackson's dispatch to the Secretary of War. The Tennesseean had assembled a ragtag army of frontiersmen, ruffians, and militiamen and put them behind a makeshift rampart of wood, mud, bales of cotton, and sugarcane. Overconfident and restless, the British made a suicidal frontal assault across a field of sugarcane stubble. Fully exposed and with no cover, the regulars were picked off by sharpshooters. The American artillery proved more accurate than expected. When the slaughter was over, more than 2,000 British lay dead or wounded. American losses numbered a minuscule 6 dead and 7 wounded. All over America, citizens rejoiced and hailed their new hero. The miseries of August quickly dissolved in a swell of national jubilation.

Reinvigorated, representatives seized the moment to invoke the name of the most revered of all patriots, George Washington. Legislators hoping to move the executive offices from the White House area to the precincts of the Capitol were accused of shamelessly trying to override the wishes of the nation's founder. Representative Lewis of Virginia flourished copies of archival correspondence proving that Washington had personally selected the sites for the White House and executive offices. Moreover, Washington had virtually pegged the Treasury, State, and War departments next to the White House (more than a mile away from the Capitol because department heads in the then-capital of Philadelphia had complained of being constantly pestered by congressional representatives quartered nearby). With almost biblical admonition, Lewis solemnly intoned, "What that man has done, let no mortal attempt to undo."[39]

Representatives who balked at the estimated $500,000 cost of re-building the public buildings were mollified by the offer of a loan of the full amount from local banks. It was ransom money, to be sure. But wealthy individuals and bankers had agreed, in contingency plans laid out four months earlier, to dangle a bulk sum as a lure to prevent Congress from bolting.[40] The Treasury would have to pay 6 percent annual interest, but it was expected that sales of public lots in the city would more than offset the principal amount before it became due.[41] Patriotic instincts and persuasive arguments convinced majorities in the House and Senate to approve the loan, which Madison signed into law on February 13, 1815.[42] Not another word was uttered, not publicly at least, about moving the executive offices away from the flanks of the White House.

The following day, exuberant Washingtonians celebrated the arrival of a copy of the Treaty of Ghent, which, with congressional and presidential approval, would bring hostilities between Britain and the United States to a close. The gloom and doubt that had hovered over the capital for months gave way to relief and optimism. The ruins might still be a reminder of civic despair, but Washington now seemed poised for revival.

Once more the capital became the focus of American national identity. It was the only part of the country that could be said to represent all Americans with its uniquely complex union of cultures and lifestyles. In this context, rebuilding the White House and Capitol took on profound symbolic import. Here was tangible proof of the Union of States, monuments to the nation-building labors of Washington, Adams, Jefferson, Madison, and the rest of the founding generation. So long as these edifices bore gashes and scars, the nation itself lay wounded. In the wake of liberation they had embodied the collective hopes and aspirations of the young republic. Now they became symbols of resilience and unity.

But influential Washingtonians remained wary, even though their city had won a reprieve. A fickle Congress could always have second thoughts, pack up its trunks, and leave. No Congress was ever bound by the decisions of its predecessors, so long as it worked within constitutional limits. To thwart any congressional change of heart, a group of three dozen affluent residents and businesspeople pooled more than $17,000 to raise a three-story building where Congress could meet more comfortably until the old Capitol was rebuilt.[43] It was a transparent ploy to stifle the grumbles of those still yearning for Philadelphia.

And it worked. With breakneck speed, workers erected what became known as the Old Brick Capitol, on a site occupied today by the Supreme Court building. In mid-December 1815 the *Intelligencer* reported triumphantly that Congress had met in the new building, where nothing but a garden had bloomed a mere five months earlier.[44] It was the largest building ever financed by private individuals in Washington. The House of Representatives would meet on a floor above the Senate, in a room seventy-seven feet long and forty-five feet wide, below ceilings twenty feet in height.[45]

The Symbolic Dimensions of Trauma and Recovery

The reappointment of Benjamin Henry Latrobe to rebuild the Capitol, and James Hoban to resurrect the White House, signaled a determination to recreate a capital at least of equal worth to the one laid waste. Latrobe was a tormented genius, overworked, understaffed, constantly on the brink of bankruptcy, and plagued for decades by a throbbing pain in his eyes that left him temperamental and incapacitated for weeks at a time.[46] Supremely confident but easily rattled, the English émigré had little patience with bureaucrats masquerading as experts.[47] Like the inspired but volatile city planner, Pierre L'Enfant, temper would be Latrobe's undoing. But before his inevitably stormy exit, Latrobe brought a singular zest to the task at hand. He, more than anyone else, embodied the resilience that enabled Washington to recover its unique status as the national capital.

Latrobe searched mightily for building materials that would convey visual delight and aesthetic appeal. High-quality freestone, hacked from quarries at Acquia Creek in Virginia before the British invasion, was now exhausted. Latrobe was forced to find an alternative stone for the long shafts of columns that would beautify the Senate chamber and his newly designed semicircular hall of the House of Representatives. Undaunted, the architect explored the wilderness southeast of the Catoctin Mountains in search of substitute stone. There he came upon the distinctive "pudding stone" marble embedded near the banks of the Potomac River in Montgomery County, and even on the other side of the water in Loudon County, Virginia. The speckled limestone breccia was a fusion of ancient rocks, uniquely multicolored with gray overtones.[48] Overjoyed that he had located a rare, home-grown American stone that could pass for marble, Latrobe rhapsodized to Thomas Jefferson about how it would bring to the public buildings a richness in "native magnificence."[49]

The Capitol was the most conspicuous landmark in the still-wooded countryside that was Washington. Before the British set it alight, it had stood like a gleaming presence above the

Figure 4.4.
Architect Benjamin Henry Latrobe, in a portrait by George B. Matthews, restored the nation's capital through vision and zest. This portrait, painted in 1930 or 1931, is a copy of a portrait by an unknown artist. Courtesy of Architect of the Capitol.

glorified village on its eastern perch. But now bureaucratic rivalry and senseless jealousies bedeviled its reconstruction. Latrobe and his nemesis, Commissioner of Public Buildings Samuel Lane, feuded publicly in a clash of personalities that would last two years. Lane pulled rank on Latrobe, demeaning the architect like a disobedient subordinate. Hard-pressed by representatives impatient to reoccupy their legislative chambers, Lane blamed Latrobe for every conceivable delay. Latrobe could only pour out his grievances in letters to friends.[50]

The plodding pace of reconstruction had much to do with the quarries that had so exhilarated Latrobe. They were undeveloped and worked by inexperienced crews who lost eighty tons of marble before they learned the proper way to cut and split the rock.[51] Sometimes the Potomac River was too low for boats to ferry the marble.[52] At other times, flood waters swirled six feet deep in the stonecutters' sheds.[53] Many of the men working the quarries spent days in wasted labor, with marble falling apart and going to waste when dry veins appeared, or seams scattered in all directions.[54] In winter, the workers' feet froze as they clambered on the chilled and slippery surfaces.[55] Brawling, gambling, and drunkenness caused further delays.[56] Costs skyrocketed: the original estimate of $1,550 per column had grown to more than $5,000 each.[57]

James Monroe brought managerial oversight to the nation's capital after his inauguration in 1817. A disciplined leader and hero of the Revolutionary War, Monroe wanted quick action and visible results. The new president regarded the Capitol and White House as the tangible symbols of America's unity and purpose.[58] Their rapid completion was vital to the spirit of national recovery and cohesion. Monroe would tolerate no further delay.

The new president nearly assumed personal command of the reconstruction effort, even trekking in foul weather to the pudding-stone quarries to judge for himself whether the celebrated rock was worth extracting. When Monroe gave his assent, Latrobe was ecstatic. The architect was already euphoric over the handful of "beautifully magnificent" finished columns that were about to give such stately dignity to his House of Representatives.[59]

President Monroe orchestrated the reconstruction of Washington's public buildings with the full authority of the executive office. Commissioner Lane appeared every Monday morning before the president

The Symbolic Dimensions of Trauma and Recovery

to present a progress report.[60] It would seem that Latrobe's work was cut out for him. But then, to the architect's great dismay, Monroe appointed two army officers and a civilian to advise him on developments at the Capitol. In Latrobe's eyes, all three were amateurs devoid of artistic bent, who would further distance Latrobe from access to the president.[61]

Meanwhile, work on the White House progressed with relative calm. Architect James Hoban was working on a commission much smaller in scope and complexity than the Capitol. Unlike Latrobe's charge, the executive mansion was not dogged by constant changes and alterations, some at the request of Congress, which led to endless delays and spiraling costs. Work proceeded so well at the White House that Hoban installed the principal rafter just days before Monroe's election, and cheerfully requested $60 for the traditional roof-raising party for his workers.[62]

Seven weeks later Hoban reported that all of the White House walls had been rebuilt.[63] But it was later revealed that he and Lane had apparently colluded in a ruse to withhold bad news from Congress: the mansion's walls were found to be more damaged than originally reported. Fearful of how Congress might react to ever-increasing costs, Lane waited until the representatives went home and then had the workers hastily tear down the damaged sections and rebuild them from scratch. When Congress returned six months later, a significant part of the White House walls had been completely reconstructed from the ground up. The extra cost was blurred in a budget bloated by increasing payouts for labor and materials.[64]

Monroe himself circumvented Congress in his rush to complete the Capitol. Congress was out of town when Lane realized there were insufficient funds to finish the building's wings. Without waiting for congressional approval, Monroe told Lane to use funds that Congress had appropriated for slating the old executive offices, purchasing fire engines, supplying water to public buildings, and constructing other parts of the Capitol. Lane was also told to run a bank overdraft up to

$50,000—an extraordinarily high sum in those days.[65] When Congress reconvened, House members berated Monroe for overstepping the limits of executive privilege and warned him about unconstitutional abuses of power. But self-interest softened their admonitions. Most representatives were plainly eager to return to their comfortable showpiece, and they excused the president on the grounds that he was justified in doing his duty to house Congress.[66]

Before leaving the capital for three months in the summer of 1817, Monroe made it clear that he expected to find the public buildings completed upon his return. It was an arbitrary deadline, and impossible to meet. Years earlier Latrobe had lectured his superiors that "rapid building is bad building,"[67] an opinion he did not abandon. When the president returned, Monroe was disappointed and angry that his deadline had not been met. True to form, Lane pointed to Latrobe as the scapegoat, charging that the architect was frequently absent from work and dilatory with paperwork.[68]

Hoban escaped the president's wrath only because enough of the White House had been completed so that Monroe could move in.[69] The move was temporary, however; the paint and plaster were still so damp that Monroe wisely vacated the mansion within days to visit family at his Virginia country home.[70] In the meantime, Lane was rapidly pushing Latrobe to the end of his tether. The architect finally lost his temper during a meeting with the president himself. Latrobe grabbed Lane by the collar and shrieked, "Were you not a cripple I would shake you to atoms, you poor contemptible wretch! Am I to be dictated to by you!" Flabbergasted by this outburst, the president calmly reminded Latrobe, "Do you know who I am, sir?" "Yes I do, and ask your pardon," said Latrobe, "but when I consider my birth, my family, my education, my talents, I am excusable for any outrage after the provocation I have received from that contemptible character."[71]

Soon after, Latrobe resigned. For the remainder of his life he was staunchly unrepentant. Staying on, he wrote, would have meant the loss of all self-respect.[72] The work went on without him, directed by his successor, a Boston architect named Charles Bulfinch. Finally, on December 7, 1819, five years after Congress agreed to rebuild the ruined city, President Monroe congratulated legislators on their return to the

The Symbolic Dimensions of Trauma and Recovery

Capitol.[73] In Bulfinch's opinion, the finished structure was equal to that of any other country.[74]

Latrobe's departure was not only tempestuous and dramatic, but also tragic. Three years later, he was dead, struck down by a bout of yellow fever. His architectural legacy at the Capitol still radiates with inspiration—from the ingenious corn-cob capitals in the vestibule adjoining the old Supreme Court, to the pioneering vaulted ceilings, to the "native magnificence" of his pudding-stone marble in the old Senate chamber and Statuary Hall.

Latrobe's vision for a Capitol worthy of the young republic yielded one of the most awesome symbols of political power and national identity ever built, architecture familiar to millions around the world. For Washington, the completion of the Capitol marked the conclusion of a triumphant comeback. The city had risen from the melancholy ashes of 1814 to assume a place in the pantheon of national capitals. It might still be a glorified village, but it was home to the president and Congress, which made all the difference.

Notes

1. Richard Rush to John Adams, 5 Sept. 1814, Richard Rush Papers, Library of Congress (hereafter referred to as LC).
2. John Strachan to Thomas Jefferson, 30 Jan. 1815, in William F. Coffin, *1812: The War and Its Moral: A Canadian Chronicle* (Montreal: Lovell, 1864), appendix 1; George Prevost to Alexander Cochrane, 3 Aug. 1814, Alexander Cochrane Papers (hereafter referred to as ACP), LC.
3. Cockburn to Alexander Cochrane, 17 July 1814, ACP, LC.
4. Mathew Carey, *The Olive Branch; or, Faults on Both Sides, Federal and Democratic*, 10th ed. (1818; reprint, Freeport, N.Y.: Books for Libraries Press, 1969).
5. Pleasonton to William Winder, 7 Aug. 1848, in John C. Hildt, "Letters relating to the Capture of Washington," *South Atlantic Quarterly* 6 (1907): 65; Pleasonton to James Buchanan, 7 Feb. 1853, Buchanan Papers, LC.
6. Oral statement, Jacob Barker to Benson Lossing, Apr. 1861, in Benson J. Lossing, *The Pictorial Fieldbook of the War of 1812* (1868; reprint, Somersworth, N.H.: New Hampshire Publishing, 1976), 935–936; Robert DePeyster to Dolley Madison, 3 Feb. 1848, Dolley Madison Papers, LC; Dolley Madison to Robert DePeyster, 11 Feb. 1848, in John H. McCormick, "The

First Master of Ceremonies of the White House," *Records of the Columbia Historical Society* 7 (1904): 183.

7. Latrobe to Thomas Jefferson, 27 Aug. 1806, in *The Correspondence and Miscellaneous Papers of Benjamin Henry Latrobe, 1805–1810*, ed. John C. Van Horne et al. (New Haven, Conn.: Yale University Press, 1986), 2: 270.

8. David Winchester to James Winchester, 25 Aug. 1814, James Winchester Papers, Tennessee Historical Society Collection, Tennessee State Library and Archives, Nashville; Logs, HMS *Albion*, 25 Aug. 1814, George Cockburn Papers, LC.

9. L'Enfant to George Washington, 22 June 1791, in Mark Mastromarino and Jack Warren, Jr., eds., *The Papers of George Washington*, presidential series 8, Mar.–Sept. 1791 (Charlottesville: University Press of Virginia, 1999), p. 290.

10. *National Intelligencer* (hereafter referred to as *NI*), 2 Sept. 1814.

11. *NI*, 28 Sept. 1814.

12. *NI*, 3 and 5 Oct. 1814.

13. *NI*, 28 Sept. 1814.

14. Annals of Congress (hereafter referred to as AC), 13th Congress, 3rd session, Column 10.

15. *NI*, 4 Sept. 1814.

16. Ibid.

17. AC, 13C 3S 353–354.

18. *NI*, 9 Sept. 1814.

19. AC, 13C 3S 312.

20. AC, 13C 3S 313.

21. AC, 13C 3S 316.

22. AC, 13C 3S 320.

23. AC, 13C 3S 322.

24. AC, 13C 3S 323.

25. *NI*, 27 Sept. 1814.

26. AC, 13C 3S 354.

27. AC, 13C 3S 359–362.

28. AC, 13C 3S 371.

29. AC, 13C 3S 372.

30. AC, 13C 3S 347.

31. AC, 13C 3S 353.

32. AC, 13C 3S 376.

33. AC, 13C 3S 389.

34. AC, 13C 3S 395.

35. AC, 13C 3S 396.

36. *NI*, 27 Sept. 1814.

37. AC, 13C 3S 218 and 220.

38. AC, 13C 3S Appendix 1728–1729.

39. AC, 13C 3S 1135. For corroborative evidence of George Washington selecting precise sites for the White House and executive offices, see George Washington diary entries, 28 and 29 June 1791, in Donald Jackson and Dorothy Twohig, eds., *The Diaries of George Washington, 1790–1799* (Charlottesville: University Press of Virginia, 1979), 6:164–165; Commissioners for the Federal District to George Washington, 30 June 1791, in Mark Mastromarino and Jack Warren Jr., eds., *The Papers of George Washington*, vol. 8, *Mar.– Sept. 1791* (Charlottesville: University Press of Virginia, 1999), 309n.; Commissioners for the Federal District to George Washington, 19 July 1792, in Robert Haggard and Mark Mastromarino, eds., *The Papers of George Washington*, vol. 10, *Mar.–Aug. 1792* (Charlottesville: University Press of Virginia, 2002), 551; Commissioners for the Federal District to Johnson, 3 Aug. 1792, Records of District of Columbia Commissioners, letters sent 1791– 1867, M371, reel 3, Record Group (hereafter referred to as RG) 42, National Archives (hereafter referred to as NA); Commissioners for the Federal District to George Washington, 31 Jan. 1797, Records of District of Columbia Commissioners, letters sent 1791–1867, M371, reel 4, RG 42, NA; William Seale, *The President's House* (New York: Abrams, 1986), 1:14, 72–73; Bob Arnebeck, *Through a Fiery Trial: Building Washington 1790–1800* (Lanham, Md.: Madison Books, 1991), 53.

40. *NI*, 15 Oct. 1814.

41. AC, 13C 3S 1137.

42. *NI*, 17 Feb. 1815.

43. Bryan Wilhelmus, *A History of the National Capital* (New York: Macmillan, 1914), 1:637.

44. *NI*, 12 Dec. 1815.

45. *Hartford* (Connecticut) *Courant*, 12 Dec. 1815, citing an undated and unavailable issue of the *Washington City Gazette*, quoted in *The Correspondence and Miscellaneous Papers of Benjamin Henry Latrobe, 1811–1820*, ed. John C. Van Horne et al. (New Haven, Conn.: Yale University Press, 1988), 3:703 n. 4.

46. *The Journals of Benjamin Henry Latrobe 1799–1820*, ed. Edward C. Carter II, John C. Van Horne, and Lee W. Formwalt (New Haven, Conn.: Yale University Press, 1980), 3:136–137.

47. Latrobe to John Trumbull, 10 Oct. 1817, in Van Horne et al., *The Correspondence*, 3:953–954.

48. Latrobe to U.S. Commissioners of Public Buildings, 8 Aug. 1815, in *Latrobe's View of America, 1795–1820*, ed. Edward C. Carter II, John C. Van Horne, and Charles E. Brownell (New Haven, Conn.: Yale University Press, 1985), 336; and William C. Allen, *History of the United States Capitol: A Chronicle of Design, Construction, and Politics* (Washington, D.C.: Government Printing Office, 2001), 106.

49. Latrobe to Jefferson, 12 Aug. 1817, in Van Horne et al., *The Correspondence*, 3:930.

50. Latrobe to Joseph Swift, 12 Apr. 1817, and Latrobe to Trumbull, 10 Oct. 1817, in Van Horne et al., *The Correspondence*, 3:879 and 953.

51. Latrobe to Commissioner of Public Buildings, 3 Nov. 1816, Records of D.C. Commissioners and of Offices Concerned with Public Buildings, Letters Received, M371, roll 19, RG 42, NA.

52. Solomon Davis to Samuel Lane, 5 Sept. 1817, ibid., roll 20.

53. Solomon Davis to Samuel Lane, 25 Mar. 1818, ibid.

54. Solomon Davis to Samuel Lane, 25 Sept. 1817, ibid.

55. Solomon Davis to Samuel Lane, 26 Nov. 1817, ibid.

56. Solomon Davis to Samuel Lane, 8 Oct. 1817, ibid., roll 4.

57. Samuel Lane to Thomas Cobb, 20 Dec. 1819, in *Documentary History of the Construction and Development of the U.S. Capitol Building and Grounds* (Washington, D.C.: Government Printing Office, 1904), 220.

58. James Monroe, First Annual Message to Congress, 2 Dec. 1817, in *A Compilation of the Messages and Papers of the Presidents* (New York: Bureau of National Literature, 1879), 2:588; *NI*, 11 Feb. 1818.

59. Latrobe to Jefferson, 12 Aug. 1817, in Van Horne et al., *The Correspondence*, 3:930.

60. Monroe to Lane, 4 Apr. 1817, in *Documentary History*, 199.

61. Latrobe to Trumbull, 10 Oct. 1817, in Van Horne et al., *The Correspondence*, 3:953.

62. Hoban to Lane, 10 Oct. 1816, M371, roll 19, RG 42, NA.

63. Hoban to Lane, 3 Dec. 1816, ibid.

64. Lane to Lewis Condict, 15 Feb. 1817, in *Documentary History*, 196; and Seale, *The President's House*, 141–142.

65. Lane to Thomas Cobb, 5 Jan. 1819, in *Documentary History*, 224.

66. AC, 16C 1S 936–937.

67. Latrobe to Commissioners of Public Buildings, 19 Apr. 1815, M371, roll 18, RG 42, NA.

68. Latrobe to Trumbull, 10 Oct. 1817, Latrobe to Monroe, 22 Oct. 1817, and Lane to Latrobe, 31 Oct. 1817, in Van Horne et al., *The Correspondence*, 3: 953, 956, and 963.

69. *NI*, 18 Sept. 1817.

70. Charles Francis Adams, ed., *Memoirs of John Quincy Adams* (Philadelphia: Lippincott, 1875), 4:7.

71. Quoted in Talbot Hamlin, *Benjamin Henry Latrobe* (New York: Oxford University Press, 1955), 477.

72. Latrobe to Monroe, 20 Nov. 1817, in Van Horne et al., *The Correspondence*, 3:968–969.

73. James Monroe, Third Annual Message to Congress, 7 Dec. 1819, in *A Compilation of the Messages and Papers*, 2:623.

74. Bulfinch to Lane, 15 Dec. 1819, in *Documentary History*, 214.

Double Restoration
Rebuilding Berlin after 1945

5

BRIAN LADD

■ As in any city recovering from disaster, Berlin, following World War II, had the opportunity to reconnect with its local traditions. The restoration of political, social, and cultural forms offered a kind of reconnection, and so did the tangible reconstruction of buildings, streets, and utility lines. Any revival of tradition was, however, enormously complicated by two problems of continuity, one temporal, one geographical—and both of them political and philosophical. First was the question of historical continuity. On the one hand, there was a desire to rebuild: to repair a damaged but extant city or, more broadly, to continue the best local traditions in architectural style, social policy, and economic development. On the other hand, everyone in charge was determined to break demonstratively with the immediate past, that is, with the Third Reich, but they did not agree about which cultural, architectural, or urbanistic traditions were the Nazi ones. The second complication arose from the fact that the city was soon divided between East and West, governed by two ideologically opposed regimes, each determined to claim the legacy of pre-Nazi Berlin, to display the clearer break with Hitler, and to prove its cultural and political superiority. Under these complicated circumstances, the rebuilding of Berlin became one of the most visibly contested venues of the early Cold War, even as it remained a matter of basic comfort and prosperity for ordinary Berliners.

The fact of Berlin's destruction in the Second World War is well known, but merely to ask the question of what caused that destruction

117

is to plunge into contested territory. In the Soviet-occupied East, for example, the official line at first informed Germans that the destruction of their land was the legacy of Hitler and the Nazis. Later, as the Cold War heated up, they were more likely to hear blame cast upon the "Anglo-American terror bombers" (with no mention of the secondary role of Red Army artillery in the battle of Berlin). In the Western zones of occupation, a version of the former story remained the official one, with perhaps more emphasis on the collective responsibility of the German people as a whole for the deeds of the Nazis. Clearly, however, many Germans in the West also continued to harbor grudges against the Western powers for the deeds of their air forces.

The sheer amount of destruction was staggering.

Many German cities, and others elsewhere, were destroyed more completely than Berlin during the war. Berlin, however, was far larger than those cities. On the eve of the war, its population of 4.3 million made it the world's third or fourth largest city. Destruction of one-third to one-half of Berlin (to cite the conventional range of estimates) was, in absolute terms, the equivalent of the total obliteration of the second-largest German city, Hamburg. A 1947 survey found that one-third of the city's apartments and 40 percent of its rooms were uninhabitable. That amounted to a half million dwellings and 2 million rooms destroyed, and at least 55 million cubic meters of rubble.[1] The fact that thousands of buildings in the vast city remained habitable in no way contradicts the photographic, film, and eyewitness accounts portraying a vast landscape of debris where a great city once stood.

Conversely, in quantitative terms, the achievement of postwar reconstruction was extraordinary. Before any construction could begin, the rubble had to be removed, itself a staggering task. The occupying powers quickly put to work teams of women (able-bodied men were few) to clear the wreckage by hand; the lines of "rubble women," passing, cleaning, and stacking bricks, became a characteristic image of the city in the immediate postwar years.[2] The reconstruction that followed is all the more impressive in light of the lack of clear authority and of any consensus about proper architectural form. Nor did Berlin regain the industrial dynamism that had fueled its prewar growth.[3] It would be reconstructed as a subsidized propaganda showcase for East and West.

The historical moment of the German defeat in 1945 quickly be-

The Symbolic Dimensions of Trauma and Recovery

Figure 5.1.
Berlin, 1949.
Landesarchiv, Berlin.

came known as "zero hour." A new beginning was obviously neces-sary—in physical terms, but also economically and ideologically. The defunct Third Reich was thoroughly discredited, but the Nazis had grown out of German society and pervaded nearly every corner of it, so it would prove impossible to agree on which authorities or traditions—people, institutions, ideas, styles—needed to be purged from a rebuilt city and country.[4] Many observers have found it easy to characterize reconstruction projects as either breaking with the Nazi past or as failing to do so—not least in Cold War propaganda on both sides. But it was not (and is not) so clear what was and wasn't a Nazi legacy in architecture and urban form, as in literature, philosophy, popular culture, economics, social relations, and even politics. Nev-ertheless, beliefs about what had gone wrong in Nazi Germany clearly shaped postwar reconstruction.

In the twentieth century, architectural styles and forms were often discredited or stigmatized because of their political associations. In Germany, an ideological battle of styles had already begun in the 1920s, with the more radical modernists (and above all their flat roofs), who were associated with the political Left, opposed and denounced by conservatives as well as by the emerging Nazi party.[5] The political labeling of architectural styles reemerged after the war, albeit with some surprising changes, and it played a prominent role in early Cold War cultural politics. As both East and West sought to distance themselves from the fascists, the politics of architecture depended on the identification of "Nazi" styles and influences.

Probably the best known visual image of Nazi Berlin is the model of the city designed by Hitler's architect, Albert Speer, although little of it was built. For Speer, destruction meant opportunity. The Allied bombers continued the work that his crews had begun shortly before, clearing large swaths of central Berlin to make way for a wide north-south axis stretching from a great domed hall to a massive triumphal arch.[6] Speer's plan, however, was in some respects a reworking of redevelopment schemes that had been proposed repeatedly through the early twentieth century, so its distinctly Nazi characteristics, beyond the sheer size of the buildings, are not easily pinpointed. Similarly, nearly every postwar plan would share certain elements in common with Speer. For example, the first postwar planners also saw destruction as an opportunity to break away from the failures of the past. Across the political spectrum, the densely packed tenement city of the nineteenth century—that is, most of Berlin—was seen as a mistake. At the time, therefore, no one supported its reconstruction.

The immediate postwar years were a time for visionary planning instead of practical planning. The few available resources went to patching up the ruined buildings in which thousands were forced to live, and uncertainty about Berlin's political status (divided, as it was, into four sectors, each ruled by one of the victorious Allies) further delayed new building programs. Hopes for the future took form in the "collective plan" developed by a group of architects led by Hans Scharoun. Their proposal for a *Stadtlandschaft* (urban landscape) envisioned an entirely new city, built around residential cells of 4,000–5,000 residents each.[7] Its basic principles were largely those of international modernism, proposing separation of homes, commerce, and industry.

The Symbolic Dimensions of Trauma and Recovery

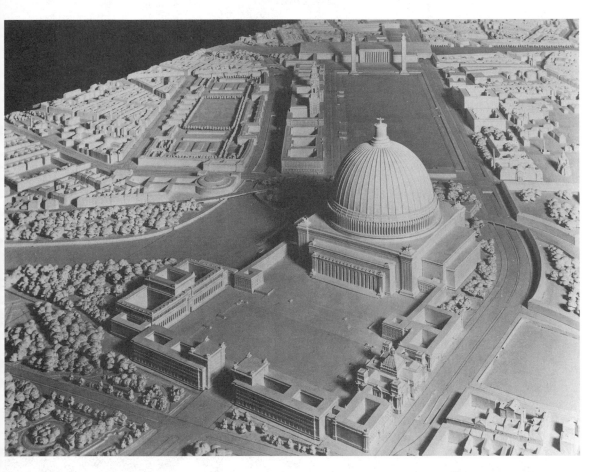

Figure 5.2.
Speer's model for Hitler's
capital: the cavernous
Reichstag building
appears very small at
lower right.
Landesarchiv, Berlin.

By virtually abandoning the destroyed city, it offered a complete break
with history—with the immediate Nazi past as well as the nineteenth-
century industrial city. Its line of orientation would be not historical,
but rather the natural landscape of the Spree River valley.[8] Nevertheless,
this vision of the *Stadtlandschaft* itself had historical roots, including
Nazi ones, in its rejection of centralized urban forms. The Nazis, too,
had wanted to break with the nineteenth-century city and embrace an
anti-urban, pastoral vision of communal life.[9]

The thinking embodied in the collective plan was influential in the
long run, but in the late 1940s it faded away. Practical objections were
raised, especially in the Western sectors, where existing property lines
were to be respected in most cases. The more compelling practical
objection was that the city was not completely destroyed: not only were

thousands of buildings still usable, but also the underground infrastructure of streets, subway lines, and utilities was estimated to be 90 percent intact; Scharoun's plan would have required its complete replacement. The collective plan also became irrelevant because the city was firmly divided into two halves by 1949 (as the three Western powers joined their sections into West Berlin, while the Soviet Union turned its sector over to its German communist allies) and then, in the East, because of a fundamental shift in architectural ideology.

The ambitions of the communist leaders of the new German Democratic Republic (GDR) became apparent in the plans for their first major reconstruction project, a boulevard extending east from the city center, which was renamed Stalinallee on the Soviet leader's seventieth birthday in 1949. The first apartment buildings there, begun that year, reflected the unadorned modernist style that leftist German architects had learned in the 1920s. However, in 1950, party leaders ordered an abrupt change in architectural style. The mile-long segment of Stalinallee was thereafter completed as an enormously wide boulevard framed by ostentatiously ornate, classically articulated apartment buildings.[10]

There was no single reason for this startling shift, which has been much studied in recent years. The ongoing struggle for control of Ger-

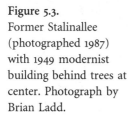

Figure 5.3.
Former Stalinallee (photographed 1987) with 1949 modernist building behind trees at center. Photograph by Brian Ladd.

The Symbolic Dimensions of Trauma and Recovery

Figure 5.4.
Former Stalinallee
(photographed 1968).
Landesarchiv, Berlin.

many played a role: the East wanted to present itself as the heir and guardian of German national culture. The explicit appropriation of national and regional styles lent its claim a visible image, one with a proven popular appeal, as opponents of austere modernism (usually conservatives) had already learned elsewhere. Communist leaders were willing to denounce modernism in populist language similar to that used by the Nazis, who had typically appealed to the "healthy common sense of the people" against avant-garde or foreign influences. The GDR minister for reconstruction, Lothar Bolz, stopped short of acknowledging any resemblance between East German plans and those of the Third Reich, but he did declare that not everything Hitler forbade was necessarily good.[11]

Western critics did not hesitate to denounce this architecture for its similarities to Speer's Nazi buildings. The communists didn't see things that way; in their own convoluted reasoning, they were reclaiming a national heritage perverted by the Nazis. To a considerable extent, they were also simply following the party line set down by Moscow. Two decades earlier, Stalin's Soviet Union had already rejected modernism because of its "formalism" (that is, its preoccupation with artistic form) and its "cosmopolitanism" that ignored local and national traditions. The East German leader, Walter Ulbricht, proclaimed that modernist architects, in their "cosmopolitan fantasies," believed that "one could build houses in Berlin that would be just as appropriate to the South African landscape."[12] In the words of another leading communist, Rudolf Herrnstadt, "egg cartons" like the first Stalinallee buildings "are the natural products of the greed for profit and contempt for humanity of the dying capitalist system."[13]

East German architects were instructed by their Soviet colleagues to regard the decentralized, horizontal city as fundamentally antithetical to the development of socialism, since it produced isolated individuals, incapable of collective action, as in the United States and England. One lecture by a Soviet planner, for example, declared, "[T]he Soviet Union is opposed to the Anglo-American theory of the desirability and efficiency of the decentralized city. It is uneconomical, it is not protected against air attack, it isolates the worker from political life and makes him into a petty-bourgeois."[14] The organization of mass demonstrations became the highest priority in East Berlin's urban planning, a fact that was decisive in the one major planning decision affecting the city center. In 1950, the immense and war-damaged royal palace was demolished to create a vast open square capable of holding larger crowds than even the Nazis had been able to assemble.[15]

In the East German view, then, the elements of the Nazi city to be repudiated did not include its neoclassical monumentality or its scale. Communist leaders pointed to the reinforced concrete bunker as the typical Nazi building, implying that the true Nazi style was the industrial modernism that characterized capitalism in its bourgeois-democratic as well as its fascist form. Ulbricht also linked both modernism and Nazism with militarism by characterizing their architecture as the "barracks style"—although this is historically inaccurate, since Nazi barracks were typically designed in a conservative Heimat style

The Symbolic Dimensions of Trauma and Recovery

that displayed pitched roofs, timber, and stucco rather than steel, glass, and concrete.[16] The communists were correct, however, in identifying the fundamental difference between Stalinallee and Speer's north-south axis: the grand buildings on the communists' boulevard provided housing, even for ordinary workers, something for which the Nazis did not provide in their Berlin plan.

Postwar Western architecture and planning saw more continuity in personnel. In contrast to the East, many leading German designers had occupied fairly high positions during the Third Reich.[17] That fact may help explain why there was less explicit vilification of Third Reich architecture, and yet also less willingness to risk anything that might be seen as resembling Nazi design. The predominant Western view (then and later) associated Nazism with classicism, historicism, monumentality, and axiality, as exemplified by Speer's Reich chancellery.[18] The rump city of West Berlin, lacking both center-city functions and, indeed, a city center, was spared any early decisions about major public buildings. The first significant reconstruction projects were small housing developments such as the Ernst-Reuter-Siedlung (1953–1955), which brought the model of Berlin's renowned 1920s modernist housing estates into the previously dense inner city, replacing solid rows of tenements with dispersed housing that turned away from the street and banishing the storefronts and industrial lofts that had filled the ground floors and courtyards of the old buildings.[19]

The West's showcase project came later, and as an explicit response to Stalinallee. Its International Building Exhibition (*Internationale Bauausstellung*, known as Interbau) of 1957 rebuilt the Hansa quarter, a large residential area near the center of West Berlin, which had been devastated by the war. Announcing the project in 1953, Berlin's construction director declared that it was intended as "a clear endorsement of the architecture of the Western world. It should demonstrate what we consider to be modern city planning and proper housing, in contrast to the false ostentation of Stalinallee."[20] Interbau's role as a showcase of international modernism was underscored by the roster of prominent foreign architects invited to contribute designs. Some declined, and Le Corbusier insisted on a large building that had to be placed elsewhere in the city, but designs by Walter Gropius, Alvar Aalto, and Oscar Niemeyer were among those built. The Hansa quarter's high-rise towers and low-rise slabs were dispersed through the landscape, not lined up along a street.

Western politicians and critics praised them as individual achievements embodying the decentralized, unregimented order of democracy and the free market. One of the planners explained that he avoided rectilinear geometry because "the free man does not want to live in an army camp, not in buildings in rows, like workers' barracks."[21] In other words, the Hansa quarter broke with the workers' barracks of the tenement city, but also demonstratively avoided what were becoming known as "totalitarian" tendencies—that is, those characteristic of both the Nazis and the communist East Germans.

This showcase had its limits as a practical model for Western reconstruction. The supposed model product of the free market had in fact been made possible by expropriating all of the private land of the old Hansa quarter and giving planners the power to redraw the streets and property lines, which they were not able do elsewhere. More important, the construction costs per housing unit proved to be unsustainably high. The Stalinallee had suffered the same problem: the extra expense that made it a showcase meant that it would remain unique.[22]

The West followed the Hansa quarter with the 1958 Hauptstadt Berlin design competition for a rebuilt and reunified capital. The 151 entries from sixteen countries offered a showcase of spacious modernist plans. Many of them resembled the postwar efforts of Scharoun's collective, with similar emphases on decentralization and circulation and a similar disregard for the extant pattern of streets and buildings. Like that plan, the winning design by Friedrich Spengelin, Fritz Eggeling, and Gerd Pempelfort remained in the realm of fantasy, since any hopes for a speedy reunification of the city were dashed by the construction of the Berlin Wall in 1961.[23]

Until the late 1950s, architecture and planning played a prominent role on the symbolic Cold War battlefield of Berlin. That is, along with the social necessities of reconstruction—above all, housing construction—both sides devoted considerable resources to designing a visible city that heralded their cause. By the 1960s, as stylistic differences faded, the Cold War in architecture came to an end, even as it continued in other venues. In other words, planning and architecture ceased to have the same compelling political purpose they formerly had. Why?

The first and most obvious reason was the shift in architectural

The Symbolic Dimensions of Trauma and Recovery

Figure 5.5.
Hansa quarter.
Landesarchiv, Berlin.

style undertaken in the East after the mid-1950s. The GDR's economic planners were increasingly aware that the Stalinallee (and comparable projects in other cities) cost far too much per unit of housing. Unlike the architects, they were not taken entirely by surprise when, in December 1954, the new Soviet leader, Nikita Khrushchev, denounced architectural extravagance and declared that prefabricated, industrialized construction methods were necessary to meet housing needs. Once again the GDR followed the Soviet lead, developing its own designs and methods for prefabricated concrete-panel construction, which thereafter accounted for the great majority of new GDR buildings.[24]

The first major project using the new methods, begun in 1959, was the segment of Stalinallee connecting the city center with the recently completed neoclassical section. (In 1961, de-Stalinization was completed by renaming the street Karl-Marx-Allee.) The buildings here differed markedly from the older segment. Most were unadorned ten-story slabs built of prefabricated panels, lacking the classical ornament and articulated facades of their neighbors down the street. Nor did they line the boulevard. They were dispersed in a large area extending back from both sides of the street. In short, they displayed many of the same design principles as the Hansa quarter, while lacking its architectural diversity. For all of the notable differences that remained, visitors to Berlin during the 1960s and 1970s were likely to be struck by the similarities between major construction projects on either side of the Wall, including centrally located commercial centers (Alexanderplatz in the East, Ernst-Reuter-Platz in the West) and large housing estates on the urban fringe. In East and West alike, a technocratic vision of modernity had triumphed, or had at least filled the void left by any more overtly political ideology of urban design. The construction of the Berlin Wall in 1961 also changed the nature of East-West competition. Until 1961, hundreds of thousands of workers, and many others, crossed the open border daily. After the Wall went up, Easterners and Westerners no longer shared the same urban spaces. As the architectural historian Francesca Rogier observes, "Without the flow of people back and forth across the border, spatial and social consciousness of built form receded, and with it the association with ideology."[25] Henceforth, the East would concentrate on competing with the West in consumer goods and the standard of living—that is, in private goods and private spaces. The shift to industrial modernism already pointed in the same direction, promoting the pursuit of a quantitative goal of many new apartments, rather than the goal of a workers' showcase promised by the original Stalinallee, which had failed to provide housing for enough workers. By the 1960s, the monumental achievement of reconstruction took the form of housing for the masses—a worthy goal, perhaps, but not one that lent itself to either clear visual expression or any obvious differences from the other side.[26]

The result, on both sides of the Wall, was an impressive job of rebuilding by most measures of quantity and also of quality, especially in West Berlin, but in the East as well. The mountains of rubble became actual mountains, fashioned into hills (now the highest points in this flat city) in city parks. Ruins yielded to new construction, and housing shortages gradually eased even as housing standards steadily improved. By the 1970s and 1980s, the new housing in East and West was coming

The Symbolic Dimensions of Trauma and Recovery

under attack for its monotony and its failure to contribute to urban and street life, but the extreme monotony in the East—where the use of one form of prefabricated concrete panel became nearly universal—contributed to a notably efficient construction industry. Its new apartments continued to find eager tenants pleased with the well-designed and well-equipped spaces. Despite its division, Berlin had proved itself to be a resilient city.

The story of Berlin's reconstruction might end here. By the 1980s, amid prosperity and political stability, the era of rebuilding seemed finally to be drawing to a close, with even East Berlin turning its attention to its last few long-neglected but prominent wartime ruins, as it prepared to declare its housing problem solved. Berlin was a rebuilt city—or rather, two rebuilt cities. The rumbles of discontent with postwar planning in East and West did not seem likely to change the city fundamentally, but the unforeseen fall of the Berlin Wall in 1989, and the subsequent necessity of melding the two cities back into one, reopened many old questions. Once again there were visible wounds in the urban fabric: those created by the Wall or left untouched because of their proximity to it. The question of how to heal these particular wounds was swept up into a broader debate about more abstract, national wounds in what would once again be the capital of a unified Germany. The result, in the 1990s, was a third restoration of the ruined city. Along with the necessity of renewed urban repair arose a widespread belief that this was a chance to do it over and get it right.

The official policy of Berlin during the 1990s was the "critical reconstruction" of the city center. That policy took the form of design rules intended to restore the scale, density, visual appeal, and lively public spaces of the early twentieth-century city. In other words, unlike the postwar reconstruction in East or West, it reflected a widespread desire to restore the urban form that the war and the Third Reich had destroyed, a goal that entailed a thorough revision of postwar reconstruction itself. Since the 1960s, in Berlin and elsewhere, there had been a growing discontent with the modernist city produced by postwar reconstruction. It had become commonplace in some circles to describe reconstruction as the "second destruction" of the city, because of the many large-scale projects that had leveled even intact buildings and neighborhoods.[27] These critics argued that the postwar regimes in East and West alike had largely replaced the fine-grained old city with megaprojects every bit as overscaled and inhumane as those proposed by the Nazis. The implication—occasionally made explicit—was that the Nazi architectural legacy was essentially the same as modernism (which was, of course, similar to Ulbricht's view).

Elements of this critique became official policy in West Berlin by the 1980s, as revealed most visibly in a second International Building Exhibition, this one known as IBA. Its lavishly subsidized and publicized projects harked back to the Cold War purposes of its 1950s predecessor, but instead of modernist purity it offered contextualist architecture and neighborhood rehabilitation. Out of IBA came the term *critical reconstruction* as well as many of the design guidelines that were subsequently applied to the city center in the 1990s.[28]

What occurred at the end of the century, therefore, deserved the name *reconstruction* in a way that the postwar efforts had not. Whereas postwar planners were determined to create a better city than had existed before, those of the 1990s turned away from the dreams of modernism and sought to recreate some fundamental characteristics of the destroyed urban fabric, which was largely a product of the late nineteenth and early twentieth centuries. Uniform limits on building height, restoration of the street grid with its narrow streets, insistence on masonry facades, and attempts to mimic (if not actually restore) the scale and diversity of individually owned and constructed parcels of land—all of these rules were derived directly from the maps and photographs of the prewar city.[29]

These design rules fed on a broad reservoir of public support, since the disillusionment with the modernist city was reinforced by the unpopularity of the defunct East German regime, which had controlled the historic core of Berlin. A belief that it was possible to restore Berlin's long-vanished visual identity also underlay the popular proposal to rebuild the destroyed royal palace as a way of restoring not a monarchy, but a visually appealing focal point for the city center. There was no shortage of critics, however, attacking either this proposal in particular or the broader restorationist tendencies. Many of them argued that the effect, if not the intention, of this restoration would be an unacceptable denial of German historical responsibility, erasing the traces of both the Third Reich and the GDR from the cityscape. Reconstruction of the palace, in fact, would require demoli-

The Symbolic Dimensions of Trauma and Recovery

tion of the prominent structure the GDR had put up on its site, the so-called Palace of the Republic.[30] More generally, the reconstruction of the city center entailed either demolishing the GDR's modernist buildings or hiding them behind new ones as the wide streets and squares (*public* spaces, as critics pointed out) shrank or disappeared under new construction.

Even where particular buildings were not at issue, critics argued that a reconstruction oriented to the city of 1900 was the product of a wish to deny, or at least not to confront, the dreadful history of the intervening decades. This was a sensitive issue in Berlin, since many postwar German intellectuals believed that their society had collectively denied its complicity in the crimes of the Nazis. The GDR had, to the end, largely subsisted on an antifascist consensus that drew a clear line between it and the Nazis. In the West, the sites of Nazi crimes had not been brought to public attention until a full generation after the war. By the 1980s, the memorial landscape of Berlin had become an important part of the rebuilt city. Memorials were not necessarily incompatible with critical reconstruction, but they implied a different connection between history and the cityscape. That was especially true of projects like the Topography of Terror, which opened in 1987 as a temporary exhibition on the desolate site of Gestapo and SS headquarters and which was intended as a kind of "open wound," eschewing any complacent embrace of tradition or normality in the cityscape.[31]

This kind of memorial—and Berlin now has many, most of them small—declares its refusal to permit rebuilding, or any return to normality, or complacency, or the past, on its particular site. But in a large and living city such a memorial can only function as a counterpoint and an exception. Reconstruction had to happen—and reconstruction, like all action, entails selective remembrance and selective forgetting. Berlin, like all cities, has traditions worth honoring, and it has (again like all cities, but presumably more than most) its shameful episodes of history. In its slow, episodic, and incomplete reconstruction, Berlin has seen an unusual degree of resistance to honoring the past in the name of remembering its shame. Whereas the extraordinarily successful rebuilding of Berlin can be seen as an act of civic affirmation, it has also been denounced as an act of historical denial. It has, necessarily, been both.

Notes

1. Statistics in Reinhard Rürup, ed., *Berlin 1945: A Documentation* (Berlin: Arenhövel, 1995), 59, 69; and Jeffry M. Diefendorf, *In the Wake of War: The Reconstruction of German Cities after World War II* (New York: Oxford University Press, 1993), 15.

2. On the "rubble woman" image, see Elizabeth Heineman, "The Hour of the Woman: Memories of Germany's 'Crisis Years' and West German National Identity," *American Historical Review* 101 (1996): 374–380.

3. See Peter Hall, *Cities in Civilization* (New York: Pantheon, 1998), 377–395.

4. Jeffrey Herf, *Divided Memory: The Nazi Past in the Two Germanys* (Cambridge, Mass.: Harvard University Press, 1997).

5. Barbara Miller Lane, *Architecture and Politics in Germany, 1918–1945* (Cambridge, Mass.: Harvard University Press, 1968).

6. On Nazi plans, see Hans J. Reichhardt and Wolfgang Schäche, *Von Berlin nach Germania: Über die Zerstörung der Reichshauptstadt durch Albert Speers Neugestaltungsplanungen* (Berlin: Landesarchiv, 1984); and Stephen D. Helmer, *Hitler's Berlin: The Speer Plans for Reshaping the Central City* (Ann Arbor, Mich.: UMI Research Press, 1985).

7. Johann Friedrich Geist and Klaus Kürvers, *Das Berliner Mietshaus 1945–1989* (Munich: Prestel, 1989), 180–250; Werner Durth, Jörn Düwel, and Niels Gutschow, *Architektur und Städtebau der DDR* (Frankfurt: Campus, 1998), 1:90–109.

8. Francesca Rogier, "The Monumentality of Rhetoric: The Will to Rebuild in Postwar Berlin," in *Anxious Modernisms*, ed. Sarah Williams Goldhagen and Réjean Legault (Cambridge, Mass.: MIT Press, 2000), 168.

9. Andrew Lees, *Cities Perceived: Urban Society in European and American Thought, 1820–1940* (New York: Columbia University Press, 1985), 275–288.

10. On Stalinallee, see Geist and Kürvers, *Das Berliner Mietshaus*, 337–353; Herbert Nicolaus and Alexander Obeth, *Die Stalinallee: Geschichte einer deutschen Strasse* (Berlin: Bauwesen, 1997); Durth, Düwel, and Gutschow, *Architektur*, 1:270–301; 2:296–413.

11. Durth, Düwel, and Gutschow, *Architektur*, 1:135.

12. Quoted in Frank Werner, *Stadtplanung Berlin: Theorie und Realität* (Berlin: Kiepert, 1976), 138.

13. Quoted in Geist and Kürvers, *Das Berliner Mietshaus*, 332–333.

14. Reprinted in *Reise nach Moskau: Dokumente zur Erklärung von Motiven, Entscheidungsstrukturen und Umsetzungskonflikten für den ersten städtebaulichen Paradigmenwechsel in der DDR und zum Umfeld des "Aufbaugesetzes" von 1950* (Erkner: Institut für Regionalplanung und Strukturentwicklung, 1995), 91.

15. Gerd-H. Zuchold, "Der Abriss des Berliner Schlosses," *Deutschland Archiv*

The Symbolic Dimensions of Trauma and Recovery

18 (1995): 178–207; Durth, Düwel, and Gutschow, *Architektur*, 2:65–67, 214–218.

16. Durth, Düwel, and Gutschow, *Architektur*, 1:176.

17. Werner Durth, *Deutsche Architekten: Biographische Verflechtungen 1900–1970* (Braunschweig: Vieweg, 1986).

18. Winfried Nerdinger, "Ein deutlicher Strich durch die Achse des Herrschers': Diskussionen um Symmetrie, Achse und Monumentalität zwischen Kaiserreich und Bundesrepublik," in *Moderne Architektur in Deutschland 1900 bis 2000: Macht und Monument*, ed. Romana Schneider and Wilfried Wang (Ostfildern-Ruit: Gerd Hatje, 1998), 97; Hartmut Frank, "Monument und Moderne," in ibid., 221–224.

19. Harald Bodenschatz, "Antworten West-Berlins auf die Stalinallee," in *Karl-Marx-Allee: Magistrale in Berlin*, ed. Helmut Engel and Wolfgang Ribbe (Berlin: Akademie, 1996), 155–157.

20. Quoted in Diefendorf, *In the Wake of War*, 149. On the Hansa quarter, see Gabi Dolff-Bonekämper, *Das Hansaviertel: Internationale Nachkriegsmoderne in Berlin* (Berlin: Bauwesen, 1999).

21. Quoted in Rogier, "Monumentality," 179.

22. Bodenschatz, "Antworten," 157–160.

23. Berlinische Galerie, *Hauptstadt Berlin: Internationaler städtebaulicher Ideenwettbewerb 1957/58* (Berlin: Mann, 1990). One might note, however, that a portion of Scharoun's *Stadtlandschaft* did come into existence in the 1960s on a prominent site: the Kulturforum near Potsdamer Platz.

24. Durth, Düwel, and Gutschow, *Architektur*, 1:462–487.

25. Rogier, "Monumentality," 184.

26. This point about housing as monumentality is made in this particular context by Rogier, "Monumentality," 184; and in a more general one, by Joseph Rykwert, *The Seduction of Place* (New York: Pantheon, 2000), 132.

27. A classic and pioneering work is Wolf Jobst Siedler, Elisabeth Niggemeyer, and Gina Angress, *Die gemordete Stadt* (Berlin: Herbig, 1964).

28. See Wallis Miller, "IBA's 'Models for a City': Housing and the Image of Cold War Berlin," *Journal of Architectural Education* 46 (1993): 202–216; and Josef Paul Kleihues and Heinrich Klotz, eds., *International Building Exhibition, Berlin 1987: Examples of a New Architecture* (New York: Rizzoli, 1986). East Berlin also began a few tentative moves in the same direction. See Brian Ladd, "Socialist Planning and the Rediscovery of the Old City in the German Democratic Republic," *Journal of Urban History* 27 (2001): 584–603. Thus 1980s postmodernism, like 1960s modernism but unlike 1950s construction, saw the Cold War rivals competing with similar architectural forms.

29. Some contributions to the debate over critical reconstruction have been collected in Alan Balfour, ed., *Berlin* (London: Academy, 1995); Annegret Burg, ed., *Neue Berlinische Architektur: Eine Debatte* (Berlin: Birkhäuser, 1994); Gert Kähler, ed., *Einfach schwierig: Eine deutsche Architekturdebatte*

(Braunschweig: Vieweg, 1995); and Michael Mönninger, ed., *Das neue Berlin* (Frankfurt: Insel, 1991).

30. On the palace debate, see Brian Ladd, *The Ghosts of Berlin: Confronting German History in the Urban Landscape* (Chicago: University of Chicago Press, 1997), 47–70; Förderverein Berliner Stadtschloss, *Das Schloss? Eine Ausstellung über die Mitte Berlins* (Berlin: Ernst und Sohn, 1993); Akademie der Künste, *Zur historischen Mitte Berlins* (Berlin: Akademie der Künste, 1992); *Kritische Berichte* 22:1 (1994); and Wilhelm von Boddien and Helmut Engel, eds., *Die Berliner Schlossdebatte: Pro und Contra* (Berlin: Spitz, 2000).

31. Ladd, *Ghosts*, 154–173; James E. Young, *The Texture of Memory: Holocaust Memorials and Meaning* (New Haven, Conn.: Yale University Press, 1993), 27–48, 81–90.

The Symbolic Dimensions of Trauma and Recovery

Warsaw
Reconstruction as Propaganda

New Warsaw is to be the capital of the socialist state. We must fight consciously and with deliberate diligence to give our town a definitely ideological stamp.
—President Bolesław Bierut, Speech to Party Congress, 3 July 1949

6

JASPER GOLDMAN

■ By any standards, the resilience displayed by Warsaw during World War II and its aftermath was awesome. The city endured three waves of destruction: during the German invasion of 1939, the Jewish ghetto uprising of 1943, and the Warsaw uprising of 1944 and their aftermaths. After the last had been put down, Adolf Hitler ordered the city to be destroyed entirely, and particular care was taken by the Nazis to individually target monuments and buildings of any historic, cultural, or aesthetic significance. This was done with grim efficiency, and by the time the Soviet army occupied the city in January 1945, over 80 percent of the buildings in the city lay in ruins. Of the 780 buildings on the historic register, only 35 survived intact.[1] One of those buildings that survived—the Lazienski Palace—still had bore holes ready for dynamite which German sappers had not had time to insert when the city was captured. On visiting Warsaw in 1945, General Dwight Eisenhower commented that he had never before witnessed destruction executed with such bestiality. There had been no military justification for the devastation. Yet almost from the moment the city was liberated, it began to recover.

In the first two months after liberation, sappers and workers were able to remove 100,000 mines and unexploded shells from the ruins, and 1 million cubic meters of rubble were removed by the end of 1947.[2] Despite a lack of electricity, water, transportation, and other basic infrastructure, the population doubled to 366,000 within four months.[3] Reconstruction of key streets and repairable buildings began immedi-

Figure 6.1.
Warsaw was nearly annihilated completely by the end of World War II, with over 80 percent of the buildings in the city damaged or destroyed. Photograph from Jan Zachwatowicz and Piotr Biegaski, *The Old Town of Warsaw* (Warsaw: Budownictwo i Architektura, 1956).

ately, and new residential areas were planned and later constructed. Within just eleven years, the city would recover its prewar population and could be said to be a fully functional capital. But the jewel in the crown of the reconstruction was undoubtedly the rebuilding of the Old Town, the historic core of the city that symbolized 700 years of Warsaw's history. Its completion—in 1961—above all suggested a rebirth of Poland's cultural and historical identity.

There has been a spectrum of resilience displayed by the city's inhabitants. There was the resilience displayed during the occupation, particularly during the doomed resistance offered in the Jewish ghetto and Warsaw uprisings of 1943 and 1944. At that time, and at great personal risk, planners undertook clandestine conservation planning that would later be important for the reconstruction.[4] After the war, the city's citizens demonstrated their resilience in almost immediately reviving the city after its liberation: "Neither the danger from mines nor collapsing buildings nor shortages of food and shelter were able to stop the returning Varsovians," comments Stanisław Jankowski, a planner present at the time.[5] The photographs of this era give a powerful impression of the Varsovians' heroic lifestyles during this period.

The Symbolic Dimensions of Trauma and Recovery

This chapter does not seek, however, to recount the heroic aspects of Warsaw's resilience, which have been told well elsewhere, particularly by actual participants in the city's resistance to the Nazis and in the later reconstruction.[6] Instead this chapter explores the reconstruction from the perspective of the communist regime supervising the rebuilding. The rebuilding of Warsaw not only offered the regime the opportunity to demonstrate the potency of state socialism and its command economy; it also offered the opportunity to design and build a "socialist capital." As the influential Communist theorist Edmund Goldzamt wrote: ". . . the spatial development of Warsaw, and especially its center, is a critical political, rather than architectural, issue. Therefore the decisions should be taken solely by our comrades responsible for waging cultural-ideological war, that is to say, by the political leaders."[7] The then

Figure 6.2.
The resilience of the returning Varsovians in 1945 is powerfully illustrated by the photographs of the era. From Bierut, *The Six Year Plan*.

preeminent political leader President Bierut went further, declaring in 1949 that: "Our Party must express itself not only regarding what and how much will be built in Warsaw but also what, where, and for whom. That is why our Party must undertake a determined struggle for a new form for our cities and settlements, and above all, our capital."[8] This "new form" would entail both rebuilding in a politically correct architectural and urban design style and the simultaneous rejection of those styles perceived to be associated with capitalism. At critical times in the rebuilding of the city, no aspect of the reconstruction was free of an ideological or political intent. Hence, this chapter explores how the resilience of the Varsovians was shaped and exploited by the regime for ideological and political ends.

This chapter focuses in particular on the most ideological era of reconstruction, the "socialist realist" period from 1949 to 1956, when the newly ascendant Communist party attempted to translate its ideology into a coherent program for rebuilding the city. Prior to 1949, the country's fluid political situation meant that reconstruction was far less visibly or comprehensively affected by politics or ideology. However, most of the reconstruction during this period focused on infra-structure and preparation for later construction projects; arguably the socialist realist period was not only the most ideological period of the reconstruction, but also the most significant in terms of the rebuilding carried out. While the party ceased to promote explicitly ideological architectural and urban forms after 1956, the course of reconstruction had largely been set by this time.

For most visitors, the ideological influence of the socialist realism period can be seen most clearly in the city's widened avenues with grim neoclassical architecture and its overscaled and unmissable Palace of Culture. It may come as a surprise that the historic core of the city, generally considered a far more valuable legacy, was also rebuilt during this period. The core consists of the Old Town and the so-called Royal Route, consisting of Nowy Świat (reconstructed in 1949–1950), Krakowskie Przedmieście (1948–1950), and Ujazdowskie Avenue, which meet at the Royal Castle, rebuilt between 1972 and 1982. While visitors are generally instinctively aware of the reconstructed, even recreated nature of these areas, it nevertheless impresses as an approximate facsimile of what was lost, and even achieves a poignancy when one realizes the lengths to which the Polish people went to restore a part of their history.

Understanding why the rebuilding of the historic core was so important to the Polish people is not difficult. The core was seen as representing their national culture and identity, which throughout Polish history had been threatened and attacked by outsiders. While the country had first been united in the tenth century and would exist in the following centuries as an autonomous dukedom or kingdom, three successive partitions in 1772, 1793, and 1795 effectively erased the country from the map. This was followed by a century of Russian, German, and Austrian domination until the end of World War I, followed by a brief twenty years of independence from 1918 until Nazi Germany reoccupied the country in 1939, the latest—and the most brutal—attempt to destroy Polish cultural identity. In response, Poles asserted ever more vigorously their national identity, which was perceived to be bound up in the country's architecture. The interwar period saw a resurgence in national styles of architecture, while the Polish parliament attempted to protect the country's architectural heritage with what is believed to

The Symbolic Dimensions of Trauma and Recovery

be some of the earliest and most comprehensive historic preservation legislation, passed in 1928.[9]

Many Varsovians would therefore have agreed with architect Jan Zachwatowicz's comment that "the issue of the documents of the past, which were purposely destroyed by the Nazis in such a barbarian way in order to eradicate centuries of the nation's history, should be treated as an indispensable element of the city—its birth certificate."[10] Not only would restoring the historic core recreate part of their destroyed city, it would also mean that the Nazis did not permanently steal a part of their national heritage. The rebuilding of the Old Town in particular carried emotional symbolism for Varsovians as the center of resistance efforts in 1944. The overwhelming popularity enjoyed by the reconstruction of the Old Town and other historic areas is indicated in part by the substantial donations collected throughout the country. In the years 1946–1964 more than 4.5 million zlotys was raised, equivalent in cost to constructing 100,000 rooms in new housing.[11] When the rebuilding of the Old Town was complete, it became—and continues to be—the city's leading attraction for domestic and international visitors.

If the motivation for popular support for historic reconstruction is clear, it is less easy to understand why the Soviet-installed communist regime—which by 1949 firmly controlled all reconstruction activity—should have sponsored the rebuilding of the historic core. This did not obviously serve the ideological agenda of the regime, reaffirming as it did popular links to a Polish past (to which the regime had no evident connection), which had little to do with the party's agenda of creating a socialist capital. Furthermore, the regime could well have argued for many other priorities besides historic reconstruction. In other communist cities, such reconstruction frequently had a low priority; as Brian Ladd recounts in the previous chapter, the most iconic historic building of East Berlin—the Royal Palace—was actually demolished, despite having survived the war relatively intact.

The weakness and lack of legitimacy of the new regime are the key to understanding why it undertook the popular reconstructions. The regime had only consolidated its control of the country in 1949 after three bloody years of civil war; it lacked a broad base of support within the country and was widely considered by the populace to be repressive, economically incompetent, and little more than an agent of the Soviet

Union.[12] The last connection was particularly unfortunate: the Soviet army had invaded the country with the Nazis in 1939, murdered thousands of Polish officers in a series of massacres (most infamously at Katyń in 1940), and had remained on the banks of the Vistula while the Warsaw uprising was put down by the Nazis in 1944.

The historic reconstructions thus presented the regime with a critical opportunity to unify the populace in a popular and unambiguously patriotic task, and thus build their support. The regime scarcely missed an opportunity to capitalize on the propaganda value of the reconstructions. The completion of key historic areas (as well as many of the newer areas) was timed to coincide with the July 22 anniversary of the founding of the People's Republic, when elaborately choreographed ceremonies and parades were held. During these events, the regime not only benefited from association with the completed buildings but also from appearing at the vanguard of the efforts to celebrate unity by repairing the damage inflicted by the Nazis. Nor was the propaganda restricted to parades and ceremonies. As one Polish author has written: "The reconstruction was one of the propaganda symbols of the success of Socialist Realism. Dozens of articles, leaflets, albums and documentaries were made to convince us that the post-War Warsaw was better and more beautiful than at any time in the past."[13]

The image of the regime abroad was unquestionably improved by the publication of expansive documents showcasing the reconstructions with extensive before and after pictures. The most famous of these were the international editions of the 1949 book *The Six-Year Plan for the Reconstruction of Warsaw*, written in Bolesław Bierut's name and derived from his speech of the same year. Perhaps the most significant propaganda triumph was the Old Town's inclusion in UNESCO's list of World Heritage sites in 1980, not as authentically restored buildings but as twentieth-century architecture. The core of the city was carefully noted to be a "near-total reconstruction."[14]

Scholars have debated, however, the extent to whether the historic core was "reconstructed" or "recreated." Certainly, the rebuilt historic core was not a literal restoration of what had existed before, but rather a carefully edited reconstruction according to Socialist Realism doctrine. As in all historic preservation or reconstruction, decisions were made about what was historically valuable, and what was preserved or reconstructed (and how it was done) revealed the political and ideo-

The Symbolic Dimensions of Trauma and Recovery

Figure 6.3.
A propaganda ceremony held on the completion of the Old Town on July 22, 1953. The poster in the image is of President Bierut. From "Warszawskie Stare Miasto: z dziejów odbudowy," edited by Emilia Borecka (Warsaw: Państwowe Wydawnictwo Naukowe, 1982).

logical priorities of the ruling class. If the decision to reconstruct the historic areas was rooted in politics, ideology determined which buildings and areas would be reconstructed and how they would be rebuilt.

Broadly speaking, the regime considered certain architectural styles to be "progressive" and others to be "reactionary." Progressive styles, such as modernized Renaissance or neoclassicism, tended to date from the period before 1830 and were considered to be from the most "Polish" and most socialist historical era. By contrast, the reactionary styles—such as art nouveau or Catholic baroque—tended to date from the late nineteenth and early twentieth centuries and were thought to represent unpleasant periods, symbolic of an era of capitalism during which Poland had been dominated by foreign powers. The communist regime considered architecture from these periods to be in conflict with the socialist, "patriotic" character that they wanted the historic core to project, and issued an edict forbidding the reconstruction of any building constructed after 1850.

If a building or its subsequent modifications dated from a reactionary architectural period, it would be creatively reconstructed. As Goldzamt explained: "The reactionaries want restoration of buildings, i.e., returning them to their previous shape.... we want reconstruction, i.e., shaping them to serve the needs of the present and the future."[15] Shaping a building to serve the "needs of the present" could mean rebuilding it to convey different architectural values and associations. Minister for Public Administration Władysław Wolski explained in 1950: "When choosing the historic period for reconstruction of a given monument, we should choose the best period for us from a cultural and social point of view. . . . we have to act boldly and avoid certain unpleasant periods."[16] The regime thus aimed to rebuild a historic core that was compatible with its ideology, to establish what historian Eric Hobsbawm terms "continuity with a suitable historic past."

Accordingly, all reconstructed buildings tended to invoke a progressive architectural style from the pre-1830 period, regardless of their appearance prior to being damaged or destroyed during the war. Hence the Old Town was reconstructed entirely in an idealized seventeenth- and eighteenth-century form; nineteenth-century modifications and additions were removed.[18] On the Royal Route, Nowy Świat was reconstructed entirely in the neoclassical style of the Congress Kingdom of Poland (1815–1830). The dozen or so nineteenth-century buildings that had existed previously were rebuilt in the earlier architectural style, and all of the heights of the buildings were homogenized. Krakowskie Przedmieście was similarly rebuilt.

Even the details of individual buildings were altered. In several buildings in the Old Town, religious elements were removed in favor of supposedly neutral decorations. On one building in the Old Town, surviving statues on its facade of the Agnus Dei and St. Mary were destroyed and replaced with a wild boar and the goddess Diana with a dog.[19] These kinds of changes were later justified by conservationists as being aesthetically, rather than ideologically, motivated.[20] This may be partly true, and the regime and the architects who carried out reconstruction were not a monolithic entity. But it was no accident that these changes to the prewar form ensured that the rebuilt buildings

The Symbolic Dimensions of Trauma and Recovery

were compatible with party ideology. Because the regime controlled all historical reconstruction activity through the institutions of the Office for Aesthetic Supervision of Production and the Art Institute of the Polish Academy of Science, it was able to ensure the sole utilization of government-approved architectural styles and details according to socialist realist rules.[21]

Outside the historic core, buildings with a reactionary architectural style that had survived the war frequently had their facades removed or were even demolished as symbols of capitalism.[22] Nineteenth-century tenement houses were particularly targeted as symbols of social injustice, as the rich had lived on the upper floors, while servants had lived in cramped quarters in the basement. Districts that had contained predominantly nineteenth-century buildings—such as the area that had come to be known as the Jewish ghetto—were never considered for reconstruction, in part because of their architectural style, but also because the urban design of the nineteenth-century tenement city was considered ideologically incorrect, a sentiment that was universally felt at the time, even outside the Communist Bloc. The city's nineteenth-century architecture finally came to be appreciated in the 1970s, but by then it was too late; Warsaw had had one of its most eclectic architectural periods largely eliminated from its physical fabric.[23]

Creative reconstruction "to serve the needs of the present" also meant altering the interiors of buildings. This was described as "modernization," but that description obscured an ideological intent. Because the new function of the Old Town was as a socialist housing district, its interiors had to reflect the perceived needs of the Polish working class and the absence of class distinctions in the new Poland. Architects therefore had to design interiors to allow for six square meters per person, the standard prescribed in the Six-Year Plan of 1949. The change of function of buildings and the housing standard frequently meant that the existing structures of surviving buildings were unusable and had to be rebuilt entirely behind the original facade. The Old Town was also rebuilt at a considerably reduced density, and many houses were not reconstructed so as to allow the area to conform to the preferred housing norms.

The need to time the completion of reconstruction for propaganda purposes also affected how buildings were rebuilt. The need to complete reconstruction in time for the July 22 ceremonies induced particularly unfortunate haste. Frequently, proper conservation and archaeological work could not be carried out, and many parts of surviving buildings—such as vaults, foundations, and wall paintings—were destroyed. Indeed, paintings were often deliberately destroyed when it became clear that conservation would have led to delays.[24] The result was that there was "far too much authorisation for replacement of old elements with new" and a great deal of unnecessary demolition.[25]

In short, the conditions under which the rebuilding of the Old Town took place—in terms of complying with deadlines, reconstructing in an approved architectural style, and accommodating changes in function and universal housing requirements—meant that it could never be an authentic recreation. It was instead a "soft" reconstruction, in which accuracy of design and materials was less important than creating the right ambience.[26] Despite considerable research on how the Old Town had looked prior to the war, little of this was actually used.[27] Even a half century later, the Old Town stills feels ersatz to many visitors, more akin to a film set than a genuine historic center.[28]

The inauthentic nature of the recreation did not stop the regime from publicizing the Old Town as an accurate reconstruction. In 1980, the research that had been done but not used for rebuilding was presented to UNESCO as evidence of how painstaking the reconstruction was, and UNESCO would later call the reproduction of the Old Town "meticulous," despite its being a recreation. Over the years, a national myth that the reconstructions *were* meticulous and accurate was propagated by the party. The publication in 1980 of the memoirs of Józef Sigalin—one of the architects in charge of reconstruction—caused an outcry because it revealed for the first time the ideological and political considerations that influenced the reconstruction, suggesting that it had been as much a political exercise as the great patriotic undertaking many Poles had believed it to be.[29]

The ideological climate in which the rebuilding of historic buildings took place is perhaps best encapsulated by the discussions surrounding the reconstruction of the Royal Castle. Long a symbol of Warsaw as the home of the country's ruler, the castle had occupied a magnificent location on the rim of the Old Town facing the Vistula until it was severely damaged in 1939 and totally destroyed in 1944 by the Nazis. In the immediate aftermath of the war, when the communists had not yet consolidated their control over the reconstruction, conservationists

The Symbolic Dimensions of Trauma and Recovery

proposed rebuilding the castle as it had been, but this was not done partly due to a lack of resources and partly because the castle was still associated with the prewar government. The question of rebuilding the castle was revisited during the period of socialist realist ascendancy. It became clear to many politicians that the castle was a necessary aesthetic and symbolic part of the Old Town. Stanisław Lorentz noted that during a meeting of party officials and architects in 1950, "It was noticed for the first time that the castle was one of those buildings that constituted the panorama of the city from the Vistula." Of particular concern was the fact that—if the castle were rebuilt in its previous form—the most prominent element in the panorama of the Old Town would still be St. John's Cathedral. It was obviously unacceptable to the communist regime to have a religious building as the most conspicuous symbol of the Old Town. As a result, Lorentz recounts, "[I]t was then that the concept of monumentalising the castle, by raising it, was born."[30] As Minister for Public Administration Wolski explained: "The Castle is situated low, lower than the Old Town. If it is to act as the symbol for the People's Government, it cannot, as a symbol be so low. . . . In this area of Warsaw the Castle should play a dominating role."[31]

Party officials therefore proposed that the castle be creatively reconstructed, as Wolski put it, "to account for the new era." This meant adjusting the architectural expression and increasing the scale. For the architectural competition held by the party in 1954, guidelines required that "the Castle should dominate its surroundings, both when seen from the Vistula and from Krakowskie Przedmieście." The castle's architecture was to "creatively refer to its historic form, but should also be a creative contribution from the architects of the contemporary Polish People's Republic." To leave no doubt what this meant, the guidelines instructed that the rebuilt castle should "harmonise in character with the Old Town, with the existing elements of the city panorama, and most importantly, with the Palace of Culture."[32]

In fact, work on the Royal Castle never began during the socialist realist period, as there was never a consensus among party leaders on how the castle should be rebuilt. During the subsequent era, from 1956 to 1970, while Wladysław Gomułka was party secretary, the rebuilding was also postponed, largely because Gomulka himself was unenthusiastic about the historic reconstructions and personally opposed the castle's rebuilding, memorably commenting, "A cactus will grow on my hand before the Royal Castle is rebuilt."[33] It was his successor, Edward Gierek, who made the decision to rebuild the castle in 1971, for similar reasons that the communist government had previously undertaken historic reconstructions: to bolster the patriotic credentials of the regime at a time of economic crisis.[34] However, by this time, the era of creative reconstruction had passed, and the castle was reconstructed quite faithfully, with the only significant change from its prewar form being the addition of two towers that had existed in the seventeenth century. However, in order to complete it in time for July 22, 1974, the construction crews cut corners. They allotted inadequate time for concrete and plaster to dry, the consequences of which are still being dealt with today.[35] Nonetheless, the way in which the castle was eventually reconstructed suggests that architects might have attempted to rebuild the historic core more faithfully had they done so after the socialist realist period.

The impact of ideology on the rebuilding of Warsaw can be seen most clearly in areas of new construction, in developments from the socialist realist era in particular. Bierut signaled the start of the era in 1949 by calling for a "new form" for a "a socialist capital." This new urban form would be principally defined by its contrast with the characteristics of capitalist urban form. As Bierut commented: "New Warsaw cannot be just a repetition of the old one, it cannot be a slightly corrected version of the pre-war jumble of private interests of the capitalists. It cannot reflect the discrepancies tearing this nation, it cannot witness and facilitate exploitation of human labour and widespread use of privileges by the class of owners."[36] The prewar capital had been defined by its fine-grained, heterogeneous urban form, which for Bierut and the party was indicative of capitalism's failure to go beyond the jumble of selfish private interests and operate for the greater good with large-scale planning schemes. As Bierut put it, prewar Warsaw had been a "chaotic, fortuitous agglomeration of buildings . . . where manystoreyed houses stood next to low ones, where shops, stores and places of entertainment were in a disordered mess." Additionally, the prewar capital reflected the low status of the working class, which had been pushed out into the suburbs, where they were denied "man's natural right to light, space and fresh air." The communist rhetoric of that time was noticeably more critical of the capitalists who created the prewar urban form of Warsaw than it was of the Nazis who destroyed it.

The Symbolic Dimensions of Trauma and Recovery

The new socialist capital, Bierut announced, would reverse the urban design characteristics of the capitalist city. Instead of capitalist disorder and small scale, the new city would contain "a balanced system of squares linked with suitably widened thoroughfares, appropriate to the task of a socialist capital with a million inhabitants."[37] The latter would be the scene of "mass meetings and demonstrations of the people on public holidays. . . . They will be the focusing point not just of the capital but the whole country." The importance of the workers to the regime would be represented by their move to the center of the city into housing blocks that would be "well spaced out in the midst of green areas" and provided with "every comfort known to modern civilisation." As a city of workers, the capital would also be a center of production, and the Six-Year Plan envisaged a "great scheme" for developing industry within the city. New housing construction would be positioned close by industrial areas, to create "rationally-planned and orderly sectors of town."

To a remarkable extent, much of the reconstruction of the city did follow the principles set out in the Six-Year Plan. The nationalization of all land in Warsaw after 1945 and the monopolizing of all urban planning and architectural activity within state organizations essentially gave the regime a free hand to reconstruct the city.[38] Accordingly, the "widened thoroughfares" became the broadened Marzałkowska and Swiętokrzyska streets; the former became ten kilometers long and fifty meters at its widest point, with the one-kilometer Constitution Square suitable for the mass meetings envisaged by the regime. Surrounding the square was Marzałkowska Dzielnica Mieszkaniowa (MDM), one of several new housing estates built for elite workers in the city center. Both the square, the two avenues, and the MDM workers' housing were used extensively for propaganda ceremonies, most notably for their opening ceremony on July 22, 1952, but also as part of an ideologically correct tourist route through the city, which entailed visitors traveling down the rebuilt Royal Route and Marzałkowska Avenue.

The striking transformation of urban form between pre- and postwar Warsaw can also be seen at Muranów, the site of the former Jewish ghetto. Previously the area was composed of narrow streets, two- and three-story buildings that had a mixture of residential, retail, and civic uses, and little open space. In its rebuilt form, its vast and open superblocks contained large towers of flats—between eight and ten sto-

Figure 6.4.
The Socialist capital: The rendering demonstrates how Marzałkowska Avenue, one of the city's main thoroughfares, was designed explicitly for parades celebrating the regime. From Bierut, *The Six Year Plan.*

ries—each containing several hundred dwelling units for 50,000 residents. Party officials considered Muranów one of the model areas of New Warsaw, and propaganda documents compared the prewar site with the modern plan in order to demonstrate how the regime had reduced overcrowding and improved living conditions for the "working man."[39]

Much of the application of socialist realism to urban form was rooted in urban movements that had been developed under capitalism. The City Beautiful movement—with its emphasis on grand boulevards, uniform architecture, and the supposedly edifying effect of good city form on the populace—was certainly a precursor to the urbanism of socialist realism, as it was to Nazi urban form. As one visitor to Warsaw commented, much of the socialist realist planning "would make Daniel Burnham and the City Beautiful movement happy, with its wide, tree-line[d] boulevards flanked by rows of controlled, cornice lined buildings."[40] The regime's planners also drew on Corbusian modernity's pro-

The Symbolic Dimensions of Trauma and Recovery

motion of a decongested urban center with wide, fast roads and "rational" urban planning. Indeed, for many of the architects and planners, the destroyed city offered exactly the sort of tabula rasa that modernists elsewhere sought through urban renewal and other mechanisms. Many of the ideas promoted in the Six-Year Plan were simply resurrected ideas that architectural radicals had promoted prior to the war, which were now practical to implement.[41] On occasion, the tabula rasa mentality of architects and planners involved in reconstruction worried even party leaders. In one session in 1946 the Polish Workers' party admonished that "building policy should be mainly concerned with renovation and reconstruction of all buildings where it is possible, no matter whether in the future they would collide with the plan for rebuilding of the city."[42] This was a clear reference to the plans for the city by the Bureau for Reconstruction of the Capital (BOS), which involved the demolition of a large number of surviving buildings. In general, while many aspects of the principles behind a socialist capital were derived from other theories, its overall package—a command economy, centrally enforced economic zones, high urban densities, and monumental boulevards and buildings designed for propaganda in the city center—marked a significant departure from its antecedents.

The contemporary architecture of the socialist realist period was as ideologically driven as its urbanism. Following the lead of Bierut's 1949 speech, the National Congress of Polish Architects proclaimed: "Two camps are realising their contradictory world pictures and ideologies. On the one hand, the camp of democracy, socialism and peace—with the Soviet Union as the main bastion—and on the other the camp of imperialism, economic crisis and warmongering. The contest between these ideologies is also being waged in architecture."[43] The ideologically correct architectural style of socialist realism became pervasive throughout the Eastern Bloc.

As with its urbanism, socialist realist architecture was principally defined by its contrast with the characteristics of capitalist or "cosmopolitan" architecture. According to Goldzamt, the latter "fetishized the construction of a building and its functional construction, always negating the ideological expression of architecture. . . . [It] is today the most powerful weapon of the imperialist bourgeois."[44] The result was architecture that "influences the consciousness of the masses, instilling in them pessimism, feelings of hopelessness in the face of the omnipotence of technology and money." By contrast, socialist realist architecture would be distinguished by being "socialist in content, national in form." As Goldzamt put it: "an architect in a nation building socialism is not only a constructor of streets and buildings, but also of human souls. He has the opportunity to influence the masses everywhere and at any time. He expresses the social ideals in the name of which the masses work and live." One example of architecture with socialist content cited by Goldzamt was the Moscow underground, whose architect had "saturated the metro architecture with ideology using rich and easily comprehensible forms." The result was that "people realize that they are landlords in their own country . . . that the nation is strong, wealthy, and uses this strength and wealth to improve the citizen's well-being and culture." Polish architects were exhorted to "study very accurately the experiences of Soviet architecture to avoid 'fatal consequences.' "

The emphasis in socialist realism on producing buildings in a national form may seem ironic, given that all of the Eastern Bloc regimes were satellite governments controlled ultimately from Moscow. However, as with the historic rebuilding, the regimes were encouraged to demonstrate their patriotism—and thus presumably build their legitimacy—by adopting a national architectural style. This would also allow the regimes to distinguish their architecture from the "international style" of the capitalists. As Ladd has shown in the previous chapter, the communist regime in East Berlin saw the Stalinallee and other projects as reviving German national architectural traditions, despite links to a template developed in the Soviet Union during the 1930s with architectural details, facades facing the street, a monumental scale, and so forth.

The national form of Polish socialist realist architecture was thus expressed by reviving and updating historical styles considered to be most Polish, while operating under a similar template. There was, however, considerable controversy over what was the most Polish—and therefore the most national—historical architectural styles. Some scholars—including Goldzamt—argued that the purest Polish architectural form was from the Renaissance period, as could be seen in the Wawel Castle at Kraków. However, generally, architects were far more accustomed to operating in the neoclassical architectural language they

The Symbolic Dimensions of Trauma and Recovery

had learned before the war and for which there were also substantial Polish and Varsovian precedents to be called upon. Hence most socialist realism resembled neoclassicism. The MDM project is one of the most striking examples of the new form, complete with tableaux in the facades depicting heroic workers engaged in industrial activity.

Arguably, the most famous example of socialist realism in Warsaw is the Palace of Culture and Science, the enormous skyscraper that still dominates the cityscape. Ironically, the building is also the most atypical example of Polish socialist realism. Although the design was in accordance with socialist realist principles in incorporating elements of national architectural form—with Renaissance motifs, particularly parapets, inspired by the Wawel Castle at Kraków—in scale and shape the building is alien to every other structure in Warsaw. The scale is colossal: the palace was designed for 12,000 people, who could use the museums, gymnasiums, congress halls, and other spaces for approved functions. Its construction required the demolition of an entire area (including a hundred houses that had survived the war) and the relocation of 4,000 people.

The building is most closely descended from similar structures in the Soviet Union, particularly Moscow State University. The similarity is not coincidental: three of the five-man team designing the palace, including the main architect, had just come from designing the university. The architects ensured that the building would have a monumental effect; it occupies only a fraction of a gigantic plot and holds an isolated position in the city's skyline, thus giving enormous symbolic importance to the building's sponsor, the Soviet Union, which paid for and constructed the building. While the building was intended as a "gift" to symbolize the "eternal friendship between the Soviet Union and Poland," it is hard to imagine that the building was not conceived as an unmistakable metaphor for Soviet dominance over Poland, just as many came to regard it.[45]

The era of socialist realism had come to an end across the Eastern Bloc by 1956. Nikita Khrushchev singled out socialist realist architecture for criticism when he attacked architectural extravagance in a speech in Moscow in November 1954, and the passing of the era can be interpreted as part of a general de-Stalinization movement in the political realm. Socialist realist projects had already come under increasing criticism from within Poland shortly after the death of Stalin in March

Figure 6.5.
The Soviet-built Palace
of Culture, constructed
in 1955, still dominates
the Warsaw cityscape.
From Aman, *Architecture
and Ideology*.

1953. As the then chief architect of Warsaw, Józef Sigalin, commented later, the regime had "made the mistake of politicizing architectural tastes. A modernist is a cosmopolitan and what follows—a reactionist. What nonsense!"[46] For a short period during the post-Stalin thaw, it looked as if Polish architects might be liberated to practice freely, but a return to central planning soon dashed these hopes.

From around this time, Polish architects began to reembrace modernism, which had first surfaced—and been vigorously debated—in Poland during the 1930s. In particular, the modernist principles of mass-produced architecture and industrialization of construction using prefabricated components were mandated by the regime. The rejection of explicitly "socialist" architecture and urban form from this period did not, however, necessarily signal an end to the role of ideology in urban development. Rather, the regime was now emphasizing its retreat from explicitly ideological urban forms in favor of a technocratic approach: instead of attempting to influence the Polish people with architectural propaganda, the regime wished to appear to be prioritizing efforts to solve their problems. The new Polish leader, Gomułka, placed enormous emphasis on obtaining quantifiable results, particularly producing as many new apartments as possible to solve Poland's housing shortage. This was undoubtedly facilitated by cheaper building technologies, but the overall impact was questionable: the architecture of the new era that was purportedly free of ideological intent was of lower quality than that produced during socialist realism. Like their counterparts in the West, the tower blocks produced during the 1970s have come under particularly heavy criticism, as producing a landscape of "emptiness, hopelessness, monotony, and nothingness."[47]

As with Warsaw's architecture and urban form, memorials remained an ideological and political barometer throughout the communist period and beyond. In choosing which monuments to rebuild, the regime faced the peculiar task of deciding which historical figures were suitable to celebrate in the communist era, despite not being socialists. Generally, the most distant historic figures were easier to place in a socialist context. Hence the party sanctioned the rebuilding of an 1898 statue on Krakowskie Przedmieście of the great poet and revolutionary Adam Mickiewicz, who had died in 1855, and a party official argued that Mickiewicz, while "not a socialist as we understand it today," was nonetheless a "symbol of progressive Polish thinking."[48]

Mickiewicz's long struggle against tsarist oppression was not mentioned.

It was the memorialization of the more recent tragedies that proved most problematic. The regime could not authorize a memorialization of the Warsaw uprising without endorsing the Armia Krajowa (AK), the Polish army that had fought against the Nazis in 1944 in part to prevent the city from falling into Soviet hands. Indeed, for the first decade after liberation, the AK was denigrated as a group of bandits who had contributed to the destruction of Warsaw, and former AK soldiers were treated with suspicion—and often oppressed—by the Soviet-backed regime. It was only after the thaw began in 1956 that the issue of memorializing the AK fighters who had died in 1944 was addressed. A competition for a memorial to remember Polish soldiers from all organizations who participated and died in the uprising in 1944 was announced by the regime. But the memorial design chosen by the regime to be built was deliberately bland and unspecific to the AK or even the uprising generally: a statue of a sword-wielding woman (the traditional emblem of the city), later known as Nike, which seemed to symbolize, in the words of one historian, "victory and retribution rather than martyrdom."[49]

In the absence of an appropriate government-mandated memorial, Varsovians took matters into their own hands. The sculptor Jerzy Jarnuszkiewicz's *Young Insurgent*, initially a thirty-centimeter maquette of an activist child wielding a machine gun and wearing a soldier's helmet, produced in 1946, became a personal emblem for Varsovians, many of whom owned a plaster copy. In the 1980s, with the communist era drawing to a close, statues of the *Young Insurgent* were authorized by the government to be placed on many of Warsaw's streets, signaling that the regime on its last legs had at last endorsed the anti-Soviet Warsaw uprising.

If we accept the central role of ideology in the reconstruction of Warsaw, we should ask: how successful were the ideological intentions of the regime? The ideological potency of communist architecture and urban planning is perhaps impossible to measure, since the effects cannot be separated from the ideological effects of other media. In terms of securing the legitimacy of the regime, the creation of the socialist capital did little, or at least not enough. The regime remained weak

The Symbolic Dimensions of Trauma and Recovery

and never enjoyed the full support of its populace. Ironically, the aspect of the reconstructions that did most to engender legitimacy for the regime had the least to do with its ideology: the historical reconstructions enjoyed nearly universal support, both domestically and internationally.

Arguably, the regime's legitimacy ultimately depended more on its ability to deliver political "goods" to the populace, rather than on an ideological message. The historical reconstructions served as one example of such a political good. But the regime consistently failed to deliver economic prosperity. This shortcoming repeatedly undermined the government and was at the root of the civil disturbances in 1956, 1970, 1976, and 1980. So while the reconstruction of the Old Town in 1950–1954 and the Royal Castle in 1971–1974 helped to appease the populace, there is little evidence that the architecture and urban planning of the socialist realist period engendered support for the regime. This was largely because at all times the reconstruction process had different meanings for different groups. If reconstruction meant the creation of a socialist capital for the party, to the majority of the populace it meant little more than the restoration of the national capital and a reversal of the Nazi destruction. Indeed, their resilience in returning to the rubble and reconstructing the city remains a hugely admirable feat. It was simply their misfortune that this resilience was shaped and exploited by a foreign ideology, mirroring the wider tragedy of 1945: domination by one foreign power with a malign ideology was simply replaced by another one. In this sense, Polish resilience did not end with the completion of reconstruction but continued until 1989, when, finally free of foreign domination, the country became free to pursue its own path.

Notes

I would like to thank the following for reading and commenting on earlier drafts: Mark Kramer, Jeffry Diefendorf, Hanna Szwankowska, Piotr Majewski, Andrzej Tomaszewski, and David Crowley. Most important, it would not have been possible to write this chapter without the collaboration of my Polish colleague Karolina Ojrzynska, who carried out the translating and research of the materials in Polish. I am extremely grateful for her invaluable assistance.

1. Maria Niemczyk, "City Profile: Warsaw," *Cities* 15, no. 4 (1998): 301.
2. Stanisław Jankowski, "Warsaw: Destruction, Secret Town Planning, 1939–44, and Post-War Reconstruction," in *Rebuilding Europe's Bombed Cities*, ed. Jeffry M. Diefendorf (Basingstoke: Macmillan, 1990), 80, 90.
3. Ibid., 81.
4. Anthony M. Tung, *Preserving the World's Great Cities: The Destruction and Renewal of the Historic Metropolis* (New York: Clarkson Potter, 2001), 74.
5. Jankowski, "Warsaw," 80.
6. A brief (and incomplete) bibliography of Polish heroism: for the activity of city planners during the occupation, see Jankowski, "Warsaw." For a detailed account of the Warsaw Uprising, see Jerzy Kirchmayer, *Powstanie Warszawskie* (The Warsaw Uprising). For an account of the Jewish Ghetto Uprising, one notable book is Marian Apfelbaum, *Dwa sztandary. Rzecz o powstaniu w getcie warszawskim*. For an account of a particularly famous incident in which the Polish Home Army (the AK) freed one of their operatives from the Gestapo in the middle of the day in central Warsaw, see Aleksander Kamiński, *Kamienie na szaniec* (Stones on the Rampart), or Stanisław Jastrzębski, *Zaczęło się pod Arsenałem* (It All Began with the Arsenal). For a general account of life under the Nazis and the Varsovians' struggle to survive, see Roman Bratny, *Kolumbowie rocznik 20* (The Columbus Generation). All of these volumes are available in multiple editions, so no publisher or year of publication has been cited.
7. Jósef Sigalin, *Warszawa 1944–80* (Warsaw 1944–80), vol. 2 (Warsaw: Państwowy Instytut Wydawniczy, 1980), 399.
8. Bolesław Bierut and Warsaw Biuro Urbanistyczne, *Sześcioletni plan odbudowy Warszawy* (The Six-Year Plan for the Reconstruction of Warsaw) (Warsaw: Ksiazka i Wiedza, 1951), pg. 15 of official English tranlation appended to Polish version.
9. Tung, *Preserving the World's Great Cities*, 75.
10. Sigalin, *Warszawa*, 301.
11. Jankowski, 88–89. 4.5M Zlotys equaled approximately $45,000 according to black market rates or $180,000 according to the official rate, as of 1957. See Krzysztof Madej, Biuro Edukacji Publicznej IPN (Public Education Office at the Institute of National Remembrance): http://www.ipn.gov.pl/bep_konwers_madej.html (5/25/04).
12. Duane Mezga, "Political Factors in the Reconstruction of Warsaw's Old Town," *Urban Design Studies* 4 (1998): 41.
13. Jerzy S. Majewski and Tomasz Markiewicz, *Warszawa nie odbudowana* (Warsaw Not Reconstructed) (Warsaw: DiG, 1989), 6.
14. UNESCO Web site: http://whc.unesco.org/sites/30.htm (5/20/04).
15. Edmund Goldzamt, "O polską architekturę socjalistyczną" (For Polish Socialist Architecture). Materials from the National Party Council (Krajowa Partyjna Narada) of architects that took place on 20–21 June 1949 in War-

The Symbolic Dimensions of Trauma and Recovery

saw. Edited by Jan Minorski (Warsaw: Państwowe Wydawnictwo Techniczne, 1950), 44.

16. Piotr Majewski, "Zamek Królewski w okresie błędów i wypaczeń" (The Royal Castle during the Times of Errors and Distortions), in *Kronika Zamkowa* (The Castle Chronicle) no. 1/39/2000, 172.

17. Eric Hobsbawm, *The Invention of Tradition* (Cambridge: Cambridge University Press, 1983), 1.

18. Majewski, *Warszawa*, 24.

19. Ibid., 137.

20. This is true even today. A guide at Warsaw's History Museum emphasized to me the aesthetic reasons that historic buildings had been rebuilt in their earlier architectural form. Conservationists then and today frequently argue for restoring buildings in their "purest" or earliest form, irrespective of any ideological implications.

21. See Mezga, *Political Factors*, 47; Majewski, *Warszawa*, 24.

22. Majewski cites two examples of nineteenth-century buildings demolished for no apparent reason other than ideology: the most precious art-nouveau tenement house in Warsaw at Sluzewska Street and another art-nouveau building at the corner of Ujazdowskie Avenue and Chopin Street. Majewski, *Warszawa*, 18.

23. Ibid., 32.

24. See Andrzej Tomaszewski, Proceedings of SARP Conference "Odbudowa Warszawy w latach 1945–1955" (Reconstruction of Warsaw in 1945–1955) (Warsaw: SARP, 1996).

25. Quote from S. Żaryn, *13 kamienic staromiejskich, strona Dekerta* (13 Houses in the Old Town, Dekert Side) (Warazawa: PWN, 1972), cited in Anna Naruszewicz, "Problemy modernizacji Zespołu Staromiejskiego w Warszawie na tle uwarunkowań okresu odbudowy" (The Problems of Modernization of the Old Town in Warsaw against the General Background of the Reconstruction Period) (Unpublished paper, Warsaw Technical University, 1995), 6.

26. Mezga, *Political Factors*, 46.

27. Author's interview with Andrzej Tomaszewski, August 2002.

28. Alistaire Horne, "Warsaw's Heroic Cityscape," *New York Times*, 17 August 2003.

29. Author's interview with Tomaszewski. Interestingly, the historic reconstructions in Leningrad tended to be far more painstaking and authentic; an enormous amount of effort was made to reconstruct the old Petrine buildings as closely as possible (author's interview with Mark Kramer, March 2002). The superior quality of the reconstructions may have been due to a greater amount of resources available and comparatively less damage in Leningrad; still, the fact that there was often less ideological influence on reconstruction in the Soviet Union seems ironic.

30. Stanisław Lorentz, *Walka o zamek 1939–1980* (The Struggle for the Royal Castle in Warsaw 1939–1980) (Warsaw: Kamek Królewski w Warszawie, 1986), 45.

31. Piotr Majewski, "Zamek Królewski," 172.

32. Lorentz, *Walka o zamek*, 47. The competition's jury concluded by recommending that the building's height be raised by 2.5 meters, although the jury did not select any of the designs submitted to be built.

33. David Crowley, *Warsaw* (London: Reaktion Books, 2003), 60.

34. See ibid.

35. Interview with Piotr Majewski, August 2002.

36. Sigalin, *Warszawa*, 397.

37. Bierut, *Sześcioletni plan odbudowy Warszawy*, 7. (Page number refers to the official English translation appended to the Polish text.) All the subsequent quotations in this and the following paragraph are from this text.

38. The nationalization of all land within Warsaw occurred with the Decree of 1945. See Jankowski, "Warsaw," 83.

39. See Bierut, *Sześcioletni plan*.

40. John Conron, "The Polish Experience," *New Mexico Architecture* 18, nos. 3 and 4 (1976): 21.

41. Increasing the quantity of green space in the city center, for example.

42. Majewski, *Warszawa*, 17.

43. Anders Aman, *Architecture and Ideology in Eastern Europe during the Stalin Era* (Cambridge, Mass.: MIT Press, 1991), ix.

44. Goldzamt, *O Polską architekturę socjalistyczną*, 25. The remaining quotes from Goldzamt in this paragraph are from the same source. This kind of sentiment was prevalent throughout the Eastern Bloc. Kurt Kiebknect, another architect, at a cultural conference of the German-Soviet Friendship Union, 1951, said: "We are against the Bauhaus. Why? We are against the Bauhaus because functionalism is the height of imperialist cosmopolitanism, the height of decadence and decay." Cited in Aman, 1991, ix. See also Brian Knox, *The Architecture of Poland* (London: Barris and Jenkins, 1971), 49; Mezga, *Political Factors*, 7.

45. For a description of contemporary opinions of the Palace, see D. Crowley, "People's Warsaw/Popular Warsaw," *Journal of Design History* 10, no. 2 (1997), 212–14.

46. Sigalin, *Warszawa*, 504.

47. Ibid., 508.

48. Crowley, "Warsaw," 70. I am particularly indebted to Crowley's volume for the material in this section.

49. Ibid., 65.

The Symbolic Dimensions of Trauma and Recovery

A Delayed Healing
Understanding the Fragmented Resilience of Gernika

7

JULIE B. KIRSCHBAUM

DESIRÉE SIDEROFF

■ For the 1937 Paris World's Fair, Pablo Picasso unveiled a vivid portrayal of human suffering entitled *Guernica*.[1] Inspired by the brutal civilian attack on a small Basque town in northern Spain, the painting became an artistic indictment of fascism, exposing the horrors of the Spanish Civil War to the world. Gernika suffered this major urban trauma on April 26, 1937, when Hitler's Condor Legion demolished the town at the request of General Francisco Franco, leader of the National Forces and subsequent dictator of Spain. While the town of Gernika lacked the global prominence and political freedom to convey its own account of the bombing, the Picasso painting, in conjunction with the international press, exposed the brutality of the attack. In the ensuing decades, the painting traveled the globe promoting a message of martyrdom and suffering. This international attention occurred in sharp contrast to Gernika's concealed recovery, which received little publicity under the censorship of Franco's fascist regime.

Franco deliberately targeted Gernika because of its cultural significance to the Basque people, for whom the town symbolized democracy and autonomy. In attacking this town, which held no military or strategic significance, Franco aimed to destroy the symbolic center of Basque self-rule and crush his enemy's morale. This deadly assault affected the lives of all of Gernika's citizens, killing many, scattering survivors, and almost completely destroying the town's physical structure.

Following the bombing, the town experienced a precarious recovery. The man who ordered Gernika to be destroyed guided its recon-

Figure 7.1.
Pablo Picasso's *Guernica* was first displayed at the 1937 World's Fair in Paris, France. Picasso created the painting to protest the destruction of the town and to generate international interest in the attack. © 2004 Estate of Pablo Picasso/Artists Rights Society (ARS), New York.

struction and dictated the rules of the Spanish public realm from 1939 to 1975. Franco simultaneously directed a rapid physical restoration and a strict program of Basque cultural subjugation. The politics of recovery meant that decades passed before town members could publicly mourn or openly place blame.

Under these circumstances, recovery in Gernika exhibited distinct physical, emotional, and cultural dimensions. *Physical resilience* denotes the ability of a city to rebuild its physical structure. It considers how the city was rebuilt, who was in charge of the rebuilding process, and the politics involved in physical reconstruction. *Emotional resilience* refers to the ability of individuals, families, and communities to cope and heal from trauma. In many Western communities for example, emotional recovery is often characterized by public and private efforts to grieve, commemorate, and memorialize the event. In Gernika, however, some survivors have also labored to prevent future violence, providing an additional dimension to emotional resilience. Finally, *cultural resilience* signifies the perseverance of cultural practices and norms through events of great cultural trauma. Outward manifestations of cultural resilience include the ability of customs, traditions, languages, or religions to survive and evolve. This chapter examines the physical, emotional, and cultural resilience exhibited in Gernika, revealing how the political circumstances in Spain forced a

The Symbolic Dimensions of Trauma and Recovery

separation between the physical recovery of Gernika and the emotional and cultural recovery of its citizens.

At present, Gernika is a small town of approximately 15,500 residents in Biscay,[2] the largest of three provinces that make up the relatively autonomous Basque region of northern Spain.[3] At the time of the bombing, Gernika was a prominent regional center of approximately 7,000 residents. Franco viewed the Basque province of Biscay as his enemy because its dominant political organization, the Basque Nationalist party (PNV), denounced his actions and instead supported the fledgling republic. Even though the PNV shared Franco's conservative beliefs and support of the Catholic church, the PNV fought for the republic because the young government promised greater autonomy for the region, a policy Franco adamantly rejected.[4]

At the request of General Franco, Adolf Hitler's German Condor Legion carried out the bombing of Gernika. It provided Hitler with the means to test newly developed weapons and military strategies out of the spotlight of international scrutiny. Lieutenant Karl von Knauer, who led the raid on Gernika, used his experience to develop training manuals for later, larger-scale campaigns of aerial bombardment, undertaken in Warsaw and London.[5]

Franco ordered the bombing of Gernika because it symbolized democracy to the Basque people. A secondary motivation aimed to instill fear into nearby Bilbao, a strategic port town that contained the majority of industrial activity for the region. The saturation-bombing techniques used during the attack did not pursue military targets. Indeed, the two most strategic sites—the Rentería Bridge (located at an important road juncture) and the arms factory—emerged unscathed, while bombs decimated Gernika's primary civilian centers, particularly the open-air market and other key locations in the downtown area. The bombing of Gernika was the second attack of this nature carried out by the Condor Legion; the nearby town of Durango suffered a similar bombardment on March 31, 1937, one month prior to the attack on Gernika. As political scientist Robert Clark observes, however, in Gernika, "the savagery of aerial bombardment of civilians was raised to its highest level," and "the name 'Guernica' has become virtually synonymous with the atrocities of war since that attack."[6]

The town's symbolic position stems from the centuries-old tradi-

Figure 7.2.
Photograph of the open-air market taken shortly after the bombing destroyed it. © Courtesy of Archivo Gernikazarra.

tion of Spanish royalty meeting in Gernika under the sacred oak tree (the Tree of Gernika) to officially recognize Basque self-rule and to agree to uphold the *fueros*, the ancient Basque system of law. In this way, the Basque Country was ruled as a democratic and autonomous region within the kingdom of Spain until the Second Carlist War (1872–1876).[7] The Tree of Gernika, a living symbol of Basque history, grows on the grounds of the Casa de Juntas, which houses the Biscayan parliament. The town has maintained this sacred tree's genealogy by planting a sapling from the mature tree.

The bombing took place during the region's Monday market, to which people traveled considerable distances to sell their wares. At 4:30 in the afternoon, while most of the townspeople and visitors socialized in the local cafés, the church bell rang to warn of an attack. Residents had become accustomed to this sound as a false alarm; however, on April 26, planes from the German Condor Legion soon appeared. The bombing of Gernika lasted approximately four hours. Planes used Vitoria, a nearby city already under the control of Franco, to refuel before returning to Gernika. As G. L. Steer reported from Bilbao to the London *Times* the following day, "The rhythm of this bombing of an open town was, therefore, a logical one: first, hand grenades and heavy bombs to stampede the population, then machine-gunning to drive them below, next heavy incendiary bombs to wreck the houses and burn them on top of their victims."[8]

Many survivors of the actual bombing perished in the aftermath, as fires trapped and burned those seeking refuge in the town's basements and crudely built bomb shelters. By the end of the day most of the downtown lay in ruins; residents and refugees were scattered across the countryside and neighboring towns, terrified and often separated from their loved ones. Fourteen-year-old Luis Iriondo escaped to the nearby town of Lumo, where he woke up at three o'clock in the morning after hearing his mother screaming his name in the town plaza.[9] The mother

The Symbolic Dimensions of Trauma and Recovery

of future mayor Alfonso Vallejo placed him—then a one-year-old infant—in the Casa de Juntas, which luckily escaped destruction.

For several reasons, it is difficult to estimate how many died in Gernika. Fires ravaged the town for days and consumed many corpses. The fate of others remained unknown as people were scattered and many of the seriously injured were sent to Bilbao or other nearby towns for medical treatment. Additionally, the baseline population in Gernika at the time of the bombing was significantly higher than usual due to the regional market and the influx of refugees. These nonresidents were most likely to die in the bombing because they had little knowledge of places to hide.[10] To this day, it remains unclear how many people were actually killed. According to the historian Hugh Thomas, experts have estimated as low as 200 and as high as 1,600.[11]

The death toll alone does not account for the impact of the attack on the town. By the fascists' own report, 71 percent of Gernika's buildings were completely destroyed and 7 percent were badly battered. The remaining 22 percent were damaged, but to a lesser extent.[12] The bomb-

Figure 7.3.
The shaded areas of this map indicate buildings that were destroyed during the attack on Gernika. © Courtesy of Archivo Gernikazarra.

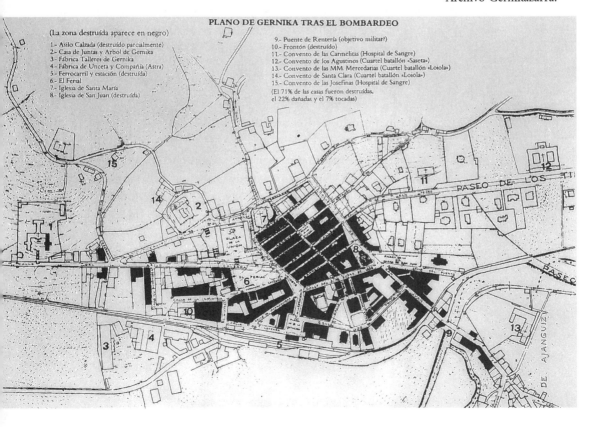

PLANO DE GERNIKA TRAS EL BOMBARDEO

(La zona destruída aparece en negro)

1.- Asilo Calzada (destruído parcialmente)
2.- Casa de Juntas y Árbol de Gernika
3.- Fábrica Talleres de Gernika
4.- Fábrica de Unceta y Compañía (Astra)
5.- Ferrocarril y estación (destruída)
6.- El Ferial
7.- Iglesia de Santa María
8.- Iglesia de San Juan (destruída)

9.- Puente de Rentería (objetivo militar?)
10.- Frontón (destruído)
11.- Convento de las Carmelitas (Hospital de Sangre)
12.- Convento de los Agustinos (Cuartel batallón «Saseta»)
13.- Convento de las MM. Mercedarias (Cuartel batallón «Loiola»)
14.- Convento de Santa Clara (Cuartel batallón «Loiola»)
15.- Convento de las Josefinas (Hospital de Sangre)

(El 71% de las casas fueron destruídas, el 22% dañadas y el 7% tocadas)

ing dramatically altered the lives of all Gernika residents. In the direct aftermath, few residents could return to their homes, and those who did were forced to share crowded quarters with other survivors. Many more left Gernika and became refugees, unable to return for years, if ever.

The attack on Gernika was a military success for both the Germans and Franco's National Forces. Franco occupied the town just three days after the bombing and was able to take over Bilbao on June 19, only two months later.[13] From the moment he entered Gernika, Franco immediately closed off the town to the international press and denied any involvement in the attack. The official story airing on National Forces–controlled radio stated that communist forces had burned the town. According to the propaganda, "Gernika was destroyed by fire and gasoline. It was set on fire and converted to ruins by the Red hordes at the criminal service of Aguirre."[14] In fabricating such a lie, denying all responsibility, and prohibiting open dialogue about the tragedy, Franco deepened the emotional wounds of the attack and prevented many residents of the town from coming to terms with the bombing. In addition to succeeding militarily and inflicting long-standing emotional damage, Franco also dealt a heavy blow to Basque culture by initiating a program of cultural suppression.[15]

Physical Resilience: Reconstruction without Emotional Recovery

■ By 1939, the year Franco won the war, the once-handsome medieval town of Gernika lay in ruins, a landscape of partially burned buildings and scattered vacant lots. He quickly initiated the rebuilding process following his rise to power, creating an extraordinary situation in which the man responsible for the town's demise led the rebuilding process. Although the physical rebuilding was carried out with speed, it was devoid of any commemoration or other efforts toward emotional healing. Residents did not enjoy the physical recovery equitably, as Franco's efforts tended to focus on his political and economic supporters, leaving the rest of the population with little assistance in satisfying their basic needs.[16]

The rebuilding process was carried out by the national Organization for Devastated Regions (ODR), a centrally controlled organization that was charged with reconstructing destroyed cities throughout Spain. The ODR initiated the rapid development of generic new towns based primarily on the architecture of central Spain, which often meant sacrificing local style and preferences.[17] The construction process was accelerated through the use of prisoner labor. To avoid rebellions, Franco used non-Basque prisoners to rebuild towns in the Basque Country and sent Basque prisoners to reconstruct other parts of Spain.

In Gernika, the work of the ODR focused primarily on the downtown area, which was almost completely destroyed during the bombing. Early plans for Gernika, heavily steeped in propaganda, indicated great fascist visions for the town, including processional streets and a 20,000-person stadium.[18] Perhaps owing to the scarcity of resources following the war, a stadium of that magnitude was never built, nor did Gernika become a great seat of fascist power.

Before any rebuilding could take place, the town was cleared and leveled to create a flat plane from which to build. This effort effectively raised the ground elevation of the town by 1.5 meters.[19] The ODR adopted a modernized version of the original medieval street grid and subsequently renamed the new streets. The formal building process was limited to the town hall and plaza, apartment buildings along the main street, a new location and permanent structure for the market, and syndicate housing for the factory workers. The new structures exhibited a human scale, which was further reinforced by restricting the downtown area to four-story apartment buildings with ground-floor commercial activity. The design of Gernika's redevelopment departed slightly from the generic ODR model because Manuel Smith de Ibarra, a native of Bilbao, designed the main square. As a result of his influence, some elements of Basque style, such as "a series of arches customary in the Basque town halls since the fifteenth century," were incorporated into the town's design.[20] However, the new design lacked enclosed porches, a signature Basque style that was prevalent in the town prior to the bombing.[21]

Only wealthy and politically powerful residents exerted local influence on the reconstruction process, and the urban form of the city shows strong evidence of this favoritism. For example, the designers of the market building compromised the plan so that a wealthy land owner would not have to give up his property.[22] Other residents' prop-

Figure 7.4.
The reconstructed Plaza de Los Fueros, featuring covered walkways, common in the region.

erty rights carried less weight, and many owners were forced to sell their land for nominal sums of money.[23] The voices of survivors who were not wealthy or powerful were never heard, nor were their needs considered. The urban form also manifested acts of negligence. While buildings were erected fairly quickly, ancillary services, such as roads, water, sewer, and electricity, often took years to install.[24]

By 1946, the ODR officially completed the reconstruction and the Francoist town government held a ceremony to honor the dictator's efforts.[25] Swift reconstruction of prominent town buildings attempted to cover up any evidence of the bombing. Functional, albeit highly

The Symbolic Dimensions of Trauma and Recovery

rudimentary, worker housing enabled the factories to continue producing goods. Outside of this celebrated center, the task of reconstructing the remainder of Gernika was left to townspeople and private enterprise. Despite the rapid physical reconstruction, the town was slow to return to normal, as the years following the Spanish Civil War were marked by famine, strict rationing, and increased suffering. Many former residents could not return for years due to the threat of imprisonment or simple lack of housing and infrastructure.[26] Those who did live in Gernika during the early 1940s experienced overcrowded conditions and lacked basic services.[27]

Although present-day residents of the town remember playing in the debris as children, vacant lots were gradually filled in and new areas developed. A period of heavy redevelopment in Gernika occurred from 1960 to 1970, coinciding with a great population surge in the Basque Country. During this period, the four Basque provinces gained a total of 202,580 new residents, many of whom relocated to take advantage of the region's abundant industrial jobs.[28] The private sector constructed numerous apartment buildings to house the workers drawn to the nearby factories. Many families living in the countryside also began to keep apartments in town to live in during the week.[29] By the end of the 1970s, this wave of new construction finally succeeded in filling in the remaining lots left vacant from the bombing. Developers also replaced older, poorly constructed buildings and initiated new construction in outlying areas of town.

Emotional Resilience: Remembrance, Memorialization, and Peacebuilding

■   Even as the physical rebuilding of Gernika took place, forty years of dictatorship significantly slowed emotional recovery. When a tragedy such as the bombing of Gernika occurs, it often produces very powerful responses. One common response is what Edward Linenthal refers to as the *toxic narrative*, where those affected by the tragedy are consumed in perpetuity by the horror of the event.[30] Emotional recovery can be measured by how well or fully individuals and communities manage to see beyond the toxicity of their traumatic circumstances. Emotional recovery is linked closely to resilience because an urban area cannot truly recuperate from an event if its people are denied a means for emotional restoration.

Franco's entry three days after the bombing signaled the start of the physical reconstruction; more important, it marked the beginning of unforeseen emotional destruction and hardship. Discussing the atrocities of the attack became grounds for imprisonment, and commemorating the event was strictly prohibited. Not only did Gernika's residents witness mass airborne destruction hitherto unobserved by civilian eyes, those who remained or later returned were not permitted to publicly honor the memories of their loved ones lost in the tragedy, or even acknowledge who was behind the attack.

Risking imprisonment, citizens engaged in clandestine activities to commemorate the bombing.[31] Each year around the time of the attack, they surreptitiously placed flowers at the collective grave and held a secret service in the Church of Santa Maria. The conclusion of the service often included great public crying and grieving. This mass later evolved into a ceremony of remembrance, developed in the late 1980s.[32]

The most famous memorialization of the bombing occurred immediately after the event itself. Picasso's *Guernica* (see figure 7.1) was the first and last effort to publicize and memorialize the event for many years. The Republican Spanish government had commissioned Picasso to paint a large-format painting for the Spanish Pavilion of the Paris World's Fair as early as January 1937. However, not until reading about the bombing of Gernika did he begin this seminal work. The surrealist black-and-white painting was an abstract representation of the horrors committed in Gernika, with no direct references to the event.[33] According to art historian Meyer Schapiro, "Picasso chose rather to convey the shock of the event and his protest through an image of animal as well as human victims, a universal suffering."[34] The painting consequently features six humans and three animals, all contorted and writhing in pain. Although he did not experience the attack himself, Picasso deeply felt the effects of the bombing both as a Spaniard supporting the Republican government and as a Parisian intellectual.

Picasso's antifascist sentiments came through clearly in the specific instructions he left after his death, indicating that *Guernica* should not reside in his homeland until Spain established a stable democratic government. Although Picasso did not even leave a will to settle his estate, he carefully laid out future plans for his most politically charged work

The Symbolic Dimensions of Trauma and Recovery

of art.[35] Per his instructions, *Guernica* and all of the preparatory paintings and drawings returned to Spain from New York's Museum of Modern Art in 1981, three years after the formation of the Spanish democracy.[36]

In the absence of local public activities, *Guernica* served as a memorial and the first step in emotional recovery throughout the years of cultural suppression. When the citizens of Gernika lacked the freedom to publicly articulate their pain, they displayed replicas of the painting as a silent protest, a condemnation of Franco's regime.[37] While other forms of personal remembrance undoubtedly occurred within private homes, such as parents teaching their children about the horrible event, no public dialogue or remembrance could legally occur.[38]

Franco's death in 1975 provided the first opportunity for reconciliation between Gernika and Spain; however, tenuous political conditions at the time precluded any discussion of blame or responsibility for the bombing. Before his death, Franco appointed King Juan Carlos, with the intention of instituting "Francoism without Franco."[39] However, rather than continuing fascism, the king introduced democracy to Spain. While many Spaniards welcomed the end of fascism, they harbored uncertainty, as the previous attempt at democracy had led to a bloody civil war followed by nearly forty years of dictatorship.[40] Additional challenges stemmed from the need for a fledgling ruler to convince oppositional Francoist and Communist parties to reach consensus. Questions regarding home rule and the degree of independence to grant to historically autonomous regions, such as the Basque Country and Catalonia, further complicated this process. The new political actors felt a need to distance themselves from the atrocities of Franco's regime and his associates and therefore took no responsibility to facilitate reconciliation efforts. To this day, the Spanish government does not officially recognize either the bombing or the culprit, considering it a past event not worth resurrecting.[41]

What the Basque Country did gain in 1980, however, was political and fiscal autonomy, which included the ability to create laws and collect taxes. With their regained freedoms, the Basque government and its local tributaries brought renewed energy to the process of emotional recovery by correcting the official story of the event and creating a forum for public remembrance.[42] As part of this belated healing effort, the town erected physical memorials, including a simple plaque in the central plaza, which states the date and location of the attack. To outsiders, this plaque may seem understated; however, its presence becomes more powerful considering the denial of the right to record even the most basic facts of the bombing for decades following the devastation.

Many Gernika residents have fought unsuccessfully to house *Guernica* in their town. To commemorate and eternalize this request, the town hall placed a ceramic reproduction of Picasso's painting on display with the words "*Guernica* Gernikara," which translates from Basque as "return the painting *Guernica* to Gernika." In lieu of receiving the painting, the town made an agreement with the Spanish government to receive a large sculpture by Henry Moore entitled *Covered Modern Figure* (1986).[43] The town also commissioned Basque artist Eduardo Chillida to create *The Broken Wall Exploded in the Name of Peace* (1988). Both sculptures are located in the Park of the Peoples of Europe, adjacent to the Casa de Juntas.

In addition to erecting public memorials, the Basque government also tried to support the personal healing of survivors. In 1987 the Basque parliament established Gernika Gogoratuz, a peace research and conflict transformation center. Since its formation, Gernika Gogoratuz has worked to "lend a voice to the survivors, so that their suffering and losses will be heard, and that issues may emerge which, for many years, had been hidden, during the occupation of the town under Francoist power."[44] Initially, Gernika Gogoratuz conducted personal interviews with all living survivors to capture the oral history of the victims. The organization also provided survivors with a venue to share their stories through the development of a documentary entitled *The Bombing of Gernika: The Mark of Men.*

The formation of Gernika Gogoratuz combated the toxic narrative by helping survivors come to terms with the tragedy. A key event in the emotional recovery of the town occurred in 1997 when Germany formally acknowledged and apologized for the bombing. Juan Gutierrez, founder of Gernika Gogoratuz, wrote to German president Roman Herzog requesting an official statement regarding the 1937 attack.[45] In response, President Herzog addressed a letter to each living survivor recognizing Germany's role in the bombing, distancing the current administration from past horrors, and yet also apologizing

The Symbolic Dimensions of Trauma and Recovery

for years of suffering. As part of the letter, he declared, "Sixty years after the bombing, new generations have emerged, but you, the victims of this attack, still have the memory and consequences of that day engraved in your heart."[46] The town of Gernika responded favorably by asking for peace and partnership: "That act while incomprehensible for us, did not leave us with feelings of hatred or vengeance, but with a huge, and immense, desire for peace.... Now we can do what we could not do then: open our arms and say welcome to Gernika, let's march together in peace."[47]

This gesture represented a highly significant moment in the aftermath of the bombing, given how long the culpability had been contested. The ability to officially attach a perpetrator to crimes committed years before enabled many residents to heal and forgive. The correspondence with President Herzog marked the beginning of a positive relationship between Germany and Gernika. Women from Gernika have traveled to Germany to discuss the bombing, and daughters of pilots from the German Condor Legion have visited Gernika to speak with survivors. Pfortzheim, a small German town, has become one of Gernika's sister cities, and young Germans can fulfill their civil service requirements by working for Gernika Gogoratuz.[48]

Cultural Resilience: Identity, Symbols, and Traditions

■ While reconciliation and memorial efforts helped individuals to heal, work was also needed to restore Franco's primary target, the Basque culture. From the moment Franco took power, he afforded the Basque people scant avenues for cultural expression. He committed acts of cultural violence, including confiscating the property of known Basque nationalists and severely persecuting Basque religious figures. Writing, speaking, and teaching the Basque language immediately became illegal, and "jail sentences were imposed for even casual conversations carried on in the language on public streets."[49] In some places, "Basque inscriptions on tombstones and public buildings were scraped off."[50]

The newly empowered fascist regime created an extensive register of Basque political prisoners and silenced many others with the threat of imprisonment. Conditions at home permitted neither political nor economic prosperity, dispersing many Basque citizens around the globe. However, even under these adverse conditions, Basque cultural norms and traditions were not lost. As one historian of the region observed, "[T]he very act of suppression provoked an attitude of resistance among the people."[51] Instead of cultural decimation, efforts to suppress the Basque people effectively turned Gernika into a symbol of Basque martyrdom and suffering.

During the dictatorship, countless clandestine acts by local residents enabled Basque culture to survive. As early as the 1950s, illegal Basque schools, *ikastolas*, began to operate in secret.[52] Significant political, educational, and financial support from the international Basque community assisted the perseverance of Basque culture under such adverse conditions. The exiled Basque government and international organizations—such as the Basque Center in Boise, Idaho—formed the backbone of this effort.

In an effort to regain the political and cultural freedoms stamped out by the dictatorship, some international and local efforts rallied around the fight for independence. By 1959, the radical military group Euzkadi ta Askatasuna (ETA; Basque Fatherland and Liberty) emerged and began employing acts of violence to challenge the dominant power structure.[53] ETA identified the Spanish state as the enemy of anything Basque and often evoked the historical significance and subsequent suffering of Gernika as part of the resistance; liberating "the symbolic oak of Guernica from foreign domination" became a primary agenda item.[54]

The activities of ETA have received significant attention from the international press, leading most foreigners to associate the Basque region with terrorism. Within the Basque Country, however, a far more complicated relationship between peace and resistance exists. For example, ceremonies promoting peace often occur in tandem with alternative activities supporting resistance.

Although ETA accrued the most international visibility, other Basque organizations promoted resistance without overtly calling for violence. After the dictatorship ended, for example, a group of historians and political activists, known as the Commission to Investigate Gernika,[55] began to meet to reflect on the past and plan for the future

The Symbolic Dimensions of Trauma and Recovery

of the town. As early as 1976, this group used the anniversary of the bombing as a time to meet with survivors and publicize the truth about the attack. The commission called for the establishment of Gernika as a city of culture and resistance for the Basque people.[56] Before disbanding in the mid-1980s, the commission had a profound impact on the political agenda of the town. Its studies informed the policies of the local government, following attainment of greater Basque autonomy. For the first time in almost forty-five years, Gernika had the opportunity to define an official response to the bombing and to reflect as a town on its own symbolic importance. Early agenda items included addressing blame and correcting the story of the bombing.

After the fall of Franco but prior to 1987, Gernika's residents observed the anniversary of the bombing with simple rituals, such as a one-hour church service held annually on April 26.[57] It was not until the fiftieth anniversary, however, that they planned a large-scale official event. In the development of the anniversary ceremonies, the Basque government and the town itself worked together to reinforce the strong cultural identity that Gernika represents for the Basque region.

The 1987 commemoration of the fiftieth anniversary of the bombing served as a turning point for the town of Gernika, marking the town's conscious reinvention as a place of peace. A deliberate decision was made to drop resistance from the town's agenda, although it remained a powerful alternative viewpoint in Gernika. There are many explanations as to why officials so strongly emphasized peace over resistance. For example, they may have felt a need to separate the image of the town from the negative international association with terrorism. Perhaps they identified reconciliation as an important healing device for survivors. Additionally, the town could have viewed peacebuilding as a more positive and sustainable form of resistance. Regardless of the motivation, pursuing the official agenda of peace allowed Gernika to relate its experiences to other global injustices and tragedies of war. Although Gernika's call for peace is not completely unique and would seem to be a clear echo of Japanese efforts in Hiroshima, it is far from a common response to urban trauma.

In an effort to reinstate Basque traditions, town officials designed an elaborate series of anniversary rituals, many of which continue today. They instituted a highly symbolic ceremony at the mass grave site

[Fig. 7.5], including group prayer, a traditional Basque song and dance, and the ringing of the bell of San Juan. The San Juan Church was a source of controversy immediately after the bombing because Franco used photographs of the church with gasoline cans "planted" in front to propagate his false claims that the communists had burned the town.[58] Local citizens managed to save the bell from the church before its destruction and now keep it in the cemetery next to the mausoleum, where it is rung only once a year, on the anniversary of the bombing.[59]

The commemorative events of 1987 inspired town officials to create a flag of Gernika that incorporates traditional imagery, including the Tree of Gernika. As part of the ceremonies, town officials also developed the town's anthem, based on traditional Basque music. These new rituals have become an integral part of the town's methods of teaching its history. Alternate meetings and resistance activities occurred in parallel to the official fiftieth-anniversary ceremony. Although the 1987 events were by far the most elaborate, the town continues to use the anniversary to publicly remember the brutality of the bombing and to promote messages of peace and community. During the anniversary week, Gernika Gogoratuz annually sponsors the International Convention on Peace and Culture, which gathers international peace workers from all fields to reflect on the challenges of advancing peace.[60]

As a result of its symbolic importance to the larger region, Gernika has received significant support from the Basque government. Since obtaining power in the early days of the democracy, the Basque government, controlled by the PNV (Basque Nationalist party), has used Gernika to reinforce and promote Basque cultural identity. Gernika plays a "central role in the spatial practice of politics of the new regime. Its historical role in Basque self-government is openly underscored and it is used in building a sense of identity and belonging in various ways."[61] For example, the Biscayan parliament continues to meet in Gernika, even though it is more remote and offers fewer amenities than the cosmopolitan Bilbao. Although most political decisions related to the broader region are made in the Basque capital of Vitoria, officials make a point of traveling to Gernika for highly symbolic decisions, such as the 1980 ratification of the Basque Statute of Autonomy.[62]

The use of Gernika as a symbol to promote Basque identity continues today through the promotion of Gernika as a steward of culture and tradition. Through the redesign of the Gernika museum and the

The Symbolic Dimensions of Trauma and Recovery

Figure 7.5.
In 1995, the town of
Gernika replaced the
original mass grave with
a marble tomb. The
front of the tomb reads
Pax, which means
"peace" in Latin.

development of cultural/historical tours of the town, Gernika has established itself as the center of the history and future of the Basque people. First opened in 1998, the Gernika museum reopened in 2003 as the Peace Museum, which relates the bombing of Gernika to other international conflicts and uses the idea of universal suffering from violence to unite seemingly disparate geographies and situations.[63] The first floor of the museum explores the pathway to peace by winding visitors through a series of interconnected exhibits that invite them to reflect on this topic. The second floor tells the story of Gernika. Visitors arrive in a room depicting the activities of the townspeople immediately before the bombs dropped. Subsequently, they enter a room showing the circumstances of those same people during and after the bombing. Another room physically and figuratively deconstructs Picasso's *Guernica* to represent its message of peace. Throughout, the museum promotes the idea of reconciliation—"the ultimate lesson which the survivors of the bombing wish to teach to future generations."[64]

Gernika's efforts to assert its cultural significance are supported by the tourist office and Basque educational institutions. Booklets for visitors offer a cultural heritage tour to all places of symbolic importance in Gernika. Small tiles imprinted with an oak leaf direct visitors to key monuments, which include the town hall, Chillida's sculpture, and the

Casa de Juntas. New generations of Basques learn about the significance of Gernika, its history and symbols in school. A visit to the town and peace museum follows as a fundamental cultural development in the Basque educational experience.

The ability of the government and the citizens to incorporate new symbols and traditions into their existing cultural lexicon is a crucial factor in the resilience of the culture. The current image of Gernika results from a series of deliberate decisions made by the Basque national government and the local Gernika government. However, this message of peace is not uncontested. The prevalence of pro-resistance graffiti in the town attests to less peaceful undercurrents, as do the alternative activities that continue to accompany the anniversary ceremonies. Gernika's residents have long accepted these two divergent symbologies for their town. It remains to be seen if these contradictory discourses will continue to coexist.

The bombing and subsequent recovery of Gernika provide an important case study of urban resilience, due both to the disjuncture between physical rebuilding and emotional recovery, and to the incredible cultural resilience demonstrated by the Basque people. Yet the case of Gernika hardly represents an ideal model for urban resilience. While the town's delayed healing is remarkable, it has come with substantial costs. The circumstances of the recovery forced victims of the attack to internalize the event for more than forty years. While officials have helped many residents come to terms with the bombing by successfully transforming the meaning of the town from victim to agent of peace and reconciliation, not everyone has responded positively to this message.

Examining the various dimensions of Gernika's resilience allows for a more thorough understanding of urban trauma and recovery. Considering the conditions under which Gernika was forced to mend, its resilience proved to be both acute and multifaceted. Through this pattern of recovery, Gernika suggests that the study of urban resilience must focus not only on the immediate aftermath of a trauma, but also on the long-term progress of the people, city, and state. Any analysis of Gernika's recovery/resilience is inevitably shaped by the time frame in which it is assessed. Further scrutiny of the town's history and the changing political regimes over sixty-five years reveals successive waves of Gernika's physical, emotional, and cultural recovery and enables new

The Symbolic Dimensions of Trauma and Recovery

perspectives on the dimensions of resilience. The conditions of Gernika's recovery have enhanced its symbolic status, enabling the town to map out its future destiny in a remarkably self-reflective manner.

Notes

1. As a native of Spain who did not speak Basque, Picasso used the Spanish spelling of the town when naming the painting. Except when referring to the painting or in a direct quote, this chapter uses the Basque spelling, *Gernika*, as an indication of respect for Basque culture.
2. Gernika-Lumo tourism Web site: http://www.gernika-lumo.net, downloaded 26 December 2003.
3. Many phrases are used to reference the Basque Country. In Basque, it translates to Euskadi (Nation That Speaks Basque) or Euskal Herria (Nation Where People Speak Basque). In Spanish, it translates to País Vasco, and in French it translates to Pays Basque.
4. The Basque provinces of Gipuzkoa and Alaba also supported the young republic. Navarra, sometimes counted as a fourth Basque province, supported the National Forces.
5. Max Morgan-Witts and Gordon Thomas, *Guernica and the Crucible of World War II* (New York: Stein and Day, 1975), p. 288.
6. Robert P. Clark, *The Basques: The Franco Years and Beyond* (Reno: University of Nevada Press, 1979), p. 70.
7. Ibid., p. 25.
8. G. L. Steer, "Historic Basque Town Wiped Out: Rebel Fliers Machine-Gun Civilians," (London) *Times*, 27 April 1937.
9. Interview with Luis Iriondo, local artist and survivor of the bombing, 29 May 2002 (translated by Anna León Herrero and Jacob Gutzmann).
10. Ibid.
11. Hugh Thomas, *The Spanish Civil War* (New York: Modern Library, rev. ed., 2001), 607.
12. Herbert Rutledge Southworth, *Guernica! Guernica! A Study of Journalism, Diplomacy, Propaganda, and History* (Berkeley: University of California Press, 1977), p. 356.
13. Clark, *The Basques*, p. 72.
14. Translated by the authors. Excerpt from *Gernika 1937: Sustrai Erreak* (Gernika: Gernikako ALDABA, 1987), pp. 32–35, in preparation for the fiftieth anniversary of the bombing. Original statement made by National Forces on 29 April 1937 on Radio Nacional in Salamanca. This same quote also appeared in *Diario de Burgos* on the same day.
15. Although this chapter focuses on the Basque people, other groups also

endured cultural suppression under Franco. The Catalan language, for example, was strictly prohibited during the dictatorship.

16. Interview with Josè Angel Etxaniz Ortuñez, 3 June 2002.
17. Interview with Jesus Aldana, municipal architect for the city of Gernika, 27 May 2002 (translated by Amaia Garcia).
18. Angel Angoso, "Projet de Reconstruction et Urbanization de la Ville de Guernica," *La Construction Moderne* 53 (June 1938): 451–454.
19. Interview with Aldana.
20. Ibid.
21. Interview with Ricardo Abaunza Martinez, manager of the Gernika Cultural House, 3 June 2002 (translated by Amaia Garcia).
22. Interview with Aldana.
23. Multiple interviewees made the same point about property rights, including Ricardo Abaunza Martinez, 3 June 2002; Maria Oianguren Idigoras, director of Gernika Gogoratuz, and Mireia Uranga Arakistain, education director of Gernika Gogoratuz, both 28 May 2002.
24. Interview with Ortuñez.
25. "Guernica Honors Franco," *New York Times*, 25 October 1946.
26. Interview with Ortuñez.
27. Multiple interviewees referenced the overcrowded living conditions and lack of services in the 1940s, including Ortuñez, Iriondo, and Martinez.
28. Clark, *The Basques*, p. 233.
29. Interview with Martinez.
30. Edward T. Linenthal, *The Unfinished Bombing: Oklahoma City in American Memory* (Oxford: Oxford University Press, 2001).
31. Interview with Ortuñez; and interview with Alfonso Vallejo, former mayor and council member for the city of Gernika, 31 May 2002 (translated by Igone Revilla).
32. Interview with Ortuñez.
33. Eberhard Fisch, *Guernica by Picasso: A Study of the Picture in Its Context* (London: Associated University Presses, 1988), p. 19.
34. Meyer Schapiro, *The Unity of Picasso's Art* (New York: Braziller, 2000), pp. 174–175.
35. Ibid.
36. Since 1981, the painting has resided in Madrid, first in the Prado Museum and later in the Reina Sofia Museum.
37. Interview with Iriondo.
38. Gernika Gogoratuz, a nonprofit agency that works to help the survivors come to terms with the bombing, is planning to undertake an extensive research project to determine how the citizens of Gernika lived in the years following the attack. Through this project, the organization hopes to discover more about the private memorialization that families conducted under the dictatorship.

39. Max Gallo, *Spain under Franco: A History*, trans. Jean Stewart (New York: Dutton, 1974), p. 357.

40. Omar G. Encarnacion, "Spain after Franco: Lessons in Democratization," *World Policy Journal* 18, no. 4 (Winter 2001–2002): 35–36.

41. Interview with Juan Gutierrez, 1 June 2002.

42. Interview with Ortuñez.

43. Interview with Vallejo.

44. Ibid.

45. Interview with Gutierrez.

46. Excerpt from a letter written by Roman Herzog, the president of Germany, to the town of Gernika, 27 March 1997. Translated by the authors.

47. Excerpt from statements made by survivor Luis Iriondo to the German president on behalf of Gernika's survivors on the sixtieth anniversary of the bombing, 25 April 1997. Translated by the authors.

48. Interview with Idigoras and Arakistain.

49. Clark, *The Basques*, p. 81.

50. Ibid., p. 80.

51. Ibid., p. 82.

52. Ibid., p. 137.

53. Ibid., p. 156.

54. Joseba Zulaika, "Tropics of Terror: From Guernica's 'Natives' to Global 'Terrorists,' " *Social Identities* 4, no. 1 (1998): 105.

55. Information about this group, Comisión Popular para la Investigación de Gernika, was provided in interviews with José Angel Extaniz Ortuñez (3 June 2002) and Ricardo Abaunza Martinez, manager of the Gernika Cultural House (3 June 2002).

56. Ibid.

57. Ibid.

58. Interview with Iriondo.

59. The San Juan Church was located near the City Hall Plaza and was partially destroyed (as a result of incendiary bombs) during the attack. It was leveled during the rebuilding process and was not replaced.

60. Interview with Idigoras and Arakistain.

61. Paulüna Raento and Cameron J. Watson, "Gernika, Guernica, Guernika? Contested Meanings of a Basque Place," *Political Geography* 19, no. 6 (2000): 729.

62. Ibid.

63. "Gernika Peace Museum," brochure published by the Gernika Peace Museum, Gernika, Spain, 2002.

64. Ibid.

Resurrecting Jerusalem

8

JULIAN BEINART

■ Jerusalem is the greatest site of physical destruction and renewal known to history. For some 4,000 years it suffered wars, earthquakes, and fires, not to mention twenty sieges, two periods of total desolation, eighteen reconstructions, and at least eleven transitions from one religious faith to another.[1] This cycle of trauma has resulted in a variety of outcomes; among them are demolition without reconstruction, repeated renewal, no destruction at all, and the conscious maintenance of ruins. This chapter explores how these divergent responses to disaster are linked to the most important buildings of the three great monotheistic religions, for which Jerusalem remains a place of special significance. In the stories and laws embedded in the documents of these religions there are clues as to how they propose to help their followers respond to losses, including the loss of life, property, territory, religious artifacts, and psychological well-being. In the loss and restitution of the major temples, churches, mosques, and synagogues, there is a similar tie between religious propositions and building form.

In the story of the earliest city in the Bible, there is a tussle between God's punishment of man and man's restitution. First, God is angry and Adam is sent from Eden. Then Adam's son Cain commits murder and is also banished, but he builds the first city and names it Enoch after his son. The first city is thus created by a criminal, but the city later becomes the place of God. There is a parallel ambiguity about Jerusalem in the texts. God is angry and he destroys, but he also loves and rehabilitates: "Here [in Jerusalem] was born the rumor of a single

181

invisible God, a father figure, authoritarian—at once petulant and magnanimous, vindictive and merciful. . . . the sadomasochism of 'in my wrath I smote thee, but in my favour I had mercy' was first articulated in religious terms."[2] For the twentieth-century theologian Jacques Ellul, Jerusalem is God's singular creation, "his own city" to be both destroyed and restored as a model for all cities.[3]

In many of the destructions of Jerusalem, brutal violence was accompanied by regret or piety. When the Babylonians took Jerusalem in 604 B.C., they only partially destroyed the city. They gave the Jews a second chance and allowed them to appoint their own king. But, dissatisfied, they returned some fifteen years later, blinded the king, murdered his children, and devastated everything, including the first of the great Jewish temples.[4] When the Romans destroyed Jerusalem in 70 A.D., Titus gave his legionnaires instructions to kill people but to save Herod's Jewish temple. In the words of the Jewish Roman historian Flavius Josephus, "Titus . . . declared that, even if the Jews were to mount [the temple] and fight therefrom, he would not wreak vengeance on inanimate objects instead of men, nor under any circumstances burn down so magnificent a work." But "against Caesar's wishes, was the Temple on fire."[5]

In 614 A.D. the Persians brutally slaughtered the Christians of the city. According to an eyewitness, "like evil beasts they roared, bellowed like lions, hissed like ferocious serpents, and slew all whom they found."[6] But then the Persian leader assembled the remaining Christians, granted them peace, selected those who knew how to do architecture, and sent them off to Persia. In 1010 the Egyptian ruler Al Hakim ordered the total demolition of Constantine's Church of the Holy Sepulchre, "to get rid of all traces and remembrance of it" despite—or perhaps because of—the fact that his mother and sister were Christians and his uncle recently a patriarch of Jerusalem.[7] Indeed, five years after the despoliation, Al Hakim's mother began "to rebuild with well-dressed squared stones the Temple of Christ destroyed by her son's order."[8]

In 1099, it was the Christians' turn.[9] The Crusaders liquidated both Jews and Muslims in probably the worst massacre in Jerusalem's history. Eyewitnesses tend to exaggerate numbers, but one suggests that 70,000 Muslims were slaughtered in the Al Aqsa mosque.[10] Flavius Josephus claimed that 1.1 million Jews were eliminated. Stepping over

The Symbolic Dimensions of Trauma and Recovery

scattered body parts and "dripping with blood from head to foot," the holy warriors marched with clergy and local Christians "to the Lord's Sepulcher and His most glorious Temple, singing a new canticle to the Lord in a resounding voice of exaltation, and making offerings and most humble supplications, joyously [visiting] the holy places as they had long desired to do."[11] But their triumph was brief. Less than a century after the rape and rejoicing of the Christians, Jerusalem was a Muslim city once again.

Ancient cities were organized around religion, their destiny determined by an omnipotent and watchful God (or gods). Few, if any, cities in history have been claimed by the faithful more than Jerusalem. The Jews have never departed from this central site of their faith. Christians, seeking converts to their new faith, spread outward from Jerusalem, taking with them relics from the city and proclaiming miracles all over Europe. In time they created new holy places in Rome and Constantinople and new pilgrimage sites such as the politically motivated Santiago di Compostela in northern Spain.[12] Islam is accused of changing the *Qibla*[13]—the direction of prayer—from Jerusalem to Mecca, and Jerusalem is regarded as its third holiest site. Jerusalem was seldom a *political* capital, except for the Jews and the Crusaders; despite their religious dedication to Jerusalem, the Zionist claim to it as the capital of Israel has never been as constant. Modern Zionists like Theodor Herzl and, fifty years later, Golda Meir, sought to build Israel's capital in Haifa, facing the Mediterranean. The poet Bialik preferred Tel Aviv because it was built by Jews; Chaim Weitzmann felt ill at ease in Jerusalem; while Ben-Gurion wanted to build a new capital, Kurnub, in the Negev.[14]

What do the monotheistic religions of Jerusalem teach us about resilience? For a modern philosopher like Arthur Koestler (who lived in Jerusalem in the late 1920s), it may be that biology is enough: the marvel of the human body lies in its capacity to regulate and repair itself. Homeostasis is man's exquisite built-in biology of resilience. Creativity, Koestler argues, "is a kind of do-it-yourself therapy, an attempt to come to terms with traumatizing challenges."[15] Sigmund Freud, the inventor of psychotherapy, was quite convinced that man's invention of God is the result of his limited abilities. Freud proposed that we need a God just as we needed a father when each of us was a young and vulnerable child. Religion is the market in which we can purchase resilience. As Freud put it, "The gods retain their three-fold task: they must exorcise the terrors of nature, they must reconcile men to the cruelty of Fate, particularly as it is shown in death, and they must compensate them for the sufferings and privations . . . imposed on them."[16] Between Koestler's extension of biology and Freud's psycho-dynamic inversion lies a contemporary Jungian thinker, James Hillman, who seeks to combine our external and internal worlds through a new and more open kind of ecological *anima mundi*—a postreligious version of an older fixing of place, the *axis mundi*.[17]

Faced with inescapable human travail, the builders of the religions of Jerusalem formulated theologies of hope. For Calvin, "Hope is nothing else than the expectation of those things which faith has believed to have been truly promised by God."[18] The pain of life and death can be managed if there is the promise that death does not terminate existence completely. In the Qur'an God promises that "[as to] the dead, God will raise them, then unto him will they return."[19] Belief in life after death was widespread in the ancient world (and still is, at least in the United States. In 1984, the midpoint of Ronald Reagan's presidency, fully 71 percent of Americans claimed to believe in life after death.)[20] In Jerusalem, ideas and practices to promote individual and social resilience were manufactured by all three faiths. Death features prominently in these eschatologies, whose texts warn the faithful repeatedly to prepare for their journey "into that good night," as Dylan Thomas put it.[21] In early Judaism the first sites of death were downward, and existence was thought to end in "the underworld of Sheol . . . a silent, dark and joyless place."[22] But at the time of Second Temple Judaism—if not before—there arose a belief, especially in the doctrines of the Pharisees, that the dead rose to a place of judgment. This invention of heaven was later emulated by both Christianity and Islam.

Earth and sky also correspond to the real Jerusalem and its heavenly counterpart. Ancient cities in the Middle East were often patterned after divine prototypes. All of the Babylonian cities were patterned after constellations: Nineveh after Ursa Major, Sippara after Cancer, Assur after Arcturus.[23] For Jews, the heavenly city is situated eighteen miles above the real Jerusalem, while in Islam it is "the highest heaven or starry firmament."[24] In September 1098, the leaders of the Crusade asked Urban II, the proclaiming pope, "to open for us the gates of both Jerusalems."[25] St. Augustine found three versions of Jerusalem, refer-

The Symbolic Dimensions of Trauma and Recovery

ring "sometimes to the earthly Jerusalem, sometimes to the Heavenly city, sometimes to both at once."[26] John, in the most famous of the Christian visions of a virtual Jerusalem, "saw the holy city, new Jerusalem, coming down from God out of Heaven, prepared as a bride adorned for her husband."[27] John's new Jerusalem is a cubic space with each side 1,500 miles long, about half the area of the United States. Looking upward is still with us as a mark of promise but looking up

Figure 8.1.
A full-page miniature from a French translation of Saint Augustine's *City of God*, 1469 to 1473. The celestial city above is guarded by angels, the earthly city below surrounded by demons. A procession from the earthly city awaits entry to the celestial city. Illustration from Schaer, Claeys, and Sargent, eds., *Utopia* (New York: Oxford University Press, 2000), 71. Courtesy Bibliothèque nationale de France.

Resurrecting Jerusalem

can also be a burden, as an Israeli poet of contemporary Jerusalem, Yehuda Amichai, has memorably conveyed:

> The air above Jerusalem is filled with prayers and dreams
> Like the air above cities with heavy industry
> Hard to breathe.[28]

There are many other concepts of resilience embedded in the religious texts of the three monotheistic religions of Jerusalem. Among these, some are spatial, others are primarily temporal. The beginning story of Genesis is of a place of loss, at first there was Eden, which was followed by an exile potentially overcome by salvation and redemption. The Jewish history that follows in the Bible is one of loss and retrieval of place and buildings. The actual locale of Eden is never specified, yet as a symbol it has been emulated throughout history. For the architectural historian Joseph Rykwert, architecture through the ages has sought to reconstruct the "implied house" in Eden.[29] The architect Stanley Tigerman has described Eden as "a sacred place, a paradigm" with major metaphorical implications for architecture. For him, the "creation of a perfect paradise lies at the center of architecture."[30] The English literature scholar William McClung has similarly asserted the spatiality of the Edenic narrative: " 'Paradise' on earth is . . . a kind of waiting room, an anticipatory suburb of kingdom come," a replica of which can be found in the nave of the religious building, a kind of promissory space before the "celestial city."[31]

There are temporal concepts of hope as well. Thomas Aquinas argued that time depends on the successive quality of events, but that eternity exists because it does not have to conform to notions of physical time.[32] Among these concepts of hope is the idea of rebirth, embodied in the central story of Christianity, the resurrection of the body of Christ. A parallel renewal concept, one that also involves time, lies in the belief of the coming Messiah, whether it is the first or the second, or whether after a millennium. Jewish belief in the messianic hope was to be achieved gradually and not according to a set date.[33] The twelfth principle of Jewish faith set out by the great twelfth-century Spanish philosopher Maimonides testifies, "I believe with perfect faith in the coming of the Messiah. How long it will take, I will await His coming every day."[34]

These themes of loss and restitution in the religions of Jerusalem

The Symbolic Dimensions of Trauma and Recovery

are given physical form in the city's architecture and urbanism. This chapter looks at four case studies of building in the history of Jerusalem over a period of about 3,000 years. The first is the series of Jewish temples, imagined and built for about 1,000 years from about 959 B.C. to 70 A.D. The second is the preeminent Christian church, the Church of the Holy Sepulchre, built in the third century after the birth of Christ and still in use. The third is the Muslim buildings on the temple site, the Dome of the Rock and the Al Aqsa mosque, completed toward the end of the seventh century A.D. and still used. Finally, there is the main synagogue of Jerusalem, the Hurva, originally built in the seventeenth century, destroyed twice, but never rebuilt. Of the four, the Jewish buildings have been destroyed and never rebuilt; the Christian church has been destroyed and rebuilt endlessly; and the Islamic monuments have never been destroyed, only damaged by nature.

The Jewish Temples

■ The first of the Jewish temples, built by Solomon, established Jerusalem as a permanent site of monotheism. Before the Jews, the city had existed for about 800 years; it was a major Canaanite city inhabited by the Jebusites.[35] The city was taken by David, whose war record and adultery apparently precluded him from building a temple. So he left it to his son Solomon, who chose the site which has been endowed with an aura ever since. The Temple Mount has been claimed as the site of the rock of the Jebusite gods, of Adam, of Cain, of Abraham and Isaac, and of Mohammed's night visit. The rock was presumably a platform in Solomon's temple as well.

The design of Solomon's temple is described in great detail in the Books of Kings and Chronicles.[36] On the basis of these literary specifications, many reconstructions of the temple building have been attempted, including in the seventeenth century by at least three celebrated Englishmen, John Wood the Elder, Christopher Wren, and Isaac Newton.[37] Its architecture includes the two entrance columns, Jachin and Boaz, which resist complete explanation. The most convincing argument may be that they were markers of light; the sixteenth line at the beginning of Genesis says, "God made the two great lights: the greater light to rule the day, and the lesser light to rule the night."[38]

Despite its aura as the first home of a single god, Solomon's temple was small, about fifty meters by fifty meters. In the words of the nineteenth-century historian Ernest Renan, it was simply "a domestic Temple, a chapel of the [grand] palace which Solomon had built next to it."[39]

Above all it was a compression fortress, with courtyards leading to a Holy of Holies supervised by priests and accessible to no one else. In this it was like many of its Middle Eastern contemporaries, whether resembling the Egyptian temple of Amon Re or similar buildings from Phoenicia and upper Syria.[40] In its holiest room was the ark, never since found and the subject of archaeological searches and, most recently, Spielberg films. Why David and Solomon chose to build such a permanent building is unclear. The Jews had been a people of movement, their religious texts always open to interpretation. David had brought the ark to Jerusalem on a cart. Even Le Corbusier's drawings of the tabernacle depict it much like a temporary tent in the desert.[41] Presumably David was primarily a political city builder who, like all mayors, wanted to impress with his building. In David's case he needed to construct a political Jerusalem to unite his tribes and centralize their new religion.[42]

The First Book of Kings describes how 22,000 oxen and 120,000 sheep were sacrificed at the dedication of Solomon's temple.[43] This is a clear Judaic borrowing from pagan practice. On the other hand, child sacrifice, apparently practiced elsewhere, was forbidden by Jewish law; in the Second Book of Kings the story is told of the pagan king of Moab, who kills his own son as a burnt offering, a sacrifice that brought down "great wrath upon Israel," his oppressors.[44] Abraham comes close to sacrificing Isaac but instead kills a lamb. Sacrificing your child, or substituting an animal—a ram if you were rich, a bird if you were poor—was a physical gift to God, a sign of spiritual dedication in the midst of material wealth.[45]

Solomon's temple stood for about 373 years before it was razed by the Babylonians, sending the Jews to their first exile in Babylon. This is possibly the first destruction of such a major building in history, and the exiled Jews in Babylon reacted in three distinct ways. The first might be called *type substitution*. The cultic temple, its priests and holy places, and its practice of animal sacrifice could not be replicated in exile. So the people of Judah invented a place of worship without any of these

The Symbolic Dimensions of Trauma and Recovery

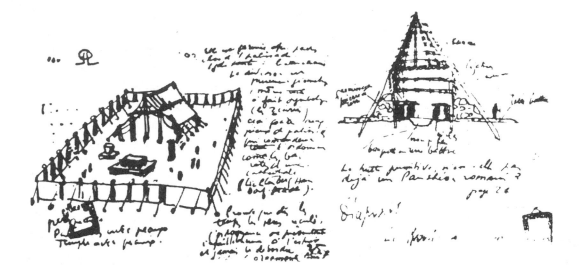

attributes, but still in recognition of the absent temple. These new places of prayer—Ezekiel called them "little temples"[46]—were a new participatory space of worship, education, and communal organization, the forerunner of the synagogue. So the loss of the remote and awesome temple was compensated by the creation of a more intimate and available form of congregation.

The second reaction to the loss of the temple might be called *envisioning*. Here substitution takes the form of dreaming of an alternative more perfect than the one lost. In the book of Ezekiel, the prophet, in exile in Babylon, writes about being put down on a mountain with a city to the south, from which he was guided by a man with a measuring line and rod in his hand. There follow seven chapters of detailed measurements of an imagined temple. Ezekiel's temple is a plan of elementary geometry and composition, removed from any actual site. The many attempts to reconstruct Ezekiel's vision stress ideality and abstraction, the plan's symmetry and perfection, and its nine-squares formula. One of the most famous of these reconstructions was by the sixteenth-century Jesuit scholar Villalpandus, who, conflating it with Solomon's temple, argued that, having been designed by God, the temples were perfect and, as a consequence, only the classical building style was appropriate.[47]

The third response to the loss of the temple and the homeland can

Figure 8.2.
Le Corbusier's sketch of the mobile Jewish tabernacle covered by a temporary tent in the desert. Figure 53 in S. Tigerman, *The Architecture of Exile* (New York: Rizzoli, 1988), 42. © 2004 Artists Rights Society (ARS), New York/ADAGP, Paris/FLC.

Resurrecting Jerusalem

be called *social reinforcement*. How does an exiled community hold itself together when faced with assimilation and disappearance? Babylon had many attractions: it had already been destroyed four times but had been splendidly rebuilt.[48] It was the largest city since the beginning of history, its buildings admired as wonders of the world. Jews were allowed to prosper and many did, even serving in Babylonian public offices.[49] To survive as Jews, they had to become more precise about themselves, and the prophets helped in this definition. In Babylonian exile, the Judeans recovered an emphasis on the Torah, the five books that contain God's directions for life, so that when the Jews returned to Israel through the good graces of the Persian king Cyrus, the Torah was renewed as the normative law of the Jews.[50] When the priest and scribe Ezra returned to Jerusalem from Babylon in the fifth century B.C., he read from the Torah of Moses to the people for the first time in public, and "all the people wept, when they heard the words of the law."[51] The Babylonian experience remained a formative one for the Jews. About 1,000 years after the exile, the codification of Jewish oral law was complete. There are two versions—the Jerusalem Talmud and the Babylonian Talmud—the latter of which is widely regarded as the more complete and authoritative.[52]

The rebuilding of the temple upon the Jewish return to Jerusalem was modest. At its inauguration in 515 B.C., only about 700 animals were sacrificed. But some 300 years later, in 169 B.C., even this humble building was desecrated by the Seleucid king Antiochus IV, whose troops pillaged it, burning the Scroll of the Law and erecting a statue of Zeus and a pagan altar on the site.[53] Despite later attempts to build walls to protect the temple, it was destroyed by the Roman emperor Pompey in 63 B.C.

Pompey's carnage foreshadowed the Roman destruction of the last and grandest of the Jewish temples about a century later. This temple, built by the Jewish king and friend of the Romans, Herod the Great, was the grandest and last of the Jewish temples. A complex and enigmatic ruler, Herod was born of an Idumaean father who had been forcibly converted to Judaism. He was a close friend of Emperors Pompey and Antony, but seemed to be a religious Jew nonetheless. On the other hand, he had nine wives and put many members of his family to death. Herod is often depicted as a cruel man, depressive and syphilitic, but he was also a titanic builder. He built the largest harbor in

The Symbolic Dimensions of Trauma and Recovery

the Mediterranean at Caesarea, as well as fortresses, palaces, roads, and sewage and water systems. Responding to what is still the region's greatest need, Herod supplied Jerusalem with water reservoirs and pools. Under his great temple, he installed sewers to carry away the loads of blood and waste left over from sacrifices.[54] Jerusalem, before its demolition by the Romans, was a magnificent and well-serviced city.

It took about forty-six years to construct the final Jewish temple. Some 10,000 workers and 1,000 priests trained as builders labored on this gargantuan enterprise; the largest stones, which still comprise the holy Western Wall, are nine to twelve meters long. The building site on the Temple Mount covered 1 million square feet, three times larger than the esplanade of the Acropolis in Athens. On its northwestern edge, Herod built the Antonia fortress; it was from this tower that Jesus' brother James was thrown, and it still plays a role in Christian rituals in the city. The plan of the temple, like those of Solomon's and Ezekiel's before, has been reconstructed frequently since the advent of Christianity.[55] It consisted of courtyard precincts leading to a central sanctuary divided into three parts; the whole complex was surrounded by an extensive system of porches. The western porch of the Gentiles connected the temple to the city. It was "the teeming crossroads of Jerusalem," where Jesus later supposedly overthrew the merchants' tables.[56] Missing from the Herodian plan are the Jachin and Boaz columns.

The historian Flavius Josephus, who, like Herod, was Jewish but a Roman sympathizer, described the horror of the Roman destruction of the temple: "the hill itself, on which the temple stood, was seething hot, as full of fire in every part of it, [but] the blood was larger in quantity than the fire."[57] This was the last chapter in a temple sequence, both imagined and built, which had lasted for a millennium. The attempts to resurrect the temple since have been both humorous and alarming. The first, in 363 A.D., was by Emperor Julian, who, during his twenty-month reign, attempted to destroy the Christianity of his nephew Constantine and restore the Roman Empire to paganism. To offend Christianity, he sent an emissary to help the few Jews in Jerusalem to rebuild the temple.[58] A fire seems to have sabotaged Julian's mission.

The destruction of Herod's temple in 70 A.D. marked for Jews the beginning of the ultimate exile. We might refer to the response to this loss as the substitution of the space and time of the building by the space and time of the text. In the Solomonic temple, we confronted the transference from the mobile form of the ark carried on a cart to the immutable form of the shrine on a holy site. For architectural historian Mitchell Schwarzer, the destruction of the temple required that the Jews find "a portable and flexible structure ... a mobile architecture that was ... as much a marking of time as of space. ... The survival of the Jewish people depended on the substitution of textual deliberation for building practice." Even the shape of the texts contained architectural ideas: "The [Babylonian] Talmud is an architecture always under construction," Schwarzer reasons.[59] The Jewish temple was gone forever; it could not be revived as architecture per se, but it could endure in the form of text, and as a message carried in "their hearts, wherever it suited them to take it."[60] Sigmund Freud, who considered settling in Jerusalem at one point, thought that its citizens were too busy making "presumptuous attempts to overcome the outer world of appearances by means of the inner world of wishful thinking."[61] With no central building and with no homeland, the Jews compensated for their loss by moving from objects to words. In the Mishna section of the Talmud, there is a law of property underscoring this trajectory from mute stone to logos:

> The people of a town who sold their town square:
> they must buy a synagogue with its proceeds;
> If they sell a synagogue, they must acquire a scroll chest.
> If they sell a scroll chest, they must acquire cloths to wrap the scrolls.
> If they sell cloths, they must acquire [religious] books.
> If they sell books, they must acquire a Torah.[62]

The Church of the Holy Sepulchre

■ For Christianity, the Church of the Holy Sepulchre—built over the putative place of Jesus' crucifixion, burial, and resurrection—is central. That it is built over a deity's grave, even a disputed one, differentiates it from the Jewish temples, which were built on multiple stories often involving a sanctified rock. There was a hill at the site called Calvary or Golgotha, defined in the Gospels as "the place of the skull"; some

Figure 8.3.
Drawing of the Church of the Holy Sepulchre. This version is an approximation of the current building, now entered from the south and more complicated than the original fourth-century B.C. Constantine church which was entered from the Roman Cardo through an open basilica on the east. From Biddle, Avni, Seligman, and Winter, *The Church of the Holy Sepulchre* (New York: Rizzoli, 2000), 70–71. © Yad Izhak Ben-Zvi, Jerusalem.

The Symbolic Dimensions of Trauma and Recovery

have even connected the dome of the church with this definition. But, in his critical history of the life of Jesus, Marcello Cravieri[63] claims that the correct name derives from Gol-Goath, a small hill mentioned much earlier in the Book of Jeremiah.[64]

Another fundamental difference between the temples and the church—critical to a discussion of disaster and recovery—is the fact that the temples, finally destroyed, departed from the physical world, while the church is a monument to the practice of reconstruction. Devastated some six times by humans, often totally, twice by major earthquakes, once by a consuming fire, and all along debilitated by

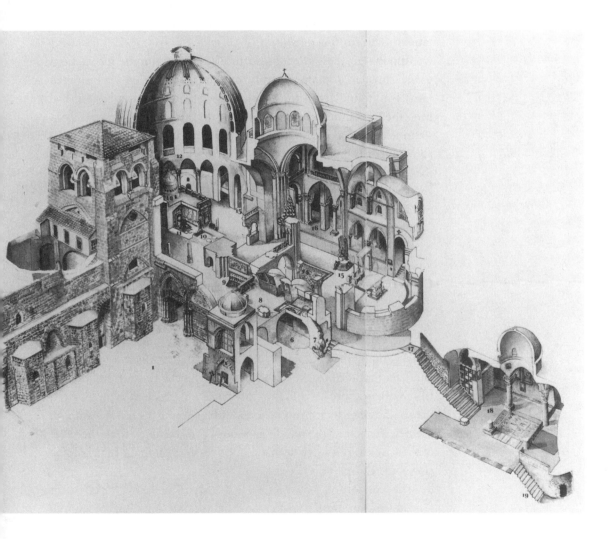

poor maintenance, the church has always been restored.[65] As recently as 1997 the dome was again renewed, this time by the Greek patriarchate of Jerusalem. It now has twelve streams of gold representing the apostles and three streams of light symbolizing the Trinity, set against a mother-of-pearl background representing the "luminous cloud of the Divine Presence."[66] Before this latest recreation, many sophisticated visitors had already been appalled by its poor taste. The American critic Edmund Wilson thought it "contains more bad taste . . . than any other church in the world"; the Russian novelist Nikolai Gogol was repelled by the gaudy decor and glossy marble, while the French writer Gustave Flaubert exclaimed: "How fake everything is! What lies! All is whitewashed, veneered, polished; calculated for propaganda and the exploitation of the customer."[67]

Almost 300 years after the death of Christ, upon the instructions of the Christian Roman emperor Constantine, Makarios, the bishop of Jerusalem, found Jesus' tomb amid piles of rubble. Just above it had been the Roman temple of Aphrodite and the statue of Jupiter. Constantine built an aedicule over the tomb and a late Roman-style edifice above it consisting of four parts. First was an atrium that connected the church to the Roman Cardo Maximus on the east, an urban link similar to the courtyards and porches of Herod's temple.[68] The three other parts of the church included a large basilica, a central courtyard or garden with the Golgotha hill in one corner, and at the western end a large open-to-the-sky rotunda covering the sites of Christ's crucifixion, burial, and resurrection.[69] The building shaped itself around Christ's passion; below the basilica, a chapel was dedicated to Helena, Constantine's mother, who apparently discovered the cross there in 327 A.D. when she searched Palestine for holy vestiges.[70]

The Constantine structure remained largely unchanged until its destruction by the Fatimid caliph Al Hakim, after which it was rebuilt and later modified by the Crusaders. The Constantine atrium and basilica were lost forever, and the church was entered, as it is today, from the south rather than from its grand urban entrance on the Cardo. In the new version of the building, a monastery complex took the place of the basilica, and a late Romanesque two-story choir and small dome closed the church on the east.

The connection between place ("a venerated site") and spirit ("promised salvation")[71] is fundamental to understanding the Church of the Holy Sepulchre and the stories of Christianity. Unlike the loss of the Jewish temples, finally permanent and leading to exile, the church stood on sites that were never lost, and could never be lost, and which were constantly recovered by a local congregation. Building and belief were integral to one another: the building's form marked the exact place of the believed events. Unlike the substitutional responses to the destructions of the temples, the reaction to the regular ruining of the church was not to invent new building types, nor to envision replacements, nor to shape religious knowledge. For Christians, the place, the body, and the spirit were fused.

This place/body/spirit fusion is found in passages from the Gospel of John. In three of the other disciples' stories, Jesus predicted that the last of the Jewish temples would be destroyed.[72] As a Jew, Jesus knew the temple well. On his last visit to it, he berated the temple's merchants, and got into an argument with the Jews, saying:

> "Destroy this temple, and in three days I will raise it up."
> Then said the Jews, "Forty and six years was this temple in building, and wilt thou rear it up in three days?"
> But he spake of the temple of his body.
> When therefore he was risen from the dead, his disciples remembered that he had said this to them.[73]

If taken literally, Jesus predicts the ruin of the temple some forty years before its actual destruction and says to Christians that his body, not another future building, will be its substitute. The persistent rebuilding of the Church of the Holy Sepulchre rests on the doctrinal acceptance of strange stories, be they as implausible as substituting a body for a building or parts of a body for food. Many ancient stories are replete with legends of recovery—after a flood, for instance, in the cases of Gilgamesh or Noah. The resilience of the Church of the Holy Sepulchre rests on people trusting that real spaces and buildings are inseparable from the stories they believe took place there.

On a less hallowed note, one might speculate whether the frequent destructions and rebuildings of the church might have increased the resilience of the building by allowing the many warring Christian factions to inhabit a portion of it. Since the fifth-century A.D. split between the Western and Eastern churches, the Holy Sepulchre Church complex has been a sanctuary of jealousy—so much so that since the Muslim

Figure 8.4.
The platform of the
Temple Mount (Haram
al-Sharif) with the two
permanent Muslim
shrines, the Dome of the
Rock and the Al Aqsa
mosque. Since their
construction in the late
seventh and eighth
centuries, they have
never been destroyed by
human hands. From
Baron Wolman, *Above
the Holy Land* (San
Francisco: Chronicle
Books, 1987), 13.

conquest of Jerusalem in 1187, the keys to the church have been owned by two Muslim families, the Joudeh, and now by the prominent Palestinian Nusseibah family. Today six Christian groups inhabit the church: the Greeks, Roman Catholics, and Armenians are the three patriarchates, and the Syrians, Copts, and Ethiopians are minority shareholders. Protestants may visit but may not hold services. There are rules about where anyone may "clean, say mass, make repairs, change a light bulb, drive a nail, open or close a door."[74] The Greeks possess about 70 percent of the space; the rest fit wherever they can into the large array of niches, chapels, courtyards, and roofs. The Ethiopians live in an "African village" on the roof. As recently as July 2002, Israeli police carried off Copts and Ethiopians who were injured during a firefight with the Palestinians.[75] Would a building never destroyed, such as the pristine Muslim Dome of the Rock, or a building destroyed and totally rebuilt, such as the Jewish temples, have been able to accommodate the divisive behavior of the Christians? It is interesting to speculate whether the form of a building, a collage added to over time, increases its resilience when its space inevitably has to be a battlefield of believers.

The Dome of the Rock and Al Aqsa Mosque

■ The Muslim buildings on the Temple Mount (or the Haram al-Sharif) represent a unique case of religious resilience in Jerusalem. Unlike all of the other major shrines in the city, the Dome of the Rock and the Al Aqsa mosque have never been destroyed by human hands, only by frequent earthquakes and occasional fires. The Al Aqsa was particularly vulnerable, having been built not on rock but on a sandy base extended from the Herodian platform. Since their construction in 691 and 705 A.D., respectively, these buildings—particularly the Dome—have been the most distinguished and memorable of all in Jerusalem. The Dome has, according to urbanist Nasser Rabbat, "no precedent in the short history of Islamic architecture. . . . it is in a class apart as a meaningful architectural monument."[76] Today it creates the silhouette of the city, particularly from the east.

That Islam chose the site of the old Jewish temples is not surprising given its awareness of the biblical role of Jerusalem and, in particular,

The Symbolic Dimensions of Trauma and Recovery

of Solomon's Holy of Holies on that piece of land. The foundation rock, now the navel of the Dome, and the stone to which so many references are made in the religious stories from Adam to Mohammed, might also have been a motive for the site's selection. There is some doubt about the event described in Kanan Makiya's recent historical novel, *The Rock*,[77] where the caliph Umar encounters the Christian bishop Sophronius after Umar's taking of the city in 638, and Umar chooses the temple site.[78] There is no doubt about the nature of the site, which was an enormous rubbish pile, as large as a quarter of the city, left as a stack of ruins by the Roman and Byzantine Christians for more than 500 years. The Christians might have felt its ruined state exemplified Christ's temple prediction,[79] but, nevertheless, it is strange that their own shrine, the Church of the Holy Sepulchre, faced toward the dump, which was only "about two bow-shots away."[80] Medieval Jerusalem's chief Muslim historian, Mujir al-Din, ascribes the site's wretched condition to more purposeful Christian actions, especially by the dowager Helena, who "ordered that the filth and scourings of the city be thrown on the Temple of Jerusalem's place. The place of the Noble Rock was transformed into a stable."[81]

To the Muslim choice of this rubbish-dump site, Nasser Rabbat also assigns a sense of identification with Judaism and an antipathy toward Christianity. Another Jerusalem historian, al-Maqudassi, suggested that the Dome might have been built to prevent Muslims from having only Christian church architecture to admire.[82] Whatever its architectural inspirations, the key dimensions of plan and height are curiously similar in the Dome of the Rock and the Holy Sepulchre.[83]

To what can we ascribe the resilience of the Muslim buildings on the Haram al-Sharif? With the exception of 150 years of Crusader rule, Muslim occupation of Jerusalem was uninterrupted for nearly 1,300 years. It may also be that the building's extraordinary quality of construction made it more likely to be preserved and reused. Architectural quality may well be a condition of resilience. The contemporary Islamic historian Oleg Grabar is sympathetic to this argument: "It is a further contention that the stunning quality of the building has helped preserve it in approximately the shape it had originally, even as the meanings associated with it have changed over the centuries."[84] There is evidence for this view in the earlier history of Jerusalem. The Roman emperor Titus, for example, decided to spare the western part of the city and its Herodian towers "to allow future generations to understand the might of the city he had fought and conquered."[85]

The vicious Crusaders could well have practiced their cruelty on the Dome and the mosque, but they did not. Instead they made these buildings the headquarters of their kingdom. The soldiers of Godfrey and Baldwin simply put a golden cross on the Dome and did some remedial interior decoration, such as covering the rock. Next to the mosque the Templars built their quarters, storerooms, and stables. They added name changes to suit their new Christianization: Templum Domini for the Dome and Templum Solomonis for the mosque (Sol-

The Symbolic Dimensions of Trauma and Recovery

omon is a curious reference considering the earlier Christian consignment of the Jewish holy site to a dump).[86]

There is a curious notion of an economy governing religious sites. Is the economy of sites a form of resilience? The nineteenth-century historian Ernest Renan was among the first to articulate this idea. He observed that "men always pray at the same sites—only the rationale for their sanctity changes from generation to generation and from one faith to another."[87] The Haram al-Sharif has been a holy site for Canaanites, then for two Jewish temples, then for a Hellenistic temple of Zeus, then for a third Jewish temple, then for a Roman temple of Jupiter, then for a Muslim complex, then for a Christian precinct, and, perhaps finally, for a Muslim shrine.

Places such as this seem to acquire resilience over time as their reoccupation adds meanings of diversity and also, somewhat paradoxically, universality to them. This can be termed the resilience of diversity through reuse and resymbolization. There is a site on Mt. Zion where Jews believe David is buried, up a staircase from a place that Christians revere as the site of the Last Supper, and where the Ottomans built a mosque. Now the Dormitian Abbey, where Mary is presumed to have died, dominates it.[88]

We should not be too sanguine about the resilience of the Haram al-Sharif, however. In 1969 a twenty-nine-year-old Australian, Denis Rohan, set the Al Aqsa mosque alight, believing its destruction would hasten the millennium. Three years later, an American named Alan Goodman killed one person and wounded three others with an M-16 rifle in the Dome of the Rock. In 1984 sixteen Jewish Kabbalists and moon worshipers were caught with explosives and sentenced, and a few months later twenty-eight yeshiva students were charged with attempting to break into the tunnels under the Haram. Twenty-eight Jewish terrorists were later convicted of plotting an explosive attack. They were supported in Israeli newspapers by an American Christian evangelical group. Many Christian sects—including Seventh Day Adventists, Evangelists, Davidists, Southern Baptists, Charismatic Christians, and others—have supported the rebuilding of the Jewish temple, publishing magazines and promoting tours to Jerusalem to propagate their cause. The undermining of the Haram continues. In July 2002, just before the annual Tisha B'Av commemoration of the loss of the last Jewish temple, the Temple Mount and Land of Israel Faithful movement announced that one of the stones of the Western Wall, fifteen meters above the ground, had started weeping, a "sign of the rebuilding of the temple" prophesied by Ezekiel and an encouragement for all of the faithful to liberate the Haram.[89]

The Hurva Synagogue

■   The Hurva synagogue, like the Jewish temples, represents a continuity of destruction and—as of yet—no reconstruction. Synagogues appear to have coexisted with the temple in Late Temple Jerusalem, even if their real emergence did not take place until after the Roman devastation.[90] At the beginning of the eighteenth century, a "messianic and Kabalistic pilgrimage" from Eastern Europe led by Rabbi Yehuda Ha-Hassid built an Ashkenazi synagogue some 400 yards west of the Dome of the Rock.[91] He died soon after; the community could not pay its taxes; and the Turks eventually burned the building. Ever since, it has assumed the name Hurva—the Hebrew word for "ruin." In 1864, when the city's population was about 18,000,[92] the synagogue was rebuilt by another messianic immigrant community from Lithuania, this time in the style of an Ottoman mosque, the putative work of the Ottoman sultan's own royal architect. Once completed, the building was described as the "most striking edifice in all of Palestine"[93] and the "glory of the old city."[94] In the 1948 war of Israeli independence, the Hurva synagogue was destroyed once again. Despite attempts between 1967 and 1982 by two famous architects, Louis Kahn and Denys Lasdun, to design its successor, it remains—true to its name—a ruin, with only one newly built arch to mark the previous Hurva synagogues.

Louis Kahn designed three versions of the Hurva, and had he not died suddenly in 1974, his project may well have been built. Despite much opposition in Jerusalem, Teddy Kollek, the mayor at the time, was committed to Kahn, who was a founding member of Kollek's Jerusalem Committee. Two aspects of Kahn's work are worth reflecting upon.

The first is what we might call the resilience of ruins. Contrary to an explicit request in the building brief, Kahn did not replace the synagogue on the same site but on land next to it, leaving the nineteenth-

The Symbolic Dimensions of Trauma and Recovery

century ruins completely in place. Kahn refers to the idea of ruins in four ways. First, ruins maintain memory: in Kahn's poetic prose, "[w]hat is not built is not really lost."[95] Second, he found a ruin, free of the obligation to perform active functions any longer, able to "fully express its spirit or form essence,"[96] often more so than whole buildings. A third aspect of Kahn's thought is the linking of ruins with the idea of silence. Kahn had experienced and commented on the never-ending silence of buildings like the pyramids. Kahn sought silence not only in the design of the new Hurva itself but, by associating the building with the adjacent ruins, his new building gained "a timelessness that links the structure to the fallen fragments that surround it."[97] A fourth Kahnian concept lies in the metaphoric idea that certain newly built forms can be seen as ruins. Already in his design for the U.S. consulate in Luanda, almost a decade before, Kahn had attacked the problem of powerful external light by wrapping an armature around an internal core, as he did in the Hurva designs, where an inner square of concrete sits within an exterior envelope of stone. "I thought of the

Figure 8.5.
Louis Kahn's first proposal for the Hurva synagogue, 1968. This view is from the ark looking toward the congregation and the surrounding light. Photograph no. 181 of K. Larson, *Louis J. Kahn: Unbuilt Masterworks* (New York: Monacelli: 2000), 148–149.

beauty of ruins . . . and I thought of wrapping ruins around buildings; you might say encasing a building in a ruin so that you look through the wall which has its apertures as if by accident."[98]

Kahn's Hurva can also be seen as a proposition about resilience through extending the space-time context of a new building following destruction. Kahn's insistence on retaining the ruins of the nineteenth-century Hurva might have departed from Jewish practice. The Book of Laws, the Shulhan Arukh, says that synagogues still maintain their holiness after they are destroyed. If grass grows, so the law says, cut it and leave it there so people will be awakened to rebuild the synagogue. But, if there is no intention of rebuilding it, you may leave the grass there.[99] A few years after Kahn's designs, a rabbi was called in to advise Kahn's successor, Denys Lasdun, about Jewish law and insisted that the Hurva be rebuilt on its original site, a constraint Lasdun obeyed.[100] Nevertheless, Kahn's proposals were very much attuned both to the built environment of Jerusalem and, to a lesser extent, to its history and memory.

In his search for spatial connection, Kahn's choice of large stones, similar to those found in the Herodian temple walls, for his own synagogue's large outer pylons was a link to the Western Wall, where Jews have prayed since the twelfth century. Another proposal, at a more extended scale, was to create a processional promenade down the hill from the Hurva to the Western Wall. Above the Western Wall are the Muslim monuments, and Kahn was unambiguous about his building's connection to them. His building does not have a dome but it sits in an elevated relationship to the Dome of the Rock and in a triadic relationship with the Holy Sepulchre. But his Hurva was to be six feet taller than the Dome.

There is a long tradition of height competition in Jerusalem. In the fourteenth century the Romanesque bell towers of the Holy Sepulchre were cut down to make them lower than nearby minarets, and, in the case of the nineteenth-century Hurva, a new minaret a few feet taller went up next door soon after the synagogue's completion. Teddy Kollek vetoed Kahn's wish for height, allegedly because he believed that the "importance of a faith need not be measured by the size of a building."[101]

Kahn made less obvious connections to the temporal past of the city. In studying the Hurva, he apparently consulted papers on the

The Symbolic Dimensions of Trauma and Recovery

origin of the synagogue. Explaining his design for the Hurva, which has large niches for candles, he alludes to the light of a candle as important in Judaism.[102] A decade before, in designing one of his American synagogues, he spoke of needing to be "in tune with the spirit that created the first synagogue."[103] And, perhaps recognizing the tradition of the word in Judaism, Kahn explained the Hurva in terms of "the words that have best expressed the spirit of that which is undefinable and to which all things are answerable to. . . . you call it God."[104] There have been suggestions that Solomon's temple played a role in Kahn's Hurva work. Coombs[105] alludes to Kahn's familiarity with a nineteenth-century Scottish architectural theorist's *History of Architecture*,[106] which contains a reconstructed plan of Solomon's temple. Today the only relation of the Hurva to Solomon may lie in the Lebanese cedar trees that have been planted on the square next to the Hurva ruins. Solomon imported cedar trees for his temple from the king of Tyre.

Kahn's proposals met opposition from many sources, religious as well as political. Some believe that, after the 1967 war that led to the Israelis possessing the Old City for the first time in 2,000 years, there was a reluctance to construct anything as bold as Kahn's work. Outside the Old City, Jewish architects could be novel and arrogant, but not in the Old City where they came face to face with history and memory. Kollek, however, did not feel these fears and, soon after Kahn's death, he invited to a competition for the design of the Hurva three members of the Jerusalem Committee: Aldo van Eyck, Richard Meier, and Denys Lasdun. When the local architectural profession objected to being excluded, Kollek canceled the competition and chose the British architect Denys Lasdun (some would argue Kollek did so because the money for rebuilding was to come from Britain). To bypass professional and religious objections, Kollek found a Jerusalem architect with religious ties to serve as Lasdun's liaison. Lasdun produced a more modest design for the Hurva than Kahn, this time built on top of the old ruins and having some resemblance to the three-part plans of the ancient Jewish temples.

In 1982 Lasdun's attempt to replace what had now become a national monument failed as well. The restitution of the loss of the Hurva could now be remembered only in terms of what might have been. The architect Kent Larson's splendid computer rendering of Kahn's unbuilt Hurva has added to this sense of potential and highlights also the failure that comes from an undelivered restitution of loss (see fig. 8.5). Losing a building is one thing; missing the opportunity to build better is a double setback. If the architectural theorist Vincent Scully is to be believed, it is not only Jerusalem that has suffered from its inability to manifest resilience; so have all of us. In his words, "[I]t is hard to believe that anything ever could have been more splendid and full of awe, more sublime in every sense, than the first project for Hurva."[107] We may all be programmed to survive, but it may take a particular culture and a special sensibility and courage to survive well.[108]

■   The stories of how the shrines of the three great religions have responded to destruction provide us with a range of mechanisms of resilience. There is a category of substitution, in which one destroyed building is replaced by another type of building. Other forms of architecturally inspired resilience include instances in which visions replace ruined reality; in which communal reinforcement occurs because of loss; in which the form and time of a building is succeeded by the form and time of words; and in which an eradicated building is transferred to the presence of a body. In line with the latter, resilience is also created by extending the body into the spirit, and marking this passion in an inevitable place. We have seen how resilience is promoted through the reuse and resymbolization of buildings and by their repeated location on the same sites, and how such allegiance to place creates a recognition of diversity and, at the same time, universality. Architects and urban designers might rejoice when supreme architectural quality contributes to resilience by suspending destruction. We might also consider whether the building of complex forms, accreted over time in response to many destructions, allows inhabitation by diverse and conflicted groups. In the work of a great architect there are lessons to be learned about the resilient attributes of ruins, both actual ruins and metaphoric ruins. Finally, there are ideas about resilience that come about through the careful and uncontrived attention that a designer pays to the attachment of new buildings to the space as well as to the time of the city.

Jerusalem, the greatest of all religious cities in the Middle East, offers these lessons to architects and planners. In the wake of more than 3,000 years of destruction, we can read in Jerusalem today the responses to these destructions in the forms of the places where the

The Symbolic Dimensions of Trauma and Recovery

three religions worship. Christians pray in a grotto reached by the city's alleys; Muslims pray in pristine pavilions that float above the city; and Jews pray in the city's open air, up against a wall of ruins.

Much of this has come about because place and building have played such a significant role in the way these religions have sought to accommodate and express their faiths. But building cannot be done without optimism. In Mother Teresa's prayer, the fifth line of supplication says: "What you spend years building, someone could destroy overnight; . . . Build anyway."

Notes

1. A. Elon, *Jerusalem: City of Mirrors* (Boston: Little, Brown, 1989), p. 20.
2. Ibid., p. 16.
3. J. Ellul, *The Meaning of the City* (Grand Rapids, Mich.: Eerdmans, 1970), pp. 105–106.
4. P. R. Bedford, *Temple Restoration in Early Achaemenid Judah* (Leiden: Brill, 2001), p. 1.
5. Flavius Josephus, *War of the Jews*, vol. 6, quoted in F. E. Peters, *Jerusalem* (Princeton, N.J.: Princeton University Press, 1985), pp. 115–117.
6. Peters, *Jerusalem*, p. 171.
7. M. Gil, "The Authorities and the Local Population," in *The History of Jerusalem: The Early Muslim Period 638–1099*, ed. J. Prawer and H. Ben-Shammai (New York: New York University Press, 1996), p. 24; and M. Biddle et al., *The Church of the Holy Sepulchre* (New York: Rizzoli, 2000), p. 44.
8. M. Biddle, *The Tomb of Christ* (Phoenix Mill, U.K.: Sutton, 1999), p. 74.
9. J. Prawer, *The Crusaders' Kingdom* (London: Phoenix, 1972).
10. Peters, *Jerusalem*, p. 286.
11. Ibid., pp. 287, 286.
12. J. Beinart, "Image Construction in Premodern Cities," in *Imaging the City*, ed. L. J. Vale and S. B. Warner (New Brunswick, N.J.: CUPR Press, 2001).
13. *The Holy Qur'an*, 2d ed. (Elmhurst, N.Y.: Tahrike Tarsile Qur'an, 1995), 2: 142–152.
14. Elon, *Jerusalem*, pp. 239–241.
15. A. Koestler, *The Ghost in the Machine* (New York: Macmillan, 1968), p. 177.
16. S. Freud, "Civilization and Its Discontents," in *The Freud Reader*, ed. P. Gay (London: Vintage, 1995), p. 695.
17. J. Hillman, "Anima Mundi: The Return of the Soul to the World," in *Spring: An Annual of Archetypal Psychology and Jungian Thought* (New York: Continuum, 1982): 71–93.

18. J. Moltmann, *Theology of Hope* (New York: Harper and Row, 1967), p. 20.

19. *The Holy Qur'an*, 6:36.

20. D. S. Katz and R. H. Popkin, *Messianic Revolution* (New York: Hill and Wang, 1998), p. 1. Reagan's secretary of defense, Caspar Weinberger, is quoted as saying: "I have read the Book of Revelation and, yes, I believe the world is going to end—by an act of God, I hope—but every day I think time is running out." *Time*, 1 July 2002, p. 47.

21. M. McC. Gatch, *Death: Meaning and Mortality in Christian Thought and Contemporary Culture* (New York: Seabury, 1969).

22. R. N. Longenecker, *Life in the Face of Death: The Resurrection Message of the New Testament* (Grand Rapids, Mich.: Eerdmans, 1988), p. 80.

23. M. Eliade, *The Myth of the Eternal Return* (Princeton, N.J.: Princeton University Press, 1974), p. 8.

24. H. Granqvist, *Muslim Death and Burial* (Helsinki: Central Tryckeriet, 1965), p. 243.

25. J. Riley-Smith, *The First Crusade and the Idea of Crusading* (Philadelphia: University of Pennsylvania Press, 1986), p. 119.

26. St. Augustine, *City of God*, 17:3, quoted in M. Turner, "Conflict of the Earthly and Heavenly Jerusalems," *Places* 8, no. 1 (Summer 1992): 10.

27. Revelations 21:2, quoted in R. W. Raven, *Death into Life* (Park Ridge, N.J.: Parthenon, 1990), p. 118.

28. Y. Amichai, *A Life of Poetry 1948–1994*, ed. and trans. B. and B. Harshav (New York: HarperCollins, 1995), p. 32.

29. J. Rykwert, *On Adam's House in Paradise* (Cambridge, Mass.: MIT Press, 1989), p. 13.

30. S. Tigerman, *The Architecture of Exile* (New York: Rizzoli, 1988), p. 13.

31. W. A. McClung, *The Architecture of Paradise* (Berkeley: University of California Press, 1983), p. 39.

32. C. J. Caes, *Beyond Time* (Lanham, Md.: University Press of America, 1985), p. 95.

33. J. Neusner and B. Chilton, *Jewish-Christian Debates* (Minneapolis, Minn.: Fortress, 1998), p. 171. A thousand years is often the term set for the arrival of the Messiah. David Koresh, the leader of the Seventh Day Adventist group who was killed with 73 others at Waco, Texas, in 1993, believed that his followers would be among the 144,000 faithful who would, according to the Book of Revelation, receive the Messiah. He took his name from David (the Jewish king) and Koresh (the Persian king known as Cyrus in Hebrew).

34. *Daily Prayer Book*, trans. P. Birenbaum (New York: Hebrew Publishing, 1977), p. 155.

35. See H. Cattan, *Jerusalem* (New York: St. Martin's, 1981), p. 20; M. Benvenisti, *City of Stone: The Hidden History of Jerusalem* (Berkeley: University of California Press, 1996), pp. 1–3; and D. Ben-Gurion, *The Jews in Their Land* (London: Aldus, 1966), pp. 47–53.

The Symbolic Dimensions of Trauma and Recovery

36. 1 Kings 5–9; II Chronicles 2–7.
37. Tigerman, *Architecture of Exile*, pp. 16, 64.
38. Genesis 1:16.
39. E. Renan, *Histoire du People d'Israel*, quoted in A. Parrot, *Golgotha and the Church of the Holy Sepulchre* (New York: Philosophical Society, 1957), p. 51.
40. Tigerman, *Architecture of Exile*, p. 61; and A. Parrot, *The Temple of Jerusalem* (New York: Philosophical Society, 1955), p. 23. With regard to borrowings from surrounding cultures, Freud claimed that Moses learned monotheism from the Egyptian king Akenaten.
41. Tigerman, *Architecture of Exile*, pp. 39, 40.
42. G. E. Mendenhall, "Jerusalem from 1000–63 B.C.," in K. J. Asali, *Jerusalem in History: 3,000 B.C. to the Present Day* (London: Kegan Paul International, 1977), p. 45.
43. 1 Kings 9:3.
44. 2 Kings 3:27.
45. J. M. Landay, *Dome of the Rock* (New York: Newsweek Book Division, 1972), p. 31.
46. Ezekiel 11:16.
47. Rykwert, *On Adam's House in Paradise*, pp. 121–130.
48. W. Schneider, *Babylon Is Everywhere* (London: Hodder and Stoughton, 1963), p. 66.
49. A. Eban, *Heritage: Civilization and the Jews* (London: Weidenfeld and Nicolson, 1985), p. 69.
50. http://www.wsu.edu:8080/-dee/Hebrews/Exile.HTM; and http://www.wsu.edu:8080/-dee/Hebrews/Afterex.HTM.
51. Nehemiah 8:9.
52. Eban, *Heritage*, p. 101.
53. Landay, *Dome of the Rock*, p. 35.
54. P. Richardson, *Herod* (Columbia: University of South Carolina Press, 1996), p. 190.
55. See H. Rosenau, *Vision of the Temple* (London: Oresko, 1979); and Tigerman, *Architecture of Exile*.
56. John 2:15.
57. Flavius Josephus, *The Jewish War* (Cambridge, Mass.: Harvard University Press, 1997), chap. 5, par 1.
58. G. Vidal, *Julian* (Boston: Little, Brown, 1964), p. 376.
59. M. Schwarzer, "The Architecture of Talmud," *Journal of the Society of Architectural Historians* 60, no. 4 (December 2001): 474, 475, 483.
60. G. Fowden, *Empire to Commonwealth: Consequences of Monotheism in Late Antiquity* (Princeton, N.J.: Princeton University Press, 1993), p. 71.
61. S. Freud, quoted in Elon, *Jerusalem*, p. 23.
62. S. Fine, *Sacred Realm* (Oxford: Oxford University Press, 1996), p. 24.
63. M. Cravieri, *The Life of Jesus* (London: Secker and Warburg, 1967), p. 410.
64. Jeremiah 31:39.

65. M. Gilbert, *Jerusalem: Illustrated History Atlas* (Jerusalem: Steinmatzky, 1977), p. 34; and Biddle et al., *The Church of the Holy Sepulchre*, p. 20.

66. http://198.62.75.1/www1/jhs/Tssplate.html.

67. Quoted in Elon, *Jerusalem*, pp. 140, 203.

68. C. Couasnon, *The Church of the Holy Sepulchre in Jerusalem* (Oxford: Oxford University Press, 1974), p. 11. The Romans had rebuilt Jerusalem as a Roman garrison town called Aelia Capitolina after the Jewish revolt of Bar Kochba some 200 years earlier.

69. D. Bahat, *The Illustrated Atlas of Jerusalem* (Jerusalem: Carta, 1990), p. 71.

70. The cross was apparently stolen by the Persians in 614 A.D. and was majestically returned sixteen years later by Heraclius, who "set [it] up unopened; for just as the Ark of the Covenant was left unopened among strangers, so was the life-giving tree of the Cross, which had vanquished death and trampled on Hell." See Peters, *Jerusalem*, p. 174.

71. The architectural historian Stanford Anderson, has used the terms "venerated site" and "promised salvation" in writing about social and disciplinary memory in architecture. See "Memory in Architecture," *Daidalos* 58 (December 1995): 23.

72. Mark 13:2; Luke 21:6; Matthew 24:2.

73. John 3:19–22.

74. Elon, *Jerusalem*, p. 201.

75. C. Nickerson, "Turf Battles Mar Peace of Christian Shrine," *Boston Globe*, 2 October 2002, p. 8.

76. N. Rabbat, "The Meaning of the Umayyad Dome of the Rock," *Muqarnas* 6 (1990): 12–21.

77. K. Makiya, *The Rock* (New York: Pantheon, 2001).

78. Peters, *Jerusalem*, p. 185.

79. O. Grabar, *The Dome of the Rock* (New York: Rizzoli, 1996), p. 35.

80. Peters, *Jerusalem*, p. 315.

81. Ibid., p. 195.

82. Ibid., p. 198.

83. Landay, *Dome of the Rock*, p. 68.

84. O. Grabar, *The Shape of the Holy* (Princeton, N.J.: Princeton University Press, 1996), p. 7.

85. Peters, *Jerusalem*, p. 226.

86. See the "Betrothal of the Virgin," in *The Life and Times of Raphael*, ed. E. Orlandi (London: Hamlyn, 1968), p. 11.

87. Elon, *Jerusalem*, p. 199.

88. See F. E. Peters, *Jerusalem and Mecca: The Typology of the Holy City in the Near East* (New York: New York University Press, 1986), p. 137; and J. Wilkinson, *The Jerusalem Jesus Knew* (New York: Nelson, 1978), p. 166.

89. http://templemountfaithful.org.

90. C. H. Krinsky, *Synagogues of Europe* (Cambridge, Mass.: MIT Press, 1985);

The Symbolic Dimensions of Trauma and Recovery

and L. I. Levine, ed., *Ancient Synagogues Revealed* (Jerusalem: Israel Exploration Society, 1981). The historian C. H. Toy, in his history of religions, suggests that the form of public worship devised by the Jews was adapted by and still exists in Christianity and Islam.

91. T. Kollek, *My Jerusalem* (London: Weidenfeld and Nicolson, 1990), p. 51.

92. Y. Ben-Arieh, *Jerusalem in the Nineteenth Century* (New York: St. Martin's, 1984), p. 304.

93. J. Phillips, *A Will to Survive* (New York: Dial, 1976), p. 12.

94. T. Kollek and M. Pearlman, *Jerusalem* (Jerusalem: Steinmatzky, 1983), p. 223.

95. R. Giurgola and J. Mehta, *Louis I. Kahn* (Boulder, Colo.: Westview, 1975), p. 183.

96. A. Tyng, *Beginnings: Louis I. Kahn's Philosophy of Architecture* (New York: Wiley, 1984), pp. 156, 168.

97. Ibid., p. 157.

98. K. Larson, *Louis I. Kahn: Unbuilt Masterworks* (New York: Monacelli), p. 38.

99. http://www.ou.org/torah/rambam.html.

100. Y. Sakr, *The Subversive Utopia: Louis Kahn and the Question of the National Style in Jerusalem* (University of Michigan Microform 9636209, 1996), p. 122.

101. Elon, *Jerusalem*, p. 74.

102. Tyng, *Beginnings*, p. 175.

103. D. B. Brownlee and D. G. de Long, *Louis I. Kahn: In the Realm of Architecture* (New York: Rizzoli, 1991), p. 364.

104. R. Wurman, *What Will Be Has Always Been: The Words of Louis I. Kahn* (New York: Rizzoli, 1986), p. 41.

105. R. Coombs, "Light and Silence: The Religious Architecture of Louis Kahn," *Architectural Association Quarterly* 13, no. 1 (October 1981): 32, 34. Coombs's reading of Kahn's Hurva in relation to Solomon's temple seems to miss more obvious connections to other Kahn buildings such as the Memorial to Six Million Martyrs in New York, which was conceived at the same time as Kahn was working on the Hurva.

106. J. Fergusson, *A History of Architecture in All Countries: From the Earliest Times to the Present Day* (London: Murray, 1876). Fergusson's views on the history of Jerusalem are strange. He, for instance, insisted that the Dome of the Rock was the church built by Constantine and was the true site of Christ's burial.

107. V. Scully, quoted in Larson, *Louis I. Kahn*, p. 9.

108. While working on this essay, I was sad to read that Jerusalem's Regional Council had just decided to rebuild the Hurva in its pre-1948 form. "The complex has become a symbol of Jewish Jerusalem to both residents and tourists alike. Its distinctive single arch dominates the Jewish Quarter's

skyline," the report adds. See http://www.jpost.com/Editions/2002. How strange, and perhaps how wonderful, that Jews now want to restore a synagogue designed by a Muslim architect back to his original design, while they rejected Jewish architects who proposed new interpretations of the synagogue.

PART III

Resilient Tokyo
Disaster and Transformation
in the Japanese City

9

CAROLA HEIN

■ Natural disasters have destroyed, in whole or in part, Japan's cities on numerous occasions. Human action, whether internal warfare or the air raids of the Second World War, has been the cause of further devastation. But regardless of the origin of the destructive force, Japan has always rebuilt its cities, and usually with astonishing speed. This chapter argues that while urban disasters can bring about an opportunity for changes in the built environment, they do not appear to induce innovation per se.[1] Many times, the Japanese rebuilt their cities much the same as they were before, innovating only slightly on building codes or urban form. At times of ongoing political, economic, and social transformation, however, the leadership sponsored urban change in the wake of destruction. These interventions, instead of responding to post-disaster conditions, were often pared-down versions of pre-disaster concepts, constrained by limited finances, the lack of appropriate planning tools, the strictures of land ownership, and the needs and desires of private initiatives that called for rapid reconstruction and the preservation of traditional urban form.

Societal transformation by itself has promoted the large-scale demolition and urban transformation of Japanese cities far beyond the areas touched by natural or human-made disasters. Rapid industrialization, urbanization, modernization, and Westernization, following the Meiji restoration of 1868 and the establishment of modern Japan, in particular buffeted Japanese cities on a grand scale. The repeated destruction of the capital, Tokyo (or Edo, as the city was called until

1868), and its rapid reconstruction provide an especially compelling means to examine disaster and rebuilding in Japanese cities. A focus on Tokyo permits comparison of reconstruction following both sudden, natural destruction and human-inflicted attack, as well as analysis of urban change in the absence of disaster.[2]

Earthquakes rattle Japan regularly; typhoons are frequent visitors; and tidal waves as well as tsunami have wiped out many settlements along the coasts. Rivers are highly susceptible to flooding, and inundation along major rivers in Edo resulted in the affluent abandoning the lowlands to the poor and lower classes and building their villas on the highlands. Traditional Japanese architecture has responded to such threats in a variety of ways. Wood construction, for example, provides flexibility in the event of tremors, and heavy roofing helps to stabilize houses buffeted by typhoon-strength winds.

But no kind of wooden structure can endure fire, which has bedeviled Japanese cities throughout history. Conflagrations were so common in Edo that they were called *Edo no hana*, the "flowers of Edo." This aestheticization of a potentially lethal natural force suggests a certain fascination with the awesome power of fire on the part of Edoites. Indeed, the Japanese seem to have accepted the recurrent advent of urban destruction in general. The location and function of many disaster-battered cities were rarely, if ever, challenged. The shogunal government (*bakufu*) attempted to reduce the spread of fires through the creation of broad open spaces (*hiyokechi*) and ordinances requiring plaster fire-proofing or the use of fire-resistant roof materials.[3] Its main intent was the protection of its own lands and those of the feudal lords (*daimyo*), which were less prone to widespread fires. The densely built commoners district, on the other hand, where most of the fires occurred, did not benefit from strong governmental intervention. Furthermore, merchants and artisans resisted adopting more expensive fire-resistant materials, and traditional wooden construction emerged again and again after each disaster. In any case, the governmental measures did little to prevent fires from spreading, particularly in winter.

The actual reconstruction of affected districts was not undertaken by the government, but rather left to the private sector. Speedy recovery was based upon individual action. It was commonly accepted that a merchant had to be back in business in three days, lest his business be

The Politics of Reconstruction

ruined.[4] Rapid reconstruction was possible because the former buildings typically had been burned to ashes, effectively clearing the sites and enabling new wooden structures to be built almost overnight. The new buildings themselves were rarely built to better withstand conflagration; instead, cheap construction continued to be favored as a means of reducing financial loss to the owners. *Yakeya*—a neologism based on the words for speculative rental row houses (*nagaya*) and burning (*yake*)—were so poorly built that they would bring profit to their investors even if they easily and frequently vanished in flames.

Even when water, fire, or earthquakes wiped away the buildings, existing land divisions and the reliance on traditional building materials and techniques favored a return to previous urban forms. Similarly, human-caused destruction in times of warfare did not necessarily lead to major transformations of city form. Changes in function, on the other hand, could severely alter a city's standing. Kyoto, the seat of the emperor, had been destroyed in the Sengoku Jidai (Period of Warring States, 1467–1568) by warring factions encamped to the north and the south of the city. It was rebuilt quickly under the rule of Toyotomi Hideyoshi, and the population quickly restored. But while the physical destruction of the city was rapidly overcome, Kyoto's political standing declined with the subsequent move of the shogun's capital to Edo in the early seventeenth century. Despite retaining the seat of the emperor, his court, and a rich artistic heritage, Kyoto was never the same.

This is not to say that fires were insignificant as forces of change. The great Meireki fire of 1657, the largest fire of the Edo era, is a good example. Some 108,000 inhabitants of Edo perished in the flames, and most of the city's buildings were destroyed, including the castle keep. Major reforms followed on the heels of the fire. By the time the Meireki fire raged through Edo, shogunal power had been firmly established, and the complicated defense system around the shogunal stronghold, built after 1590, was no longer necessary. It became possible to open firebreaks to the north and west of the castle and to extend the growing city into the surrounding areas as well as on landfill.[5] The feudal lords were given land on either side of the outer moats to build secondary residences, and many even built third estates, in order to hold goods for the other residences and to serve as a refuge in case fire destroyed the main residence.[6] All temples and most shrines were moved beyond the outer moats and even beyond the Sumida River, extending the city farther. The Meireki fire thus enabled the Tokugawa shogunate to adapt Edo's urban structure to the needs of the expanding feudal metropolis and enabled the city to effectively become the political capital and administrative center of Japan.[7]

In the following centuries, urban change in Edo remained limited, even though big fires burned down thousands of houses in the city almost every winter. Rather than upgrading building standards to prevent such conflagrations, the authorities instead directed their energy toward improving fire-fighting capabilities through the creation of fire brigades.[8] Large-scale urban transformation, even in the wake of slate-clearing disasters such as the Meireki fire, did not take place unless there was a broader societal mandate for change.

Such a mandate came about in 1868 with the Meiji restoration. Industrialization brought about rapid urban growth, while the cities—and particularly the capital, Tokyo—had to provide the physical framework for the regime's new bureaucratic and corporate needs and representative functions The rapid transformation of Japan from a secluded island nation into a world player did not allow for an overall urban makeover. Instead, the government selected specific places for intervention. Governmental policy was to create first and foremost those buildings and urban structures crucial to industrial development and modernization—such as factories, ministries, and infrastructure—leaving most of the city, particularly neighborhoods and the homes of ordinary citizens, relatively unchanged or only transformed under the influence of private investment.

The Meiji restoration introduced national and prefectural government as well as a system of municipal administration—all of which were invested in the development of the capital city. New economic opportunities and social hierarchies led to the emergence of business leaders whose interests further transformed the built environment. While these new public and private actors at times used disasters as catalysts for change, the emerging political and economic forces of Meiji Japan themselves transformed many urban areas untouched by disaster. An examination of Tokyo's history since the Meiji restoration allows us to compare different types of destruction, consequent strategies of reconstruction, and their impacts on the urban landscape.

The brick district in the Ginza area at the heart of Tokyo stands out as an early attempt at fire prevention, modernization, and West-

The Politics of Reconstruction

ernization through reconstruction. After a major fire in 1872, which destroyed nearly 3,000 houses, the governor decided that reconstruction in the Ginza area should set an example for fireproof residential construction, and he retained the English engineer Thomas J. Waters to rebuild the entire district with brick buildings. The Ginza then became the first Japanese example of urban planning based on the creation of a unified streetscape and the separation of traffic, common in many European cities at the time. The speedy creation of the new plan was, in part, the result of a government still in flux, effectively run by only a handful of people, and the absence of a mature body of planning law and planning responsibility.[9] The new scheme laid out streets fitted with footpaths and brick buildings adorned with arcades governed by a strict design code. Projected as the modern entrance to Tokyo, the Ginza formed the connection between the new train station at Shinbashi and the European settlement in Tsukiji.

While the architectural transformation of the Ginza was striking, changes to its urban structure were less dramatic. The new plan largely preserved the traditional layout of the area after attempts to unify the land rights of the district failed. While the widening of many streets was proposed, in only a few instances did the plan create new roads, unify blocks, or alter directions in traffic flow. The Ginza took three years to build; reconstruction with traditional methods would have been much faster. Tokyoites were slow to warm to the new development. Buildings looked expensive and not particularly earthquakeproof. Moreover, they were ill adapted to Japanese lifestyles. Many remained empty for years, and the entire project was brought to a close in 1877. The Ginza was the first and last attempt at transforming Tokyo along the lines of a major European city. Because the district was destroyed again in 1923 and 1945, these historic planning efforts have largely vanished, and the typical chaotic Japanese cityscape has again prevailed.[10] While public authorities promoted street widening and the use of fire-resistant building materials as practices in the best interests of all, the need for a uniform architectural streetscape had no historical basis in Japan and was subsequently scrapped. While the Ginza project may be considered a failure in its early years, it laid the basis for the commercial development of the area, making it a long-term success in regard to land values.[11]

Fires provided opportunities for punctual urban improvement

planning at the end of the nineteenth century, but Tokyo's leaders also attempted to establish a more comprehensive plan for a modern infrastructural network. Such a plan could then serve as a guide for more limited renewal projects, as well as for planning in other Japanese cities. Since 1876 a committee under the Tokyo prefectural governor, Kusumoto Masataka, had been working on urban improvement, and by 1880 his successor, Matsuda Michiyuki, presented a plan and budget estimate for the most urgent fire-prevention works. To Matsuda, the *yakeya* row houses were the source of fires and epidemics, and he proposed to eradicate them from central Tokyo by using a combination of tactics—widening streets, building new canals, and introducing fireproof construction (brick, stone, and plaster) along the main thoroughfares. None of these urban planning techniques directly addressed the problem of the *yakeya*, which existed in the interiors of the blocks. However, the imposition of new fire-resistant roofing materials—which led to rising rents and the exclusion of this inexpensive rental housing from the city center—was intended to hasten the departure of the poor, while enabling the rich to remain.[12]

Under Matsuda's governorship, the city endured several major fires, as well as the first planning responses to such disasters. During the winter of 1881, four large fires broke out successively across the city. One, the Matsuedachō fire, destroyed more than 10,000 houses. In response, the city authorities enacted a number of successful planning interventions intended to create firebreaks, including the widening of fifteen streets and the construction of three canals. These punctual planning interventions, together with ongoing discussion of more general planning issues, led to both the 1888 Tokyo Urban Improvement Ordinance and the 1889 Tokyo Urban Improvement Plan.[13]

While the latter may be viewed in part as a reaction to earlier disasters and fires, the 1889 plan was neither a reconstruction blueprint nor a project limited to fireproofing. Rather, it outlined a comprehensive strategy focused on infrastructural improvement. Although realization of the 1889 Tokyo plan was impeded by the Sino-Japanese (1895) and Russo-Japanese (1904–1905) wars, the 1888 ordinance became the forerunner of the first Japanese Urban Planning Law of 1919 and established the template for subsequent rebuilding efforts. Fire prevention remained the main focus of Japanese urban planning, but at a

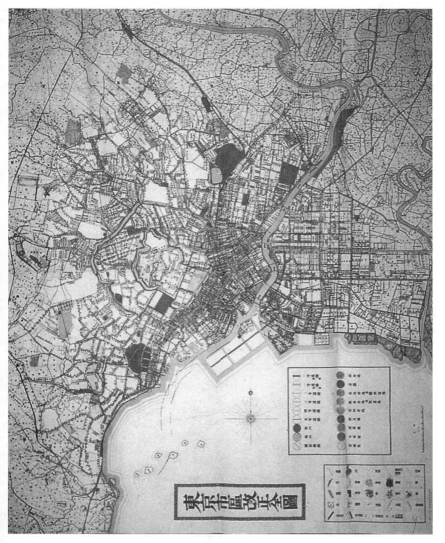

Figure 9.1.
Tokyo Urban
Improvement Plan, 1889.
From Ishizuka and
Ishida, *Tokyo: Urban
Growth and Planning*
(Tokyo: Center for
Urban Studies, Tokyo
Metropolitan University,
1988). This map has been
turned sideways to
facilitate comparison
with Fig. 9.2.

time of major political change, the government pursued *any* opportunity for the adaptation of Tokyo to modern needs.

The transforming capital of Meiji Japan could not wait for natural disasters to unexpectedly create opportunities for the accommodation of modern functions. Huge urban areas were needed, and fast. The political transformations were already in motion to provide the necessary land. The introduction of land-ownership laws after the Meiji

Resilient Tokyo

restoration made land a tradable, taxable good, while the abolition of the former aristocratic domains and the return of most of their land-holdings brought large parcels into the hands of the new government. Many of these areas were strategically well situated for government and business districts or factories. As a first step, such land was partly cleared of existing buildings and subdivisions and used for military purposes (such as exercise grounds), government offices, factories, agriculture, or other public functions. While these sites were scattered throughout the city, much of the land formerly attributed to major *daimyo* lay just beyond the gates of the former shogunal castle, which had become the Imperial Palace after the Meiji restoration.

This area—the contemporary Hibiya and Marunouchi districts—became a central element in the transformation of Tokyo, providing space for all of the elements of a modern metropolis: a political center, major park, business district, central train station, and so forth. In 1890, the Mitsubishi Company purchased from the military the land not used or defined in the Tokyo Urban Improvement Plan. Mitsubishi was influenced to make the acquisition by the example of London's central business district and the decision to site a new central rail station near Marunouchi. There was little immediate demand and it took more than two decades to fill the Mitsubishi Meadow, an area of about seventy acres.

Today, none of the original red-brick buildings survive. Nevertheless, the Marunouchi-Hibiya district remains a landmark in Japanese urban development. Few cities anywhere have had a comparable occasion for such a tabula rasa–style urban reorganization. With the combined effects of a compelling urban vision for Tokyo and the availability of extensive areas of land at Marunouchi, the modernization of Tokyo and its transformation into a modern capital proceeded smoothly. The Marunouchi-Hibiya area itself, once home to the most powerful *daimyos*, has retained its role as the political and economic heart of Tokyo and Japan through successive changes of leadership.

Other former *daimyo* areas supported large-scale reconstruction as well. Mitsubishi also purchased the Kanda-Misakichō area in 1890 and rebuilt it with wide streets and one thoroughfare bordered by *renga-nagaya*—wooden row houses separated by a brick wall for fire protection purposes.[14] The use of brick reflects the advent of new building materials that the Ginza development had attempted to implement. In

The Politics of Reconstruction

contrast to the Ginza, however, there was no insistence on a Western-ized design. The new Tokyo thus kept many of Edo's urban patterns, while the functions themselves changed.[15]

Where overall plans did exist prior to a disaster, they were used as a framework for comprehensive reconstruction, but the existence of such plans and planning tools did not necessarily guarantee innovative reconstruction. In the 1920s, modern planning had taken root in Japan. In 1919, the Home Ministry passed the Town Planning and Urban Building acts, developed with the help of its City Planning Section under Ikeda Hiroshi. This legislation introduced a system of zoning, land readjustment, and building lines, which applied to the entire built-up area, including the urban extension. Visionary public leaders—above all, Gotō Shimpei, who held major administrative posts in the colonies and in Japan—also developed concepts aimed at shaping To-kyo's urban future.[16] But these first steps at modern planning neither prevented the vast destruction unleashed by the 1923 Great Kantō earth-quake and its consequent fires, which affected large parts of two major cities, Tokyo and Yokohama, nor did they guide the reconstruction effort in its wake.

Gotō, the former mayor of Tokyo who was named home minister on the second day of the disaster, attempted to promote the recon-struction work as a national project.[17] While his efforts were dogged by a bureaucratic structure and a decimated budget, a comprehensive plan—the Tokyo Reconstruction Plan—was prepared. This document concentrated on land readjustment and the creation of roads and parks in the built-up areas of the city. But the plan was neither progressive nor responsive to the needs of the expanding metropolis; it was even more conservative and pragmatic than plans discussed before the dis-aster.[18] It ignored the developing suburbs and did not provide guide-lines for urban extension, although many people rebuilt their liveli-hoods in the suburbs after the earthquake.

The Tokyo Reconstruction Plan resulted in approximately 8,895 acres of land-readjustment projects, the construction of 157 miles of roads, and the building of some 55 parks. It also included a unique bridge allocation plan based on urban design principles. The plan re-mained in effect until 1930 and helped to establish land readjustment as the main Japanese planning tool.[19] Land readjustment has a partic-ular character in Japan. It does not consist of overall expropriation of

Figure 9.2.
Tokyo Reconstruction
Plan, 1923. From
Ishizuka and Ishida,
*Tokyo: Urban Growth
and Planning* (Tokyo:
Center for Urban
Studies, Tokyo Metro-
politan University, 1988).

a site followed by a completely new urban plan, but rather street widening and straightening, which strive to keep the new lots as close as
possible to the old ones and thus maintain elements of the traditional
urban form.

In the end, the opportunity to transform the city following the
earthquake's destruction was not fully captured. In its immediate aftermath, the citizens wanted stability and relief and thereafter they
strongly opposed major changes. While citizen opposition did not succeed in stopping major land-readjustment projects at the time, assem-
bling land for large-scale interventions, even after major disasters,
nonetheless remained a challenge to urban authorities. The longing on
the part of citizens to quickly rebuild their lives, and the Edo "habit"
of fires, further promoted rapid rebuilding according to traditional
protocols. To aid the citizenry, construction of temporary barracks in
preassigned firebreak zones was permitted. But the removal of these

The Politics of Reconstruction

dwellings was never strictly reinforced, and so large areas of Tokyo turned once again into densely settled districts of highly flammable wooden buildings.[20]

Beyond the reconstruction activities that it caused, the earthquake of 1923 brought to light existing social problems and spurred a variety of changes already under way. It sparked violence against Koreans, for example, who were rumored to be poisoning wells. It also accelerated the move of the wealthy to the outskirts of the city, a trend that had begun around 1900 and was further impelled by the great flood of 1910. At the same time, people began moving from the countryside to these suburban districts, furthering their growth. New road and rail infrastructures were built to connect the emerging suburbs with the center city and to accommodate the burgeoning traffic needs. Specifically, these involved the construction of terminal stations and of interchanges, such as Shinjuku and Shibuya.[21]

While the development of Shinjuku as a major subcenter of Tokyo was prompted by disaster, it was reinforced by earlier planning decisions. In 1919, Fukuda Shigeyoshi, a technical officer of the city of Tokyo, had proposed the development of subcenters like Shinjuku to promote deconcentration of the growing metropolis. The concept was taken up in later plans, and Shinjuku's west side has since evolved into Tokyo's high-rise business district and the home of the Tokyo metropolitan government. Such development was not directly a result of the 1923 Great Kantō earthquake; rather, it was made possible through the availability of the eighty-four-acre site of the Yodobashi water purification plant, which had been built in the late nineteenth century.

Just as the land formerly owned by the military aristocracy had allowed for the creation of new urban functions, the waterworks became the condition for the creation of the Shinjuku business district. A disaster may destroy buildings in a large area, but land ownership and private initiative will determine the rebuilding trajectory if strong expropriation laws and planning tools do not exist or are not effectively applied. The reconstruction after the 1923 Great Kantō earthquake illustrates how urban development and radical change depend both upon private and public intervention and their interaction, as well as on the larger political, economic, social, and cultural conditions prevailing at the time. While the earthquake accelerated the modernization

Figure 9.3.
The site of the Shinjuku subcenter before construction, featuring the Yodobashi water purification site From City Planning Institute of Japan, *Centenary of Modern City Planning and Its Perspective* (Tokyo: City Planning Institute of Japan, 1988).

of urban functions and social structure, the catastrophe did not bring about a progressive project for the Japanese capital.

A new urban plan could have emerged following the Second World War, when the occupation army transformed Japanese politics and economics. But after the air raids of 1945, production capacity was crippled and the economy could not support a massive reconstruction effort. In contrast to the 1923 earthquake—which left the rest of the country capable of sustaining the revitalization of the capital region—the Second World War touched nearly every major Japanese city. More than one hundred urban areas, not just Hiroshima and Nagasaki, were severely damaged by air raids and were designated for restoration according to the War Damage Restoration Plan.[22] Only a handful of cities survived the war intact, including Sapporo and the historic cities of Kyoto and Nara. In response to the national scope of the destruction,

The Politics of Reconstruction

Figure 9.4.
Photo of war destruction
in Tokyo. From Tokyo
Metropolitan Govern-
ment, *Tokyo: The Making
of a Metropolis* (Tokyo:
Tokyo Metropolitan
Government, 1993).
Courtesy Asahi Shinbun.

the government created a central planning office for reconstruction on November 5, 1945. In December, the cabinet decided on the policy for the reconstruction of war-damaged areas, and in September 1946, the Special City Planning Act was passed. Despite the national planning, the outcome of postwar reconstruction efforts varied in each city, as did their prewar experiences with urban planning.[23]

Moreover, Japan in the postwar years was an occupied country and did not enjoy complete freedom in the reconstruction of its cities. This was particularly the case in Tokyo. Based on its strong tradition of prewar planning, Tokyo was well equipped for comprehensive redevelopment, but progress was, nevertheless, slow. To begin with, Allied forces had taken over part of the city's central business district, as they had done in Yokohama.[24] While the American occupation forces rarely interfered with urban issues, the larger postwar changes they set into motion were manifested in the built environment. There was also a symbolic dimension to keeping Tokyo in check. This was the national capital that had hatched the Japanese war machine; grand plans for a

Resilient Tokyo

return to its past glory were not encouraged by the Allied victors. Moreover, the reconstruction policy specifically favored the rebuilding of local cities and did not allocate supplementary funds for the reconstruction of the capital.

The manager of the Tokyo metropolitan government planning section, Ishikawa Hideaki, had led Tokyo's planning since 1933 and was also in charge of Tokyo's War Damage Restoration Plan. Ishikawa had very specific ideas about the future of the city, suggesting decentralization and deconcentration of the urban population. Based on his ideas for "living spheres" proposed during the war, Ishikawa sought a ward-area population of around 3.5 million and the development of satellite and outer towns all over the Kantō plains to accommodate population and industrial growth. Ishikawa developed a plan for monofunctional towns containing 200,000 to 300,000 people, set apart by greenbelts (an inheritance from air defense planning during the war), and structured by a ring- and radial-shaped road network. Ishikawa's original plan projected land readjustment on about 50,000 acres, exceeding the burned-out area. But the nation's financial difficulties and the Fundamental Policy for the Reconsideration of Reconstruction Planning of 1949—based on the American-imposed so-called Dodge line[25]—forced reconstruction projects to be scaled down or abandoned, and curtailed Ishikawa's idealistic concepts.

Ishikawa's plan for a general reconstruction of Tokyo failed, as did similarly large-scale schemes drawn up by Hans Scharoun and his group for postwar Berlin—in part because it called for demolition beyond the destruction of the war in order to create a coherent infrastructural network. Citizens objected to such action. Faced with the need for housing and the enormity of the destruction, they longed for quick rebuilding and not a city built from scratch. Moreover, existing property rights and limited finances prevailed against such large-scale transformations.

After 1949, Tokyo's projects were reduced from the original 50,000 acres to a mere 3,000. These were implemented mainly in the districts of Shinjuku, Ikebukuro, and Shibuya, a move that promoted deconcentration through the creation of the subcenters that had been suggested decades earlier. Similar reductions applied to the street and park plans, and none of the proposed 100-meter-wide streets were realized.

The Politics of Reconstruction

Once more, planning in response to fire prevention succeeded, while efforts to create monumental cityscapes failed.

The curtailment of the Tokyo reconstruction projects occurred shortly before the economic boom of the 1950s, which was triggered by the Korean War. Had the reconstruction projects remained in place, they might have guided building in later years. Once the economy revived, a building boom ensued and land prices soared, making it even more complicated to implement planned improvements. By 1960 Tokyo's ward population exceeded 8 million, more than double Ishikawa's projection for the population maximum.[26] The infrastructural improvements of the boom period, hastened by the 1964 Olympics, concentrated on public land and often involved multilayered highways built over the old moats and canals. The war reconstruction had, after all, not provided land for such developments. Beyond infrastructural improvement, Tokyo's reconstruction was largely left to the private sector, which quickly reestablished the metropolis as the economic heart of Japan.[27] While the decades following the Second World War saw change on multiple levels, the physical form of the city and intangible laws of urban tradition helped to maintain continuities with the traditional city amid changes in architectural design and building materials.

By the 1970s Tokyo had fully recovered its prewar functions and gone beyond reconstruction to become a global city.[28] Moreover, it seems to have forgotten its own legacy of past destruction. Hiroshima instead has eclipsed Tokyo as the archetype of urban trauma in Japan. Hiroshima's potent symbolism derives not so much from the number of lives lost in the atomic blast (in comparison, for example, more people perished in a single Allied air raid on Tokyo on March 10, 1945), but because it was the first time the terrible force of an atomic explosion had been unleashed on a human population. Remarkably, in spite of Tokyo's many cycles of destruction and recovery, the city has built no memorials on the order of the Hiroshima Peace Center.[29]

A general discussion about political, economic, social, and cultural aspects of planning in Tokyo was largely absent in the years after World War II. This was because reconstruction relied mainly on land readjustment to provide the framework for rebuilding, reconfirming it as a tool of choice for Japanese planning. As in the aftermath of the 1923

Figure 9.5.
Hiroshima Peace
Memorial, under
construction. From
Ishimaru Norioki,
"Reconstructing
Hiroshima and
Preserving the
Reconstructed City," in
*Rebuilding Urban Japan
after 1945*, ed. Carola
Hein, Jeffry Diefendorf,
and Yorifusa Ishida
(London: Palgrave
Macmillan, 2003).

earthquake, land-use plans and building regulations were not fully implemented, and Tokyo (as well as other cities) once more saw the growth of the kind of traditional temporary housing that was partic ularly vulnerable to fires.

Tokyo has not seen a major natural catastrophe in seven decades. Street widening and the use of fire-resistant construction materials particularly in large-scale recent developments have limited the spread of fires. The continued existence of large traditional areas with predominantly wooden housing and narrow lanes, however, raises fears that a future earthquake and its consequent fires could still wreak havoc on large areas of Tokyo. Statistically a major earthquake is anticipated, and planning specialists are gearing their proposals toward the next major disaster. As history has shown, the post-disaster reconstruction trajectory depends strongly on the existence of plans and methods that frame rebuilding not only on the site destroyed, but also in areas that may experience secondary impacts of the disaster. In particular, reconstruction plans need to be laid out early enough to permit adequate citizen participation, as the example of the reconstruction of Kobe after the Great Hanshin-Awaji earthquake in 1995 demonstrates.

When the earthquake hit—spurring large-scale fires in the older sections of the city, but also destroying reinforced-concrete structures from highways to skyscrapers—the city of Kobe had just approved a new master plan. This projected two subcenters for the city, one of which was to be in the Shin-Nagata area, which was largely destroyed in the quake. The catastrophe enabled realization of the plan, but rendered its implementation more difficult. In the earliest period after the earthquake, the government took charge and promoted plans for a major infrastructural development program and general improvement plan without allowing room for participation; only later could traumatized citizens voice their opinions. The master plan did not recognize the population's urgent needs, especially for housing. Recovery and reconstruction efforts in those areas of the city with established citizen initiatives proceeded more smoothly than those without.

This overview of disasters in Japan and their role in the transformation of cities demonstrates that the response to urban trauma depends upon the larger political and socioeconomic, as well as cultural and technological situation and the special conditions of the city prevailing at the time. Societal changes more than disasters per se are thus

key to understanding Japanese urban transformation. New urban and architectural forms were introduced after a disaster only when urban planning authorities, public- and private-sector actors, and citizens were all in alignment, or when extraordinary conditions prevailed, as in Hiroshima. The form of destruction and its scale appear to be less important than the time and the (natural or human-made) context in which these occur. Natural destruction rarely changes the general political and economic conditions by itself. It is usually localized, destroying a part of a city or even an entire city, but leaving the national government in a position to help with the rebuilding. In the case of war destruction, particularly on the losing side, the overall political, economic, and societal conditions often change dramatically and—in contrast to natural disasters, which provoke overall compassion—war reconstruction is morally charged and requires taking sides.[30] Destruction in the Second World War was also not limited to one area or one city, but affected many cities and all areas of society—military as well as civilian. The American occupation forces provoked political, socio-economic, and larger cultural changes, which stimulated further transformation.

Disasters alone do not revolutionize planning. Once people have settled back into their lives, initiatives to improve the cityscape often slow down, just as attempts to prepare Tokyo for a major earthquake have not made much progress in spite of the devastation of the Great Hanshin-Awaji earthquake in Kobe. Unless citizen initiatives are strengthened through education initiatives (*machi sodatte*) and the decentralization of planning powers, and unless their aims are integrated with a larger analysis of future urban needs and the changing composition of society, reconstruction efforts will invariably fall short of their lofty goals.[31] And the cycle of destruction and reconstruction will continue without improving the lives of the citizenry.

Disasters may serve as opportunities for change, but they may also provoke the desire to retain the past—as the postwar rebuilding of Warsaw shows. This, however, is more typical for Europe. With their stone-building culture and relative absence of natural disasters, European cities do not have many opportunities for physical change. Thus, disasters may provoke more transformation (or provoke even more regret over what disappeared) than similar disasters in, for example, Edo-period Japan, where physical destruction of buildings occurred regularly, and the intangible urban culture and power structures stayed the same.

Political, economic, social, and cultural changes or technological innovations can occur rapidly, while transformations of urban and built forms need more time, unless a disaster hits. Although buildings disappear easily, lifestyles have changed only gradually, and they keep traditional Japanese building elements alive. While the height, form, material, and appearance of all types of buildings are very different today from a century ago, houses in particular are still built of wood and contain traditional features and spaces, such as rooms laid out with reed mats (*tatami*). Contemporary architectural design and building materials differ strongly from traditional construction, but land ownership and the structure of the traditional neighborhoods remain largely unchanged.

Legal systems further regulate change, creating long-time continuities, even when the actual construction disappears. Urban land with small lot divisions strongly resists change, even as technological innovations demand urban transformations. The increase of horse-drawn carriages and other types of wheeled traffic in the largely pedestrian Japanese cities since the mid-nineteenth century and the introduction of the railroad necessitated infrastructure changes. It took years, for example, to build parts of the Yamanote ring line through densely built areas north of Tokyo station or around Shinbashi station. These same innovations doomed many aspects of traditional Edo, such as canals, waterways, and narrow streets, but did not provoke a complete rebuilding, as it proved much easier to follow former streets, canals, or moats than to build a whole new pattern.

The existing urban structure has proven resistant to any type of reconstruction—be it post-disaster or due to other types of change—unless a complex set of political, economic, and social forces promotes change and there are large tracts of land available for comprehensive transformation.

Inside the existing city, major changes happen on land that is in the hands of a single authority. Large estates, military land, industrial sites, or railway holdings make major urban transformation possible. Outside the city, in spite of being somewhat limited by agricultural land patterns, planners theoretically have a larger chance to implement new forms—if they can overcome resistance by speculators and private land owners. The creation of new towns, for example, has been a major theme of postwar urban growth. A future decline in urban population and the end of urban growth, however, may limit such new development to existing lands. If planners are to intervene in the future transformation of a city, they must lay out a long-term plan based on the existing urban structure—one that can be implemented whenever a site is freed through disaster or societal transformation. They also must limit themselves to a handful of ideas that are applicable to that city's culture and traditions. Preserving green spaces and improving public spaces may be one important aspect of their work. Knowing that the urban structure changes slowly, planners should develop principles rather than fixed plans for the future.

The history of Japanese destruction and rebuilding has shown that even the best political and planning intentions do not prevent disasters from striking cities and that even though the dangers of future disasters are often known, possible preventive measures are not always implemented. Nonetheless, as long as cities fulfill their functions of sheltering and protecting trade, politics, and everyday life, national and local leaders will promote their rebuilding and citizens will move to cities even though new disasters loom. Urban resilience is thus anchored in the resilience of an intangible urban culture as well as remnants of the physical urban past. A city is more than built form; it is a complex phenomenon of political decisions, economic powers, social structures, cultural experiences, and legal heritage. As long as these intangible elements survive, the physical destruction of the city and even the deaths of large numbers of people do not cause the death of the city. Even when an urban culture dies, the geographic location, remnants of an older culture, and traces of built form can influence a reconstruction centuries later. It is thus not surprising that pride and urban resilience are often stronger than the memory of a disaster.

Notes

1. See, for example, the argument by Geneviève Massard-Guilbaud that catastrophes often serve as catalysts for change: Geneviève Massard-Guilbaud, "Introduction: The Urban Catastrophe—Challenge to the Social, Economic, and Cultural Order of the City," in *Cities and Catastrophes: Villes et Catastrophes*, ed. Geneviève Massard-Guilbaud, Harold L. Platt, and Dieter Schott (Frankfurt am Main: Lang, 2002), 9–42, esp. 38.
2. On the urban history of Tokyo, see in particular, Roman Cybriwsky, *Tokyo: The Shogun's City at the Twenty-first Century* (New York: Wiley, 1998); Hiromichi Ishizuka and Yorifusa Ishida, *Tokyo: Urban Growth and Planning* (Tokyo: Center for Urban Studies, Tokyo Metropolitan University, 1988); Hidenobu Jinnai, *Tokyo: A Spatial Anthropology* (Berkeley: University of California Press, 1995); Edward Seidensticker, *Low City, High City: Tokyo from Edo to the Earthquake: How the Shogun's Ancient Capital Became a Great Modern City, 1867–1923* (Cambridge, Mass.: Harvard University Press, 1991); Edward Seidensticker, *Tokyo Rising* (Tokyo: Tuttle, 1990).
3. On the recurrence of fires in Tokyo and attempts at fire prevention, see also Ishida, Yorifusa, "Finding a Way to Overcome Tokyo's Big Fires," unpublished paper presented at the International Conference of Asia Scholars meeting in 1998 in Noordwijkerhout, Netherlands; and William W. Kelly, "Incendiary Actions: Fires and Firefighting in the Shogun's Capital and the People's City," in *Edo and Paris: Urban Life and the State in the Early Modern Era*, ed. James L. McClain, John M. Merriman, and Kaoru Ugawa (Ithaca, N.Y.: Cornell University Press, 1994), 310–331.

4. Seidensticker, *Tokyo Rising*, 8. Early visitors to Japan had made similar remarks; see Edward S. Morse, *Japanese Homes and Their Surroundings* (New York: Dover, 1961), 317.

5. Paul Waley, *Tokyo: Now and Then* (New York: Weatherhill, 1984), 331–333.

6. Ibid., xiii.

7. Ishida, "Finding a Way to Overcome Tokyo's Big Fires."

8. On the creation of fire brigades, see Waley, *Tokyo*, xxv.

9. On the construction of the Ginza brick district, see also Terunobu Fujimori, *Meiji no Tōkyō keikaku* (Tokyo: Iwanami shōten, 1990); Yorifusa Ishida, *Nihon kindai toshikeikaku no hyakunen* (Tokyo: Jijitaikenkyūjo, 1987); André Sorensen, *The Making of Urban Japan: Cities and Planning from Edo to the Twenty-first Century* (London and New York: Nissan Institute/Routledge Japan Studies Series, 2002), 61–62.

10. On the long-term development of Ginza, see Satoshi Okamoto, "Destruction and Reconstruction of Ginza Town," in *Destruction and Rebirth of Urban Environment*, ed. Norihiko Fukui and Hidenobu Jinnai (Tokyo: Sagami Shobo, 2000), 51–83.

11. See also Fujimori, *Meiji no Tōkyō keikaku*; Okamoto, "Destruction and Reconstruction of Ginza Town."

12. On the preparation of the Tokyo Urban Improvement Plan, see Ishida, "Finding a Way to Overcome Tokyo's Big Fires," 2.

13. See Ishizuka and Ishida, *Tokyo*, 12.

14. On Kanda-Misakichō, see Masao Suzuki, *Meiji umare no machi, Kanda-Misagichō* (Tokyo: Seiobō, 1978).

15. On the continuous presence of Edo-time urban patterns in contemporary Tokyo see, in particular, Jinnai, *Tokyo*.

16. Gotō Shimpei, mayor of Tokyo from 1920 to 1922, had laid out a large-scale public investment project for Tokyo. See Ishizuka and Ishida, *Tokyo*, 19.

17. Ishizuka and Ishida, *Tokyo*, 5.

18. As Japan scholar Edward Seidensticker argues, the earthquake sped up social and spatial transformations, such as the decline of the "low city," destroying remnants of the Edo period and its culture which had survived the Meiji restoration. Seidensticker, *Low City, High City*, 9; Seidensticker, *Tokyo Rising*, 5.

19. Carola Hein and Yorifusa Ishida, "Japanische Stadtplanung und ihre deutschen Wurzeln," *Die Alte Stadt* 3 (1998): 189–211.

20. The Dojunkai Foundation provided only 5,663 houses, including temporary dwellings in 1924 and 1925. See Ishizuka and Ishida, *Tokyo*, 21.

21. See also Akira Koshizawa, *Tōkyō toshi-keikaku monogatari* (Tokyo: Nihon Keizai Hyōronsha, 1991), 76–91.

22. The war damage encompassed an area of 63,153 hectares; 2,316,000 houses had been burned. Moreover, 331,000 of the citizens in these areas had been killed and 427,000 were injured. All data on the damages during World

War II exclude Okinawa. On the general framework of reconstruction in Japan, see Yorifusa Ishida, "Japanese Cities and Planning in the Reconstruction Period: 1945–55," in *Rebuilding Urban Japan after 1945*, ed. Carola Hein, Jeffry Diefendorf, and Yorifusa Ishida (London: Palgrave Macmillan, 2003), 17–49.

23. Ishida establishes six categories of war-damaged cities; see Ishida, "Japanese Cities."

24. The historian John Dower calls the area "Little America"; see John W. Dower, *Embracing Defeat: Japan in the Wake of World War II* (New York: Norton, 1999), 206.

25. The so-called Dodge line was an austerity budget devised by Lt. Joseph Dodge and imposed by the General Headquarters, which targeted national budget allocations for public works projects and especially for the war-damage reconstruction projects.

26. See Ishizuka and Ishida, *Tokyo*, 27.

27. On the reconstruction of Tokyo, see Hiroo Ichikawa, "Reconstructing Tokyo: The Attempt to Transform a Metropolis," in *Rebuilding Urban Japan after 1945*, ed. Carola Hein, Jeffry Diefendorf, and Yorifusa Ishida (London: Palgrave Macmillan, 2003), 50–67.

28. Book titles refer to Tokyo as a global city; see, for example, Saskia Sassen, *The Global City: New York, London, Tokyo* (Princeton, N.J.: Princeton University Press, 1991).

29. The decision to memorialize the atomic destruction of Hiroshima was also realized because there was abundant international support for such a memorial. Indeed, several elements came together to allow for the realization of the Hiroshima Peace Park: international interest, a special law providing supplementary funding (the Peace City Law), a comprehensive project chosen by competition, and a sensitive architect, Tange Kenzō. It is nonetheless surprising that Tokyo does not offer a memorial of a scope and scale at least similar to the pagoda commemorating the 1923 Great Kantō earthquake by Itō Chuuta. See also Carola Hein, "Hiroshima: The Atomic Bomb and Kenzō Tange's Hiroshima Peace Center," in *Out of Ground Zero: Case Studies in Urban Reinvention*, ed. Joan Ockman (New York: Temple Hoyne Buell Center for the Study of American Architecture, Columbia University, 2002), 62–83.

30. See Judith Lewis Herman, *Trauma and Recovery* (New York: Basic, 1992), 5.

31. On the concept of *machi sodatte*, see also Yasuhiro Endō, *Machi Sodatte wo hagukumu: Taiwa to kyōdō no dezain* (Tokyo: Tokyo Daigaku Shuppankai, 2001).

The Politics of Reconstruction

"Resist the Earthquake and Rescue Ourselves"
The Reconstruction of Tangshan after the 1976 Earthquake

10

BEATRICE CHEN

■ At 8:02 A.M. on the morning of July 28, 1976, approximately five hours after an earthquake struck Tangshan in northeastern China, a MIG-8 fighter jet landed at the People's Liberation Army base nine kilometers from the sprawling industrial city of Tangshan. Two army officers quickly ran toward the plane and an officer named Lee asked, "What is the flight's mission?" The pilot replied, "We are looking for the epicenter of the earthquake." Without checking the identity or credentials of the other passengers, Lee anxiously asked the pilot to fly over Tangshan and confirm his suspicion that the epicenter lay under the city. As Lee watched the plane fly toward Tangshan, he radioed the pilot, "Can you see Tangshan yet?" Through the speakers came the pilot's shaky voice, "Yes, where it used to be!"[1]

When the earthquake shook Tangshan out of its slumber in the early hours of that summer morning, nobody imagined that it would turn the city into a vast ruin. Not a single structure in this city of thirty-three square kilometers escaped unharmed from this earthquake, which registered 7.8 on the Richter scale. Fully 78 percent of Tangshan's industrial buildings and 97 percent of its residential buildings were leveled.[2] The enormity of the physical destruction could only mean a comparable scale of human calamity. The official death toll stands at 240,000, but outside sources have posted much higher figures.[3] Some current residents still believe that the death toll is at least twice that of the official tally. One third-generation Tangshan resident pointed out, "Not one single building escaped earthquake damage. How can the

Figure 10.1.
Immediate aftermath of
the 1976 earthquake.
Courtesy of Tangshan
Earthquake Museum.

government officials say that only one quarter of the Tangshan population perished in this disaster?"[4] To this day, the true death toll remains
a haunting unknown.

What is certain is that within three seconds on July 28, 1976, Tangshan was obliterated from the earth by a natural force roughly 400
times that of the atom bomb dropped on Hiroshima.[5] It is conceivable
that if the earthquake had not been detected by a number of seismo-
logical centers around the globe, the news of this great catastrophe
would never have reached the outside world.[6] When pressed for details,
the Chinese government remained reticent about the earthquake. Even
a year later, the only thing authorities were willing to reveal was that
the Tangshan earthquake was the deadliest in four centuries of Chinese

The Politics of Reconstruction

history.[7] They were so reluctant for the outside world to find out about the impact of the earthquake that they closed the city to foreigners for the next two years.[8]

What happened during the year after the earthquake and why the secrecy and silence? This chapter will uncover the events in Tangshan following the earthquake and show that, beneath the shroud of secrecy, Chinese authorities were urgently recovering and rebuilding Tangshan under extraordinarily challenging conditions. Despite foreign predictions that rebuilding Tangshan would require at least twenty years, a modern earthquake-resistant city rose from the rubble in a mere decade. Tangshan has been rebuilt into a fully functioning and populous city that continues to be dominated by the industries that existed prior to the earthquake. However, to conclude that a city is resilient by virtue of its complete reconstruction, however rapid, is perhaps too simplistic in the case of Tangshan. An exploration into Tangshan's recovery reveals how post-disaster urbanism can be driven by powerful political forces.

The Chinese Communist party not only controlled the design and reconstruction of Tangshan but also the people's behavior and perceptions about the recovery efforts. The reconstruction process mirrored larger changes in the Chinese political agenda. Without the Chinese Communist party, today's Tangshan would be a very different city, or might not even exist at all. Tangshan has been an important industrial center of Hebei province since the late Qing dynasty, blessed with an abundance of natural resources, including coal, iron, gold, oil, and natural gas. Tangshan's growth into a densely populated city prior to the earthquake can largely be attributed to industrial development and the exploitation of these resources. Hailed as the "cradle of China's modern industry," Tangshan was the home of China's first modern coal pit, first standard-gauge railway, first steam locomotive, and first cement works.[9]

In 1953, Mao Zedong's communist regime launched its first Five-Year Plan, which, following the Stalinist model, placed a great emphasis on a centralized economy, collectivization, and extensive development of heavy industry. Many state-owned factories were established in Tangshan in this period. Until the earthquake in 1976, Tangshan's industrial output grew steadily each year: the annual coal output alone increased from 3.3 million tons in 1953 to 26.9 million tons in 1975.[10]

The sociospatial organization of Tangshan in this period also re-flected typical Maoist urban development. The principle units of urban form in the Maoist city were the work units, or *danwei*. Each was a compound akin to a miniature, self-contained city with its own fac-tories, residential areas, recreational and medical facilities, schools, and communal meeting and dining spaces.[11] While work and residential areas were housed in different buildings, these were typically adjacent to each other. Workers enjoyed the convenience of a short walk to their workbench or desk (few people commuted to work in the Maoist city). The majority of the housing stock in Tangshan prior to the earthquake consisted of single-story houses made of brick and stone. During the late 1950s and 1960s, new multistory concrete buildings for residential and administrative uses were added in the western part of the city. But even then, Tangshan remained a predominantly low-rise city. An em-phasis on low-cost construction also meant that none of the new mul-tistory buildings had appropriately reinforced steel structures, nor were other measures taken to ensure resistance to tremors. Furthermore, the political turmoil of the Cultural Revolution during the 1960s and 1970s led to the abandonment of any control over urban construction: build-ings could be constructed on any available site, with virtually no su-pervision by relevant authorities.[12] Unlike Beijing, with its imperial complex and dense mat of ancient neighborhoods, Tangshan lacked the form or fabric of a traditional Chinese city. As Beijing was shaped by centuries of dynastic rule, Tangshan was crafted in the image of doctrinaire Maoist industrialization.

The Tangshan earthquake was an inauspicious event in an extraor-dinarily inauspicious year. That year, 1976, had scarcely begun when the Chinese people learned of the death from cancer of their revered premier, Zhou En-Lai. The so-called Gang of Four, fearful that Zhou and his chosen successor, Deng Xiaoping, were looming in popularity even above Mao, prohibited any public mourning for the expired pre-mier. Meanwhile, Mao's own health was failing fast, and rumors began to fly of the helmsman's imminent passing. An internal power struggle among senior party members was already under way, pitting the Gang of Four and other Maoist ideologues against a more reform-oriented opposition. Despite Mao's fading power and declining health, he and his followers were still effectively in control at the time of the earth-

quake and its immediate aftermath. Hua Guofeng, whom Mao had designated as his successor, managed the Tangshan disaster largely in
accordance with the chairman's wishes, promoting national self-reliance and mobilizing
the masses. Then, on September 9, only weeks
after one of the greatest earthquakes in Chinese
history, Mao Zedong was dead. The rebuilding
of Tangshan would now proceed without him.

To the astonishment of the world community, the Chinese government refused all
foreign aid for earthquake rescue and recovery
operations. Just three days after the disaster, the
Department of Foreign Affairs issued a statement: "Under the leadership of Chairman Mao
and the Chinese Communist Party, the people
of China are eagerly participating in the earthquake relief efforts. The Chinese have decided
to rely on themselves to overcome this disaster."[13] Mao and his supporters believed that to
accept foreign assistance in any form would
ruin the dignity of the Chinese. Given China's

Figure 10.2.
A row of single-story
homes that survived the
earthquake. Photo by
author.

closed-door policy during the Cultural Revolution, it is not surprising
that rescue and recovery efforts were conducted in such a highly se-
cretive atmosphere.

The Maoists seized the opportunity to propagate the chairman's
ideology of national self-reliance by launching the recovery campaign:
"Resist the Earthquake and Rescue Ourselves" (*Kang zheng Jiu zhai*).[14]
The masses were still Mao's most potent political weapon. He had spent
a lifetime finessing the art of manipulating the popular sentiment; his
strategy of indoctrinating a population into scrutinizing each other and
reporting on errant behavior ensured mass participation and self-
regulation. Anyone who dared to stray from Mao's ideologies would
be exposed to public scrutiny and penalized.[15] Under his rule, millions
meekly followed his orders.

Rather than seeking a new strategy to tackle a disaster of such great
magnitude, the Chinese government continued using the effective party

propaganda to exert Mao's influence. In contrast to China's guarded response to the international community, the post-earthquake events on the domestic front were heavily publicized on Mao's terms. He chose what to reveal and what not to reveal based on his political agenda of building a strong and self-reliant nation. What made possible the reign of fear during the Cultural Revolution also allowed Tangshan's recovery process to develop efficiently.

The authority of Mao's political leadership facilitated Chinese post-disaster management because it was essentially orchestrated from the top down. There was no lengthy discussion process to reach a consensus or develop a strategy; relevant parties were mobilized on command; and no disobedience was tolerated from below. The People's Liberation Army was sent in as soon as the central government was informed about the extent of the earthquake damage; groups of physicians arrived the next day from Beijing and other cities in Hebei province. The Communist party issued a statement requesting all provinces to deliver medical supplies, food, clothing, and lights. It demanded that anyone participating in the rescue and recovery mission have his own vehicle and provide his own food.[16]

Even the distribution of aid was coordinated by the central government. Each province was directed by the Central Party Committee as to which supplies it should provide for Tangshan: Inner Mongolia donated 1.8 million yuan in food, Shanghai delivered 2.4 million yuan in medication, and Shanxi province sent thousands of cooking utensils.[17] The efficient communication among Chinese Communist party members throughout China ensured that the orders were disseminated within a day.

Without Mao's legacy of organizing and mobilizing the masses, disaster relief would likely have been chaotic and slow. His supporters in the party were aware that the Chinese must present a united front if they were to overcome this disaster unassisted; thus they continued to advance Mao's doctrine of the "mass line" through "education."[18]

Many of the stories that emerged from post-disaster Tangshan were about the strength and selflessness of the people. In one unlikely account, a man went to save the local Communist party official before he began to look for his wife among the rubble;[19] a mother carted the body of her nineteen-year-old son to the airfield and asked the doctor, "Can my son be saved? If not, I'm going to go save the others."[20] The

The Politics of Reconstruction

Figure 10.3.
The People's Liberation Army was mobilized for the rescue effort. Courtesy of Tangshan Earthquake Museum.

narratives often referred to the party as their savior: people who had been buried for days would declare, "Long live the PLA!" when pulled out of the rubble and would inform everyone that contemplating Mao's teachings had helped them endure and survive.[21]

Many of the narratives present the Tangshan people as almost superhuman, endowed with such strength and forbearance that they could carry on with their lives unaffected by the physical and psychological trauma of a terrible disaster. These narratives of heroic resilience were intended to be both inspiring and didactic, instructing the people on how a model Chinese citizen might cope with sudden disaster and underscoring the wisdom and glory of the Maoist way. The narratives also attempted to cultivate what the Chinese call the ability to "eat bitterness," or withstand great suffering stoically, a notion that Mao's political regime believed to be crucial to the sustainability of China as a great nation. The underlying message was that the Chinese could survive this disaster only because they followed Mao's teachings of self-reliance and resilience.

Since the government had the power to control the kinds of information disseminated to the masses, imposing particular strands of thought on the population was an easy task. The regime ensured that only approved party narratives dominated northeastern China immediately. Moreover, because the government was considered all-powerful, when it issued a command, the people generally felt obliged to follow state directives.[22] It is not surprising that the only published personal account of the earthquake at that time was penned by a People's Liberation Army cadre, Qian Gang, who praised the Maoist regime's disaster relief efforts: "When a disaster strikes," wrote Qian of communist China:

> help pours in from all over the country. The people unite, get organized and conquer nature. Our socialist system has fully demonstrated its superiority. The people in the disaster area put it well: "The new and the old societies are as different as day and night. We cannot find enough words to express our gratitude to Chairman Mao and the Communist Party! Earthquakes cannot subdue a heroic people. We'll keep on working energetically in building socialism."[23]

The emergence of personal accounts published after the completion of reconstruction in 1986 provided a wholly different perspective on the aftermath of the Tangshan earthquake. Detached now from the political strategizing of the party, the new narratives put a more human face on the disaster and the recovery process. Chen Zhu-Hao, who lost his daughter in the earthquake, observed that the survivors mourned for the dead, but every day they would continue to dig through the rubble, hoping to find other loved ones, friends, neighbors, and compatriots. At night, they remained among the ruins, in tents built with wooden sticks and plastic sheets.[24] Chen never even mentions the Communist party in his narrative:

> It only took half a day to build our new home. We also found some pieces of timber and laid them on the ground so it would not be so wet. Since we didn't have many things, we did not need the entire plastic sheet so we left the unused portion on the ground. In about ten days, my neighbor Liu and his two daughters came back to Tangshan from the countryside. They only had one tent so Liu used the rest of our plastic sheet to build another tent for his daughters. Alone in the tent at

night, I forgot the misery of recovering the bodies under the scorching sun but only to be occupied by other concerns,

This is my home. I'm going to be living here, my new home, a new beginning . . .

Will my eldest daughter be safe in the countryside?

We were a family of five, but now there are only four of us left. Here, I'm all alone sleeping in the tent . . . and another one lying in the dirt.[25]

Such personal reflection on trauma and loss had no place in Chinese society under the Maoist regime. If the people could recover from the earthquake, they would have achieved a great human triumph which served to confirm the superiority of Mao's leadership and the victory of his leftist ideology within the Chinese Communist party. Therefore Mao sought to take advantage of his cult of personality and power of governance to ensure that the people would obediently follow his directives to overcome the disaster quickly despite the hardship.

During the recovery process, the succession struggle continued to escalate within the Chinese Communist party. The ensuing political transformation reinforced the concentrated power of political leadership in China and altered the course for the reconstruction of Tangshan. When Deng Xiaoping eventually consolidated power by 1978, following the legendary struggle between Premier Hua Guofeng and the Gang of Four, he abandoned many of Mao's ideologically driven policies, such as promoting an egalitarian society and maintaining state control of the economy.[26] He encouraged the learning of Western science, technology, and economic methods but, at the same time, he believed in the importance of traditional Confucian values. His objectives for reform were to integrate the best from the East and the West so that China could become competitive in the international community.

Although both leaders wanted to prove China's superiority, they chose opposite approaches to this goal. While Mao espoused the ideology of building power through national self-reliance, Deng believed that China could not improve without learning from more developed Western nations. Unlike Mao, whose ideology prevailed over other considerations and whose state intervened in all aspects of Chinese society, Deng was more concerned with the concrete results of policies rather than their symbolic nature. In fact, he was often criticized for prioritizing economic development above political ideology.[27] Compared to Mao's politics, Deng's regime was characterized by pragmatism and efficiency, as exemplified by his use of the famous parable of the two cats: "It does not matter whether the cat is black or white. So long as it catches the mouse, it is a good cat."

As such, the planning for the new Tangshan was transformed from a political football into an exercise of pragmatic science. The methodical approach toward the creation of the 1976 Comprehensive Plan of Tangshan was a dramatic departure from the slogans and heroic narratives of resilience that dominated the recovery process under Mao's regime. For the first time in modern China, the central government seemed willing to delegate its political authority and leave the planning of the city to experts. As a result, the plan for new Tangshan was created by experienced planners and academics more interested in building a city than in constructing a particular ideology. Instead of mobilizing the usual masses, the central government mobilized a group of urban planning experts that included academics from Tsinghua University, Beijing University, and Tongji University, and brought them to Tangshan in order to evaluate the possibilities for its reconstruction.

Before they even began to propose potential designs, the experts reviewed the reasons for the large-scale destruction of Tangshan. One observer noted that in the Lubei district, the only thing standing was the pagoda on top of Phoenix Hill overlooking the ruins of the city. All but a few of the recently built multistory buildings had been leveled, and the empty spaces between the buildings were filled with broken bricks and debris. In the Lunan district, the rooftops of the one-story homes that had crumbled during the earthquake were all that was visible. Piles of debris blocked the narrow lanes and streets of Tangshan.[28]

While the experts recognized that the magnitude and the timing of the earthquake contributed to the extensive damage, they also observed that the poor design of the old Tangshan may have increased the devastation. They concluded that the structures were of low quality and were not built to prevent earthquake damage. The high density of Tangshan made the earthquake even more deadly. In 1976, 70 percent of the area of Tangshan had a pre-earthquake population density of 15,000 people per square kilometer.[29] In addition, the most populous district of Tangshan was built on a fault line, which led to the complete collapse of all the buildings and a death rate that was twice the average of the city. The experts also pointed out that buildings were too close together, and the roads too narrow and irregular. Many T-junctions reduced the flow and connections throughout the city, making it difficult for people to escape in the event of a disaster. Furthermore, the consultants reminded the Chinese leadership that the lifelines of the city, including water, electricity, communications, and transportation, completely broke down after the earthquake because the infrastructure had been poorly designed.[30]

The experts' analysis made clear that the development of Tangshan was less than adequate for the contemporary era. In response to their official report, the vice chair of the State Council concluded:

> We cannot use the old Tangshan as a blueprint for the reconstruction; we must build a new Tangshan. This region is an important base for coal and steel production, therefore we must create a plan for Tangshan that integrates the development of the entire region. In other words, we must strive for a comprehensive plan for a new Tangshan by considering Tangshan as one entity.[31]

The central government looked upon the reconstruction of Tangshan as an opportunity to improve the city through systematic planning, an exercise that was largely neglected under Mao's leadership. Deng foresaw the potential of using a rationally reconstructed Tangshan to show the outside world China's ability to modernize and to affirm the superiority of Deng's socialist regime over Mao's outdated leftist ideology.

The new design would correct the mistakes of the previous urban form of Tangshan and build upon the principles of modernity espoused by the new political leadership. The 1976 Comprehensive Plan aimed to transform Tangshan into a modern, earthquake-resistant city with an improved living environment. The plan sought to seize the opportunity of disaster to solve the problems of urban sprawl in pre-quake Tangshan, characterized by chaotic land use, a disorderly street system, and railway lines bisecting the city proper. The planners also aimed to improve the functionality of the city by increasing the number of streets, expanding public green space, and dividing the city into three parts: the central district, the eastern industrial district, and a new urban area in Fengrun.[32]

According to the proposed plan, the area of the city would expand from thirty-three to eighty-one square kilometers in order to allow the creation of more open space and to reduce the population density. The new spatial design of Tangshan ensured that the urban population would not be concentrated in a single area of the city in the event of another deadly earthquake. Furthermore, the plan divided the city into residential and industrial zones separated by a green belt. With this single act, the government vastly improved the quality of life for the residents. No longer would they have to live literally next door to a factory or endure the heavy pollution that had plagued the city prior to the earthquake. At the same time, the industries that were critical to the national economy could be preserved. Finally, the overall layout of the city was redesigned into a simple grid system with wider tree-lined roads and designated open space. The roads, however, were not widened to symbolize the power of the communist regime but to allow people more room to escape in the event of another earthquake.[33]

In keeping with Deng's objective of modernization, the new plan for Tangshan promoted the principle of efficiency. The reconstruction efforts would transform Tangshan into a functional city that would encourage future economic development. The ultimate goal of the reconstruction plan for Tangshan was to contribute to the national political agenda of economic development. Unlike Mao, Deng was much more concerned with the functions of the resultant design than with the design itself. His priority was to rebuild a city that would continue its pre-earthquake level of industrial output and could withstand another disaster with minimal damage. The symbols and values of urban design did not hold much meaning for Deng; it was the future of the city that mattered.

The Chinese had repudiated urban planning in 1960 during the National Economic Planning Meeting, and the urban reconstruction plan for Tangshan was one of the first efforts to bring planning back into favor.[34] The prepared scheme, however, was subject to challenge by the physical, political, and economic conditions of the time. One major difficulty of Tangshan's reconstruction stemmed from the experts' recommendation (and the government's preference) to rebuild on top of its ruins.[35] Tangshan could have moved to a new location but the natural resources available in the existing location were crucial to the survival of Tangshan's (and China's) economy. For this reason

Figure 10.4.
The creation of open space between residential buildings was also critical to the reconstruction plan of Tangshan. Photo by author.

Tangshan could not be altered too drastically from its pre-earthquake form, if it were to regain its pre-quake industrial economic base.

The strategies adopted for the reconstruction of the city emphasized the restoration of urban life and industrial production in situ. In addition to rebuilding the factories, the regime prioritized residential construction and reconstruction of the city's central business district. According to a news article published in 1979, Tangshan officials stated that "all 730,000 urban residents are expected to have new homes by the end of 1982."[36] Faced with the urgency to build housing for the residents, the central government adopted a uniform typology of modern housing to speed reconstruction. Each apartment was composed of living rooms, bedrooms, a storage room, a kitchen, a toilet, and a balcony. In addition, it was equipped with heat and running water. Since Premier Hua Guofeng insisted on an architecture that reflected the building technology of the 1970s, concrete became the construction material of choice ("bricks," it was said, "are for the Qin dynasty!").[37]

As a result, Tangshan today is filled with slabs of almost identical concrete housing. Ironically, this uniformity of housing has given Tangshan a distinctly socialist urban identity among modern Chinese cities.

Mao had successfully shaped a population that was willing to "eat bitterness" throughout the reconstruction period. For at least two years, the people of Tangshan had to make do with primitive living conditions before their permanent homes were rebuilt, while participating in the labor-intensive rebuilding process.[38] But by the end of 1979, 820,000 of the 2.76 million square meters of housing had been completed, and the city was well on its way toward renewal.[39] Rebuilding the city on top of its ruins, however, proved costly, and the Chinese government was now suffering great financial hardship. In 1982, the state council made the decision to scale back the scope of the reconstruction plan due to a shortage of funds.[40] As a result, several goals of the reconstruction plan were not achieved. The local government did not foresee the difficulty of relocating the residents and industrial enterprises out of the center of the city, especially since the new urban area was being constructed at such a slow pace that it was unable to attract many residents. The new urban area never attained the targeted population while the old city center quickly achieved a population density that was higher than recommended by the guidelines of the reconstruction plan. Also, nearly all of the industrial factories were rebuilt in the same places so the distribution of land use in Tangshan did not change much from the chaotic mixture of land use that had existed prior to the earthquake.

Even though the government had hoped for a bigger and better Tangshan, fiscal realities limited the options for expansion. Nevertheless, the government was able to rebuild and restore the essential aspects of Tangshan city within ten years after the earthquake. In total, the central government allocated 600 million yuan for direct disaster relief, 2.5 billion yuan for reconstruction, and the city was exempted from contributing revenue to the central government until 1983.

The new Tangshan has undergone few dramatic changes since the reconstruction was completed in 1986. The result is an orderly built environment, which stands out in comparison to other contemporary Chinese cities, especially those that underwent rapid growth and expansion in the 1990s. The major axis of the city, which extends from the entrance of the new train station, is boulevard-like but not lined

Figure 10.5.
A new Tangshan rises
out of the rubble. Photo
by author.

with grand, imposing architecture, as in Paris or Berlin. Instead, rows
upon rows of slab housing no more than six stories in height are lined
up equidistant from one another behind neat patches of green space.
These residential zones also include schools, shops, restaurants, post
offices, kindergartens, theaters, and bath houses.[41] As one moves toward the center of the city, brightly painted blue and red roofs, similar
to that often found on European houses, adorn the tops of buildings
and break up the monotony of the slab housing. In the distance, huge
smoke stacks disrupt the view of rolling hills. If not for a memorial at
the center of town, one would never suspect a devastating earthquake
had once destroyed the city.

Without help from the rest of China, Tangshan could have never
been rebuilt into a modern Chinese city and its people might well have
lost the will to go on. Tangshan's significance in the national economy

"Resist the Earthquake and Rescue Ourselves"

also accelerated its recovery. Under harsh conditions of limited technology and time constraints, the people of Tangshan worked to resume their city's pre-earthquake production output, a goal they met within two years.[42] While Mao dictated that the people rescue themselves, the enduring spirit of resilience was fostered by the nation's support of Tangshan and the desire of the people of Tangshan to express their gratitude. Yet, without the rational objectives of Deng's regime and the combination of communism, socialism, and economic reforms, Tangshan would not have become the city it is today.

Although many Chinese people believed that the Tangshan earthquake was an ominous sign (millions regarded it as a portent of the death of Mao and that he wanted to take many along with him), the political upheavals that followed positively and unexpectedly affected the reconstruction. The change in political leadership shifted the focus from the recovery of the people's spirit to the physical recovery of the city. Under Deng Xiaoping's leadership, the state became less involved with the daily lives of the Chinese people, but the reconstruction of Tangshan was still dominated by state intervention. Deng made sure that the plan would transform Tangshan into a modern, earthquake-resistant city with an improved quality of life, while using it to his political advantage.

The reconstruction of Tangshan marked a departure from the old ways of communist China and became one of the first experiments in reforming modern China, part of the effort to construct a nation-state on a par with the international community. The product of its country's transformation, Tangshan was able to rise from its rubble and become a source of pride for China. When the central government announced the completion of reconstruction efforts in 1986, Tangshan was revealed to the world as the celebrated paradigm of modern Chinese urban planning.[43]

Had Mao lived, Tangshan would have been designed by party cadres, rather than by experts in urban planning and design. Correspondingly, as one resident pointed out, "If China had accepted foreign aid, today's Tangshan would be a modern city with skyscrapers."[44] Similarly, Tangshan would look very different if it had been rebuilt during China's current transition from a planned to a market economy. The recovery and rebuilding of Tangshan reinforce the inextricable link between planning culture and Chinese politics and reveal the significance of

The Politics of Reconstruction

urban reconstruction as an arena for the display of political authority in the communist regime.

Notes

1. Hebei Province Bureau of Seismology, *Tangshan Kang Zhen Jiu Zhai Jieu Che Ji Zhai* [Post-disaster Management of the Tangshan Earthquake] (Beijing: Di Zhen, 2000), 20.
2. Wang Tzi-Ping, *Di Zhen Wen Hua Yu Shu Hui Fa Zhan* [The Culture and Development of a Post-earthquake Society] (Beijing: Di Zhen, 1996), 6.
3. It was not until June 1977 that Chinese officials disclosed, via a Mexican husband-and-wife research team, the scale of the destruction brought by the Tangshan earthquake. Even so, an estimated death toll was not given; Chinese officials only revealed that the Tangshan earthquake was the deadliest in four centuries. However, they neither refuted nor agreed with the previous published estimated death toll of 655,000. The officially listed death toll, however, stands at 240,000; Andrew Malcolm, "Chinese Disclose that 1976 Quake Was Deadliest in Four Centuries," *New York Times*, 1 June 1977.
4. Zhang Tian, interview with the author, August 2002.
5. Gang Qian, *The Great China Earthquake: A Revealing Account of the Worst Quake in Recorded History* (Beijing: Foreign Language Press, 1989), 53.
6. Jasper Becker, "Remembered with a Shudder," *South China Morning Post*, 7 July 1996.
7. Ibid.
8. Patrick Tyler, "After Eating Bitterness, 100 Flowers Blossom," *New York Times*, 28 January 1995.
9. Li Chengzhen, "Tangshan Da Di Zhen" [The Great Tangshan Earthquake], *China Business and Information News*, 11 February 2003, 33.
10. Gao Dao Sen, ed., *Feng Huang Gong Huo Zhong Zai Sheng* [The Rebirth of a City] (Tianjin: Tianjin People's Publishing, 1996), 12.
11. Piper Rae Gaubatz, "Urban Transformation in Post-Mao China: Impacts of the Reform Era on China's Urban Form," in *Urban Spaces in Contemporary China*, ed. Deborah Davis et al. (New York: Cambridge University Press, 1995), 30.
12. Wang, *Di Zhen Wen Hua Yu Shu Hui Fa Zhan*, 416.
13. *Tangshan Da Di Zhen* [The Great Tangshan Earthquake] (Hebei), 134.
14. Patrick Tyler and Lori Reese, "An Ominous Rumbling," *Time Asia*, 27 September 1999.
15. John King Fairbank and Merle Goldman, *China: A New History* (Cambridge, Mass.: Belknap, 1998), 325.

16. Hebei Province Bureau of Seismology, *Tangshan Kang Zhen Jiu Zhai Jieu Che Ji Zhai*, 38.

17. *Tangshan Da Di Zhen*, 180.

18. Fairbank and Goldman, *China*, 325.

19. Xinhua News Agency, 9 January 1977.

20. Hebei Province Bureau of Seismology, *Tangshan Kang Zhen Jiu Zhai Jieu Che Ji Zhai*, 49.

21. Qian, *The Great China Earthquake*, 123.

22. Li Jinfang, "Social Responses to the Tangshan Earthquake," University of Delaware Disaster Research Center, Preliminary Paper No. 165 (1991), 7.

23. *After the Tangshan Earthquake: How the Chinese People Overcame a Major Natural Disaster* (Beijing: Foreign Languages Press, 1976), 4.

24. Chen Zhu-Hao, *Tangshan Di Zhen Tsing Li Ji* [Journal of Tangshan Earthquake] (Beijing: Ming Tzu, 2001), 120.

25. Ibid., 124.

26. Fairbank and Goldman, *China*, p. 407.

27. Wang, *Di Zhen Wen Hua Yu Shu Hui Fa Zhan*, 20.

28. Tsao Chi Jia, *Tangshan Di Zhen Zai Qu She Hui Hui Fu Yu She Hui Wen Ti Yan Jiu* (Beijing: Di Zhen, 1997), 417.

29. Ibid.

30. Ibid.

31. Ibid., 421.

32. Mao Qizhi, Wu Liangyong, and Wu Weijia, "Reconstruction of the City of Tangshan Twenty Years after a Major Earthquake: Planning, Achievement and Experience," in *Innovative Urban Community Development and Disaster Management: Proceedings of the International Conference Series on Innovative Urban Community Development and Disaster Management*, Kyoto, Japan, 26 September 1995, ed. James F. Goater, UNCRD Proceedings Series, no. 13 (Nagoya, Japan: United Nations Centre for Regional Development, 1996), 253–261.

33. Tsao, *Tangshan Di Zhen Zai Qu She Hui Hui Fu Yu She Hui Wen Ti Yan Jiu*, 416–417.

34. A. G. O. Yeh and F. Wu, "The Transformation of Urban Planning Systems in the Midst of Economic Reform in PRC," *Progress in Planning* 51, no. 2: 167–252.

35. Interview with Mao Qizhi, professor of urban planning, Tsinghua University, 18 August 2002.

36. Xinhua News Agency, "Construction of Housing Projects in Full Swing in Tangshan," 3 December 1979.

37. Tsao, *Tangshan Di Zhen Zai Qu She Hui Hui Fu Yu She Hui Wen Ti Yan Jiu*, 425.

38. Hebei Province Bureau of Seismology, *Tangshan Kang Zhen Jiu Zhai Jieu Che Ji Zhai*, 133.

39. Xinhua News Agency, "Construction of Housing Projects in Full Swing in Tangshan."

40. Mao, Wu, and Wu, 255.

41. Xinhua News Agency, "Construction of Housing Projects in Full Swing in Tangshan."

42. "A New Tangshan Rises from the Rubble," *Beijing Review*, 15–21 July 1996.

43. "Reconstruction of Tangshan," exhibition at the Tangshan Earthquake Memorial Museum, Tangshan, China.

44. Li Tian, personal interview, 12 August 2002.

Reverberations
Mexico City's 1985 Earthquake and the Transformation of the Capital

11

DIANE E. DAVIS

■ On September 19, 1985, at 7:14 A.M. an earthquake reaching a magnitude of 8.1 on the Richter scale and lasting almost two full minutes hit the coast of Mexico, rocking its capital city and shaking its buildings and its people. The next day, at 7:38 P.M., Mexico City experienced a second tremor of an almost equal magnitude on the Richter scale, 7.5. What has come to be known as the Mexico City earthquake, then, was in actuality two earthquakes, although those who experienced it lived through a single disaster whose longer-term reverberations were as powerful as the first set of tremors that hit the city on that initial day in September.

The earthquake, or those two days of tremors big and small, produced a physical disaster on a scale not seen since the destruction of the city in 1521, when Hernán Cortés's forces defeated the ancient Aztec city of Tenochtitlan. This same battle site later served as the seat of eighteenth- and nineteenth-century Spanish colonial power and subsequently marked the place where the majority of the 1985 earthquake damage occurred. After the first day alone, 250 buildings were completely destroyed with 50 more at risk of collapsing; thousands of others were damaged or considered to be unusable. Five thousand people were injured with more than 1,000 still trapped under the debris; more than 250,000 people were homeless. The city lacked telephone and electricity services. After the second day's quake, when more reliable statistics began flowing in, 2,000 were officially confirmed dead (although close to 7,000 cadavers had been identified) with 28,000 still listed as missing;

255

Figure 11.1.
The immediate aftermath, Pino Juarez complex, Mexico City, September 1985. Photo by Jorge Núñez.

Figure 11.2.
Homeless earthquake victims, Mexico City, September 1985. Photo by Jorge Núñez.

more than 7,000 victims were being treated at relief stations, with 30,000 at gyms and other sites turned into shelters. More than 800,000 residents were ultimately forced to abandon their homes and sleep in the open air.[1] Official statements later acknowledged 5,000 killed and 14,000 injured; but an independent final tally accounted for 2 million

The Politics of Reconstruction

Figure 11.3.
Remains of the Jalisco apartment building, downtown Mexico City, September 1985. Photo by Jorge Núñez.

residents temporarily made homeless and thousands dead, tens of thousands injured, 100,000 damaged building units (mostly residential), and hundreds of thousands of residents made permanently homeless. The city suffered billions of dollars of material damage and tens of millions of dollars in the tourist trade were lost, as were hundreds of millions of dollars in wages by workers who became unemployed as a result of the earthquake.[2]

The bulk of the damage was centered in the heart and symbolic center of the city, which held close to 20 percent of the entire metropolitan area's population and contained a large variety of colonial monuments, key government buildings, educational institutions (both secondary schools and colleges), medical centers, and most of the city's major commercial and retail establishments, principal hotels, and theaters. The main plaza that defines this historically central area is a large cement expanse called the Zócalo, which traces its origins to precolonial times and is now surrounded by the Presidential Palace, the main political and administrative offices of the Mexico City (or federal district) government, and several historically significant Aztec ruins

Reverberations

exposed during underground construction for the subway during the 1960s. Over the years the Zócalo has served as the main location for popular protests against governing authorities, both local and national.

Yet the downtown areas damaged by the quake, generally speaking, were not merely recognized as locations for activist pilgrimages or as the embodiment of political power. These areas housed, employed, and provided basic services for hundreds of thousands of residents. Multitudes of Mexico City residents still shopped on these downtown streets for their children's first shoes or to purchase the food, electronics, clothing, and general consumer goods sold in the fixed and street markets of the area—especially in a very hard-hit area called Tepito. The zones most destroyed, in short, were often the first stop for all but a few of the city's wealthy elites, who were dispersed to the far ends of the metropolitan area; and this meant that the earthquake affected almost every principal cultural, political, and economic institution in the city. Thus the question arises: how does a city recover from a disaster of this social and physical magnitude? And also, to return to some of the themes of this inquiry, *what* exactly does it recover?

One way to answer these questions is to think primarily in physical terms. Yet on this account, the record is not entirely clear. To be sure, if one were to visit Mexico City today, roughly twenty years after the earthquake, there would be significant evidence of major building reconstruction and restoration. The residential areas hardest hit by the quake now boast more than 48,000 new or fully reconstructed housing units, provided by a program called Renovación Habitacional Popular.[3] This program has been routinely lauded for its successes, with its achievements recognized in the form of several international awards for its capacity to redesign housing and transfer ownership in accordance with the immediate housing needs, property rights claims, and cultural and historical significance of the affected areas. Additionally, much headway has been made in terms of repairing many of the estimated 240 damaged government buildings, or relocating government services to alternative sites so as to facilitate long sought-after goals of decentralizing public administration out of the central city. More than 150,000 public employees eventually had their work successfully relocated elsewhere.[4]

However, the short- and long-term successes in reconstructing housing and recovering government services delivery have not been matched in all affected realms. A considerable number of the privately owned buildings damaged by the quake were not fully recovered; several were still visibly damaged more than fifteen years after the quake. This was especially true for a good portion (though clearly not all) of the downtown hotels and private office buildings. Many of those damaged by the earthquake were not attended to for years, and some closed down immediately while others went out of business within a few years. This was especially so for those appealing to a more modest clientele, that is, locally owned and operated hotels or offices servicing Mexican nationals, not international hotel chains catering to foreign tourists. But even some of the larger hotels catering to the more affluent crowds were not refurbished until after 2000, as the city saw the beginnings of a downtown real estate boom.

The record on reconstruction of the housing stock also was mixed, despite the large number of new apartments offered by the Housing Renovation Program. This owed to the fact that these new apartments were not always built as physical replacements for the existing (but damaged) housing stock, due mainly to ambiguities in ownership and tenure. Much of this housing stock was owned by absentee landlords who had nothing to gain from the Housing Renovation Program, which offered housing ownership options as a lure to move long-standing residents away from damaged buildings into new housing stock.[5] In fact, landlords who owned these downtown properties and had for years written them off as productive investments, owing to more than four decades of rent control, preferred to wait until the longer-term effects of the Housing Renovation Program heated up the local land market enough to raise the value of their practically worthless lots. This, in turn, meant that a good number of the damaged apartment buildings remained standing during the long process of property rights transfer, despite the construction of new housing alternatives. Of the affected buildings that remained standing, some continued to serve their original functions, even in their damaged state. Residents preferred to stay in less than perfect quarters despite the comfort (and ownership) sacrifices this entailed if it meant being able to live in proximity to downtown. Other buildings remained completely abandoned, however. A couple of areas not far from the downtown railroad station covering a two- to three-block area remained in a state of pure destruction, although they were a stone's throw from downtown areas that were entirely reconstructed. In short, in a purely physical sense, even the housing reconstruction record appears mixed at best.

Some of this clearly has to do with the scarcity of public and private funds for reconstruction, an issue related to financing as well as to the magnitude of the damage. At the time, disaster research experts considered this earthquake to be one of the most destructive and economically costly of the century in terms of overall loss, exceeded only by San Francisco in 1906 and Tokyo in 1923, with estimates for reconstruction and rehabilitation costs hovering between $5 and 10 billion.[6] But it goes without saying that the source and character of financing for reconstruction directly shapes recovery and affects what gets recovered and by whom. Another thing to consider, of course, is the time frame of reference. In a period of twenty or so years, is it reasonable to expect full reconstruction and recovery? Perhaps not. Even taking into consideration the very real temporal and financial limitations on reconstruction generally, it still is worth pondering the record of partial reconstruction in Mexico City, especially if it reflects other dynamics, such as the urban, political, and economic context of this disaster.

Mexico City's earthquake hit right in the midst of a deepening economic crisis, which placed limits on financial resources—both public and private—for the city's reconstruction. Even more important, the spatial location in which the earthquake occurred also affected reconstruction and recovery efforts. And this meant that in addition to the economic situation in Mexico, the contested cultural, social, and economic character of Mexico City's downtown areas, as well as the administrative capacity of the local and national governments both downtown and citywide, directly affected the dynamics of recovery, producing mixed results.

This chapter explores this mixed record by explaining what was reconstructed or recovered in Mexico City after its earthquake, what wasn't, and why, and asking whether—given its mixed record of reconstruction—Mexico City should qualify as a resilient city. The inquiry is organized around three interrelated propositions that guide the discussion of Mexico City's post-earthquake recovery and resilience and situate it in the larger themes of this volume.

I begin with the initial proposition that a city is more than its buildings, and thus resilience must be understand as more than physical reconstruction. I then turn to two additional propositions: reconstruction is not necessarily recovery (or vice versa), and resilience is not always a good thing (and can even be a bad thing). The chapter concludes with more general remarks about how, given the record on recovery and resilience presented here, we might analyze and rethink the longer-term significance of trauma and physical crisis in cities. In order to know whether or not a city is resilient, and in order to make sense of what was or was not recovered or restored after a disaster, it is absolutely critical to both recognize and embrace the idea that a city is much more than its buildings. Put another way, cities are not just built environments: they are composed of people, social and political institutions, economic activities, and infrastructure; they have histories and symbolic meanings; and they generally are internally differentiated in social and spatial terms, so that different parts of the city often host different concentrations of these attributes or activities. Mexico City's earthquake exposed this claim in ways that no text or body of theories could.

The 1985 earthquake had multiple reverberations in all aspects of life and livelihood in Mexico City, ranging from political and economic to social and spatial. And this meant that struggles over and plans for post-earthquake reconstruction and recovery were very much struggles over the city itself: its meaning and the institutions and practices that were to give it life, form, and character in the days, months, and years after the earthquake. When the September 19 and 20 quakes shook Mexico, it was immediately obvious to both the government and Mexico City citizens that one of the most pressing problems to be addressed was the fact that the daily routine of urban life for almost all of the city's residents had been completely disrupted if not irredeemably transformed. This entailed disruption of key commercial services (food, consumer goods, and so on), the provision of urban services throughout the metropolitan area, and the routine patterns of urban governance. For days and sometimes weeks or longer, hundreds of thousands of people had no homes, no work, no transportation, no food, no water, no telephones, no hospitals to visit for treatment of the wounded, no place to bury their dead, and no reliable authorities to whom they could turn for assistance.[7] This was the case not just because of the high Richter scale magnitude of the earthquake, but because by hitting the center of the city, most of the services and institutions that sustained the city as a whole were disabled if not destroyed. This state of affairs owed to the history of urban development in Mexico, which had preserved the traditional character of the center city, centralized its key institutions and services, and prevented the outward movement of its residential populations and public institutions.[8] Had an earthquake of the exact same enormity pounded any other spatial location in the metropolitan area, the magnitude of the urban disruption would not have been as great. Perhaps then the main task at hand would have been to think about replacing buildings. But because the hardest hit area was the metropolitan center—which was also the center of the entire country—a multiplicity of essential services, economic activities, and institutions were at risk.

Important communications and electricity providers were concentrated in the area decimated by the earthquake, and their disruption affected the administrative capacity to restore services to the entire metropolitan area. Through the damage incurred by one single building in downtown Mexico City, local, national, and international telephone service for the city was completely suspended. As Elena Poniatowska asked incredulously in her compelling ethnography of the earthquake, "How is it possible that 55,000 branches that connect the south with the north of the country and the whole country with the world were all concentrated in one single old building on Victoria Street?"[9] A large majority of the city's electricity substations were also in these central areas, leading to power outages for an extended period of time. Also, almost all of the metropolitan area's transport services were paralyzed, especially buses, since they crisscrossed the center of the city. Subway service was also disrupted, albeit temporarily, because it depended on electricity.

The city's main medical institutions were also affected by the earthquake, since many of these public medical services were located in an area that housed the Centro Médico. Along with most of the city's secondary schools,[10] all of the city's principal medical services were concentrated in the hardest-hit areas. Five major hospitals were destroyed and twenty-two were damaged, leading to disruption of 30 percent of the entire city's medical capacities.[11] With the city's major public health services suspended or disrupted, the government lost much of its capacity to respond to the medical crisis, creating yet a new set of social and health problems and concerns for authorities.

Granted, officials and citizens ultimately constructed makeshift locations for treatment of the injured, and the three most damaged medical buildings were by no means the only hospitals in the city. But they were the principal ones. Moreover, these particular institutions had special symbolic presence and meaning for the city's residents, representing one of the most lauded social services provided to the public by Mexico's postrevolutionary state. When the medical center's obstetrics unit was all but destroyed, and a few newborns and orphaned infants were found clinging to their lives in the face of death, dust, and destruction, scores of residents streamed to the familiar halls of these public hospitals to offer their services and to aid the doctors who, historically, had played an important role in both serving the public and challenging the Mexican state in years past.[12]

The fact that so many key services were disrupted or destroyed posed a recovery problem for the authorities, as did citizens' natural instincts to become involved in restoring them, since this created an additional management challenge. Differences of opinion further stalled the process. Most government officials felt that reconstruction efforts should be targeted toward the immediate restoration of economic services and activities as much as housing. Shelter, of course, was a concern, but with the government's eye on essential services there was little initial attention paid to the issue of temporary shelter. The neglect of basic shelter needs motivated those without homes to start making vocal demands on the government. Complicating matters most was the fact that within the urban population, different groups held different priorities; those in the farther reaches of the metropolitan area pushed authorities to restore services, while those within the most damaged areas sought shelter and medical services. This, too, complicated government decision making about how to distribute disaster relief funds.

Some disagreement about recovery priorities should be expected, of course. But with the Mexico City earthquake, there were a large number of conflicting priorities because of the location of the earthquake and the spatial concentration of its effects in downtown areas. If the area hit by physical destruction had preserved only one key function, or if the earthquake had destroyed only houses or businesses or services, authorities would have been better able to prioritize and develop a coherent or easily implementable plan for reconstruction. In the Mexican case, reconstruction was determined as much by political pressures as by questions of efficiency or a coherent rebuilding plan.

Despite conflicting social, political, and economic priorities, the government eventually did restore most of the key services that gave the city its social and economic dynamism. But reconstruction and restoration unfolded unevenly, affecting various parts of the city differently, initially following a logic of money and power. This meant, for example, that the government first devoted its energies to those services, like telephones and electricity, that allowed the economic wheels of the city to start moving again, often at the expense of attention to the primary food and shelter demands of the most damaged areas. It also meant that infrastructural and recovery services geared toward small-scale producers were not high on the priority list, despite the fact that they were heavily concentrated in earthquake areas. Some of this owed to the fact that these small-scale producers did not hold political or social power in the ruling party (the Partido Revolucionario Institucional, or PRI) that governed Mexico's capital city and the nation as a whole. But it also stemmed from the fact that the PRI-led government was most concerned about restoring the functioning and reputation of the capital city as a whole, which threatened to shut down in its entirety owing to myriad service disruptions emanating outward from the center. For the PRI, then, damaged areas downtown—and their populations and buildings specifically—were to be treated first if their recovery helped in this larger urban recovery aim, not merely because they were the most damaged parts of the city.

Part of the logic underlying these decisions was that if Mexico were to keep its macroeconomic standing vis-à-vis the international lending community, big ticket concerns like the financial and large-scale manufacturing services, neither of which were downtown but both of which were dependent on electricity and phones, needed to be revived immediately. That this became an overriding reconstruction concern owed in no small part to the fact that Mexico City had long served as the nation's economic engine of growth. It also owed to the highly centralized character of Mexico's political system, which gave the president the power to subordinate local reconstruction efforts to larger macroeconomic aims, especially those at the national level. This became quite evident even to capital city residents when President Miguel de la Madrid initially insisted that Mexico did not need and would not accept any foreign aid to help recovery from the earthquake. On September 24, five days after the first quake, the president publicly stated that the earthquake would "complicate the management of Mexico's foreign debt."[13] A Harvard-trained economist, de la Madrid had come to the presidency with great plans to recover from the 1982 debt crisis, mainly by fostering more liberalization of the economy and working closely with the International Monetary Fund (IMF). In the three years prior to the earthquake, he was considered to have made great headway toward this goal. When the earthquake hit, concern about preserving progress on economic liberalization drove his initial decision to shun foreign aid. Eventually, de la Madrid retreated from this stance, but the delay stalled reconstruction, lost essential time, and unnecessarily angered citizens. Moreover, since the World Bank provided many of the loans for recovery (more than $500 million), this further fueled citizens' suspicions that the administration was concerned with recovery only for macroeconomic purposes.[14] So too did the events surrounding First Lady Nancy Reagan's personal handing over of a check for $1 million to aid in the recovery to President de la Madrid. "Once endorsed the check was given back to Nancy, asking her to credit it to the national debt, since during the time that it took to get the pen out and sign, the debt grew by $12 million because of interest."[15]

Medical services came next in order of attention, but only after many resources were devoted to policing the city in order to stop looting and other crimes against property. This stance raised questions among some citizens, who felt it reflected undue concern for the wealthy and the primacy of the market and disregarded human suffering. Again, the administration's concerns about economic liberalization and foreign investors may have played a role in these calculations about policing. They also factored into health-care systems' recovery. Even before the earthquake hit, the de la Madrid administration had been struggling against opposition from citizens and health professionals to the decentralization of the country's health care system, as part and parcel of the president's plan to decentralize public financing and services.[16] Thus, when the government turned to the recovery of health services, it used the opportunity to push forward the original decentralization plans in ways that smacked of opportunism. It was only at the end of this list of other priorities, then, that the government acknowledged the need to provide temporary shelter. And when this did occur, the government initially paid much greater attention to the middle-class areas of the city damaged by the quake, including Colonia Roma, than to the poorer tenement areas of downtown.

Over the long term, plans for renovated housing for poorer folks displaced from downtown areas were essentially implemented quite successfully. Initially this program was not on the agenda, however. Originally, authorities mandated that reconstruction funds be used only for schools and hospitals.[17] They approved the new program for housing renovation only eighteen months later. Until then, most of those displaced who later received housing were living in tents. Many remained there indefinitely, with the last temporary shelters disappearing fifteen full years after the original quake.

The failure to deal with popular housing in the initial post-earthquake period had major repercussions on a variety of levels. In addition to fueling general dissatisfaction, the early public inattention to downtown housing reconstruction meant that even private investors did not rush to recover, redevelop, or reinvest in downtown areas. They had little incentive to invest in restoring hotels, offices, and other damaged buildings until people were out of makeshift housing, which created a low-rent character in the area, and until property rights issues were resolved. This further explains why many damaged downtown properties were left untouched, with both vacant and half-vacant lots peppering the city for more than a decade.

Even as it dragged its feet on housing, a much more concerted effort was made by the government to rebuild or recover the major offices of the ruling party and the government, many of which had been seriously damaged or destroyed. In his initial tours of the damaged areas, moreover, President de la Madrid made a great effort to visit building sites and assess physical damage. It did not go unnoticed that he did not visit any of the victims nor meet with displaced citizens.[18] These stances further alienated citizens, who felt that people should come before the party/state in any recovery plan. To be sure, in a disaster of this magnitude, everything cannot be recovered, and again there are the issues of cost, which limits reconstruction efforts. But it is not necessarily the case that only rich cities can recover from disasters because they have the resources to reconstruct or restore multiple activities, areas, and buildings. Recovery—and perhaps even resiliency—also has to do with establishing legitimacy, which means understanding and responding in some fashion to the priorities that citizens hold for their city. Such concerns entail a concerted effort at social and political reconstruction, not just physical reconstruction. And if a government or other reconstruction actors have legitimacy—even if physical reconstruction is uneven and slow—citizens will not necessarily feel that recovery has been thwarted or denied. The fact that most residents in Mexico City felt denied both in the immediate aftermath as well as years down the road (even though some reconstruction eventually did materialize) directly affected the recovery efforts and their longer-term impact on the city.

Mexico's governing authorities clearly believed that recovery of the city's economic functions, which depended on reassuring external lenders and investors, was as important (if not more so) than the reconstruction of buildings. But it is also important to emphasize here that—from the citizens' perspective—reconstruction was not the same as recovery. Citizens wanted to recover or restore many other things besides their homes. In particular, what became most evident during the days and weeks after the earthquake was that citizens were eager to recover what they called "dignity," as well as government accountability. These two important aspects of government legitimacy mattered as much as buildings in the everyday dynamics of urban life.

To be sure, the active struggles of citizens to recover both dignity and accountability ultimately helped ensure that the government would eventually reconstruct their houses; the same social movements that gave life to these accountability concerns also empowered the struggle for housing. And in that sense, there is some relationship between physical reconstruction and recovery. But for a series of reasons, including the fact that the earthquake exposed in ways never seen before the existing institutional structures of power, authority, and abuse that destroyed the meaning of the city for many of its residents, attending to corrupt political and institutional practices became recovery priorities in and of themselves. One of the most high-profile discoveries in the aftermath of the earthquake was the exposure of clandestine garment factories peppered through downtown areas. Many were concentrated on one street, San Antonio Abad, where single buildings of seven or eight stories each held as many as fifty-five different garment factories. When the earthquake hit, these buildings collapsed under the weight of the sewing machines and heavy rolls of textiles crammed into old dilapidated structures. One particular eleven-story downtown building that collapsed in the first early morning quake held a group of seamstresses, mainly young girls and women who had been working all night. For months prior to the event they had been trying, to no avail, to organize themselves in order to demand better working conditions. The earthquake did more than expose the horrendous conditions under which they were working; citizens became enraged because, when the earthquake hit, the local governing authorities immediately sent in police to protect the garment factory owner as he—with police help—salvaged the machines and sewing equipment, leaving scores of injured women and bodies buried under the rubble without any attempt to extricate them. This highly publicized incident came to represent the ways that residents of the city had been exploited in life, through collusion between downtown business interests and authorities, and were exploited even in death. As one survivor put it, "My family was not killed by the earthquake; what killed them was the fraud and corruption fostered by the government."[19] This sort of realization not only spurred a delegitimization of government authorities, but also motivated citizens to shun government assistance and attempt to recover their own forms of urban justice.

The earthquake also exposed serious violations in construction standards, motivating residents to shun government help even in this time of crisis. Many of the buildings that collapsed were not old buildings, but those that had been constructed relatively recently, between 1950 and 1970, during the heyday of government-led public construction. A good number of the most decimated buildings, in fact, were the massive public housing projects built for middle-class workers, like the Nuevo Leon building at the Tlatelolco housing complex and the Multifamiliar Juarez. In the Tlatelolco-Nonoalco complex alone, 43 out of 102 buildings were completely destroyed.[20] This destruction, tragic in itself, highlighted a corrupt government's failure to comply with building standards and its use of low-quality construction materials.

The earthquake also exposed two other noteworthy examples of government exploitation and abuse, which further intensified citizens' efforts to restore dignity and accountability. The first was the discovery of numerous bodies, many of them showing evidence of torture, in the basements of various collapsed police stations and other public build-

The Politics of Reconstruction

Figure 11.4.
Miguel Aleman housing
project, 1985. Photo by
Jorge Núñez.

ings in the city. The second was the initial decision by authorities to use some of the earthquake reconstruction aid to repay Mexico's foreign debt, something that was seen as helping the country's financial institutions and elite at the expense of the thousands of (mainly poor) citizens who were left homeless. It was bad enough that the government first refused to accept foreign aid for the earthquake, but to then appropriate these belated funds for the country's banking elite only added insult to injury.

At its core, the earthquake conveyed a larger message about the meaning and character of the city itself: Mexico City had been treated for far too long as a place—or conglomeration of spaces and practices—where privileged people got rich on the backs of modest residents, and where people were abused (even to death) by authorities who acted in collusion with the nation's economic elite. This surely oversimplifies the situation but, for many citizens, the earthquake's trauma generated just this kind of interpretation and lasting memories.

Reverberations

Moreover, until a few years after the earthquake, Mexico City citizens had been denied the rights of mayoral elections and democratic participation in the governance of the capital city. Thus the earthquake also became a catalyst for Mexico City's citizens to do something about this political situation and to actively recover urban accountability, justice, and dignity. The reconstruction of buildings paled in relation to these larger goals.

Within days of the earthquake, people began to organize on their own and reclaim the city for themselves by taking over the business of recovery and reconstruction without assistance from government authorities.[21] Their efforts ensured that certain activities were recovered or restored, ranging from housing to medical services (many public sector doctors set up makeshift triage units near their homes or in subway stations). With these actions, citizens consistently highlighted social justice and equity concerns, in direct contrast to the government's elitist approach.[22] Most important, citizens' self-organization around recovery efforts in turn produced lasting changes in the politics of this city. In the words of Elena Poniatowska, when citizens asked, "Is it possible that we can still believe in the efficacy of the government when, at the crucial moment, it was the people who did everything?" their answer was a resounding no.[23] When they stopped believing in the current government, they began to struggle for a new one, forming more expanded social movements, new tenants' rights organizations (especially in Guerrero), and new economic coops—thirty-seven in the badly hit downtown barrio of Tepito alone—with the aim of governing and caring for themselves.[24]

The proliferation of social movements and self-help organizations also had longer-term impacts, including a slow but steady change in both the practices and the form of Mexico City's government, not to mention the housing composition and spatial structure of the city itself.[25] Out of the post-earthquake ashes, Mexico City saw a new coordinated movement of citizens' organizations, which boldly demanded a "right" to housing. Their existence motivated subsequent governments to introduce new housing stock in areas of the city that had long been neglected. The housing rights movement, moreover, served as a central political force in subsequent struggles for the democratic reform of the city government. And when the PRI finally caved in to citizens' demands on this issue, many of those who had honed their political skills and social networks in these social movements became the key political base for the city's first democratically elected administration in more than sixty years.[26]

Of course, it would be a mistake to suggest that the widely cast recovery efforts guided by social movements were only targeted at non-material aims, like dignity, accountability, and political or democratic reform. Citizens also struggled to recover their lives, their social networks, and their places of work, as well as to bring new political leaders into city government. Yet, these aims were not always consistent with building reconstruction aims, due to the peculiar mixed character and modes of land use in downtown areas. For example, a good proportion of those who joined neighborhood associations and social movements in the aftermath of the earthquake were interested in recovering the urban economic life they had before the earthquake, which meant a return to street vending, small-scale commercial activities, and traditional land-use patterns, which mixed small-scale commercial and residential land use. This did not always square with the larger aims of the city's political leadership. Moreover, some of the most ardent advocates of housing reconstruction were those who saw this as a necessary first step toward the recovery of yet another possible potential land use for downtown areas—a higher-scale commercial, office, and tourist center, as in other major urban areas.

Figure 11.5.
Displaced residents encamped at the Tlatelolco housing project, 1985. Photo by Jorge Núñez.

In short, the earthquake fundamentally shook the foundations of political and economic life, producing a conflict over what exactly should be recovered, in terms of social and economic activities. This conflict had implications for the character, type, and scale of building reconstruction as well as for recovery more generally. And in many ways, the recovery and reconstruction process as a whole revolved as much around hopes for what the city could or should be in the future as around what it had been in the past. Many of these issues came to the surface in the housing renovation program itself, which reflected these competing interests. On one hand—and for political reasons, relating to the strength of social movement organizations that materialized among downtown residents—the authorities committed to rebuilding homes for low-income, downtown residents, despite being under pressure from real estate forces and some planners to move them elsewhere in the city. But at the same time, in the process they also revised the property rights of many of these long-standing residents, giving ownership options to people long under rent control restrictions. Building owners and real estate developers—not the residents themselves—advocated this tenure shift as a way to help along the process of downtown land revalorization.[27] In this sense, at least, the earthquake provided an opportunity to lay the foundations for a more substantial reconstruction and renovation of downtown areas, fifteen to twenty years down the road. Along with the political reforms in local government and the new political leadership in the city that emerged in the aftermath of increased social mobilization, this transformation in property rights and land usage was one of the most lasting consequences of the earthquake.

The story so far underscores the possibility that in the Mexico City case, the notion of resilience might be applied as much to the people as to the city itself. While the resilience of Mexico City's citizens is something to be lauded, it is worth pondering whether or not Mexico's capital city would have experienced the political and spatial transformations that now define it without the tragedy of the earthquake. After living under decades of nondemocratic government, with urban conditions deteriorating, perhaps an earthquake was just the visceral catalyst Mexico City residents needed to spur them into action. After all, Mexican citizens had long organized themselves to make demands on the government, but this had propped up the government more than challenged it, in no small part because citizens were willing to give the government the benefit of the doubt in terms of showing its responsiveness to their claims and needs.[28] The earthquake seemed to put an end to this cycle of protest and cooptation, perhaps because the government's failures and incapacities to respond to citizens were so blatant—or perhaps because the extent of death and destruction wrought by the earthquake was felt so deeply that citizens threw all caution to the wind and took their lives into their own hands.

In the face of trauma, there are always multiple resiliences, and different people and different activities may be resilient in ways that do not necessarily contribute to recovery. Not only can conflict emerge in the face of multiple resiliences, but the more specific evidence from the case of Mexico City shows that it was precisely the resilience of some of the most corrupt and unjust people and institutions in the capital that made the post-earthquake recovery and reconstruction efforts so dreadful, at least initially. Indeed, among the most resilient forces were the local police, the army, and the political leadership of the PRI, which governed the city and the nation. In the days and weeks immediately after the earthquake, these groups actively struggled to reinforce their own positions and practices, using the earthquake and the trauma it produced among citizens to strengthen their power base.

This unabashed resiliency of some of the city's most authoritarian and least laudable forces took several forms. Even after so much death, destruction, and human and physical trauma, business as usual seemed to continue. Police looted cadavers and buildings, and government authorities made no effort to stop them. The army distributed blankets and other rescue supplies among its soldiers rather than passing them to earthquake victims. Government-appointed authorities (in customs and elsewhere) took bribes for the delivery of rescue equipment, sold rescue materials, and skimmed money out of the coffers of rescue aid.[29] Many citizens reported being forced to pay bribes to police in order to get the bodies of their loved ones or to return to their homes.

Yet it was not just the resilience of corruption that was so troubling in the aftermath of the earthquake. The ruling party also seemed intent on showing that it was business as usual, not just with respect to macroeconomic policy, but in its efforts to wield power and authority over citizens. The PRI's resolve in this regard seemed to strengthen as citizens themselves began organizing in reaction to the failures and corruption in the clean-up. Less than a week after the initial quake, the government officially declared that only governmental authorities— not neighborhood organizations—had the right to assist with rescue and clean-up.[30] Some of this concern surely owed to the confusion and chaos generated by thousands of volunteers who showed up to aid in the efforts.[31] But much of it owed to the government's fear that social mobilization would be used to lay blame at the evident incompetence of authorities and, worse yet, to politically challenge the government for its failures. President de la Madrid, in fact, publicly acknowledged this when he announced that, in addition to establishing emergency programs, the government was going to work actively to stop citizens who "used the legitimate demands of residents for purposes of social agitation."[32]

Ultimately most of these offensive postures backfired, because citizens continued to mobilize and to decry government incompetence and heavy-handedness, despite subsequent efforts to show some responsiveness to the crisis and to the overall concerns of citizens. Neither a continual reshuffling of Mexico City authorities in the weeks and months after the disaster nor the resignation of the government's secretary of Housing and Urban Development within a year of the quake could stem the intense tide of dissatisfaction and political opposition. A year after the earthquake, more than one-third of Mexico City's citizens still held a negative view of the handling of the crisis. They most consistently maligned the police and military, but they also criticized the Mexico City government authorities and the president himself.[33] Even moderate political observers and academic commentators later questioned the wisdom of government efforts to stifle, or "pacify," the increasingly active citizenry.[34] It may have been precisely the bullheaded resilience of the authoritarian PRI and its corrupt policing and administrative apparatus—as exposed by the earthquake—that led to the defeat of the ruling party in both the city and the nation several years later. That is, the eventual defeat of the PRI emerged in the context of the struggle between resilient citizens and this surprisingly resilient state. Thus it might be more accurate to say that the desire of each to direct or dominate the recovery and reconstruction process together led to the political transformation of the city and the nation.

Given the disastrous results for the government in charge, one may well ask: why did authorities continue to pursue actions that so clearly alienated citizens? Why did the PRI and its administrative apparatus try to remain resilient, especially in times of trauma and especially when that resiliency entailed corrupt and unprincipled actions that led to delegitimation, mobilized social opposition, and political defeat? Part of the answer to these questions might rest on a closer understanding of the nondemocratic nature of the Mexican state. One could speculate that the corrupt and abusive practices of this state were so well entrenched and institutionalized that even in the face of trauma, they were immutable. Yet one also could argue that it was precisely the extent of the crisis and trauma that reinforced or perhaps even produced these problems. Indeed, the highly centralized and hierarchical character of one-party rule had created an entrenched bureaucracy that was rigid and highly inflexible, with all directives controlled from above, on the level not just of the city but also of the nation. When faced with a local crisis of this dimension, one that called for rapid and flexible decision making and response, Mexico City authorities were unable (and maybe even politically unwilling, at first) to rise to the occasion. And their failures in these regards are precisely what angered many citizens and led many to take matters into their own hands. It may be worth considering, then, that in highly traumatic situations, like earthquakes and other major physical disasters that hit cities, authorities in highly centralized political systems are more likely to fall back on routine behavior, making them incapable of responding to the new circumstances. And if routine behavior is predicated on a hierarchical structure of political decision making, authorities may actually fail to address the challenge of major crises adequately. Their "resilience"—expressed as an insistence on continuing business as usual—may prevent them from acting in ways that most constructively promote recovery and reconstruction.

If resilience cannot inherently be seen as good or bad, what should we be talking about when we examine cities that experience major disasters? It may make best sense to focus on what gets transformed rather than on what parts return to the pre-disaster status quo. But how then should we understand the character or extent of change in a post-disaster situation? This is where the notion of resilience is still helpful, especially if that transformation comes in response to conflicting or multiple resiliences, which together set parameters for how cities recover from disaster.

The Mexican case can be conceptualized as a competition among citizens and authorities, each of them resilient in some fashion. This enabled the earthquake to be truly transformative of urban life, politics, and society. The massive tremors themselves—and the ways in which the authorities responded to them—empowered urban citizens to mobilize on their own behalf to challenge a corrupt and highly bureaucratized local government. It also exposed the political biases of government authorities, diminishing their legitimacy in the eyes of citizens. Together, these developments hastened a grassroots challenge to the power of the ruling party in Mexico City, bringing about an urban democratic reform and, eventually, the defeat of the old guard politicians and the election of a leftist mayor committed to housing and employment for the city's low-income residents. Both of these changes helped to signal the end to one-party rule in the nation as a whole, owing to the demise of the PRI in the social, political, and economic center of the capital.[11] The reverberations of the earthquake, in short, were deep and long lasting, and they extended far beyond the built environment to the social and political life of the city.

Of course, all change is neither unassailable nor only for the good. The earthquake also exposed fissures in the capacity of downtown residents to retain central areas of the city for small-scale commerce and low-income housing, and led to large-scale investment in tourism and financial activities, which are starting to displace long-standing residents. The earthquake—and the renovated housing that was eventually constructed under the new property rights regime—also produced new conflicts and divisions among downtown residents, including an explosion of violence among street vendors that has reached new heights in recent years. As a result, Mexico City now faces new pressures to gentrify local property markets, and the displacement of residents has become a problem of great proportions, as big investors now find opportunities in downtown properties. The direction of these changes in the built environment is still unclear, and it is not certain that the major reconstruction of hotels, tourist establishments, and financial headquarters, which many investors want, will actually materialize. It all depends on the continued resilience of advocates and downtown opponents. In any event, Mexico's capital might never have arrived at this point if the earthquake had not shaken the city's foundations so deeply.

Notes

1. These figures come from Elena Poniatowska's *Nothing, Nobody: The Voices of the Mexico City Earthquake* (Philadelphia: Temple University Press, 1995), pp. 16, 21.
2. For these and other figures, see Russell R. Dynes, E. L. Quarantelli, and Dennis Wenger, *Individual and Organizational Responses to the 1985 Earth-*

quake in Mexico City, Mexico (Newark: Disaster Research Center, University of Delaware, 1990), pp. 3–4.

3. For more details on the program, see Marcelo Ebrard and Jorge Gamboa de Buen, "Reconstruction in Central Mexico City after the 1985 Earthquake," *Ekistics* 346 (January–February 1991): 18–27.

4. Dynes, Quarantelli, and Wenger, *Individual and Organizational Responses*, p. 4.

5. Owing to rent control laws first introduced in the 1940s, few downtown buildings were owner-occupied. In some instances, owners had relinquished an interest in these properties for so long that when their residents were turned out into the streets by the earthquake or offered new housing in alternative spots, the original owners failed to materialize.

6. Dynes, Quarantelli, and Wenger, *Individual and Organizational Responses*, p. 4.

7. This assessment draws from a general reading of several personal and official published chronicles. Generally speaking, the most informative chronicles were included in Elena Poniatowska's *Nothing, Nobody*; Adolfo Aguilar Zinser, Cesáreo Morales, and Rodolfo Peña, eds., *Aún tiembla: Sociedad política y cambio social: El terremoto del 19 de Septiembre 1985* (Mexico City: Grijalba, 1986); and Presidencia de la República, *Terremotos de Septiembre: Sobretiro de las razones y las obras crónica del sexenio 1982–1888* (Mexico City: Fondo de Cultura Economica, 1986).

8. For a historical account of the politics of growth and land use patterns in Mexico City, see Diane Davis, *Urban Leviathan: Mexico City in the Twentieth* Century (Philadelphia: Temple University Press, 1994).

9. Poniatowska, *Nothing, Nobody*, p. 32.

10. Dynes, Quarantelli, and Wenger, *Individual and Organizational Responses*, p. 4, report that more than half of the city's 3,000 public schools suffered "structural and/or non-structural damage, interrupting the education of over 650,000 children according to some reports."

11. Ibid., p. 5.

12. Some of the most important strikes and challenges to the authoritarian government in the 1960s were led by doctors, either on their own or in alliance with prodemocracy students. Historically speaking, the social programs of the postrevolutionary state revolved mainly around the expansion of medical services, much of which can be traced to the active social and political role of doctors who took positions in the government to lead these efforts.

13. Quoted in Dynes, Quarantelli, and Wenger, *Individual and Organizational Responses*, p. 26.

14. The destruction of downtown areas and monuments did indeed cut directly into Mexico's foreign exchange earnings. Tourism has long been Mexico's second-largest export item, after oil.

15. Poniatowska, *Nothing, Nobody*, p. 99.

16. For more on this issue, see Guillermo Soberón, Julio Frenk, and Jaime Sepúlveda, "The Health Care Reform in Mexico: Before and After the 1985 Earthquake," *American Journal of Public Health* 76, no. 6 (1986): 673–680.

17. Antonio Ortigoza Aranda, Luis Granovosky, and Ruben Paz Hurtado (with the collaboration of Roberto Macías Ballesteros, Silva Hernández Martínez, Carlos Vázquez Cargallo, and Angel Madrid Valderrábano), *19 Negro: Génesis del terremoto en México* (Mexico City: Editorial Roma, 1985), p. 173.

18. Poniatowska, *Nothing, Nobody*, p. 32.

19. Ibid., p. 78. For more on the factory sweatshops, see ibid., pp. 142–144.

20. Dynes, Quarantelli, and Wenger, *Individual and Organizational Responses*, p. 4.

21. Poniatowska, *Nothing, Nobody*, p. 193. For a more general analysis of urban popular organization after the earthquake, see Juan Briseno Guerrero and Ludka Gortari Kraus, *De la cama a la calle: Sismos y organización popular* (Mexico City: Centro de Investigaciones y Estudios Superiores en Antropología Social, 1987); and Alejandra Massolo and Martha Schteingart, *Participación social, reconstrucción, y mujer: El sismo de 1985* (Mexico City: El Colegio de Mexico, 1987). For a focused discussion on one of the important organizations that got stronger in the aftermath of the earthquake, the Asamblea de Barrios, see Angelica Cuellar Vazquez's *La noche es de ustedes, el amanecer es nuestro: Asamblea de Barrios y superbarrio Gomez en la ciudad de México* (Mexico City: UNAM, 1993).

22. The case of the recovery actions by doctors is quite interesting in this regard. One of the contentious issues in the debate over the decentralization of public health services had been whether to continue supporting the Hospital Juarez, one of the hospitals destroyed in the earthquake. One of the issues at stake was whether it would continue as a teaching and research hospital with services open to the public. The liberal reformers in the government sought to privatize these services to a great extent, and doctors affiliated with this hospital opposed this change. These same doctors were quite active in freely offering their services to the injured in the days and weeks after the earthquake. For more on this, see Poniatowska, *Nothing, Nobody*, pp. 160–165.

23. Ibid., p. 97.

24. Ibid., pp. 270, 281.

25. For more on this, see Armando Cisneros, "Organizaciones sociales en la reconstrucción habitacional de la ciudad de México," *Estudios Demográficos y Urbanos* 3, no. 2 (May–August 1988): 339–352; Jorge Gamboa de Buen and Jose Angonio Revah Locoutery, "Reconstrucción y política urbana en la Ciudad de México," *Foro Internacional* 30, no. 4 (1990): 677–694; and Ernesto Ortega Valadez, "Reflexiones sobre los efectos del sismo en la organización vicinal," *Estudios Demográficos y Urbanos* 2, no. 1 (1987): 141–147.

The Politics of Reconstruction

26. This was initially evident in the first democratically elected mayoral administration of Cuauhtémoc Cardenas, who swept into office with the support of urban social movements and a commitment to reforming government around the urban political participation long demanded by social movement activists. His successor, Andres López Obrador, was even more linked to housing movement activists who emerged on the scene in the post-earthquake period not merely in the form of social movements, but as leaders of the program to distribute new housing in the city. For more on the longer-term constraints of having these social movement activists as their political base, see Arturo Alvarado and Diane Davis, "Citizen Participation, Democratic Governance, and the PRD in Mexico City: The Challenge of Political Transition," in *The Left and the City: Attempting Participatory Democracy in Latin America*, ed. Benjamin Goldfrank and Daniel Chavez (London: Latin America Bureau, 2003).

27. For more on the Programa de Renovación Habitacional Popular and its impact on land use and private property dynamics in Mexico City, see Emilio Duhau, "La formación de una política social: El caso del Programa de Renovación Habitacional Popular en la ciudad de México," *Estudios Demográficos y Urbanos* 2, no. 1 (1987): 75–99.

28. For elaboration of this argument about the historical relationship between citizen demand-making and government responsiveness, and how this worked over the last forty years in Mexico, see Diane Davis and Viviane Brachet Marquez, "Rethinking Democracy: Mexico in Historical Perspective," *Comparative Studies in Society and History* 31 (1997): 86–119.

29. This was reported in Poniatowska, *Nothing, Nobody*, pp. 83, 85.

30. Aranda, Granovsky, and Hurtado, *19 Negro*, p. 170. It also is worth noting that the Tlatelolco housing complex was the one stormed by authorities in the 1968 student movement protesting the Olympics, resulting in many deaths and defining the beginning of Mexico's own "dirty war." Thus these buildings embodied their own memories of repression and abuse, which combined with the newly exposed pattern of corruption to enrage citizens.

31. Dynes, Quarantelli, and Wenger, *Individual and Organizational Responses*, p. 40. Interviews demonstrate that government agents found the challenge of feeding and coordinating thousands of volunteers almost as great as that of helping victims.

32. Translation by author. De la Madrid is quoted in Adolfo Aguilar Zinser, "El temblor de la República y sus réplicas," in Zinser, Morales, and Peña, *Aún Tiembla*, p. 100.

33. Dynes, Quarantelli, and Wenger report that of the Mexico City residents sampled for their survey, 35 percent had an overall negative evaluation of the police, with 32.1 percent the corresponding figure for the military, 17 percent for the Mexico City authorities (i.e., Departamento del Distrito Federal [DDF]), and 10 percent for the president. Among the greatest complaints were that the police and military acted in a nonhumanitarian, non-

compassionate, and inappropriate way, while the authorities acted in an inappropriate and disorganized fashion (p. 94). A survey one year later failed to note any change in attitudes, at least about the president (p. 109). For more, see their study of the earthquake, *Individual and Organizational Responses*.

34. See, for example, Manuel Villa A., "La politización innecesaria: El régimen político mexicano y sus exigencias de pasividad ciudadana a los damnificados," *Estudios Demográficos y Urbanos* 2, no. 1 (1987): 27–51.

35. See Diane E. Davis, "Mexico City: The Local-Dynamics of Democratization," in *Capital City Politics in Latin America: Democratization and Empowerment*, ed. David J. Myers and Henry A. Dietz (Boulder, Colo., and London: Lynne Rienner Publishers, 2002), pp. 227–264.

A Vital Void

Reconstructions of Downtown Beirut

I looked this way and that way. I could not believe what I saw: level ground, empty, like an open palm of the hand, a horizontal expanse, leveled and paved over, its even surface unmarred by any stray objects or protrusions. . . . The sea, I said. I must find the sea. . . . If I cannot find the sea, then I am either dreaming or mad. I will walk down to the sea. From there, I will try to see where I am, pinpoint my location. And from there, I will figure out the direction the shop lies in, or I'll see some landmark, something to guide me, so I can reorient myself to go on.

—Hoda Barakat, *The Tiller of Waters*

12

HASHIM SARKIS

■ A few lines before the end of *The Tiller of Waters*, the protagonist, Nicholas Mitri, wakes up after his death in a void.[1] Once he orients himself, he realizes that this void is actually the center of Beirut that he has inhabited alone during the 1975–1990 civil war and that he has been desperately trying to narrate and preserve throughout the novel. Mitri, a Greek Orthodox man from the predominantly Muslim West Beirut, had been forced out of his house by Shiite Muslim refugees from South Lebanon who had, in turn, been displaced by an Israeli invasion. Homeless, he drifts to his father's textile shop in downtown Beirut, the contested battle zone between Christian East and Muslim West Beirut. There, he lives alone like Robinson Crusoe in the wilderness of the city center and recounts his family's story and the history of the different peoples and religious groups that inhabited his life and the prewar city.

The house where he lived with his Greek Alexandrian parents and with the Kurdish maid he loved, the shop owned by a Sunni Muslim next to his father's in the bazaar of downtown Beirut, and the parlor where his mother was trained by an Armenian piano teacher are all eventually wiped out—not by the war but by the reconstruction project. The void, at the end of the story, represents the futility of his efforts

281

to preserve the places. The buildings and streets, it turns out, are more fragile than the memories that inhabit them.

The civil war that entrapped Mitri was triggered in 1975 by disagreements between Lebanon's Christians and Muslims over the presence and power of the Palestinian militias in Lebanon. The war would briefly stop in 1977, with the intervention of Arab forces led by Syria, only to be resumed again, this time with the participation of the Syrians on the side of the Palestinians and Muslims. When the Israelis invaded Lebanon in 1982 to support the Christians and expel the Palestinians, the war took on an international scope with a failed American and European military intervention. The period between 1983 and 1990 witnessed a rapid deterioration of the Lebanese economy and a series of battles among Christian and Muslim militias. It was not until a Saudi-brokered constitutional amendment evened out the distribution of power between Christians and Muslims—and until the Americans reluctantly accepted Syrian hegemony over Lebanon—that the civil war officially came to an end in 1990. A decade and a half of war displaced more than half of Lebanon's population of 3 million and killed about 150,000 people. It also inflicted physical damage throughout the country and particularly in Beirut. Downtown Beirut stood as an evacuated demarcation area within the divided city throughout most of the violent and quiet chapters of the fifteen years of war.

Almost fifteen years after the war, the city center that had been cleared for new development is slowly being filled. The restoration work and the new road networks have been completed. Judging by the crowds that swarm the restaurants and shops of the restored quarters and by the high real estate prices, this restored district has been deemed a popular success. A residential neighborhood on the southeastern corner has been too brightly restored, as have the religious monuments. Based on the phasing of the master plan, the period between 2000 and 2008 is supposed to bring the most construction activity, reaching beyond 2 million square meters. Four years into this period, however, only a handful of new buildings have been added.

Significantly, Beirut is still looking for the shape of its old center and of its primary space, Martyrs' Square. The proposed designs for this important part of the city's center remain sketchy, and they vary from drawing to drawing in the technical plans and promotional brochures of SOLIDERE, the private real estate holding company in charge of the redevelopment of the city's center. One drawing shows a broad perspective opening toward the sea in the north, highlighting this rather than the activity in the square. Another favors the smooth flow of traffic, transforming the square into a boulevard. Yet another exaggerates the vegetation in the middle, turning it into a public garden. Based on the current or proposed adjacent uses, it is difficult to imagine a public space that could unify a mosque to its south, a Virgin megastore in its middle, and an archaeological glacis on the north. Collective space seems no longer possible.

During the ten years after the launch of the plan to rebuild the city center, thousands of articles and hundreds of books and reports were written against the clearing of downtown Beirut.[2] Many critics argue that the razing of about 85 percent of the buildings in the old center was unnecessary, especially since not all of them were damaged beyond repair. Critics also contend that handing over the development to a private real estate company was a way to exclude average land owners and tenant citizens from participating in the rebuilding of their city. Economically, the clearing has been criticized for being grandiose and unrealistic, incommensurate with the city's capacities to actually develop it. As in Hoda Barakat's novel, the clearing has also been associated with the political and psychological amnesia that followed the civil war. Instead of reconciling their differences, the fighting factions and religious sects have chosen not to come to terms with their belligerent past but to switch from military to tacit confrontation.

The physical clearing bore out some of the predictions of the critics. The reconstruction has been expensive and has resulted in a dramatic drop in the value of SOLIDERE's stock. It excluded average citizens and favored a more affluent clientele. The clearing was simply too extensive to be filled by an economy exhausted by international debt and regional conflicts. Yet there have been significant side and lag effects resulting from this strategy of rebuilding that are worth examining. Based on a study of the reconstruction from the early 1990s into the early twenty-first century, this chapter argues that the process of refilling the physical void of downtown Beirut has itself generated unexpected patterns of development that may be as important in the shaping of the postwar city as the reconstruction plans. These patterns are similar to those that have guided much of the construction in the rest of Beirut—both after the war and throughout its modern history.

Equally unexpected has been the way the reconstruction of downtown continues to be a platform on which contending claims over urban life are being played out even if the process of reconstruction has eliminated many of the old players. In the absence of an open political arena, the claims tend to revive political discourse even if they are made on grounds of aesthetics or good urban development.

Once the downtown was cleared for redevelopment, the debate moved to determining the degree of restoration of the center. The plans prepared by Dar al-Handasah, a large corporate design firm, and ratified by the Lebanese parliament for implementation by SOLIDERE, were supposed to be final, but they tended to emphasize regulation over form. They also deferred many key decisions to individual developers and left it up to them to negotiate their way with SOLIDERE, the supervisor of the plan's execution. Even matters of historic preservation, which appeared at first to be clear and straightforward, were open for such negotiations.

According to the plan, building essential infrastructure and restoring the salvaged buildings was to precede any new construction. As planning and legislation for reconstruction and the transfer of property and development rights progressed in the early 1990s, numerous citizens' groups formed in response to the broad scope of change proposed by the plan. Many of these groups called for the restoration of the city as it was before the war. Amsterdam and Antwerp were evoked as models when the feasibility of such an undertaking was questioned. Such total restoration of the pre-trauma city met considerable opposition from the plan's supporters, who argued that Beirut—now a fragmented and overextended metropolis—needed a larger center and that the congestion and traffic problems had to be solved.

When the traffic engineers announced plans for wider roads, developers for larger parcels, and archaeologists for deeper pits, it became evident that a total restoration of the center was going to be impossible. Even the number of structures to be restored dropped to fewer than 15 percent of the historic building stock. Parameters for preservation were set based on photographic and other forms of available documentation, but it soon became evident that Beirut had multiple and competing pasts. To which of these would the restoration efforts be anchored? Many downtown buildings had changed over time, and many of those chosen for preservation, generally located in two districts dating back to the French Mandate (1918–1943), were not as architecturally interesting as the preservationists claimed. As a result, the restored buildings and streets turned out to be overdecorated with references to a variety of pasts—and sometimes to pasts they never had. Interestingly, the few new buildings constructed during this first phase also bore the impact of this historicism and were forced to mimic the preserved buildings, however false.

Recollection of the war itself—the painful but necessary process of social healing—is what the urban planners and architects neglected to respond to, according to many critics and citizens' groups. A small park, known as the Garden of Forgiveness, was forced to absorb all of the pressure of remembering the war in the downtown area, but most of the remembrance is in the name.

The rest of the district is shorn of such references. On the other hand, it is difficult to imagine how such a longing for remembrance might be translated into built form without turning macabre or reducing architecture to sentimental scenography. The task is made even more difficult given the implicit political moratorium against a historical assessment of the war. Among the arts, novels and occasionally cinematic and video works have tackled the problem of dealing with the emotional and psychological remnants of war much more effectively than have architecture or urban design. In confronting these ghosts, many such novels have acquired either an epic or documentary form.

Paradoxically, the amnesia of Beirut's postwar physical reconstruction has played an important role in providing historical continuity between the city's defining myths—the myth of self-consumption and the myth of self-renewal. Since the formation of Lebanon in 1920, after the Versailles Treaty attached the Mount Lebanon region to the coastline on the west and the Bekaa Valley on the east, Beirut has seduced mountain peoples with its cosmopolitanism and permissive, liberal culture. The French Mandate that ruled Lebanon between the two world wars had earlier envisioned Beirut as the main port of the country, but not as its capital. It was as if the administrators feared the eventual consumption of the mountain by the city.

Despite its religious, sectarian, and regional overtones, the fifteen-year conflict has been interpreted by several revisionist historians as a struggle between Beirut and the country, the urban and the rural, or the cosmopolitan and the national. Before the war, nobody came from Beirut, but everybody yearned to go there. Like New York, New York, Beirut refers only to itself. But such self-indulgence is ultimately punished. As perpetuated by folk culture and history alike, Beirut was propelled into history by a moral judgment, passed long ago, that the city deserves destruction. The fifteen-year war was just another punishment for the same excesses of self-consumption that so endowed Beirut with seductive appeal and notoriety. Beirut's self-consumption, the foundational problem of Lebanon, presents a necessary condition for the cyclical myth to be realized.

The second defining myth relates that Beirut will be destroyed but that it will rise from the ashes. Popular songs and poetry to this effect reassured the citizens in their makeshift shelters that the city would be rebuilt. Even the warlords who were overseeing fulfillment of the myth of self-consumption always insisted that the phoenix would eventually rise.

The myth of self-destruction feeds the myth of resilience. These two myths recur like outcome following destiny. But a historical survey of this cycle quickly reveals that most of the calamities in the history of Beirut were natural, not manmade. Importantly, the transition from destruction to construction has rarely been the responsibility of the same generation. Sudden turning points that appear in the historical narratives of other cities confirm that a radical, if only momentary, clearing of the air is necessary for the same generation to make its way from mortar guns to mortarboards. Lebanon's war crimes were exonerated by a general amnesty issued in 1991, absolving everybody in order to move on. It is not surprising that it is mostly the younger video artists and novelists and returning expatriates who are calling for and taking on the responsibility of recollection, not those who were active during the war years. Amnesty and amnesia share more than an etymological root.

Over the years of reconstruction, amnesia has played another historical role, again manifesting itself urbanistically. The clearing of downtown created a collective homesickness for Beirutis even if they still resided in Beirut. All manners of nostalgia and sentimentalized recollection were unleashed. Hundreds of coffee-table books were published, covering the different periods of the city's history.[3] So were personal memoirs of the "good old days," along with fictional accounts of life in the city center. Relics salvaged from the clearing—including old doors, decorative railings, and column capitals—have found new life in the decor of homes and restaurants.

The literary critic Svetlana Boym distinguishes between two kinds of nostalgia, *restorative* and *reflective*.[4] The restorative form seeks the truth in recovering what has been lost. Boym describes this as an undertaking that tends to be associated with nationalist, often oppressive, regimes. The moratorium on history may have spared Beirut this form of nostalgia, allowing the reflective form to prevail. Reflective nostalgia favors fragmentary, selective, and highly personal attributes in the recovery of lost places. Here, individual architects selectively express personal accounts of the past, a past—Boym argues—that is devoid of politics. Whereas restorative nostalgia fetishizes the past, the reflective form makes possible a grassroots, collective process of recovery. In Beirut, individual developers and religious groups that reclaimed and restored their buildings operated largely in this manner. All parties have managed to evade the overbearing and ultimately untenable responsibility of "truthful" recovery. Instead, alternative histories were created through highly individuated, freely applied motifs: a hyper-Moorish style verging on Indian; an arabesque baroque; a Mameluke vernacular; and other fusions that extend beyond recognition. Amnesia, it turns out, allowed a playful mingling of multiple, competing histories. It also passed along the responsibility of recovery from a central authority to a diverse array of architects, decorators, and artisans.

These side effects of nostalgia might have seemed peculiar to postwar reconstruction, but a survey of the history of the city's center reveals that these patterns flow smoothly out of the city's past, a series of contests between groups over the center and the major urban spaces associated with it—primarily Martyrs' Square. Martyrs' Square makes its historical appearance in late seventeenth-century drawings and literature as a clearing outside the walls of the city to the east, as a caravan-staging place prior to their entering the city. This kind of loosely defined open space, known in Arabic as a *maydan*, also provided a visual clearing that aided defense of the city from invaders. As the city grew beyond its walls in the nineteenth century, the *maydan* slowly transformed into a large urban square. Given the density of the inner city and the rapid pace of development to its east and south, the square soon emerged as the center of business and transportation

Figure 12.1.
Martyrs' Square in its
1960s heyday. Aga Khan
Trust for Culture,
Ecochard Archive.

activity in town. A road linking the city to Damascus was later constructed, connecting the southern tip of the square to the countryside beyond.

In the late nineteenth century, Ottoman modernization initiatives accelerated Beirut's rise, enabling the city to become the main port on the eastern Mediterranean. These initiatives included introducing electricity and water networks and building wider roads in the old city. With the help of local donations, the Ottoman ruler of Beirut also transformed the square into a major public garden. Its primacy in the

The Politics of Reconstruction

city was now formalized by the building of the Little Serail—the new government quarters—on its northern side. The tramway lines introduced at the beginning of the twentieth century intersected in the square and further altered the space.

The name of the square changed often during this period, but the assassination of Arab nationalists there by the Ottoman military during the First World War gave it its current name. Significantly, some of the old names, mostly the *Bourj* or *Balad*, are still used for the same square, particularly by the pre–civil war generations. The armistice brought the 400-year Ottoman rule to an end and yielded a new nation-state called Greater Lebanon under the supervision of a French Mandate. An international trade fair at the beginning of the French Mandate was held in the square as well as in an area just west of it, where the Ottomans had cleared part of the medieval fabric for an avenue they never built. The French eventually shaped this area into a small plaza with radiating streets and baptized it Place de l'Etoile.

But even after l'Etoile and the abutting parliament were built, Martyrs' Square continued to function as a multiplicity of urban spaces. It provided the formal grounds in front of the government headquarters as well as the public garden; it served as a transportation hub for Beirut's citizens; it provided accommodations for visitors and cafes for politicians and intellectuals. The square also created a convenient buffer between the city's red light district on one side and its major religious buildings on the other. But this eclectic collage of functions ultimately spawned competing claims over the city center and the square; in the process, the different functions of the space were gradually eliminated while its symbolic role increased.

The French Mandate did not propose major changes to the form of the city center until 1932, when the combined effects of a modern new port in Haifa and the Great Depression threatened Beirut's economy. The Brothers Danger, a French planning group, were asked to put together a master plan for the city of Beirut that would support economic recovery ideas that focused on trade and the seaport. Danger proposed the creation of different urban centers for the extramural neighborhoods of the city and a ring road to connect these centers to each other and to Martyrs' Square. A further articulation of the plan of the square prepared by the French architect Delahalle removed the Ottoman Serail, opened its northern face to the sea, and cascaded the square toward the port, the source of economic vitality. Delahalle also proposed Phoenician facades for the buildings abutting the square. References to the Phoenicians abound in this period as the nascent nation searched for ways to ground and justify itself historically. Much of the new architecture of the period would also replace the Levantine motifs with Moorish and Egyptian ones and would otherwise attempt to reclaim a national—as opposed to a regional—architecture. Although neither Danger's plans nor Delahalle's designs would be implemented, the connection to the sea remained a goal for many of the subsequent plans.

A study prepared in 1942 by French planner Michel Ecochard shifted from shaping spaces to laying out networks. In his correspondence with the French authorities during the Second World War, Ecochard emphasized the need to create an open network of circulation between the city's main port and airport, bypassing the city center and its main square in order to quickly mobilize the troops in the event of an Axis invasion. Ecochard's plan remained mostly at the level of road networks, but his side projects included a literal bypass in the form of a multilevel road to the north of the square. With this bypass, Martyrs' Square lost its transportation function. As in the Danger plan, the square also lost its administrative role, this time to a new government complex to be located between the Place de l'Etoile and Serail Hill to the west.

Ecochard's plan inspired some of the new roads built in the 1950s, which in the process planted the seeds of urban decentralization. A more explicit attempt to move the administration out of the center and out of the city came from a report by the Greek planner Constantinos Doxiadis in 1959. Doxiadis proposed creating a new administrative center for Beirut outside the city's municipal boundaries where the road to Damascus intersected with the peripheral road. Rather than revise the layout of the old center, the welfare government of the time opted for the creation of an altogether new administrative capital that would move government away from the city and closer to the country. This move followed a short but serious civil war in 1958 that brought about numerous confrontations between the state and the opposition in the city center. In the end, only the presidential palace moved out of the city, and the resultant vacuum would often be taken for a vacancy to be filled by competing powers.

The Politics of Reconstruction

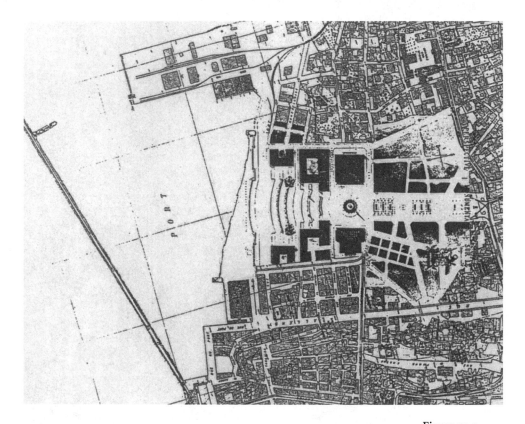

Figure 12.2.
The plan of Delahalle
for Martyrs' Square.
Courtesy of May Davie.

In 1963, Ecochard was brought back to Lebanon to propose a master plan for the metropolitan district of Beirut. This time he envisioned a new modern city south of Beirut that would release the pressure from the traditional old city. He also proposed the creation of a new business center south of Martyrs' Square that would draw business out of the center and place it between the old and new cities. Whereas the plan for a new city would eventually be abandoned, the drive for decentralization gained momentum in subsequent years and culminated in the emergence of a new business center in the Hamra area near the American University of Beirut.

In parallel, an infatuation with the possibility of redressing and reclaiming Martyrs' Square preoccupied the Beirutis. With the removal of the Serail, the square acquired a much larger statue commemorating the martyrs. A constant reworking of the landscape in the square and of the layout of bus and taxi stops attests to the increasing presence of

Figure 12.3.
The new commercial
center proposed by
Michel Ecochard in 1964.
Aga Khan Trust for
Culture, Ecochard
Archive.

the square in the popular imagination, even if its urban functions were
reduced. In the late 1960s and early 1970s, the square became the location of many of the increasingly violent student and labor demonstrations. Grassroots movements and political parties were filling the
vacuum created by the state.

A radical inversion of this decentralization tendency took place after the 1975–1977 war episode. During a brief lull in the fighting in 1977,
a plan was proposed calling for reconstruction of the city center. Authored by the French planning agency APUR and strongly preserva-

The Politics of Reconstruction

tionist in tone, this proposal concentrated on manicuring and highlighting the city's open spaces. Interestingly, the plan called for Martyrs'
Square (which reacquired its role as *maydan*, as a clearing between East
and West Beirut during the war) to be furnished with trees and wide
sidewalks as if offering the citizens a space in which their differences
and animosities could be peacefully played out.

The war resumed soon afterward, but the downtown—particularly
Martyrs' Square—continued to play an important role in maintaining
the image of the city as a coherent entity. Despite its division into two
entities (and its subsequent splintering into even smaller ones), the

Figure 12.4.
The APUR plan of 1977,
the first "return" to the
centrality of Martyrs'
Square. APUR and
Ministry of Public Works
(Beirut).

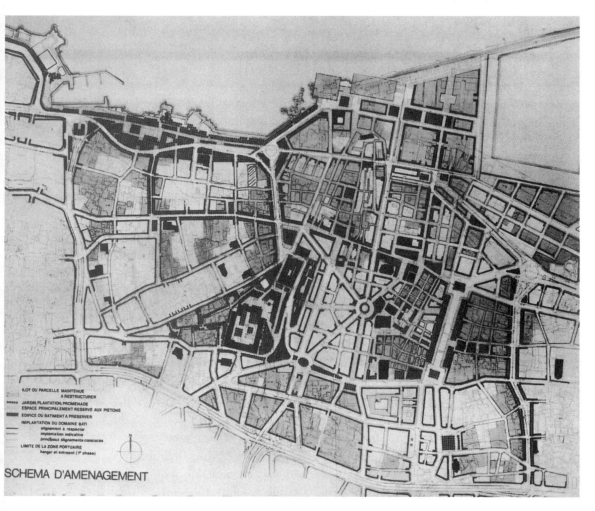

ILOT OU PARCELLE MAINTENUE
A RESTRUCTURER
JARDIN, PLANTATION, PROMENADE
ESPACE PRINCIPALEMENT RESERVE AUX PIETONS
EDIFICE OU BATIMENT A PRESERVER
IMPLANTATION DU DOMAINE BATI
alignement à respecter
implantation indicative
principaux alignements constatés
LIMITE DE LA ZONE PORTUAIRE
hangar et entrepol (1ª phase)

SCHEMA D'AMENAGEMENT

A Vital Void

Figure 12.5.
The present clearing around Martyrs' Square. Photo by Mark Dwyer.

center became like the Forbidden City in Beijing, holding the city together by the power of its ubiquitous image and by its inaccessibility.

The end of the war in 1990 and the Dar al-Handasah/SOLIDERE plan brought the city back to its center. Governmental institutions rushed back; so did the different religious groups. Businesses, particularly larger ones, are slowly returning to the center, and glittery restaurants and shops are crowding the streets and sidewalks. But the role of the center in relation to the rest of the city—especially at the levels of business, transportation, and public life—remains unclear. This lack of clarity is most glaring in Martyrs' Square. Against the backdrop of the restored neighborhood, this clearing now serves as spillover parking, exhibition or concert space, or as a site for invariably tacky installations. It seems to have returned to its previous role as a vital void, as a *maydan*, outside of downtown. Absorbing the various speculations about urban development, while resisting being taken over by any one of them, has been one of the most vital, albeit ignored, functions of this public space.

A major dynamic in urban development in Lebanon is based on the fact that the value of the land is often much higher than the value of the buildings that sit upon it. While location and size, as is always the case, do figure prominently in the evaluation of property, the historical value of the building does not contribute as much to the assessment of the property. Given a weak mortgage market, real estate in Lebanon is not linked to the fluctuations in interest rates. Moreover, property taxes are low. Investment and speculation in real estate can continue even if the demand is not high, because real estate still provides the most secure sector for investment (in spite of a vacancy rate of about 30 percent in the 1970s, particularly in luxury residential buildings). It was therefore not surprising when planners proposed 4.7 mil-

The Politics of Reconstruction

lion square meters of built-up area in downtown Beirut, including 2 million square meters to house some 40,000 inhabitants.

With a building code that keeps getting revised to increase the land exploitation factors, especially in the business districts of the city, it is difficult to see how the urban fabric can hold against this kind of change. Buildings dating back to the early 1950s and 1960s are routinely torn down and replaced by parking lots, as owners play a waiting game with prospective developers. These clearings serve as development indices, particularly in neighborhoods like Ras Beirut and Ashrafieh, where competing claims and scenarios for development help to increase the value of the vacated property as well as the properties around it. Another example of this in the downtown area is the reconstruction of the old souks, the city's old bazaar.

Most of the actual development in the downtown is supposed to be handled by private developers, who purchase the land from SOLIDERE and build it up according to plan. However, SOLIDERE has reserved the right to build about 25 percent of the land itself, including key sites that would serve as pilot or seed projects to encourage development around them. One of these key sites was the souks project, the reconstruction of the city's bazaar, located just south of the historic harbor. Given unanticipated political changes and financial difficulties, the project was halted for four years during which most of the sites around it continued to be purchased and built by private developers—despite economic stagnation and the absence of a pilot project. While the anticipation of the souks' reconstruction has not triggered as much development as their realization would have, speculative development has clearly overwhelmed rational planning and may require certain changes in the land uses of the new bazaar. The clearing around Martyrs' Square may be interpreted as a larger version of this pattern in

A Vital Void

Beirut's development culture, particularly in the way it affords extraordinary view corridors to different sectors under construction.

These patterns of development are not unique to the postwar period, nor are they unique to downtown Beirut. However, given the limited political platform in Beirut after the war and the highly charged location of the downtown in the country's geopolitics, they prove that urban life can overcome exclusionary practices. Today, the main questions regarding politics are being asked through means other than religious sectarianism or party politics. When interrogated carefully, the city's built environment, architectural heritage, and public spaces expose a highly political content that can still be debated and challenged.

The political theorists Ernesto Laclau and Chantal Mouffe have argued that the dynamic of democratic politics stems from the fact that the central position of power remains open for contest.[5] The center is constantly cleared and kept at an equal distance from everybody's reach in order for democracy to maintain the potential for constant debate and change. The voids produced by the development culture in Beirut may not fully correspond to this operative void in democratic politics. Furthermore, public spaces cannot be as fluid if they are to maintain their public roles. However, the constant redefinition of Martyrs' Square over its recent history asserts that Beirut's development culture and its political life intersect at many unforeseen points. Much of the square's resilience and vitality can be explained by its constant change rather than through an examination of its salient features. Against the past and current plans for Martyrs' Square, which limit its role by fixing its shape and function, architects and urban designers today are challenged to imagine ways in which the vitality of constant change might be enhanced and reified by design. In this, perhaps, lies the key to the continued resilience of downtown Beirut.

Notes

1. Hoda Barakat, *The Tiller of Waters*, trans. Marilyn Booth (Cairo: American University in Cairo Press, 2001).
2. See, for example, Nabil Beyhum, *Reconstruire Beyrouth: Les Paris sur le Possible* (Lyon, France: Maison de l'Orient, Etudes sur le Monde Arab,

The Politics of Reconstruction

1991), n. 5; Peter G. Rowe and Hashim Sarkis, eds., *Projecting Beirut: Episodes in the Construction and Reconstruction of a Modern City* (Munich: Prestel, 1998); and Samir Khalaf, *Beirut Reclaimed* (Beirut: Dar An-Nahar, 1993).

3. See, for example, Fouad Debbas, *Beirut: Our Memory* (Beirut: Naufal Group, 1986); Ghassan Tueni and Fares Sassine, eds., *El Bourj: Place de la Liberte et Porte du Levant* (Beirut: Dar An-Nahar, 2000); and Fares Sassine and Nawaf Salam, eds., *Liban: Le Siecle en Image* (Beirut: Dar An-Nahar, 2000).

4. Svetlana Boym, *The Future of Nostalgia* (New York: Basic Books, 2002).

5. Ernesto Laclau and Chantal Mouffe, *Hegemony and Socialist Strategy: Towards a Radical Democratic Politics* (London: Verso, 2001 [2d ed.]).

After the Unrest
Ten Years of Rebuilding Los Angeles following the Trauma of 1992

13

WILLIAM FULTON

■ It is always difficult to measure urban resilience, but never more so when the trauma results from civil unrest, as opposed to a natural disaster or enemy attack. With natural disasters, it is frequently difficult to place blame, even if "acts of God" are sometimes all too intertwined with ill-advised decisions to site buildings in vulnerable areas. Wars and other attacks usually entail clear enemies, and eventually come to some negotiated halt, accompanied by greater territorial clarity. With riots and civil unrest, by contrast, destruction is community-based. Victims and perpetrators live in close proximity; violence is often inflicted within the very neighborhoods that feel most aggrieved; and recovery entails the need to redress not just physical damage but also deeply ingrained mistrust. Rebuilding, in this sense, requires not just investment in real estate, but also a variety of human capital—local infusions of community dynamism, neighborly cooperation, and no small measure of hope.

In the United States, Los Angeles, California, stands out as the site of two generations of civil unrest: the Watts riots of 1965 and the civil unrest of 1992. The 1992 disturbance was the most damaging urban riot in American history, killing fifty-four people and causing hundreds of millions of dollars in property damage. Touched off by the acquittal on April 29 of white police officers accused of beating black motorist Rodney King, the rampage lasted several days and spread to an area much larger than the earlier riots in Watts. The disturbance ranged across dozens of square miles, mostly along the lengthy commercial strips in the southern part of the city of Los Angeles, including many areas not traditionally viewed as part of South Central. It even spilled northward above the Santa Monica Freeway into Hollywood, the traditionally Jewish Fairfax district, and other neighborhoods far from the traditional centers of African-American residence. This chapter investigates a full decade of efforts to rebuild South Central Los Angeles, following the trial of King's assailants.

In so many ways, Los Angeles is a city like no other—a vast but low-rise city, dense and sprawling at the same time. Auto-oriented and generally without high-rises, Los Angeles might seem different from a more traditional metropolis such as New York. But in many ways this is not really true. In overall statistical terms, the five-county metropolitan Los Angeles area is almost identical to the tristate New York area. One study found that in 1997, metro L.A. had a population density of 8.31 persons per urbanized acre (15.8 million people living on 1.9 million acres of urbanized land) while New York had a population density of 7.99 persons per urbanized acre (18.6 million people living on 2.33 million acres of urbanized land).[1]

With 10 million people, Los Angeles County is the nation's most populous local government unit. And with almost 4 million people, the city of Los Angeles is the second most populous city in the United States, far ahead of number three, Chicago. The riot-torn areas of southern Los Angeles were mostly located inside the city of L.A., but they also included some areas in unincorporated Los Angeles County. These areas were poorer than most other parts of L.A.—and, thanks to recent immigration trends, more crowded as well—but in physical terms they were not atypical.

Even in these parts of town, Los Angeles is very much a city of neighborhoods—a city low to the ground, consisting of commercial strips, single-family homes, and two-story apartment buildings. The commercial strips vary dramatically in quality and intensity around the city. Affluent neighborhoods have large and successful strip commercial centers, while the strips in poor neighborhoods often have a combination of older stores, swap meets, vacant lots, and modest neighborhood-serving facilities such as churches. But no matter what the socioeconomic differences between neighborhoods, the residential streets are often a similar low-rise mix. This general similarity, however, cannot mask the fact that different sections of Los Angeles are very

The Politics of Reconstruction

different indeed. As a western city that did not really come into being until the early twentieth century, L.A. experienced only rare instances of the overt Jim Crow segregation common in the South. But as the modern notion of L.A. took hold in the 1910s and 1920s, African Americans and Mexican Americans—who had previously lived throughout the city—were increasingly segregated into large but definable ethnic enclaves.[2] Mexican Americans were contained in the neighborhoods to the east and southeast of downtown—hence the origin of the East L.A. barrio. At the same time, virtually all African Americans were segregated in neighborhoods along South Central Avenue to the south of downtown, which is why the area became known as South Central.

Especially during World War II, the African-American population grew dramatically, but the boundaries of South Central did not spread much. In the half-century after the war, South Central grew very slowly, quite literally a block at a time, as the African-American population moved to neighborhoods such as Crenshaw and cities such as Inglewood and Compton, which were located to the west, south, and southwest of South Central. In keeping with L.A.'s general structure as a city of massive ethnic enclaves, South Central is not small. Stretching from the University of Southern California southward to Watts and beyond, and from Alameda Street on the east at least to Crenshaw Boulevard, South Central covers perhaps fifty square miles—larger than most cities.

During the postwar era, this vast area was also isolated from the rest of the city by the freeway system—which eliminated the need for outsiders to drive through the neighborhood on surface streets—and by the structure of metropolitan life. For example, at the time of the 1965 Watts riots—and for close to a decade afterward—South Central was not integrated into L.A.'s larger bus system. Rather, it was served by a private company that was separate from the regional system.

The Watts riots had erupted from an altercation between African-American men and Los Angeles police. It led to days of looting and violence, especially along 103d Street, the "Main Street" of the African-American neighborhood known as Watts. The looting and civil unrest was fairly localized, and it took place in the context of widespread urban unrest, especially in African-American neighborhoods, during the 1960s.[3]

It also accelerated the process of white flight from South Central and surrounding neighborhoods—and, indeed, black flight as well. Beginning in the 1970s, African Americans who could afford to do so began to leave South Central. Some of them went to the adjacent neighborhoods and communities, whose racial characteristics gradually changed, while others skipped over dozens of white communities before settling in outlying towns such as Oxnard, Colton, and Perris (40 to 60 miles away), or even Las Vegas (300 miles away), which had traditionally welcomed black residents.

At the same time, immigrants from Asia and Latin America began to move into the traditionally African-American parts of South Central, altering the area's demographics for the first time in decades. This move was part of a larger change in central Los Angeles, where rapid immigration and high fertility rates among immigrant families dramatically changed the city's demographics in a short period of time. Many African Americans of all economic classes remained in the residential neighborhoods of South Central, and so did the major African-American institutions—at least for a while. But, gradually, a new population emerged, one that was reflective of the growing Latinization of Los Angeles. Many were recent immigrants and their families; many more were established Latinos looking for good prices on single-family houses.

So, when the police officers accused of beating Rodney King were acquitted in 1992, South Central was a very different place than it had been during the Watts riots in 1965. It still had an unusual concentration of poverty, and it still had a strong concentration of industrial jobs. But it was characterized by declining commercial strips, a remaining African-American population that was, on the whole, much poorer than the blacks who had inhabited the area in 1965, and a growing and diverse Latino population that had a much different history than the African Americans. On top of all this was the fact that the built environment of South Central—like the rest of Los Angeles— was aging fast. Roads, houses, stores, water and sewer lines were all getting older and, for the first time, Los Angeles was facing the issue of becoming a mature city.

Unlike the incident that sparked the 1965 Watts riots, the King beating—which had received widespread publicity because it happened to be captured on videotape by an onlooker—occurred nowhere near

South Central. It happened in a remote section of the San Fernando Valley, perhaps thirty miles away from Watts. The actual trial of the police officers did not even take place in Los Angeles County; nervous prosecutors moved it to Simi Valley, a town in Ventura County just west of the San Fernando Valley.

Nevertheless, the outrage was felt first—and primarily—in the historically African-American neighborhoods of South Central. Looting and rioting initially occurred in the vicinity of the intersection of Florence and Normandie, a major intersection in South Central. Over the next three days, violence and looting focused on the retail strips up and down South Central. Some of it also spilled over into other areas to the north, including Hollywood and the Fairfax district. During the disturbance, a pattern emerged: a commercial strip or series of mini-malls would be set on fire—presumably by African-American gang members, who were widely believed to be responsible for the arson—and then the stores would be looted by a multiethnic population that included poor Latina mothers in search of bread, diapers, and other basic commodities.

The 1992 civil unrest was a much more complicated event than the 1965 Watts riots. It was more widespread; it apparently involved more—and more different types of—people; and it came after a lengthy series of tense racial incidents between African-American residents and Korean retail store owners. As an urban riot, it was isolated; that is, unlike the Watts riots, it was not followed by similar incidents in other cities in subsequent years. However, it was just one of many incidents that led to a gloomy sense of foreboding in Los Angeles in the early 1990s, which was perhaps best reflected in the dystopic tone of Mike Davis's landmark book, *City of Quartz*.[4] The unrest came near the beginning of a major recession, and it was followed by the Northridge earthquake of 1994 and the O. J. Simpson trial of 1995. Furthermore, it occurred in an era when the moral issues associated with racial discrimination and urban poverty were much more ambiguous than they were in the 1960s. In contrast to the Watts riots, there was relatively little investigation by any official body into the underlying social and economic conditions that caused the riots. The investigations that followed focused mostly on the practices of the Los Angeles Police Department, and few if any of the arsonists were ever prosecuted. Moreover, at a time when "political correctness" was important, there was little agreement even on what to call the sequence of events that led to the destruction.

The word *riot* appeared out of fashion, suggesting as it did that the participants were responsible for the disorder. African Americans tended to favor terms that would lend the incidents a political cast, such as *uprising* or *rebellion*. Those seeking middle ground tended to call the incident an episode of *civil unrest* or a *civil disturbance*. But no one disputed that the events were tragic and that they provided further evidence that—almost thirty years after the Watts riots—the task of reviving L.A.'s poorest neighborhoods remained monumental.

There was also no doubt that, a generation after the freeway system first permitted most people in Los Angeles to circumvent it on a daily basis, South Central was back on everyone's radar screen. Much of the early post-riot effort was focused on repairing damaged race relations—not just between whites and blacks, but also between blacks and Koreans. Local leaders also focused a great deal of attention on providing the Los Angeles Police Department with new leadership, who could encourage more community-friendly policing techniques.[5]

In the wake of the disturbance, Los Angeles undertook a crisis-driven rebuilding effort on a scale rarely seen anywhere in the United States since the urban renewal programs of the 1970s. Using the public-private model that he had applied to many other problems during his tenure—including the 1984 Olympics—Mayor Tom Bradley, an African American then in his fifth term, created a private organization, Rebuild L.A., and entrusted it to businessman Peter Ueberroth, the former baseball commissioner and Olympics czar. The organization raised more than $300 million in investment commitments from major corporations, many of them retailers, and attempted to engage both businesses and neighborhood leaders in the rebuilding effort.

Most everyone recognized that an underlying reason for the persistent urban decay was a lack of investment in both businesses and buildings in the southern parts of Los Angeles, and the city's main recovery efforts eventually focused on these. Mayor Bradley's Rebuild L.A. group attempted to stimulate business investment in South Central. The city's Community Redevelopment Agency also moved toward the quick creation of several new projects in the riot-torn areas as a means of stimulating new investment in real estate development.

This renewed attention proved a double-edged sword. On the one hand, after decades of neglect, many South Central residents welcomed any attention at all. On the other hand, for a poor and neglected area, South Central turned out to be far more turf-controlled than anyone expected, as the business leaders and investment specialists deployed to the riot area by Mayor Bradley quickly discovered. There was an African American power structure of long standing—and this power structure was not united but, rather, rent with equally long-standing factional disputes. There were young community development specialists of all races, many of whom also had friends and enemies in the power structure. There were many groups of local business owners, and there were advocacy groups representing the new immigrant communities that were also struggling for recognition. As one young community development specialist said shortly after the riots, "The whole idea of rebuilding L.A. is a joke. What have we been doing down here all these years?"[6]

As a result, neither the business investment effort nor the real estate investment effort worked out exactly as planned. Although it eventually did some good, Rebuild L.A. quickly turned into a public relations fiasco for Mayor Bradley. Even though he designed the organization to lean on businesses to make investment commitments in South Central rather than simply dole out money, Bradley was quickly forced to retreat from his original plan to put white businessman Ueberroth solely in charge. Instead, he appointed five cochairs, representing different racial and ethnic groups. Rebuild L.A. publicly worked to extract investment commitments from a wide variety of businesses—especially supermarket chains, as markets remained a particular hot-button issue in South Central.

Meanwhile, the city's attempt to use the Community Redevelopment Agency and encourage private banks and real estate companies to invest ran into a similar buzzsaw. The state of California changed the redevelopment law to expedite the creation of new project areas, but, as a successor to discredited urban renewal efforts, redevelopment had been suspect in South Central for decades. Even private efforts to reinvest ran into turf difficulties. Seeking a "good guy" image, First Interstate Bank sponsored a design competition for a mixed-use affordable housing and retail project on a vacant lot on Vermont Avenue near Manchester and selected Dan Solomon, California's leading affordable housing architect, to design it. The project had the support of the area's African-American city councilman, Mark Ridley Thomas. But it was opposed by neighboring middle-class African-American home owners—including the powerful U.S. representative, Maxine Waters—who wanted more retail and less affordable housing in their neighborhood. Waters and her neighbors persuaded the new mayor, Richard Riordan (a white Republican), to delay the project, at least temporarily.[7] Such turf wars were not uncommon.

Ten years after the civil unrest, both statistical indicators and anecdotal reports suggested that the ravaged parts of the city were still doing poorly and that the whole Rebuild L.A. effort had made little difference. Poverty in the entire five-county Los Angeles region was still extremely concentrated in the areas commonly identified in the media as "South Central L.A."[8] The vast majority of buildings damaged in 1992 had not been rebuilt, and those that were housed small businesses with few employees, who were paid low wages. Several studies concluded that, while the riot area still had lots of jobs, those numbers were low compared to other parts of the city, especially when measured as a ratio of jobs to population.[9] Similarly, the southern parts of the city lagged far behind the rest of Los Angeles in retail and housing construction.[10]

In terms of actual investment in new real estate development projects, the southern parts of Los Angeles did not seem so resilient in the years after the civil unrest. Disappointing as they are, however, these statistics do not mean that L.A. was not a resilient city in the decade after the civil disturbances of 1992. Rather, the task of rebuilding Los Angeles turned out to be much larger and more complex than simply reconstructing damaged buildings. And the nature of the community and its resilience turned out to be different than they appeared to be when rebuilding efforts began.

So perhaps Los Angeles did not recover in the manner or to the extent that scholars and commentators expected. There was less investment in the built environment than anyone expected, and life remained difficult for the people who lived in the affected neighborhoods. But if by resilience we mean confidence, energy, and sheer *chutzpah*, then Los Angeles clearly showed considerable resilience in the decade after 1992. The recent wave of immigration had given the city—and even its most troubled neighborhoods—new life. And the economic

The Politics of Reconstruction

recovery of the late 1990s gave the city a new confidence that helped it to overcome a whole series of depressing events in the early to mid-1990s—not just the civil unrest of 1992, but also a series of devastating fires and earthquakes, as well as the emotionally wrenching spectacle of the O. J. Simpson capture and trial.

On April 29, 2002—ten years after several days of civil unrest traumatized Los Angeles—local leaders gathered for the groundbreaking of a 60,000-square-foot retail center at the corner of Vermont and Slauson avenues in South Central Los Angeles. No street had suffered more damage during the unrest of 1992 than Vermont Avenue. Once a proud thoroughfare that contained some of the area's finest retail stores, its lengthy retail strip had been devastated by the riots of 1992, and more than 120 stores had been damaged.[11] Retailers had been reluctant to return to the area, and many neighborhoods—even those with middle-class home owners near the commercial strips—were left without basic goods and services.

In the aftermath of the unrest, more effort had been put into reviving basic retail in that area than into any other revitalization endeavor. The new Vermont/Slauson center—the second developed in the neighborhood by the Vermont/Slauson Economic Development Corporation—was a manifestation of this effort, and it simultaneously represented everything that the intervening ten years had wrought: progress, change, and frustration. It did not contain Macy's or Niketown or even a furniture store. It contained Burger King but no sit-down restaurant—a reflection of the restaurant industry's view that sit down diners could be accommodated at the edges of the neighborhood, where the perceived costs and risks were lower.

It also contained a supermarket, but even that reflected a new trend. Supermarkets in South Central had been devastated during the civil unrest, and much of the revitalization effort had been focused on bringing them back. The new supermarket was not Ralph's or Albertson's or Von's, the three big chain markets that dominate most of Los Angeles, nor even one of their discount markets. Rather, the market was Gigante, Mexico's third-largest supermarket chain, which had recently announced plans to open more than twenty stores in the Los Angeles area catering to Mexicans and Mexican immigrants.[12] Even Gigante came to the neighborhood carefully, only after working with the Vermont/Slauson group to ensure that its marketing techniques and store operations could attract African-American shoppers who still lived in the neighborhood, while also meeting the needs of the Mexican immigrants, who represented Gigante's core market.[13]

When L.A.'s leaders envisioned rebuilding devastated neighborhoods after the 1992 unrest, they probably were not thinking about a Mexican supermarket chain working with a historically African-American community development corporation to ensure cross-cultural balance in daily marketing. Yet, more than a decade after the devastating civil unrest, this is what resilience has turned out to mean in Los Angeles.

South Central Los Angeles today looks little different than it did a decade ago. Despite all of the business commitments, redevelopment efforts, and battle for the glory of revitalization that followed the unrest of 1992, the rebuilding has, generally speaking, not occurred. A few new commercial centers have been built, but many of the commercial buildings damaged during the civil unrest have simply been torn down, leaving vacant lots on the commercial strips that are sometimes populated by swap meets. According to one analysis, only 19 percent of the buildings located in South Central that were damaged in 1992 had tax-paying businesses located in them in 1999. On average, those buildings housed only one or two small businesses, which employed an average of seven workers and paid an average monthly wage of only about $1,700. For damaged neighborhoods in the central parts of Los Angeles, north of the Santa Monica Freeway, the numbers were somewhat better. The same analysis also noted that the number of jobs per resident in South Central, which was already far below the citywide average, dropped dramatically during the seven-year period.[14]

Similarly, the many supermarkets promised in the wake of 1992 did not materialize. With Rebuild L.A.'s help, thirty new markets had been promised. According to research conducted by Occidental College, in 1992 there were thirty-two chain supermarkets and twenty-three independent markets in the area affected by civil unrest. In 2002, there were thirty-one chain markets and twenty-six independent markets. One major chain promised twelve stores and built six, including one far outside the riot area, one that was a reconstruction of a store damaged by the unrest, and two that have since closed.[15]

Meanwhile, the area affected by the civil unrest did not seem to be attracting much residential development either, despite being targeted by affordable housing developers and their funders. The affordable housing project at Vermont and 81st was eventually built—with Mayor Riordan's approval and according to architect Solomon's stately design. But an analysis of multifamily construction in Los Angeles during the years 2000 and 2001 found that only 3 percent of the construction (208 units out of a total of 6,571) occurred in the South Los Angeles planning area, compared with 2,600 units in West Los Angeles and 1,600 in the southern San Fernando Valley.[16]

These gloomy results mostly reflected the failure of institutional Los Angeles to respond effectively to the events of 1992. Informally, however, there is improvement, thanks in large part to the influx of immigrants into the historically African-American neighborhoods. Although the number of jobs per resident in South Central Los Angeles was far below the city average, the area did retain a large number of jobs, especially in manufacturing. In 2000 the area had more than 2,700 manufacturing companies that employed 84,000 workers. Manufacturing accounted for 27 percent of total employment in the area, even more than the service sector. And part of the reason that the jobs-per-person ratio was going down was because of the nature of the population, not the nature of the jobs.

South Central L.A.'s population grew dramatically between 1980 and 1990 and again between 1990 and 2000.[17] Most of the new population comprised large immigrant families from Latin American countries. Many of these families were desperately poor, and the neighborhoods of South Central continued to suffer as a result. But many were upwardly mobile working-class families who chose South Central because of its proximity to jobs and its relatively affordable housing. These immigrant populations brought new life and vitality to declining neighborhoods—and after 1996 they began to vote in large numbers as well, which will also have an impact on physical investments in South Central.

In contrast to many inner-city neighborhoods throughout the nation, South Central has a consistent and healthy home-buying market that provides low-end single-family ownership opportunities. Between 1999 and 2002, more than 300 homes per year were bought and sold in each major zip code in South Central, at prices averaging $100,000 to $150,000 and increasing gradually over time.[18] This is the first time in a half-century or more that a new group of upwardly mobile home buyers has looked to South Central as a vehicle to achieve a middle-class life.

There is little doubt that other public investments, especially in schools and parks, will follow. Los Angeles Unified School District has passed several billion dollars in school bonds—largely because of overwhelming support from Latino voters—and is in the process of building eighty new schools all over the city. The Trust for Public Land and other groups are working in inner-city neighborhoods in South Central and elsewhere to expand and improve the parks available to local residents.

These kinds of improvements—low-end home ownership, more schools, improved parks, a manufacturing base that appears to be holding its own—may not be the kinds of dramatic or sexy changes that anybody envisioned following the events of 1992. But they do represent the nature of L.A.'s resilience.

In the last piece he wrote before he died, Carey McWilliams—one of the most insightful observers the city has ever seen—called L.A. "a very special city in spite of itself."[19] He meant by this that Los Angeles had emerged as one of the great cities of the world even though it had been built on the basis of a suburban mindset—a mindset that was shared equally by the upwardly mobile upper-middle classes of the Westside and the San Fernando Valley and the working class of southern Los Angeles County. Although the city is much different now, McWilliams's observation applies equally to the Los Angeles that has emerged since 1992.

To be sure, some problems in South Central L.A. remain stubbornly resistant to solutions. These include the neighborhood's persistent African-American poverty, the resistance of retailers to moving to the area, and the general difficulty in moving public-private building projects forward in ways that will revitalize the built environment, as had been envisioned following the civil disturbances. Yet the very melding of the First and Third worlds that causes so many of L.A.'s problems also provides the basis for the city's resilience. People and money flow into the city from everywhere in the world. They don't always wind up in the same place—people tend to flow to poor parts of town, money to affluent parts of town—but the constant flow of both is consistently creating new assets. And as L.A. ages, the very liabilities created by an earlier age may turn into assets too. The vast commercial strips of South Central, for example, will almost surely serve as the stock of land required to build housing and make other improvements to the built environment in the future, as the project at Vermont and 81st suggests.

With this kind of energy constantly flowing into town, eventually Angelenos get things done. It may not always be pretty or timely, and it may not work out the way that planners and strategists envision. But Los Angeles remains a city of such remarkable energy that it doesn't stay down for long. The Los Angeles of 1992—the gloomy L.A. depicted in *City of Quartz*—seems very distant now. In its place, we see L.A. as the resilient city, the city that remains, despite all of the changes, a very special city in spite of itself.

Notes

1. William Fulton, Rolf Pendall, Mai Nguyen, and Alicia Harrison, *Who Sprawls Most? How Growth Patterns Differ across the U.S.* (Washington, D.C.: Brookings Institution Center on Urban and Metropolitan Policy, 2001).

2. Kevin Starr, *Material Dreams: Southern California through the 1920s* (New York: Oxford University Press, 1990).

3. Robert Fogleson, "White on Black: A Critique of the McCone Commission Report on the Los Angeles Riots," in *The Los Angeles Riots*, comp. Robert Fogelson (New York: Arno, 1969), 111–143. See also Robert E. Coot, *Rivers of Blood, Years of Darkness* (New York: Bantam, 1967).

4. Mike Davis, *City of Quartz: Excavating the Future in Los Angeles* (London: Verso, 1990).

5. Ironically, in the wake of the riots, the long-time African-American mayor Tom Bradley was succeeded by the white businessman Richard Riordan, and Riordan replaced white police chief Darryl Gates with African-American Willie Williams.

6. William Fulton, "Whose Riot Is This, Anyway?" in his *Reluctant Metropolis: The Politics of Urban Growth in Los Angeles* (Point Arena, Calif.: Solano, 1997), 285–311.

7. The 1992 civil unrest occurred one year before the end of Mayor Tom Bradley's fifth term. At age seventy-six, he decided to retire in 1993. He was succeeded by Richard Riordan; despite his long-standing ties to Bradley and the City Hall power structure, Riordan was elected largely on the strength of white votes in the San Fernando Valley. He served two terms and was succeeded in 2001 by James Hahn.

8. Bureau of the Census, Census 2000 Summary File 3, Table P87, "Poverty Status in 1999 by Age," http://factfinder.census.gov.

9. Mark Drayse and Daniel Fleming, *South Los Angeles Rising: Opportunities for Economic Self-Sufficiency Ten Years after the 1992 Civil Unrest* (Los Angeles: Economic Roundtable, 2002).

10. William Fulton, *Multi-Family Housing Is Being Constructed on Los Angeles's Commercial Strips* (Ventura, Calif.: Solimar Research Group, 2002). Downloaded from www.solimar.org.

11. Peter H. King, "Searching for a Legacy," *Los Angeles Times*, 21 April 2002, p. 1.

12. Elena Gaona, "Gigante Breaks New Ground," *Los Angeles Times*, 30 April 2002, p. C-2.

13. William Fulton, "L.A. Powerhouse," *Planning* 68, no. 6 (June 2002): 24–25.

14. Drayse and Fleming, *South Los Angeles Rising*.

15. Amanda Shaffer and Robert Gottlieb, "1992 Riots: Promise of Renewal Broken," *Los Angeles Times*, 10 March 2002, p. M-1.

16. Fulton, *Multi-Family Housing*.

17. U.S. Census.

18. Calculated by the author based on information available from the *Los Angeles Times* and Dataquick at http://www.latimes.com/classified/real estate/la-dataquick.ssipage.

19. Carey McWilliams, "Los Angeles: A Very Special City in Spite of Itself," in *Los Angeles, 1781–1981: Commemorating the 200th Birthday of Nuestra Señora La Reina de Los Angeles* (suppl. to *Los Angeles Times*, 31 August 1980).

Cyborg Agonistes
Disaster and Reconstruction
in the Digital Electronic Era

14

WILLIAM J. MITCHELL

ANTHONY M. TOWNSEND

■ Palma Nova near Venice, with its famous star-shaped fortifications, is a city of two tales.[1] You can read complementary narratives from the plan.

One tale is of enclosure. The walls, as in other ancient, medieval, and Renaissance cities, protected the concentrations of assets and settled populations within from nomadic bandits and mobile armies without. In addition, as Lewis Mumford cogently put it, "[T]he power of massed numbers in itself gave the city a superiority over the thinly populated widely scattered villages, and served as an incentive to further growth."[2] Density and defended walls provided safety, economic vitality, and long-term resilience. At the extreme, under siege, the gates were closed, soldiers manned the battlements, and the city became self-contained for the duration. To attack it, one needed some technology to breach the defensive perimeter—Joshua's trumpet, Achilles' wooden horse, Francesco di Giorgio's tunnel beneath the walls of Castel Nuovo, a battering ram, or a siege engine.

The second tale is of connection. The central piazza, surrounded by public buildings, is both the focus of the internal street network and the local hub of a road network that extends through the gates and out into the countryside, linking the city to others. The piazza is—like the server of a local Internet service provider (ISP)—a node at which nearby and larger communities are connected. When the gates are open, the city functions as a crossroads rather than as a sealed enclosure, a place of interaction rather than one of exclusion.

Urban history is, from one perspective, a struggle of these narratives for dominance. Eventually, the network won. Mumford associated this victory with the rise of capitalism—a new constellation of economic forces that "favored expansion and dispersal in every direction, from overseas colonization to the building up of new industries, whose technological improvements simply canceled out all medieval restrictions." For cities, "[T]he demolition of their urban walls was both practical and symbolic."[3]

Superficially, modern Manhattan resembles a scaled-up version of Palma Nova; it is a regularized street grid, surrounded by water, and accessed by a limited number of bridges and tunnels. But the networks are denser and more numerous; they extend the city's connections much farther out into the world, and they provide many more functions. Road, rail, water, and air transportation links connect to local, regional, and global destinations. Water supply and sewer networks extend the island's hydrological footprint over a huge area and establish vital connections to distant collection, storage, and treatment sites. Mechanical air supply networks make the interiors of large buildings and the city's many underground spaces inhabitable. Pipes for hydrocarbons and wires for electricity densely blanket the built fabric with delivery nodes and extend the supply network to tank farms and power stations far out in the hinterland. There is a wired telecommunications network that began with the telegraph, evolved into an analog telephone network, and is now transforming into a multifunctional digital system. And there are multiple forms of wireless networking—particularly broadcast radio and television, microwave, cell phone, pager, and the 802.11 wireless data protocol. Horizontal network links make use of terrestrial, subsurface, and aerial real estate, while vertical links run through the service cores and chases of buildings.

Today, in the era of the network triumphant, the technologies of attack and defense have correspondingly transformed. A city can still, of course, be obliterated with explosives and bulldozers, but there are now subtler means. By bringing down the networks it depends upon, a city can be killed. Those networks can also be hijacked and turned against their creators—delivering destruction by appropriating the very transfer and distribution capabilities that motivated their construction.

Furthermore, since digital networks increasingly control other networks, there is an entirely new type of threat to contend with. Not only

The Politics of Reconstruction

may there be direct physical attacks against the "real property" components of critical urban networks, but there may also be cyberattacks against the computers and networks that control those infrastructures. As the U.S. Congress Committee on Security in the Information Age reported in May 2002, a computer hack may cause "the same damage as a strategically placed bomb."[4] The same report added:

> A cyberattack can originate from any part of the globe and from any nation, group or individual. The low cost of equipment, the ready availability of technology and cybertools, and the otherwise modest resources needed to mount a cyberattack makes it impossible for governments, much less businesses, to identify or track all potential cyberadversaries.[5]

The simplest way to crash a network is to block or sever a crucial link. Networks fail—sometimes catastrophically—when backhoes cut telephone or power cables, just as blood clots block arteries and accidents jam the 405 Freeway. They are particularly vulnerable to this form of failure at points where there is no alternative route for traffic to take (or, at least, no efficient one). That is why links such as the Khyber Pass or San Francisco's Bay Bridge are of such strategic importance; break them, and large chunks of network on both sides are disconnected from each other.

It is even more effective, in general, to shut down a node—particularly one at which many links converge. If an earthquake destroys a freeway interchange, for example, travel in several directions is blocked at that point. Or, if a major airline hub is closed, such as Chicago's O'Hare airport, a major air travel disruption results. Furthermore, nodes often concentrate more crucial functionality than links. Sever a vein, and you may survive, but stop your heart and you're a goner. Yank a cable at the periphery of a LAN (local area network) and most of the network continues to function, but crash the central server and the whole network goes down.

If part of a network fails to perform its function, the trouble may propagate to other links and nodes—particularly where the network is tightly coupled. A sewer blockage can produce a back-up to a house's sink or toilet, and a fender bender can quickly propagate traffic jams far back through a freeway network. This becomes particularly troublesome when there are no escape mechanisms, such as pressure valves and off-ramps. It's why New Yorkers dread getting stuck in the Holland Tunnel.

Even worse, the propagation of loads can cause progressive failure of network infrastructure. In an electric power network, for example, the burnout of a transformer can propagate excess loads to other parts of the network, which fail in turn, and so on. It is much the same with nuclear chain reactions, and with progressive structural failures, like that of the World Trade Center towers; floors collapsed onto lower floors, which then became overloaded and collapsed themselves, and so on, with gathering force. To protect them against progressive failure, networks need devices such as fuses or circuit breakers, which sacrifice themselves for the sake of the system.

In large, high-speed networks, such as modern power grids and the Internet, patterns of overload propagation and progressive failure are potentially very complex, hard to predict, and frustratingly difficult to control. Once they get started, even in a small way, there is an ever-present danger that they will grow explosively to produce large-scale, long-term damage. In 1998, for example, the power grid of Auckland, New Zealand, experienced a cascading failure that badly damaged all four of the central business district's main power arteries. The New Zealand Stock Exchange shut down until it could switch to back-up power; the central business district was darkened for many weeks; air conditioners and refrigerators went out during the summer months; and the pubs had to serve warm beer—something the locals took particularly hard.

The largest-ever system failure of the highly interconnected eastern North America power grid occurred on Thursday, August 14, 2003. The blackout apparently began in Ohio when three transmission lines came into contact with trees and short-circuited.[6] This produced a cascade of power failures that, within ten minutes, left around 50 million consumers without power. New York, Detroit, Cleveland, Toronto, and other major cities were blacked out for many hours. Months of investigation were required to establish the precise path of failure propagation through this huge, complex network.

In addition to hardware failures, software failure can also propagate alarmingly. In January 1990, a minor mechanical malfunction in an AT&T telephone-switching center in lower Manhattan caused the switch to shut down and automatically reset its control software. When the switch came up again, it notified other switches around the country that they could begin routing calls to it. Unfortunately, these notifications triggered a control software bug, which shut down the switches that received it. When these switches restarted, they further propagated the problem, and so on. Before the problem could be diagnosed and corrected, it had affected all 114 switching centers in the AT&T system, severely disabled the system for nine hours, prevented 70 million of the 138 million long-distance and 800-number calls placed on the system that day from getting through, and caused hundreds of millions of dollars in business losses.[7]

And it can get even worse. Since different types of networks are often functionally interdependent, failure of one type can produce failure of another. Telecommunication and electrical supply networks are particularly closely intertwined. Telecommunication devices require electric power, and increasingly, power grids are managed by means of sophisticated telecommunication systems. Similarly, if the power grid goes out, the traffic lights cease to function, and the traffic network rapidly snarls up. And, where pumps power water and air supply networks, power failures quickly render many buildings uninhabitable. Even where there is no direct functional interdependency, the physical co-location of network links can propagate failures; for example, the tunnels into Manhattan provide both transportation and telecommunication conduits, so destruction would simultaneously affect both types of networks.[8] The destruction of the World Trade Center towers, for example, took out both a major subway transportation node in the basement and a concentration of wireless telecommunication nodes on the roof.

One often-told, dramatic tale of cross-network cascading is that of a Worcester, Massachusetts, kid who hacked a telephone switch—wiping out custom settings and disabling telephone service in the area.[9] The automated control tower of the local airport used the telephone network to activate runway landing lights. Thus, when an approaching plane signaled the tower to switch on the lights, the lights failed to operate, and the airport had to be closed.

The August 14, 2003, blackout of Manhattan provided the most dramatic illustration so far of large-scale, cross-network failure in a modern city. When the grid went down, the lights and the air conditioners went off in buildings without emergency back-up systems, so large numbers of workers were quickly forced out of office towers. They found that the subway was not running, and traffic lights were inoperative, so the streets were jammed with commuters walking home. Most telephones did not work either, so communication and coordination were difficult. The water supply soon gave out in many buildings, since electric-powered pumps had failed. And many hotel guests were locked out of their rooms all night when card-key access systems ceased to function.

Sometimes large networks fail—unsurprisingly—due to general destruction of their infrastructure. When an ice storm hit Quebec in January 1998, for example, it brought down trees, poles, pylons, and tens of thousands of miles of power line spread over a huge area. As a result, large parts of Montreal were left without power for most of a freezing month, and the emergency repair effort was enormous. But, under some circumstances, highly localized failure or destruction can also produce major outages.

At the very dawn of the computer network era, pioneering researchers began to realize that the capacity of a network to continue functioning after damage depended a great deal upon its structure. Paul Baran introduced his seminal paper on distributed communications networks with a diagram showing three types of networks: centralized, decentralized, and distributed.[10] The *centralized networks* consist of links radiating from a central node, exactly as with the radial roads of Palma Nova and other centrally planned cities. They are, as Baran noted, "obviously vulnerable as destruction of a single central node destroys communication between the end stations."[11]

The *decentralized network* is a "set of stars connected in the form of a larger star," much like the patterns of major streets radiating from public places in the Wren plan for London, the Haussmann plan for Paris, and the L'Enfant plan for Washington, D.C. The centers of stars were still points of vulnerability, but the destruction of one such subcenter would not be a complete disaster; this would disconnect nodes directly linked to it, but the rest of the network could continue to function. Thus decentralization provided a way of scaling up and of isolating the effects of damage.

The *distributed network* is a nonhierarchical mesh, as in the street grids of Manhattan and Chicago, though not necessarily as regular. Its redundancy provides robustness; if nodes or links are destroyed, traffic

The Politics of Reconstruction

can simply route around the damage. But there is an efficiency penalty; to get from one node to another typically requires passing through many intermediate nodes, which are potential points of inefficient transfer and congestion. With a street grid, there are always many stop signs and traffic lights and many travel options, but one is unlikely to get stuck if there is a blockage somewhere. Similarly, if high-rise towers were interconnected by sky bridges, they would enhance safety through the increased redundancy and wider spatial distribution of their escape networks, but they would be harder to control by means of security checkpoints at entry-level elevator lobbies.

In practice then, large transportation, communication, and other networks are often combinations of stars and meshes—seeking a balanced combination of the advantages of both. So Palma Nova has not only its radial arteries, but also several rings of streets concentrically around the central piazza, and smaller piazzas (forming minihubs) at the centers of its wedge-shaped segments. The radial streets of Paris and Washington are superimposed upon meshes and grids of more minor streets, and the radial transportation links of many modern cities are supplemented by ring roads and ring lines. Air transportation networks are increasingly organized around major hubs but continue to include links that do not pass through the hubs. And the vast structure of the Internet has turned out to be highly hierarchical, with a dominant pattern of major hubs, but also with significant amounts of meshing in many regions.[12]

The large, decentralized networks that increasingly dominate our globalized world have turned out to be remarkably resistant to random accidents and failures. Nodes and links may go down here and there, but unless they unfortunately happen to be vital hubs or critical arteries, the effects are usually brief and localized. But deliberate attack is another matter; intelligent attackers can pick out the most attractive targets—going simultaneously for several major hubs, for example, rather than wasting their ammunition on peripheral nodes. Even a structure as large and heavily meshed as the Internet is probably very vulnerable to coordinated pinpoint attacks. There are good reasons to conceal, harden, and defend major switching nodes.

The attack on New York's World Trade Center towers vividly drove home these lessons about network structure. In the immediate aftermath, the surface street network, which is highly redundant, continued

Figure 14.1.
Telecommunications infrastructure clustered on the World Trade Center towers.

to function effectively. The New York subway system is much less redundant, so destruction of a major node beneath the towers produced significant, long-term transportation outages. But the attraction of the target to the terrorists was not only the concentration of human life and the powerful symbolism of the towers, but also the role of lower Manhattan as a key node in the global financial network—supported by an astonishing concentration of telecommunications infrastructure. In September 2001, there was more fiber optic cable under the streets of Manhattan than in all of Africa. The two main telephone switches in the financial district had more lines than many European nations. And there were more than 1,500 antenna structures on top of the World Trade Center's north tower alone.

The destruction of telecommunications infrastructure was extensive. Verizon served more than 3 million local phone lines from its 140 West Street central office, which was badly damaged by debris, smoke, and water. AT&T had a central office in the basement of the World Trade Center; this survived the buildings' collapse, but the office lost its electric supply and eventually went down when back-up battery power gave out at 4 P.M. on September 11. Its service included 20,000 T1 lines and 1,200 T3 lines for customers throughout lower Manhattan and as far away as Long Island, so outages occurred not only locally, but also in a random pattern throughout the region. At least fifteen cellular telephone base stations were lost, while many others had their landline connections knocked out by the damage to Verizon's

Figure 14.2.
Telephone outages in Lower Manhattan immediately after 9/11 (from New York City Office of Emergency Management).

The Politics of Reconstruction

facility. And, of course, the antennas on top of the north tower were all gone.

This loss of infrastructure combined with a surge in demand for telephone service, with the result that the telephone network became severely overloaded. On September 11, telephone traffic in the New York area was at about double the normal levels. Cell phone networks were jammed; during the morning, fewer than 5 percent of calls were connected. Nationally and internationally, AT&T connected 431 million calls—about 20 percent more than normal. To keep outgoing lines from New York and Washington open, AT&T blocked incoming calls. It required an enormous telecommunications recovery effort to get the New York Stock Exchange back in operation six days later.

Figure 14.3.
A portable cell phone site deployed on Water Street in Lower Manhattan immediately after 9/11.

The Internet continued to operate much as its designers had hoped.[13] There were some localized outages due to infrastructure damage and power failures; there was a surge in e-mail traffic, and major news Web sites quickly became overloaded, but this had little effect on the global Internet. However, the New York metropolitan area was, at that point, the Internet's largest single international bandwidth hub, and several of its major switching centers (carrier hotels) were all within close proximity on the west side of lower Manhattan. It became apparent that a coordinated attack on the carrier hotels might have disconnected New York from the rest of the world, or the United States from Europe—though connections from the West Coast of the United States to Asia would still have continued to operate.

For an attacker, it can be a better strategy to exploit, rather than destroy, an enemy's networks. If access to a large-scale network can be gained, it eliminates the need to expend a lot of effort and energy to get to them. It isn't even necessary to possess comparable forces. Violence and destruction can be delivered with modest means but pinpoint accuracy, by infiltrating or hijacking those networks.

The AIDS epidemic provided a brutal preview of this strategy. The HIV virus, as we quickly discovered, efficiently propagates itself through the network established by human sexual contact and by blood transfer—a network that has, in recent decades, been vastly ex-

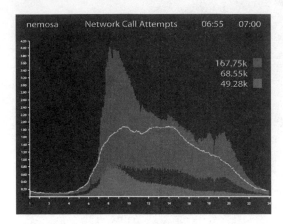

Figure 14.4.
AT&T call volume after
9/11.

tended through high-speed travel and population mobility. It has infiltrated itself into this
human construction and has hijacked it for its
own purposes. And in doing so, it has created
a distributed state of siege—not the geographically focused sort, such as the type for which
Palma Nova's walls were designed, but one
manifested at a million condoms. Unlike the
plagues of old, which required population density to flourish and could often be kept at bay
by isolating and quarantining populations,
AIDS depends upon the existence of connected
paths—maybe extending over vast distances—within a global network.

Computer viruses are chunks of mobile code in digital form, rather
than genetic code in bioformat, but they turn out to operate in much
the same way. They are too familiar, now, to require detailed explanation, and their potential for destruction has grown exponentially
with the Internet. Just a week after September 11, for example, the
Nimda virus struck 85,000 servers throughout the world, producing
far more Internet congestion, outages, and economic damage than the
infrastructure losses resulting from the World Trade Center attack.[14]
Such viruses dramatically illustrate the downsides of decentralizing
production and dematerializing functionality; they can be produced by
even the moderately computer literate (right down to modestly skilled
script kiddies) at any of the world's millions of Internet nodes and
propagated rapidly from those nodes. They can even be injected wire-
lessly into the Internet, from mobile and transient locations. And, like
the HIV virus, they generate a globally distributed state of siege—this
time manifested at e-mail filters that exclude suspicious incoming messages, virus-protected personal computers, and corporate network fire-
walls.

Miniaturization, biotechnology, and nanotechnology provide yet
more opportunities to infiltrate networks and turn them destructively
back upon themselves. Small quantities of powerful toxins, virulent
bioagents, or even vicious little nanobots can be produced and potentially distributed precisely where they will do the most damage, through
air and water utility networks.[15] Air conditioning duct networks some-

times seem as if they had been designed expressly for this purpose; they provide efficient conduits from conveniently accessible intakes to all of the inhabited spaces of a building, bypassing guards and locked doors. In this case, the distributed siege points (now being put in place, in some contexts, as the danger is recognized) are filters, valves, and electronic sensors designed to sniff out and divert threats.

Finally, the miniaturization of destructive power has extended the possibility of infiltration to all forms of transportation networks. The Unabomber did not need B-52s or million-dollar missiles to deliver heavy bombs; he could use the mail system to put sufficiently deadly quantities of explosives right into the hands of his victims. For anthrax spores, the mailed packages can be even smaller. Suicide bombers can just drive a car, hail a cab, or take the bus to their destinations. A fertilizer bomb can be delivered by van or truck to a building's loading dock or underground garage, or simply driven up to the front door— hence the rows of bollards, Jersey barriers, and other ad hoc fortifications that now deface many urban landscapes. Nuclear weapons can be introduced via shipping containers right into the hearts of major cities. And, particularly in the aftermath of the September 11 hijackings, airport check-in gates have become the most vivid and obtrusive reminders of the emerging state of distributed siege.

The densely, globally networked world is emphatically not (as early cyberspace utopians had sometimes imagined) inherently one of self-regulating, libertarian harmony. The proliferation and geographic distribution of access points—the very essence of the benefits of networks—also multiply and distribute opportunities to create threats to the safety and well-being of those who have come to rely upon network capabilities. The entry barriers often aren't high: many network-friendly destructive devices can be fashioned without much specialized knowledge, skill, or resources, and much of the information can be downloaded or ordered from the Internet. (As Martin Amis wrote in the immediate aftermath of September 11, "a score or so of Stanley knives produced two million tons of rubble."[16]) High-speed, efficient transfers within networks make these threats difficult to localize and isolate, so that destructive effects may be felt far from the site of an initial security breach. And effective, inexpensive, widely deployable filters and barriers are not easy to devise.[17]

As a result, the characteristic fear of our times is no longer the barbarians beyond the gates (or beyond the Cold War missile shield), but foreign bodies networked into our midst.[18] In the context of transportation networks and human movement, it manifests itself in the understandable fear of the terrorist infiltrator and the suicide bomber, and in the indefensible—sometimes overlapping—ugliness of antiimmigrant, antirefugee, and antiminority demagoguery (the associated pathologies are closed borders, apartheid, and ethnic cleansing). At another level, it is the fear that containers and vehicles—from letters to airliners—will be infiltrated, hijacked, or redirected to serve as carriers of explosives and toxins.[19] Within communication networks, it is the fear of viruses, worms, hackers, and crackers. And within networks of water and air transfer, and body-to-body contact, it is the fear of deadly contagion.

To avoid becoming an easy and perpetually anxious target in a world of networks and distributed siege, one of the best strategies is to decentralize. Instead of being concentrated in a conspicuous downtown office tower, a business organization can be dispersed to a collection of electronically interconnected suburban locations. Instead of running a terrorist organization from a base that is subject to preemptive and retaliatory attack, a network can scatter its members throughout the community. In both cases, however, there is something to lose: intercommunication becomes more difficult and less effective, economies of scale may disappear, and loss of regular face-to-face contact may result in declining trust and cohesion. But as the effectiveness of telecommunication increases—and the risks of centralization increase—the balance may shift in favor of greater dispersal.

September 11, 2001, drove home the lesson that centralizing an organization at one location, such as a skyscraper carrying the corporate logo, does make it terribly vulnerable. As one New York real estate manager commented in the wake of the World Trade Center attack, "I'm not sure that tall trophy office buildings will ever be popular again."[20] And as William Safire proposed in his column: "We're a big, roomy country. Physically decentralized government, tied together electronically, would be the strength of our nation if DC were paralyzed."[21] These responses were probably exaggerated (particularly by antiurban conservatives), but it was clear that the tradeoffs in the bal-

The Politics of Reconstruction

ance of centralization versus dispersal would henceforth be evaluated differently.[22]

Technically, the agglomeration economies that motivate the clustering of functions within organizations, and of businesses in industrial clusters, are offset by the risks of intense spatial concentration. Where the benefits of agglomeration remain high relative to the risks of natural disasters, localized network failures (such as power blackouts), or terrorist attacks, clusters are likely to remain. But, where the risks of agglomeration are higher relative to the benefits (and, perhaps, where these risks are reflected in insurance rates and taxes to support protective services—the so-called terrorism tax) and where efficient network interconnection reduces the advantages of agglomeration, organizations are more likely to spread risk through decentralization.

By taking advantage of wireless connection and miniaturized, portable equipment, the strategic benefits of mobility combine with those of dispersal. This is by no means an entirely new idea among theorists of conflict; there have long been scattered, mobile guerillas, irregulars, and resistance groups. But inexpensive, efficient, mobile telecommunication adds a new dimension; such groups can now act in much more effectively coordinated ways. In offensive mode, they can mount simultaneous attacks on key nodes in widely dispersed networks, such as the servers and switching hubs of a computer network, or the transformer stations of a power grid. They can converge on a target, in coordinated fashion, from many directions at once. And they can swarm—suddenly and unexpectedly materializing at some location in order to accomplish their goal, then rapidly dispersing once again to avoid containment or retaliation. Electronically coordinated street demonstrators at the 1999 World Trade Organization meeting in Seattle demonstrated the efficacy of swarming.[23] The Critical Mass anticar bicyclists in the San Francisco Bay area have done even better at suddenly appearing out of nowhere to "cork" intersections and choke traffic,[24] and "swarm warfare" has become a fashionable topic among security analysts.[25] When George W. Bush visited London in November 2003, Scotland Yard tried to get cell phone system operators to shut down service in the vicinity of the president's motorcade, so that demonstrators would be deprived of their capacity to swarm effectively.

The same logic extends to telecommunication infrastructure. Even where nodes are multiplied and widely distributed, as with the Internet and cellular systems, they remain fixed targets. If nodes become wireless and mobile, however, the network itself transforms into a swarm that can rapidly reconfigure, elude attack, and move into areas of damage to restore service. After the 1994 Northridge earthquake, for example, cell phone providers developed a strategy of deploying trailer-mounted mobile cell sites, together with temporary, point-to-point microwave links to replace lost landlines, to rapidly restore service in damage zones. After September 11 in New York, this strategy was effectively used to reconstruct cell phone coverage and reweave it into the larger network (see fig. 14.3). And military strategists have begun to contemplate swarms of collaborating, robotic aircraft interconnected by an "Internet in the sky."[26]

If dispersal, mobility, and elusiveness do not sufficiently reduce vulnerability, other options are replication and replaceability. This is not a new idea either: generals have frequently been prepared to throw replaceable foot soldiers into the breach; automobiles have reserve tanks; and building codes require alternative fire exits in case one gets blocked. But the availability of cheap, plentiful electronic devices gives the concept a new spin. The Internet, for example, is built from relatively inexpensive channels and switches—which make extensive redundancy feasible, and thus enables routing around damage. Even better, a mobile, ad hoc network, supported by portable, disposable wireless devices, would combine the advantages of fluidity and redundancy. This would be particularly difficult for enemies to root out of communities: nodes could be scattered quickly; they would not have fixed locations; and a lot of them would have to be found and eliminated to take down the network. If enemies did succeed in destroying some nodes, new ones would just pop up anyway.

Defensive strategies that rely upon redundancy work even better with software than with hardware, since software can quickly and inexpensively be replicated, and the process of replication can readily be decentralized. Thus, file back-up and the distribution of back-up copies to distant locations have become standard computing practice. Whereas work on PCs was once saved to floppy disks or tapes; backup is now, increasingly, a network function. Every e-mail sent, for example, has copies created on multiple servers—and those servers are

The Politics of Reconstruction

automatically backed up at regular intervals. On networked computers, it is increasingly difficult to assure that a file is *not* getting backed up somewhere.

Organizations that rely upon digital data and that cannot afford downtime frequently create redundant sites with both duplicate hardware and replicated data. Financial firms, in particular, have come to depend upon back-up "hot sites"—with duplicate hardware, replicated software and data, and a crew of operators—that are ready to take over at a moment's notice. When Lehman Brothers' Manhattan data center was destroyed in the September 11 collapse of the World Trade Center towers, the chief technology officer was able to activate a back-up facility in New Jersey from his Blackberry text messenger, while he was escaping down the stairs. The firm was trading again the next day.[27] By noon on the day of the attacks, all major New York banks had activated their disaster recovery plans. Cantor-Fitzgerald, which lost 700 employees, was trading from back-up centers in New Jersey and London when the bond market reopened two days later.[28] Many other affected financial firms used their disaster recovery contractors (SunGard, Comdisco, and others) to retrieve data from off-site back-up locations.[29] But law firms, which depended more upon original documents on paper, had much more difficult recoveries. And at least one architecture firm, which did not have off-site back-up, had to retrieve files piecemeal from the servers of its collaborators and consultants.

If instant recovery capacity is not necessary, back-up sites can disperse over great distances. But, where large amounts of data must be transferred to and from back-up sites, and where high-speed recovery is imperative, network capacity limits dispersal. For example, the ES-CON protocol used by IBM mainframes to connect to remote mass storage devices is limited to about a forty-kilometer radius. And the back-up sites for Manhattan financial firms are mostly to be found elsewhere in Manhattan, in New Jersey, and in Brooklyn.

Since September 11, 2001, there has been heightened interest in putting distance into distributed computing architectures, so that computer clusters can extend beyond potential disaster footprints. This requires a combination of high-speed data links capable of operating over hundreds of kilometers and servers and storage systems designed to absorb an increased load and to continue operating seamlessly when some of the nodes in the cluster go down. It seems likely that this sort of enterprise continuity technology will continue to develop.[30]

Switching to a back-up site is not, of course, a possibility for a small deli adjacent to the large financial firm. In fact, the electronic relocation of its neighbor's center of activity may leave it without customers. Strategies of electronic back-up and redundancy are powerful, but their effects are differential.

Shift this principle to a metalevel, and the process of replication and dispersal can, itself, be replicated, dispersed, and mobilized. This makes it more robust than a process centralized at a single, potentially vulnerable production facility. Parasites, bacteria, and viruses provide the model for this; under favorable conditions they are self-replicating, and they can distribute themselves simultaneously through multiple channels—making them particularly difficult to stamp out.

Since the operation of writing information in memory is fundamental to digital computation, the logic of replication quickly manifested itself on early computers. Programmers learned to code loops that would write the same information repeatedly into memory—rapidly filling it to overflowing. With slightly trickier logic, and abandonment of the distinction between program and data (easy in languages like Lisp), they could write chunks of code that replicated themselves. At that stage, the worst outcome of out-of-control replication was crashing an isolated computer, which could easily be fixed by rebooting. But the interconnection of computers into networks instantly changed that. It became possible to send destructive code from computer to computer—either explicitly, or more insidiously, by clandestinely attaching it to e-mail or other transfers. Furthermore, it was quite trivial to write code that automatically replicated itself whenever it landed on a new host, and then attached itself to outgoing e-mail to propagate further. Thus, in the Internet era, computer viruses successfully imitated their biological predecessors.

Mobile, self-replicating code can be benign (like many biological viruses), and it can even provide an efficient way of performing useful functions on a large scale, but it can also wreak destruction. As Internet users have discovered, maliciously circulated viruses can overwrite memory, erase files, make software misbehave, display offensive messages, take over one machine to attack others, and crash the entire system. The varieties of damage that viruses can inflict are limited only

The Politics of Reconstruction

by the imagination and technical skill (and it often doesn't take a lot) of programmers with bad intentions and network connections.

By now, a standard (indeed, often essential) defense against viruses is software that scans incoming mail to detect and block attached viruses and that also scans disks to detect and eliminate any viruses that may have lodged there. But the difficulties are just like those encountered with defenses against biological viruses; different remedies are required for different viruses, there is a continual threat of new viruses for which there aren't yet any defenses in place, and some viruses may replicate themselves with mutations that allow them to elude the defenses. Thus there is a problem of scale and complexity, and an ongoing, escalating battle between virus and antivirus forces.

Code replication not only provides the means to propagate viruses, it also provides a way to amass forces for sudden, large-scale attacks from multiple directions. In distributed denial-of-service attacks on Internet servers, hackers surreptitiously take over many machines, then employ them simultaneously to fire streams of packets at target servers, thus overloading and bringing them down. Furthermore, denial-of-service attacks can be directed not just at a single server, but at multiple servers all at once, potentially providing a way to overcome the Internet's defensive redundancy. In October 2002, for example, a denial-of-service attack was directed against nine of the Internet's thirteen root servers scattered around the globe.[31] A sustained, successful denial-of-service attack on all thirteen of the root servers would crash the Internet.

By destroying digital resources, disabling the computers we have come to rely upon, and disrupting communications, Internet viruses can inflict immense economic damage, but they mostly aren't a direct threat to human life and safety. However, this will change as embedded networked devices proliferate, as our bodies become network nodes, and as transportation, power distribution, water, and air supply networks are increasingly intertwined with telecommunication networks. The price we will pay for integration and intelligent management of large-scale networks is that of continuously and resourcefully defending them against more and more potent virus threats.

As capacity for the fabrication of physical artifacts shifts from centralized factories to small-scale, networked, personal fabrication facilities, traditional monopolies on the production and distribution of weapons begin to break down. Personal fabrication of printed texts, toys, or electronic components may be unambiguously a good thing, but personal fabrication of guns and nuclear detonators, from downloaded designs and apparently innocuous materials electronically ordered from scattered suppliers, certainly is not. Personal biotechnology—maybe the fabrication of viruses from online genetic information and mail-order supplies—is even scarier. By 2002 researchers had, for example, fabricated infectious polioviruses using a publicly available genome sequence, inert chemicals, and modest laboratory equipment.[32] Self-replicating nanobots (which eliminate the distinction between production machinery and the products of that machinery) are not inconceivable. And the most apocalyptic scenario is of a world suddenly overwhelmed by runaway, self-replicating gray goo. As the well-known computer technologist Bill Joy has suggested, we now have the possibility "not just of weapons of mass destruction but of knowledge-enabled mass destruction (KMD), this destructiveness hugely amplified by the power of self-replication."[33]

Where cities from Troy to Palma Nova defended their encircling walls, New York and other twenty-first-century cities must defend their distributed networks against accident and attack. They must protect physical network infrastructure against destruction, not only locally, but also at its far-flung extremities. They must assure that there is sufficient redundancy in vital networks, so that these networks are not vulnerable to failure or destruction of a few key nodes or links. They must introduce circuit breakers, relief valves, and similar protections against failure propagation. They must find effective ways to guard against introduction of explosives, toxins, bioagents, portable code, and other destructive agents, and against hijacking for unintended purposes of vehicles, servers, and similar delivery devices. And they must contend with both threats of physical destruction and threats to the logical integrity of networks from viruses, worms, software attack tools, and the like.

Conversely, if cities can keep their networks operating in times of disaster, they can quickly mobilize regenerative resources. Transportation networks can bring in relief supplies from distant parts of the globe. Mobile wireless nodes can swiftly restore telecommunications. And, increasingly, high-speed digital linkages to distant back-up sites and geographically distributed enterprises can keep economic activity cranking along.

Traditionally, there was safety in numbers and in surrounding walls. Now, urban security and resilience are grounded in patterns of connectivity. And defensive rings have fragmented and recombined. They no longer surround entire settlements and separate them from the countryside, but enclose countless, scattered network access points—from airport departure gates to password-protected personal computers.

All this dramatically compresses the time scale for measuring urban resilience. Until now, we have mostly conceived of it in terms of years-long cycles of economic decline answered by regeneration, and of physical decay or destruction followed by rebuilding. But twenty-first-century cities face the threats of swift and stealthy attack, of network failures that suddenly propagate from far away, and of large-scale, unexpected system collapses. They cannot afford to go down in the face of them—even for short periods. Increasingly, they need the capacity to respond instantly, and to bounce back from disasters within minutes.

Notes

Portions of this chapter are based on work supported by the National Science Foundation's Urban Research Initiative under Grant No. SBR-981778, "Information Technology and the Future of Urban Environments."

1. Construction of Palma Nova commenced in 1593. It was intended to serve as a fortified, garrison outpost of Venice. The design is usually credited to the Venetian architect and urban theorist Vincenzo Scamozzi, author of the treatise *L'Idea dell'Architettura Universale*, which deals extensively with fortified cities. Today, Palma Nova is a sleepy country town, one of the best surviving examples of what Lewis Mumford sardonically called the "asterisk plan."
2. Lewis Mumford, *The Culture of Cities* (New York: Harcourt, Brace, 1960).
3. Lewis Mumford, *The City in History* (London: Secker & Warburg, 1961), p. 410.
4. Joint Economic Committee, U.S. Congress, *Security in the Information Age: New Challenges, New Strategies*, May 2002, p. 2; http://www.house.gov/jec/security.pdf.

5. Ibid., p. 42.

6. U.S.–Canada Power System Outage Task Force, *Interim Report: Causes of the August 14th Blackout in the United States and Canada* (Washington, D.C.: U.S. Department of Energy, 2003).

7. Leonard Lee, "The Bigger They Are," in his *Day the Phones Stopped* (New York, Donald I. Fine, 1991), pp. 71–97.

8. Sandeep Junnarkar, "Keeping Networks Alive in New York," www.CNETNews.com, downloaded 28 August 2002.

9. The story is recounted in Scott Charney, "Transition between Law Enforcement and National Defense," in *Security in the Information Age*, May 2002, pp. 52–60.

10. Paul Baran, *On Distributed Communications: 1. Introduction to Distributed Communications Network*, Memorandum RM-3420-PR (Santa Monica, Calif: RAND, August 1964).

11. High-rise towers suffer from a similar vulnerability when, as in the World Trade Center, their vertical access routes are concentrated in central service cores. Building codes do require multiple, separated means of escape, and this may suffice in the case of relatively small fires, but it is insufficient when catastrophic events destroy cores entirely.

12. Bill Cheswick's beautiful, widely published Internet maps illustrate this. See http://research.lumeta.com.

13. National Research Council, *The Internet under Crisis Conditions: Learning from September 11* (Washington, D.C.: National Academies Press, 2002).

14. The scale of attacks has escalated with that of the Internet itself. When Robert Morris's notorious worm struck in 1988, it crashed about 6,000 servers—roughly 10 percent of the Internet's total at that time.

15. On the distribution of bioagents, and the potential consequences, see Richard Preston, *The Demon in the Freezer* (New York: Random House, 2002).

16. Martin Amis, "Fear and Loathing," *Guardian Unlimited*, downloaded 18 September 2001, http://www.guardian.co.uk/Archive/Article/0,4273,4259170,00.html.

17. Filters and barriers are relatively cheaper and easier to deploy in the digital world than in the physical world, though advances in miniaturized, inexpensive sensor technology may begin to change this. It is likely that water, air, and other supply networks will increasingly be equipped with early warning systems that permit operators to swiftly quarantine affected sections.

18. For a more detailed discussion of this point see Thomas Homer-Dixon, "The Rise of Complex Terrorism," *Foreign Policy*, January/February 2002, downloaded from http://www.foreignpolicy.com/issue_janfeb_2002/homer-dixon.html.

19. See, for example, John R. Stilgoe, "Observation: Terrorism, Box Trucks and the American Elite," *Topic* 1 (Summer 2002).

20. Charles V. Bagli and Leslie Eaton, "Seeking New Space, Companies Search Far from Wall St.," *New York Times*, 14 September 2001, pp. A1, A6.

21. William Safire, "An Optimist's What-if," *New York Times*, 29 October 2001, p. A15. He elaborated: "House members at home in their districts could be called into virtual session, as could the Senate; debates could be on the Internet, deals made in conference calls and votes taken (as they now are) electronically."

22. For a typical polemic in favor of increased decentralization, motivated by the World Trade Center attacks, see Oliver Morton, "Divided We Stand," *Wired*, December 2001, pp. 152–155. For some anecdotal indications of a shift in this direction several months after September 11, see Charles V. Bagli, "Seeking Safety, Manhattan Firms Are Scattering," *New York Times*, 29 January 2002, pp. A1, A24. For some analysis from an economic perspective, see Edward L. Glaeser and Jesse M. Shapiro, "Cities and Warfare: The Impact of Terrorism on Urban Form," Harvard Institute for Economic Research Discussion Paper 1942, December 2001, downloaded from http://papers.ssrn.com/abstract=293959, and William C. Wheaton and Jim Costello, "The Future of Lower Manhattan, Signals from the Marketplace," MIT Center for Real Estate, 2002, downloaded from http://web.mit.edu/cre/www/news/ncnyc.html.

23. Paul de Armond, "Netwar in the Emerald City: WTO Protest Strategy and Tactics," in *Networks and Netwars*, ed. John Arquilla and David Ronfeldt (Santa Monica, Calif.: RAND, 2001), pp. 201–235.

24. For a more detailed discussion of Critical Mass, with pointers to Web sites and newspaper accounts, see David Ronfeldt and John Arquilla, "What Next for Networks and Netwars?" in Arquilla and Ronfeldt, *Networks and Netwars*, pp. 336–337.

25. See, for example, John Arquilla and David Ronfeldt, *Swarming and the Future of Conflict*, Document DB-311-OSD (Santa Monica, Calif.: RAND, 2000). The idea of swarming was given considerable popular currency by Kevin Kelly, *Out of Control: The New Biology of Machines, Social Systems and the Economic World* (Reading, Mass.: Addison-Wesley, 1994).

26. Lakshmi Sandhana, "The Drone Armies Are Coming," *Wired News*, 30 August 2002.

27. "Lehman Brothers' Network Survives," *NetworkWorldFusion*, 26 November 2001.

28. "Cantor-Fitzgerald: 47 Hours," *Baseline*, downloaded from www.baselinemag.com/article2/0,3959,36807,00.asp.

29. "Businesses Start the Recovery Process," *NetworkWorldFusion*, 12 September 2001.

30. See, for example, Sun and Nortel's Enterprise Continuity System, introduced in 2002. "Partners-System Integrators and Alliances—Sun." Viewed on July 15, 2004. http://www.nortelnetworks.com/prd/sia/sun/ecs.html.

31. Associated Press, "Powerful Attack Upsets Global Internet Traffic," *New York Times*, 23 October 2002, p. A19.

32. Rick Weiss, "Polio-Causing Virus Created in N.Y. Lab: Made-from-Scratch Pathogen Prompts Concerns about Bioethics, Terrorism," *Washington Post*, 12 July 2002, p. A-1.

33. In his well-known article "Why the Future Doesn't Need Us," *Wired* 8, no. 4 (April 2000), Bill Joy drew widespread attention to the dangers of runaway, destructive self-replication in genetics, nanotechnology, and robotics. As he remarked, "Gray goo would surely be a depressing ending to our human adventure on Earth, far worse than mere fire or ice, and one that could stem from a simple laboratory accident. Oops." http://www.wired.com/archive/8.04/joy_pr.html.

Conclusion
Axioms of Resilience

■ What can we conclude about the nature of urban resilience from this global tour of disaster and recovery? Do the wide range of historical and contemporary accounts presented in this book reveal common themes that can help us understand the processes of physical, political, social, economic, and cultural renewal and rebirth? Or are the trajectories of recovery simply too diverse to distill common elements sufficient to develop an interpretive framework? Are cities resilient because their recovery has followed some particular identifiable model, or are they resilient only because interpreters choose to define resilience in such fluid and malleable ways?

We began this book with the observation that, at least for the last two centuries or so, nearly every traumatized city has been rebuilt in some form. This historical fact raises the question of whether it is possible for a city to be rebuilt *without* being resilient. What does the concept of a *resilient city* mean if every city appears to qualify? Is it even prudent to compare a city like Jerusalem, challenged throughout its many centuries with profound suffering and repeated bloodshed, and a swaggering upstart like Chicago in 1871? In short, the contents of this book demand that we question its very title.

What, then, is urban resilience? On one level, urban resilience implies a physical capacity to bounce back from a significant obstacle, much like a rubber ball dropped on the pavement. But cities are not rubber balls, nor is a disaster like an asphalt plane, from which a rebound can be definitively predicted by a set of mathematical equations.

LAWRENCE J. VALE

THOMAS J. CAMPANELLA

This constraint has not prevented some scholars from seeking systematic analyses of post-disaster recovery. Perhaps the best comparative study is *Reconstruction following Disaster*, a project focused on natural disasters, which was sponsored by the U.S. National Science Foundation in the mid-1970s.[1]

Its team of researchers proposed and tested a "model of recovery activity" that classified the recovery process into four distinguishable (if overlapping) stages: "1) Emergency responses; 2) Restoration of the restorable; 3) Reconstruction of the destroyed for functional replacement; and 4) Reconstruction for commemoration, betterment and development." These stages follow a curious temporal predictability: the time required for each activity period (except the last) is approximately ten times as many weeks as the previous one. Thus, when plotted on a logarithmic scale, the four stages appear as a series of approximately equal intervals. Each stage encompasses a set of actions: the emergency phase is marked by efforts to cope with the injured, with the loss of life, and with the presence of debris and is a period when "normal social and economic activities cease or are drastically changed." Depending on the scale of societal resources, this phase may last from a few days to many weeks. Its end is signaled by the cessation of search-and-rescue operations, the "drastic reduction in emergency mass feeding and housing," and the reopening of principal streets.[2]

The second period—restoration—entails the reestablishment of "major urban services, utilities, and transport, the return of those refugees intending to return, and substantial clearance of the rubble." This phase, again depending on available resources, lasts from several months to more than a year. The third phase—dubbed the "replacement reconstruction period"—is marked by the rebuilding of the capital stock to pre-disaster levels and the "replacement of the population." In areas that suffer high death tolls, of course, such reference to a replacement population is no more than a statistical convenience, meant to signal that the area once again contains adequate housing, jobs, and amenities to support the pre-disaster population. During this period, these scientists and social scientists observed, "social and economic activities return to predisaster levels or greater." Finally, with the return to prosperity and sociability, the fourth stage is defined by "commemorative, betterment and development reconstruction." These large projects—usually government-financed—serve "three varied but

The Politics of Reconstruction

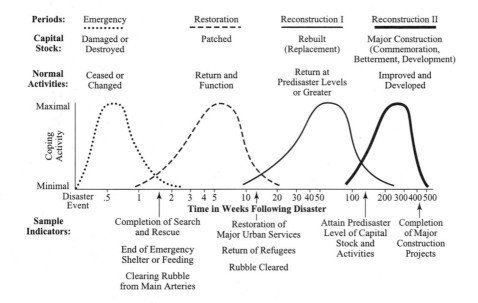

Periods:	Emergency	Restoration	Reconstruction I	Reconstruction II
Capital Stock:	Damaged or Destroyed	Patched	Rebuilt (Replacement)	Major Construction (Commemoration, Betterment, Development)
Normal Activities:	Ceased or Changed	Return and Function	Return at Predisaster Levels or Greater	Improved and Developed

Coping Activity — Maximal / Minimal

Disaster Event   .5   1   2   3 4 5   10   20   30 40 50   100   200 300 400 500

Time in Weeks Following Disaster

Sample Indicators:	Completion of Search and Rescue	Restoration of Major Urban Services	Attain Predisaster Level of Capital Stock and Activities	Completion of Major Construction Projects
	End of Emergency Shelter or Feeding	Return of Refugees		
	Clearing Rubble from Main Arteries	Rubble Cleared		

sometimes interrelated functions: to memorialize or commemorate the disaster; to mark the city's post-disaster betterment or improvement; or to serve its future growth or development."[3] Applied to the recovery of San Francisco following the earthquake and fire of 1906, the model does indeed seem to yield the hypothesized pattern of quadruple-phased activity.

In the course of a thousand weeks (approximately twenty years), San Francisco demonstrated its resilience, rebounding from disaster in all of the measures judged relevant by the team. Since such patterns seemed to hold in other cases as well, the authors concluded, "[D]isaster recovery is ordered, knowable, and predictable." Still, they acknowledged that the rate of recovery is "directly related to the extent of the damage, the available recovery resources, the prevailing predisaster trends, and such qualities as leadership, planning and organization for reconstruction."[4] This sort of analytical framework is certainly a valuable contribution to the task of explaining post-disaster urban recovery, yet it masks as much as it reveals. It is not enough to pose general models for urban recovery; in this book we have been asking *who* recovers *which* aspects of the city, and by what mechanisms.

The extent, pace, and direction of urban recovery are chartable only in very general terms and present a woefully incomplete picture of

Chart C.1.
A model of disaster recovery activity. Redrawn from *Reconstruction Following Disaster.*

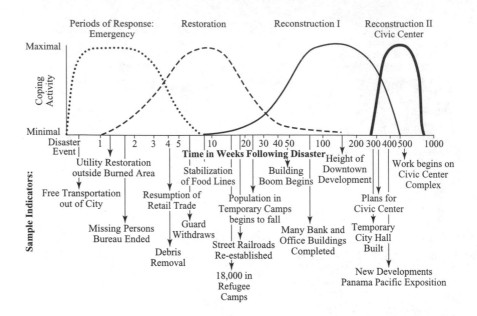

Periods of Response: Emergency | Restoration | Reconstruction I | Reconstruction II Civic Center

Coping Activity — Maximal / Minimal

Time in Weeks Following Disaster

Disaster Event | 1 | 2 | 3 | 4 | 5 | 10 | 20 | 30 | 40 | 50 | 100 | 200 | 300 | 400 | 500 | 1000

Sample Indicators:

Utility Restoration outside Burned Area

Free Transportation out of City

Resumption of Retail Trade

Missing Persons Bureau Ended

Stabilization of Food Lines

Guard Withdraws

Debris Removal

Building Boom Begins

Population in Temporary Camps begins to fall

Street Railroads Re-established

18,000 in Refugee Camps

Many Bank and Office Buildings Completed

Height of Downtown Development

Plans for Civic Center

Temporary City Hall Built

New Developments Panama Pacific Exposition

Work begins on Civic Center Complex

Chart C.2.
San Francisco after 1906:
A model of disaster
recovery activity.
Redrawn from
*Reconstruction Following
Disaster.*

reality. Moreover—even if every disaster follows a predictable pattern of rescue, restoration, rebuilding, and remembrance—it is not this generality that is interesting; what matters are the variations. We can only conceptualize the pattern of recovery if we delve into what drives the variation. It matters, for instance, that the Chinese central government viewed the devastation of Tangshan in 1976 as a threat to national industrial development, or that the contending governments of postwar Berlin viewed the reemergent city as an ideological battleground of the Cold War. Likewise, the particular priorities undergirding the reconstruction of Warsaw are incomprehensible without taking into account the parallel mandates of Polish nationalism and Soviet communism. The reconstruction of Mexico City after the 1985 earthquake was similarly prodded by the dominant political party's efforts to retain legitimacy in the face of countervailing social movements that threatened to unseat it. Jerusalem, traumatized more than perhaps any other city in history, has undergone repeated cycles of destruction and renewal, but each time the process of reconstruction and remembrance was carried out in profoundly different ways.

Although the history of urban destruction and resilience offers few direct parallels to any specific event that may occur today (however tempting conflation may be), the leaders who must cope with a disaster often have nowhere else but the past from which to seek guidance. At the end of the tumultuous day of September 11, 2001, New York mayor Rudolph Giuliani returned home to read Winston Churchill's recollections of coping with the London Blitz.[5] Journalists interpreting the events of 9/11 quickly converged on the term Ground Zero to describe the site of the World Trade Center attacks, even though that term had historically referred to the epicenter of a nuclear test or strike, from which blast and radiation effects could be measured. More generally, ever since Pliny the Younger dutifully penned his eyewitness account of the last moments of Pompeii, local disasters have gained an increasingly global reach. In 1902, the volcanic demise of St. Pierre on Martinique was front-page news across the Atlantic in Paris, just as the earthquake and fire of San Francisco dominated global headlines four years later. Whatever the cause, the world trade in disaster narratives continues to increase, as each battered place attempts to extract lessons and parallels from the plight of distant others—and to telegraph its own significance and suffering to an empathic global audience. This has produced a kind of trans-historical metacommunity of victimized cities, places, and peoples.

It is no simple task to extract common messages from such wide-ranging stories of urban resilience, let alone lessons that might be applied in the future. Yet several themes do stand out clearly, and the following twelve will be of particular interest to those planners, urban designers, politicians, and other professionals responsible for the well-being of the urban built environment.

1. Narratives of Resilience Are a Political Necessity

■ The ubiquity of urban rebuilding after disaster results from, among other things, a political need to demonstrate resilience. In this sense, resilience is primarily a rhetorical device intended to enhance or restore the legitimacy of whatever government was in power at the time the disaster occurred. Whatever its other effects, the destruction of a city usually reflects poorly on the government in power. If the chief function of government is to protect citizens from harm, the destruction of densely inhabited places presents the greatest possible challenge to its competence and authority. Cultivation of progress-oriented uplift therefore remains a priority for governments. Of course, governments conduct rescue operations and channel emergency funds as humanitarian gestures first and foremost, but they also do so as a means of saving face and retaining public office. Everyone loses if Linenthal's "toxic narrative" is ever allowed to become the predominant public sentiment.

In a sense, the notion of a resilient city is a societally and economically productive form of denial. Even the most horrific acts of destruction have been interpreted as opportunities for progressive reform, and the process whereby this narrative is assembled often happens very quickly. In Beirut, for example, the city's collective memory was tapped selectively to form an almost impressionistic collage of the past, one that studiously avoided the pain of literal reconstitution. In short, recovery entails real-time physical reconstruction of the built environment, but also the construction of a suitable interpretive framework that enables psychological, emotional, and symbolic recoveries.

2. Disasters Reveal the Resilience of Governments

■ In the aftermath of disaster, the very legitimacy of government is at stake. Citizens have the opportunity to observe how their leaders respond to an acute crisis and, if they are not satisfied, such events can be significant catalysts for political change. Even something as minor as a snowstorm can threaten or destroy the reelection chances of a mayor who is too slow in getting the plows out.[6] In Mexico City, residents saw that the existing bureaucracy lacked the flexibility and the will to place the needs of homeless citizens first. By criticizing the PRI's overriding interest in calming international financial markets, grassroots social movements gained new primacy.

At an equally basic level, the sudden disruption of a disaster causes governments to exercise power quite directly, revealing an often disquieting repertoire of techniques they can and will use when confronted with emergencies. In places that have undergone more substantial transformation in the aftermath of a major destructive act, this has most often entailed government expropriation of land. In postwar Warsaw, for instance, both the edited reconstruction of the Old Town and the modernist housing estates in adjacent areas depended on the power and flexibility assumed by a strong central government. Similarly, the extensive construction of new low-income housing in post-quake Mexico City required government expropriation of damaged properties. By contrast, the 1992 civil unrest in Los Angeles prompted local leaders to engage the private sector in the Rebuild L.A. campaign.

Rebuilding—whether seen through the lens of the creative destruction of capitalism or through the industrial agenda of some socialist five-year plan—is an economically necessary means to jump-start employment and spending, and thereby casts in bold relief the values and priorities of government.

3. Narratives of Resilience Are Always Contested

■ The rhetoric of resilience is never free from politics, self-interest, or contention. To many, the dominant progressive narrative is a premature assertion of closure, a call to move onward before everyone is on board (the term *closure*—much overused in the language of trauma and recovery—itself has a strident tone of finality to it). Narratives centered on promises of progress are often bankrolled by those who control capital and the means of production. They are manipulated by media pundits, politicians, and other voices carrying the greatest influence.

In any traumatic societal event, some people will always be more resilient than others, and so the notion of a resilient *city* is always inherently incomplete and unpredictable (a city is, after all, the sum of its citizenry). There is never a single, monolithic *vox populi* that uniformly affirms the adopted resilience narrative in the wake of disaster. Instead, key figures in the dominant culture claim (or are accorded) authorship, while marginalized groups or peoples are generally ignored in the narrative construction process. No one polled homeless people in Manhattan about how we should think about 9/11. Nor were the views of left-wing atheists solicited in Oklahoma City as that faith-based community struggled to recover from the 1995 terrorist bombing. The power politics of any resilience narrative makes it inherently controversial, and changing power dynamics within each affected community will determine just how contested the construction of resilience becomes.

4. Local Resilience Is Linked to National Renewal

■ A major traumatic event affecting a particular city often projects itself into the national arena. Recovery becomes linked to questions of national prestige and to the need to reestablish standing in the community of nations. In this sense, resilience takes on a wider ideological significance that extends well beyond the boundaries of the affected city.

In the wake of World War II, Warsaw's architects and planners confronted the nearly total obliteration of Polish heritage and painstakingly sought to use architecture and urban design as mechanisms of national renewal. Their Soviet overseers added their own ideological layer to this effort, interpreting Warsaw's renewal through the rosy lenses of socialist workers' housing and industrial development. But the common progressive thrust was unmistakable: the new Warsaw would be purged of the housing inequities of its capitalist past, relieved of the inefficiencies of its medieval street network, and stripped of the architectural accretions imposed by centuries of non-Polish overlords (even as new and highly visible buildings sponsored by Russians were dutifully welcomed).

Other cities have pursued modernity without Warsaw's heavy dose of retrograde nationalism, yet hardly abandoned the nationalist impulse. A disaster affecting a capital city carries an especially heavy burden, since any city that is host to many national institutions is swiftly equated with the nation-state as a whole.[7] When a Mexico City, a Beirut, a Warsaw, or a Tokyo suffers, all of Mexico, Lebanon, Poland, or Japan feels the consequences. Whether the trauma is a natural disaster, a war, or a terrorist strike, it is almost impossible not to conflate the local with the national. And in the case of a superpower like the United States, the chain of meaning extends to the global sphere as well.

5. Resilience Is Underwritten by Outsiders

■ Increasingly, the resilience of cities depends on political and financial influences exercised from well outside the city limits. Usually, in a federal system, urban resilience depends on the emergency allocation of outside funding from higher levels of government. In the United

The Politics of Reconstruction

States, this holds true for every federally designated "disaster area"—whether caused by a hurricane, snowstorm, heat wave, power outage, earthquake, flood, or terrorist act. Sometimes, where recovery is costly and local resources meager, funding comes from international aid sources (often with strings attached, in the form of political agendas of one sort or another). Chinese leaders recognized this potential in 1976 and refused to let international aid organizations get involved in the rebuilding of Tangshan—a decision that may well have cost many lives. The postquake Mexican leadership also initially shunned outside aid, part of an effort to reassure international investors about the nation's progress on economic liberalization. By contrast, the reconstruction of Europe under the American Marshall Plan was generally well received. In an extreme example of resilience underwritten by outsiders, Franco rebuilt Gernika to disguise his own earlier efforts to destroy the symbolic heart of Basque nationalism. The global influx of humanitarian aid to assist the Iranian city of Bam, leveled by an earthquake in late 2003, entailed far more than reconstruction of a vast mudbrick citadel; it also carried implications for rebuilding international relations with Iran.

Of course, at least in wealthy places, the underwriting of resilience is also expected to come from the insurance industry, even as legislative action in the United States seeks to limit insurer exposure in the case of terrorist events. The 9/11 attacks resulted in the most expensive loss in the history of the insurance industry. As one executive put it, "Terrorism was covered by insurance prior to Sept. 11 but never priced into insurance."[8] This is no longer the case. Downtown has now been euphemized as a "concentration of risk," and premiums on certain properties—especially prominent office skyscrapers—soared as much as 300 percent following the 2001 attacks on the Pentagon and World Trade Center. A year later the Boston-based company Applied Insurance Research attracted national attention when it unveiled a database of likely terror targets. Anthony Flint of the *Boston Globe* termed this "a landscape of fear in an Excel file"—a doomsday catalog of "high-visibility corporations, the tallest buildings in major cities, government facilities, and so-called trophy locations," including the White House, Disneyland, and the Golden Gate Bridge. The AIR database was assembled by a team of former FBI and CIA agents to enable insurers to accurately set premiums and coverage for a post-9/11 world.[9] Resilience, it seems, will continue to depend on both the terms of insurance deals and on the broader connectedness of national and global terms of assistance.

6. Urban Rebuilding Symbolizes Human Resilience

■   Each human lives a life that is centered on the well-being of self, family, and friends—all of which can be suddenly and totally shattered by a single cataclysmic event or the more protracted horrors of war. By contrast, urban reconstruction is a highly visible enterprise that conveys an almost heroic sense of renewal and well-being. Whatever our politics, we rebuild cities to reassure ourselves about the future. The demands of major rebuilding efforts also offer a kind of succor in that they provide productive distraction from loss and suffering and may help survivors to overcome trauma-induced depression. Architecture and urban design are, of course, central to the reconstruction and reimagining of traumatized places. Oklahoma City, for example, needed not just a memorial to those lost in the attack on the Murrah Building, but a replacement federal office facility, which was completed nearby in 2003.[10] In the effort to shore up the scattered and shattered lives of survivors, post-disaster urbanism operates through a series of symbolic acts, emphasizing staged ceremonies (such as the removal of the last load of debris from Ground Zero) and newly constructed edifices and memorials. These symbols, along with the processes needed to bring them about, constitute a key element of urban resilience. They link the ongoing psychological recovery process to tangible, visible signs of progress and momentum.

7. Remembrance Drives Resilience

■   Urban resilience, at least in its American form, is inextricably linked to the process of memorialization. In the 1970s, the team sponsored by the National Science Foundation could still put together a four-stage model of urban reconstruction that relegated the commemorative function to the fourth (though longest) stage. Yet, at least in the case

The Politics of Reconstruction

of terrorist attacks, the memorializing impulse now seems to demand more prompt and urgent attention.

In the past, many significant urban disasters have gone largely unmarked. Toronto created a waterfront park to memorialize those who lost their homes and lives following hurricane Hazel (1954) as a sensible response to the hazards of floodplain construction, but most cities have refrained from deliberate attempts to keep devastated areas un-rebuilt. Chicago memorialized its famous fire not with an open clearing but by long-standing adulation for the stone water tower that survived the conflagration. (Architect William Le Baron Jenney designed a fire memorial, to be "built out of safes and columns recovered from the debris," but the mayor refused to let it be built.)[11] Survivors of the great fires of London (1666), Boston (1872), Seattle (1889), Baltimore (1904), and Toronto (1904) devoted little or no land to memorials, although each fire dramatically altered the architectural fabric of its city. Hiroshima, on the other hand, built its Peace Park memorial—an island of open space in what quickly became again a dense industrial city—with the full support of the American occupation forces.[12] Usually, where emptiness persists, its cause is lack of market interest, not deliberate public policy. Such sites are far too valuable in the recovery process to remain empty.[13]

8. Resilience Benefits from the Inertia of Prior Investment

■ In most cases, even substantial devastation of urban areas has not led to visionary new city plans aimed at correcting long-endured deficiencies or limiting the risk of future destruction in the event of a recurrence. Wherever disasters are not accompanied by significant regime changes, the post-disaster era typically inherits the institutional structure and planning practices of the pre-disaster establishment. The aftermath of disaster is a time of desperate efforts to restore basic services—and to ensure that survivors are assisted with food, shelter, medical aid, and clothing; it is not generally deemed an appropriate moment to introduce radical changes in public policy or urban form. After London's Great Fire of 1666, architects including Christopher Wren, John Evelyn, and others proposed bold new plans for the city's street network. Yet, as Kevin Lynch has written, the most ambitious plans were thwarted by entrenched property interests and "a complicated system of freeholds, leases and subleases, with many intermixed ownerships."[14]

As was demonstrated in London, the power of property rights to stabilize the forms of cities—or stymie their evolution—cannot be overemphasized. Particular building codes and practices may change in an effort to limit future vulnerability to disaster or attack, and destruction may even inspire new types of architecture, but larger urban patterns are not easily or readily altered. This is not surprising in the United States or in parts of Western Europe, but it also extends to places such as Japan, where the long-standing preference for "land readjustment" practices has been exercised after disasters to alter the width of streets and the exact locations of property boundaries, but these changes have been implemented without fundamental changes to the larger pattern of urban structure.

In New York City, reconstruction of the World Trade Center has involved scores of powerful players in state and local government as well as community and professional organizations. The large number of "chefs" has resulted in a contentious planning and design process. In Manhattan, successful rebuilding entails a double inertia: a push to "heal" the lower Manhattan skyline and restore its pre-disaster drama, and an effort to restore parts of the original street pattern (i.e., that which preceded the WTC superblock). Whatever ultimately gets built will need to accommodate public demands for open space and memorials as well as private demands to restore huge amounts of office space and retail facilities—demands driven as much by insurance provisions as by market conditions.

More generally, the inertia of urban resilience is produced by a combination of undiminished geographic advantages, long-term investment in infrastructure, and place-dependent business networks. As Homer Hoyt wrote of post-1871 Chicago, "Many of Chicago's commercial rivals hoped that [the fire] would permanently halt the industrial and commercial progress of the city whose growth had amazed the world. . . . The railroad bands of iron and steel and the trade connections of Chicago, however, were too thoroughly established to permit that happening." Tellingly, in *Nature's Metropolis*, William

Cronon's magisterial account of the growth of nineteenth-century Chicago, the Great Fire warrants a scant four pages. The conflagration did little to derail the city's prodigiously productive relationship with its hinterland since "the main flow of capital that sustained Chicago's economy had precisely the same sources as before the fire."[15] Much the same could be said about London after 1666; however charred, the City still marked the center of world trade connections. Disaster spurs reinvestment and creative destruction as long as the source of urban economic strength remains fundamentally unaffected. Capitalism, in this sense, outflanks catastrophe.

9. Resilience Exploits the Power of Place

■ The immutability of policy-making organizations and the resilience of land planning are also linked to the great attachment many people have to particular places, even after such places have been substantially destroyed. As Kevin Lynch puts it, "A city is hard to kill, in part because of its strategic geographic location, its concentrated, persisting stock of physical capital, and even more because of the memories, motives, and skills of its inhabitants."[16] Mere cost accounting fails to calculate the most vital social and psychological losses—and the resultant political engagement—that are so often tied to the reclamation of particular places. No place better illustrates this than Jerusalem. For Jews, Christians, and Muslims, there is simply no *replacing* Jerusalem: "Men always pray at the same sites," religion scholar Ernest Renan observed of the city. "[O]nly the rationale for their sanctity changes from generation to generation and from one faith to another."[17]

Rebuilding cities fundamentally entails reconnecting severed familial, social, and religious networks of survivors. Repairing, improving, and reusing the pre-disaster physical infrastructure are means to reestablishing the human connectivity that such networks fostered. Urban recovery occurs network by network, district by district, not just building by building; it is about reconstructing the myriad social relations embedded in schools, workplaces, childcare arrangements, shops, places of worship, and places of play and recreation. Surely, this is at the heart of the Warsaw Old Town story (at least as it has been idealized), but it is also central to the reclaiming of downtown Mexico City after the earthquake, the struggles over Martyrs' Square in postwar Beirut, and the hard-fought campaign to retain Washington, D.C., as the national capital after its destruction in 1814. Attachment to particular places often trumps the economic temptation to clear a damaged site and begin anew in accordance with some more efficient or ideal pattern. The wholesale redesign of China's Tangshan is the exception, not the rule—and it was dependent upon an official government view that "new and modern" are always preferable to ideologically discredited past practices. The selective reconstruction of Warsaw's Old Town perfectly captures these twin impulses of nostalgia and opportunism; its planners found a way to recall past glories and also reduce traffic congestion by erecting an underground highway tunnel. Mussolini accomplished much the same thing in Rome through urban renewal, by pairing archaeological excavations with new multilane traffic axes through the city.[18]

10. Resilience Casts Opportunism as Opportunity

■   There is a fine line between capitalizing on an unexpected traumatic disruption to the fabric of a city as an opportunity to pursue some much-needed upgrading of infrastructure and facilities and the more dubious practice of using devastation as a cover for more opportunistic agendas yielding less obvious public benefits. The dual reconstruction of Chicago after the 1871 Great Fire illustrates the problem perfectly: the razed city was rebuilt once in a shoddy form and then—in reaction to this—rebuilt again with the grand and innovative skyscrapers that gave the resurrected city a bold new image and lasting fame.[19] The annals of urban recovery are replete with such examples where rebuilding yielded improvements over the pre-disaster built environment. Following the 1906 earthquake and fire, San Francisco clearly emerged as a much more desirable city, just as its boosters had boldly predicted. Across the continent, the explosion of a munitions ship in the Halifax harbor killed nearly 10,000 people in 1917 and destroyed more than two square miles of the city, yet the recovery "set off a chain reaction": "A new port was built, the retail section improved, the hospital enlarged, a new health center and central park [were] created, a new street railway [was] built, and telephone connections were laid to the rest of Canada and to the United States."[20]

In the decades that have followed, many city leaders have continued to take full advantage of disaster-borne opportunity. San Francisco officials exploited the damage done to the Embarcadero Freeway by the 1989 Loma Prieta earthquake as the opportunity to demolish this eyesore and augment the public amenities of 1.5 miles of downtown waterfront by creating a music pavilion, the new Harry Bridges Plaza, an extended trolley line, a revitalized historic ferry building and farmers' market, and enhanced ferry service.

Shortly after a massive IRA bomb devastated parts of the city center in 1996, government officials in Manchester, England, established Manchester Millennium, Inc., a public-private task force charged not only with the immediate recovery but also with longer-term regeneration. The redevelopment included new office, retail, and entertainment facilities, as well as a multilevel pedestrian plaza and a new museum highlighting urban life around the world. Kobe, Japan, capitalized on the devastation of the Great Hanshin-Awaji earthquake of 1995 to launch an ambitious ten-year plan to rebuild and modernize its port, and used earthquake debris and industrial waste from the Kansai area to reclaim land for a new island-airport.[21] Oklahoma City did not rebuild the Murrah Federal Building, largely destroyed in the terrorist bombing of 1995; instead, the government commissioned a nearby new high-security "U.S. federal campus" intended to link the north downtown neighborhood to the central business district. Moreover, the new Oklahoma City National Memorial, built on the Murrah site, was expected to greatly enhance tourist attention to a previously neglected part of the city. Most recently, debate about how to rebuild Ground Zero in New York has focused in part on improving the area as a regional transportation hub.

Of course, disaster-triggered opportunism can just as easily work against the best interests of the affected city. Following the 9/11 attacks in New York, many downtown firms either fled the city or established secondary operations in the suburbs—a process of decentralization that brought new growth to a number of communities around New York, at the city's expense.

11. Resilience, Like Disaster, Is Site-Specific

■ All disasters, not only earthquakes, have epicenters. Those who are victimized by traumatic episodes experience resilience differently, based on their distance from the epicenter. When speaking of traumatized cities, there is an understandable temptation to speak as if the city as a whole were a victim. September 11 was an "attack on New York"; the truck bomb that destroyed the Murrah Building was the "Oklahoma City bombing"; all of London faced the Blitz. Even in the largest experiences with devastation—such as the Tangshan earthquake—it was significant that the quake leveled vast residential and commercial areas but spared some industrial facilities, as this forced the government to consider vast new schemes for housing workers. In Mexico City, it was all-important to the subsequent process of recovery that the earthquake wreaked its greatest havoc on the highly symbolic city center. In Berlin, especially once the postwar city was divided into zones of occupation, it mattered mightily which parts of the city had been destroyed and which regime thereby inherited the debate over how to proceed with each particular reconstruction challenge.

The site-specificity of resilience will increasingly follow a different trajectory, given the global flow of electronic data and information. Information and communication networks can all too easily be obstructed by a disruption at some key node. When such a node is destroyed—as in the case of the Mexico City telephone and electrical substations during the 1985 earthquake—an entire country may suffer the consequences. Alternatively, the very nature of a digital electronic network provides redundancies and "work-arounds" that guard against a catastrophic breakdown of the system. Indeed, this is the power of the Internet: the instantaneous rerouting of data around a blockage is not generally associated with any particular place; even though a particular disaster may be site-specific, the network is not. Resilience in this case is a systemwide phenomenon. Distributed and redundant networks helped mightily in New York City during September 2001 but, conversely, meant little to mud-brick Bam in 2003. Inevitably, though, the world's ongoing litany of disasters will continue to intersect with the hyperconnected realm of the cybercity. The digital electronic era offers tempting new targets for mayhem but also affords new possibilities for resilience.

The Politics of Reconstruction

12. Resilience Entails More than Rebuilding

■ The process of rebuilding is a necessary but, by itself, insufficient condition for enabling recovery and resilience. We can see this most acutely in Gernika, where the trauma inflicted on the Basque town and its people by Hitler's bombers—and Franco's will—remained painful for decades, even after the town was physically rebuilt. Only with a regime change—forty years after the attack—did citizens feel free to express the full measure of their emotional sorrow, or attempt to reestablish the Basque cultural symbols that had been so ruthlessly destroyed. In a different way, the struggle of Angelenos in South Central to recover from the traumatic destruction of the 1992 civil disturbances can only partly be measured by the modest efforts to erect new buildings in devastated areas. Of equal import, resilience has depended on the influx to the area of new people, not just new money. The energy of demographic change, often led by immigrants, has buoyed resilience and given it a human face.

The Los Angeles story, however, underscores the extent to which the economic hardship caused by civil unrest may be the most daunting challenge to recovery and resilience. How should we measure the resilience of cities that struggle to retain their economic base? Los Angeles remains vibrant, but other cities have lost large percentages of their population and building stock—not because of some destructive act such as a war or a natural disaster, but because industries moved away, or wealthier residents decamped for the suburbs, or misguided urban renewal efforts scattered whole populations of "blighted" neighborhoods.

Historically, cities have experienced many forms of economic irrelevance or abandonment. From the Silk Road to the Rust Belt, trade patterns have changed and sources of production have shifted, bypassing the economic bases of urban outposts once regarded as central. New York's devastated South Bronx faced the prospect of "planned shrinkage" in the 1970s although it later rebounded.[22] Once vibrant North Carolina cities like Durham and Burlington have suffered mightily as their major industries—textile manufacturing, railroads, and tobacco processing—went into decline. Other American cities have experienced major population and housing losses, sustained over a period of decades, that are comparable with the declines usually associated with some sudden disaster. As one extreme example, industrial Detroit has lost nearly a million people since 1950. Unlike earlier eras, however, today's nation-states seem far less willing to let cities disappear, even if their economic relevance has been seriously questioned. National governments provide special programs—such as urban renewal funds or empowerment zones—to assist particular cities, refusing to let them sink on their own. Although the effectiveness of such programs is often questioned, the will to rescue cities and spur additional economic development remains real.

One may well ask, then, whether a Durham or a Detroit ranks as a resilient city. Most growth in both places has been at the regional scale—in the burgeoning suburbs—while the cities themselves have struggled for decades. Yet at the same time, repopulation and rebuilding have commenced in earnest. In Durham, sprawling old tobacco warehouses are being transformed into chic condo complexes, while in Detroit new lower-density subdivisions, suburban in image, have risen on the bone piles of old, dense row housing (along with denser, more urban housing options in some places).[23] Clearly, even these much-battered cities have gained from resilient citizens, ambitious developers, and a dogged insistence that recovery will still take place.

■ Twelve axioms can hardly cover every facet of urban resilience. We have said relatively little, for instance, about efforts to plan in advance for the possibility of disasters. Nearly every city and country makes some attempt at pre-disaster planning, usually focusing on efforts to cope with whatever sorts of calamities are judged most likely to occur, or those feared to be most devastating. Civil defense agencies prepare plans to protect civilians in every conceivable circumstance, from floods to nuclear fallout to the effects of chemical or biological weapons. Inevitably, many such plans prove to be of limited value and have often been subject to ridicule. Basement bomb shelters, lined with cans of Campbell's soup, or the infamous "duck-and-cover" films of the Cold War era are still routinely parodied, and the more recent national run on duct tape and plastic sheeting, prompted by ill-considered advice from the U.S. Department of Homeland Security, fueled a legion of jokes on late-night television.

Still, humanitarianism alone will dictate that those cities and nations that can afford to provide protection in advance will continue to do so. Similarly, intelligence agencies operate to root out potential terrorists or stave off civil unrest, even in the face of growing criticism for threatening civil liberties. Whatever the merits, pre-disaster planning often exposes official priorities to provide disproportionate assistance to certain kinds of people and certain kinds of places, and is very revealing about the relationship between the government and the governed.[24] Flood-control projects often pass the problem downriver; dictators often provide bomb shelters for "essential personnel" but not for average civilians; costly "earthquake-proof" buildings are normally not used for low-income housing—and the list goes on. Despite the shortcomings, however, any full measure of urban resilience must take account of all such efforts to mitigate disaster a priori.[25]

This volume has also underplayed some aspects of the institutional response to disasters. There is a vast and growing literature on the management of disaster, but some of the cases described here do not focus on these aspects of urban resilience. Those accounts that do address institutional disaster management—in Mexico City, Oklahoma City, Los Angeles, Tangshan, and Beirut—still cannot convey the full range of issues. Thousands of books and articles have emphasized the behavior of rescue workers, the psychological effects of trauma on victims (and on frontline professionals trying to assist them), and the institutional arrangements that hasten recovery or cause it to lag. Close analysis of these factors—the micropractices of recovery—is also a necessary part of interpreting resilience.

Ultimately, the *resilient city* is a constructed phenomenon, not just in the literal sense that cities get reconstructed brick by brick, but in a broader cultural sense. Urban resilience is an interpretive framework proposed by local and national leaders and shaped and accepted by citizens in the wake of disaster. However equitable or unjust, efficient or untenable, that framework serves as the foundation upon which the society builds anew. "The Cities rise again," wrote Kipling—not due to a mysterious spontaneous force, but because people believe in them. Cities are not only the places in which we live and work and play, but also a demonstration of our ultimate faith in the human project, and in each other.

Conclusion

Notes

1. J. Eugene Haas et al., eds., *Reconstruction following Disaster* (Cambridge, Mass.: MIT Press, 1977).
2. Ibid., pp. 1–3.
3. Ibid., p. 3.
4. Ibid., pp. xxvi, 1, 3–5.
5. Described in the documentary *In Memoriam*, HBO, May 2002.
6. Chicago's Michael Bilandic learned this the hard way in 1979. Ten years earlier, New York mayor John Lindsay nearly suffered the same fate in his own reelection bid; Vincent J. Cannato, *The Ungovernable City: John Lindsay and His Struggle to Save New York* (New York: Basic, 2002), pp. 395–397.
7. The rhetoric of resilient cities shares a great deal with that of those cities built from scratch to serve as new capitals. Like the resilience phenomenon itself, the idea of designed capital cities is largely a product of the post-1800 era of the modern nation-state. The urban audacity to build a Washington, D.C., or a Canberra, New Delhi, or Islamabad—a spirit carried to the extreme by the construction of Brasilia and of several subsequent cities in Africa—reveals a peculiar value assigned to newness in the pursuit of international recognition, combined with a cultivated disdain for the overcrowded and morally suspect conditions of older cities. See Lawrence J. Vale, *Architecture, Power, and National Identity* (New Haven, Conn.: Yale University Press, 1992).
8. P. J. Crowley, Insurance Information Institute, quoted in Katherine Roth, "Getting Insured in New York Tougher—and Costlier—since Sept. 11," *Abilene Reporter-News*, 22 August 2002.
9. Anthony Flint, "Security Analysts Trying to Narrow List of Possible Targets," *Boston Globe*, 6 September 2002, p. A25.
10. Ron Jenkins, "New Oklahoma City Federal Building Opens for Business," *Boston Globe*, 9 December 2003, p. A21.
11. Ross Miller, "Out of the Blue: The Great Chicago Fire of 1871," in *Out of Ground Zero: Case Studies in Urban Reinvention*, ed. Joan Ockman (New York: Prestel, 2002), p. 50.
12. See Carola Hein, "Hiroshima: The Atomic Bomb and Kenzo Tange's Hiroshima Peace Center," in *Out of Ground Zero*, pp. 62–83.
13. There are exceptions, however. Large swaths of the center of Kuwait City remain unbuilt since these parcels are the sites of cemeteries. In Bangkok, significant center-city parcels have been withheld from development because they are regarded as cursed. For the most part, pluralist America lacks the common religious tradition of such Buddhist or Muslim cultures, and city officials have long ignored the claims of "sacred ground" expressed by minority voices. Still, ongoing efforts by Native American groups to

recognize the importance of burial grounds, as well as the long controversy over how to deal with the rediscovery of the large African Burial Ground in lower Manhattan (whose records were tragically destroyed by the World Trade Center collapse), suggest that debates over urban archaeology, urban development, and memorialization will continue to pose nagging questions.

14. Kevin Lynch, *What Time Is This Place* (Cambridge, Mass.: MIT Press, 1972), 3–4. See also Neil Hanson, *The Great Fire of London: In That Apocalyptic Year, 1666* (New York: Wiley, 2002).

15. Homer Hoyt, *One Hundred Years of Land Values in Chicago: The Relationship of the Growth of Chicago to the Rise of Its Land Values, 1830–1933* (Chicago: University of Chicago Press, 1933), pp. 101–102; William Cronon, *Nature's Metropolis: Chicago and the Great West* (New York: Norton, 1992), pp. 345–346.

16. Kevin Lynch, *Wasting Away* (San Francisco: Sierra Club, 1990), p. 109.

17. Cited in Amos Elon, *Jerusalem: City of Mirrors* (Boston: Little, Brown, 1989).

18. See Spiro Kostof, *The Third Rome, 1870–1950: Traffic and Glory* (Berkeley, Calif.: University Art Museum, 1973).

19. Ross Miller, *American Apocalypse: The Great Fire and the Myth of Chicago* (Chicago: University of Chicago Press, 2000); and Miller, "Out of the Blue," pp. 56–60.

20. Lynch, *Wasting Away*, pp. 109–110.

21. Timelines for these reconstructions are provided in Van Alen Institute, *Information Exchange: How Cities Renew, Rebuild, and Remember* (New York: Van Alen Institute, 2002).

22. Eugenie Ladner Birch, "From Flames to Flowers: The Role of Planning in Re-imaging the South Bronx," in *Imaging the City: Continuing Struggles and New Directions*, ed. Lawrence J. Vale and Sam Bass Warner, Jr. (New Brunswick, N.J.: Center for Urban Policy Research Press, 2001), pp. 57–93.

23. See, for example, Brent Ryan, "The Suburbanization of the Inner City," Ph.D. diss., Massachusetts Institute of Technology, 2002.

24. See Kenneth D. Rose, *One Nation Underground: The Fallout Shelter in American Culture* (New York: New York University Press, 2001); Laura McEnaney, *Civil Defense Begins at Home* (Princeton, N.J.: Princeton University Press, 2000); and Jennifer Leaning and Langley Keyes, eds., *The Counterfeit Ark: Crisis Relocation for Nuclear War* (Cambridge, Mass.: Ballinger, 1984). For a comparative study of civil defense policy, see Lawrence J. Vale, *The Limits of Civil Defence in the USA, Switzerland, Britain and the Soviet Union* (London: Macmillan, 1987).

25. See, for example, Raymond J. Burby et al., "Unleashing the Power of Planning to Create Disaster-Resistant Communities," *Journal of the American Planning Association* 65, no. 3 (Summer 1999): 247–258.

Appendix
Suggestions for Further Reading on Urban Disasters and Recovery

■ Given the great range and frequency of traumatic events in the history of cities worldwide, it is hardly surprising that the literature on urban disasters and their aftermaths is vast. What follows is little more than an introduction to that literature, an initial survey of some of the many books that have been written to document, analyze, and interpret the destruction and recovery of cities. This literature embodies an equally vast array of perspectives on the meaning of disaster, recovery, and resilience. Some authors have written about "lost cities" that linger on today only as ruins,[1] while others have taken a pragmatic preservationist stance, less concerned about the cause or meaning of disaster than about the urgent need to retain the heritage encoded in the fabric of threatened or destroyed cities.[2] In recent years both before and after the terrorist attacks of September 11, 2001—several projects (including this one) have attempted to set urban disasters in comparative perspective. The following is a sampling of these and other kinds of scholarship in the fluid and burgeoning field of urban destruction and renewal. Other suggestions for readings about specific types of disasters may be found on the Resilient City Web site: http://resilientcity.mit.edu.

The most wide-ranging single work on the aftermath of urban disasters is a three-volume research compendium entitled *Destruction and Reconstruction of Towns*, published in 1999 and 2000 by the International Commission for the History of Towns.[3] The commission, a diverse group of mostly European scholars, sought to "observe on a com-

357

parative level those behavioural patterns of the city population that were triggered by an unexpected physical destruction of cities, total or partial, and continued until the task of rebuilding was finished." Despite this broad aim, the report's editor correctly acknowledges that the contribution of these volumes provides "more information on destruction than on reconstruction" and concludes that questions about the latter "should be marked for research in the future."[4]

Cities and Catastrophes: Coping with Emergency in European History, an edited volume released in 2002, emerged from the Fifth International Conference on Urban History, held in Berlin in 2000. Like *Destruction and Reconstruction of Towns*, much of this volume covers premodern Europe, though some chapters do discuss nineteenth- and twentieth-century catastrophes. It addresses only "natural" disasters—especially earthquakes, fires, and floods—and also contains material on epidemic diseases and on the structure of relief efforts in eighteenth-century British North America.[5]

Other recent work has taken up the challenge to examine post-disaster recovery. Most notable is *Out of Ground Zero: Case Studies in Urban Reinvention*, which evolved out of a symposium organized by the Temple Hoyne Buell Center for the Study of American Architecture at Columbia University. Edited by Joan Ockman, this volume includes analyses of Lisbon following the earthquake of 1755 and Chicago after the Great Fire of 1871, and accounts of efforts to rebuild following the destruction of World War II in Rotterdam, Hiroshima, and Plymouth (UK) and to reconstruct Balkan cities after the "urbicide" of the 1990s. Similarly, New York's Van Alen Institute hosted an exhibition (with a follow-up catalog) illustrating comparatively how Beirut, Berlin, Kobe, Manchester, Oklahoma City, San Francisco, and Sarajevo have coped with major disasters of all kinds.[6] Other edited collections have brought together essays on disasters and recovery but paid little specific attention to cities, grouping accounts of urban fires and earthquakes together with widespread non-urban catastrophes such as the sinking of the *Titanic* and the *Exxon Valdez* oil spill.[7] The inimitable Mike Davis, in *Dead Cities*, ranges even further, assessing destruction from terrorism, global warming, riots, and "runaway capitalism."[8]

While these various volumes add a great deal to our understanding of how specific places coped with disaster, they were not expressly written to develop a theory of urban resilience. There is, nonetheless, an entire literature devoted to theorizing on "disaster" or "catastrophe" and to modeling "disaster response." Many authors have grappled with the interface between natural disasters and the human interventions that have enhanced the vulnerability of places, whether deliberately or by accident.[9] Others have stressed the impact of specific traumatic events on particular individuals, social groups, or communities.[10] Still others have emphasized the efforts to plan or prepare for potential disasters and to manage (and pay for) their aftermath,[11] or have emphasized the role of the media in disaster relief.[12]

Crucibles of Hazard: Mega-Cities and Disasters in Transition provides a broad introduction to the impacts of natural disasters on major urban areas. Edited by Rutgers University geography professor James K. Mitchell, the anthology considers the environmental risks posed by catastrophic earthquakes, storms, floods, and other events in a number of the world's cities and concludes that "[m]ega-city hazards are profuse, burdensome, symbolically potent, incompletely understood, and addressed by public policies that typically make use of just a few types of possible adjustment." As Mitchell puts it, "Urban hazards and disasters are becoming an interactive mix of natural, technological, and social events," in ways that affect more people, and make it difficult to isolate environmental hazards into separate types of phenomena. *Crucibles of Hazard* identifies a number of innovative policy opportunities that could reduce a city's risk exposure to environmental hazards, including capitalizing on the differential risk of hazards to combat trends toward urban uniformity; broadening the scope of hazard-based contingency planning models to enable "the public and private sectors of metropolitan areas . . . to take disjunctive events into account systematically and deliberately, not just as inconvenient disruptions of 'normalcy' "; and mobilizing the "symbolic value" of hazards "as fertile sources of metaphors and myths about appropriate human behaviour in an uncertain universe." The book examines Tokyo, Seoul, Dhaka, Sydney, London, Lima, Mexico City, San Francisco, Los Angeles, and Miami.[13]

Another useful overview is *The Vulnerability of Cities* by British geographer Mark Pelling. This book approaches the problems of natural disaster preparedness and response by examining what makes a particular city more or less resilient to disasters. Pelling uses three case studies—Bridgetown, Barbados; Georgetown, Guyana; and Santo Domingo, Dominican Republic—to explore the relationships among the ecological, political, and economic dimensions of urban development patterns. Using this information, the author identifies connections between chronic and catastrophic disasters and pinpoints adaptive potential as a key to the social resilience of cities to disaster.[14]

Much of the vast literature on disasters is, of course, tied specifically to particular times and places. As the chapters in this volume make clear, despite important patterns, each disaster generates its own interpretive framework, its own symbolism, and its own politics. Examining the richness of such social and cultural forces in other cities will provide ample material for future studies.

Notes

1. Paul G. Bahn, ed., *Lost Cities: 50 Discoveries in World Archaeology* (London: Weidenfeld and Nicolson, 1997).

2. Anthony M. Tung, *Preserving the World's Great Cities: The Destruction and Renewal of the Historic Metropolis* (New York: Clarkson Potter, 2001).

3. Martin Körner, *Destruction and Reconstruction of Towns: Topic, Statement of the Questions and the Results of Research*, vol. 3 (Bern: Haupt, 2000).

4 Ibid., pp. 77, 84.

5. Geneviève Massard-Guilbaud, Harold L. Platt, and Dieter Schott, eds., *Cities and Catastrophes: Coping with Emergency in European History/Villes et catastrophes: Réaction face à l'urgence dans l'histoire européenne* (Frankfurt am Main: Lang, 2002).

6. Joan Ockman, ed., *Out of Ground Zero: Case Studies in Urban Reinvention* (Munich and New York: Prestel, 2002); Raymond W. Gastil and Zoë Ryan, eds., *Information Exchange: How Cities Renew, Rebuild, and Remember* (New York: Van Alen Institute, 2002).

7. See, for example, Steven Biel, ed., *American Disasters* (New York: New York University Press, 2001); and Michael Barton, "Journalistic Gore: Disaster Reporting and Emotional Discourse in the *New York Times*, 1852–1956," in *An Emotional History of the United States*, ed. Peter N. Stearns and Jan Lewis (New York: New York University Press, 1998), pp. 155–172.

8. Mike Davis, *Dead Cities* (New York: New Press, 2002).

9. J. Eugene Haas et al., eds., *Reconstruction following Disaster* (Cambridge, Mass.: MIT Press, 1977); Kenneth Hewitt, ed., *Interpretations of Calamity* (Boston: Allen and Unwin, 1983); Ian Burton, Robert W. Kates, and Gilbert F. White, *The Environment as Hazard*, 2d ed. (New York: Guilford, 1993);

Risa I. Palm, *Natural Hazards: An Integrative Framework for Research and Planning* (Baltimore, Md.: Johns Hopkins University Press, 1990); Graham A. Tobin and Burrell R. Montz, *Natural Hazards: Explanation and Integration* (New York: Guilford, 1997).

10. Martha Wolfenstein, *Disaster: A Psychological Essay* (Glencoe, Ill.: Free Press, 1957); William Spangle and Associates, *Rebuilding after Earthquakes: Lessons from Planners* (Portola Valley, Calif.: William Spangle and Associates, 1991); Claire B. Rubin et al., *Community Recovery from a Major Natural Disaster* (Boulder: Institute for Behavioral Science, University of Colorado, 1985); Robert Bolin and Patricia Bolton, *Race, Religion, and Ethnicity in Disaster Recovery* (Boulder: Institute for Behavioral Science, University of Colorado, 1986); Mary B. Anderson and Peter J. Woodrow, *Rising from the Ashes: Development Strategies in Times of Disaster* (Boulder, Colo.: Westview/UNESCO, 1989).

11. Richard J. Healy, *Emergency and Disaster Planning* (New York: Wiley, 1969); H. Paul Friesema et al., *Aftermath: Communities after Natural Disaster* (Beverly Hills, Calif.: Sage, 1979); James D. Wright et al., *After the Clean-Up: Long-Range Effects of Natural Disasters* (Beverly Hills, Calif.: Sage, 1979); Mary Comerio, John D. Landis, and Yodan Rofé, *Post-Disaster Residential Rebuilding*, Working Paper 608 (Berkeley: University of California, Institute of Urban and Regional Development, 1994); Mary Comerio, *Disaster Hits Home: New Policy for Urban Housing Recovery* (Berkeley: University of California Press, 1998); U.S. Department of Housing and Urban Development, *HUD Disaster Recovery Guidebook: Promoting Recovery, Hope and a New Beginning* (Washington, D.C.: HUD, 1997); Rutherford H. Platt, *Disasters and Democracy: The Politics of Extreme Natural Events* (Washington, D.C.: Island Press, 1999); Neil Middleton and Phil O'Keefe, *Disaster and Development: The Politics of Humanitarian Aid* (London: Pluto, 1998); Jennifer Leaning and Langley Keyes, eds., *The Counterfeit Ark: Crisis Relocation for Nuclear War* (Cambridge, Mass.: Ballinger, 1984); Lawrence J. Vale, *The Limits of Civil Defence* (London: Macmillan, 1987).

12. Committee on Disasters and the Mass Media, *Disasters and the Mass Media: Proceedings of the Committee on Disasters and the Mass Media Workshop* (Washington, D.C.: National Academy of Sciences, 1980); Jonathan Benthall, *Disasters, Relief and the Media* (London: Tauris, 1993).

13. James K. Mitchell, ed., *Crucibles of Hazard: Mega-Cities and Disasters in Transition* (New York: United Nations University Press, 1999), pp. 473, 484, and 497.

14. Mark Pelling, *The Vulnerability of Cities: Natural Disasters and Social Resilience* (London: Earthscan, 2003).

Index

Beirut, downtown reconstructions in
(*continued*)
and political amnesia, 283–286, 296, 340
and port functions, 288, 290
post-1990, 282–286, 294–296
and property rights, 284
and religious groups, 281–283, 287, 294, 296
and restoration versus modernization, 284
and self-destruction myths, 285–286
and self-renewal myths, 286, 294
and SOLIDERE, 20, 282–284, 294–295
and urban versus rural culture, 285–286
Berlin, postwar reconstruction of
and the "barracks style," 124
and the Berlin Wall, 126, 128
and Bolz, Lothar, 123
and classicism, 122, 125, 133
as Cold War propaganda, 117–120, 126, 128, 350
cost of, 126–127
and decentralization, 124, 126
East German narrative of, 118, 122–124
as erasure of history, 17, 121
and the Ernst-Reuter-Siedlung, 125
and expropriation, 126
and the German Democratic Republic (GDR), 122, 127, 130–131, 133
in the Hansa quarter, 125–126, 128
and Hauptstadt Berlin design competition, 126
and "historical responsibility," 130–131
and housing, 125, 127–129
and infrastructure, 122
and Interbau, 125
and Khrushchev, Nikita, 127
and land use, 120–121
and mass assembly, 124
and memorials, 131
and modernism, 120, 122–126, 128–131
and nationalism, 123–124
and Nazi past, 5, 117, 119–121, 123–126, 130
as opportunity, 120
and pre-Nazi architectural traditions, 117, 120–121, 129–130
and resilience, 129

and reunification, 129–130
and the royal palace, 124, 130, 134
and rubble removal, 118, 128
and "rubble women," 118, 132
and scale of wartime destruction, 118
and Scharoun, Hans, 120, 126, 133
as the "second destruction," 129
and the second International Building Exhibition (IBA), 130, 133
similarities in, 127
and Stalinallee, 122, 125, 127–128
and Ulbricht, Walter, 124
Western architects of, 125
Western narrative of, 118, 125–126
Bhopal, industrial accident at, 6
Bierut, Bolesław, 137, 146–147, 149
biological weapons, 6–7, 323–324, 330
Birmingham, Alabama, 1963 church bombing in, 59
Bloomberg, Michael, 60
Boston
and fire of 1872, 345
urban renewal in, 7
Bradley, Tom, 304–305, 311
Budapest, population loss in, 3
Bulfinch, Charles, 112
Bush, George W., 90

capitalism (*see also* social structure)
and class discrimination, 32
and communication networks, 314
and corporate order, 44
and "creative destruction," 15, 31, 78, 341
and disaster narrative, 15, 31–32, 40
and global disparity, 47
and innovation, 31
and minority discrimination, 32
and resilience, 5, 15, 31–32, 40, 342, 347
and Schumpeter, Joseph, 78–79
spread of, 5
and urban development, 31
and World Trade Center attack, 47
capital punishment, 59
chemical weapons, 6–7
use of at Halabja, Iraq, 6
Chicago, fire of 1871 at, 4, 6
and aid organizations, 53

as result of disaster, 4, 9

Erikson, Kai, 31

Franco, Francisco, 18, 159, 161, 163–164,
    168, 171, 173–174, 343, 351
Freud, Sigmund, 35, 183–184

Gernika, reconstruction of
    and anniversary of 1987, 173–174
    and Basque autonomy, 161–162, 169,
        173–174
    and Basque identity, 18, 159–161, 163,
        171–173, 174–175, 343, 351
    and Basque National Party (PNV), 161,
        174
    and Basque resistance movement, 172–
        173, 176
    and censorship, 161, 163, 168–169
    and Condor Legion destruction of, 159,
        161–162
    and "cultural resilience," 160, 171–177
    and democratization, 169
    designing for, 164–165
    and "emotional resilience," 160, 167–
        171, 176
    and Euzkadi ta Askatasuna (ETA) 172
    and Franco, Francisco, 18, 159, 161, 163–
        164, 168, 171, 173–174, 343, 351
    and German apology, 170–171
    and Gernika Gogoratuz, 170–171, 174,
        178
    and housing, 165, 167
    and infrastructure, 166–167
    and King Juan Carlos, 169
    and memorialization, 168–170, 172, 173
    and Organization for Devastated
        Regions (ODR), 165–166
    and the peace movement, 170–171, 174–
        176
    and the Peace Museum, 174–175
    and "physical resilience," 160, 164–167,
        176
    and Picasso's *Guernica*, 18, 159–160, 168–
        170, 177
    and population growth, 161, 167
    and prisoner labor, 165
    as propaganda, 165
    and scale of destruction, 162–163

and tourism, 175
and toxic narrative, 167, 170
and the Tree of Gernika, 162
Giuliani, Rudolph, 62, 88, 90, 339
Goma, volcanic destruction of, 4
    scale of, 10
Gomułka, Władysław, 153
Gotō Shimpei, 221
Guernica (*see* Gernika)

Halabja, Iraq, chemical attack at, 6
Halifax, 1917 ship explosion at, 348–349
Hillman, James, 184
Hiroshima
    destructive scale of nuclear attack, 10
    and disaster fiction, 82
    and Hiroshima Peace Center, 227–228,
        345
    and memorialization, 227, 234
    nuclear attack at, 4, 6, 224
Hitler, Adolf, 5, 120, 123, 159, 161
Hurva Synagogue, 18, 187, 200–204, 209–
    210
Hussein, Saddam, building programs
    and, 5

immigration, in American culture, 38, 79–
    80, 83
insurance industry, 5, 12, 343
Ishikawa Hideaki, 226

Japan, post-disaster reconstruction in
    and American occupation, 224, 230,
        234
    and architecture, 214–215, 217, 230
    consistency of, 231
    costs of, 213
    and deliberate disaster, 213, 215–216,
        228–230
    and education, 230
    and fire prevention, 214
    and industrialization, 213, 216
    and legal systems, 230
    and Meiji Restoration, 213, 216, 219–
        220
    and memorialization, 227, 234
    and modernization, 213, 219–220, 230–
        231

in disaster fiction, 75–76, 79–88
and economic decline, 83, 87, 351
growth of, 78, 91
and immigration, 79–80, 83
infrastructure of, 314
and Le Corbusier, 78
and mass media, 75
memorials in, 69
and modernism, 78
and pre-2001 disasters, 69, 77, 79
and racism, 80
and resilience, 88, 90–91
symbolism of, 86
Nichols, Terry, 59
Norick, Ron, 64
nuclear accidents, at Chernobyl, 6
nuclear weapons
fallout from, 7
use of, 4, 6
Nyala, Sudan, starvation at, 6

Oklahoma City, Murrah Federal Building
attack
and American identity, 66
and the arts, 64
and blame, 66
commodification of, 63, 66
and the death penalty, 59
destructive scale of, 10
and education, 63
and Fifth street closure, 60
and heroism, 14, 61
and mass media, 62, 67
and McVeigh, Timothy, 59
memorializing of, 13, 14–15, 55, 58, 62–
63, 65, 69, 344
and the Murrah "footprint," 60
and Nichols, Terry, 59
and Norick, Ron, 64
and Oklahoma City National
Memorial, 70, 349
and Oklahoma City National
Memorial Foundation, 60
and outreach to September 11 victims,
72
and patriotism, 14
psychological effects of, 69
and religion, 14, 341

and resilience, 14–15, 61, 341
and use of site, 61, 349
*Out of Ground Zero: Case Studies in
Urban Reinvention*, 358

Partido Revolucionario Institucional
(PRI), 264, 270, 273–274, 276, 340
Pataki, George E., 47
Picasso, Pablo, 18, 159–160, 168–170, 177
Pompeii
destruction of, 4, 6
and Pliny, 339
tourism at, 4
pre-Columbian settlements
abandonment of, 4
and education, 4
and tourism, 4

Rebuild L.A., 21, 304–306, 308, 341
religion
in American culture, 34, 74, 79
and ancient city design, 183–184
and architecture, 188, 204
and death, 184
and disaster fiction, 74
and disaster narrative, 34, 79
and eternity, 184
and existentialism, 184
and Freud, 183–184
and Hillman, James, 184
and memorializing disaster, 14
and resilience, 14, 183, 186, 204, 347,
354
and sacrifice, 188
and space, 186
and time, 186
remembrance (*see* memorializing
disaster)
resilience
versus abandonment, 3–4, 351, 357
and aid, 5, 13, 342–343
in American culture, 28, 32, 34, 46, 74,
79–80
and architecture, 13, 18, 186, 204
and biology, 183
and blame, 39, 299, 340
and capitalism, 5, 15, 31–32, 40, 342, 347
and capitol building, 354

and memorializing United flight 93, 71–72

in national memory, 71

and war against terrorism, 71

Silverstein, Larry, 89

social structure

and disaster narrative, 32, 34, 39, 51, 339–340, 348, 353

and fear, 39

and hostility, 38–39

and immigration, 38

and modernization, 39

and resilience, 12, 14, 19, 27, 39, 253, 262, 267, 273, 339–340, 348, 353

SOLIDERE, 20, 282–284, 294–295

Speer, Albert, 5, 120, 123, 125

Springsteen, Bruce, 47–48

Tangshan, post-1976 earthquake reconstruction of

and academic disaster analysis, 244–245

and building technology, 247

and censorship, 20, 236–237, 241–243, 251

and Comprehensive Plan of Tangshan (1976), 244–245

costs of, 248

counter-narratives of, 242–243

and Cultural Revolution, 238–240

and decentralization, 245–246

and disaster response planning, 246

and domestic aid, 240

and economic liberalization, 20, 247, 249–250

failures of, 248

and foreign aid, 20, 239, 250, 343

and heroism, 240–242

and housing, 247–249

and industry, 237, 246

and infrastructure, 245

and land use, 245–246, 248–249

and Maoist ideology, 237–245, 248, 250

and Maoist legacy, 240

and Maoist urban development, 238

and Maoist versus post-Maoist agendas, 250

and mass mobilization, 239–240

and memorialization, 249

and modernization, 246, 348

and natural resources, 237, 246

and open space, 245

party control of, 237, 240, 250–251

and People's Liberation Army, 235, 240–242

and political reform, 20, 244–245, 250, 338, 348

and relocation debate, 246

and scale of destruction, 4, 6, 10, 235–236, 244, 251

and self-reliance, 20, 239, 241, 250

and temporary shelter, 248

terrorism, 4

and communications disaster, 323–324

and intelligence, 353

and memorialization, 65, 345

and symbolism, 8

the war against, 71

and weapons, 6

Timgad, 4

Tokyo, post-disaster reconstruction in

and American occupation, 225–226

and architecture, 217–218

and canal construction, 218

and class discrimination, 218

and class polarization, 223, 233

compared with postwar reconstruction of Berlin, 226

and decentralization, 223, 226

and deliberate disaster, 214

and destructive scale of 1923 earthquake, 10

after earthquake of 1923, 10, 217, 221–223

and fire prevention, 216–218, 220, 222, 228

in Ginza area, 216–217, 233

and Gotō Shimpei, 221

and housing, 226

and industrialization, 215

and infrastructure, 218, 221–222, 231

and Ishikawa Hideaki, 226

and land readjustment, 221–222, 227, 346

and Matsuda Michiyuki, 218

and Meiji restoration, 215, 220

World Trade Center attack (*continued*)
   and Bloomberg, Michael, 60
   and Bush, George W., 90
   and capitalism, 47–48, 54, 59, 320
   commodification of, 16, 74
   and counter-narratives, 48
   and cultural expectations, 48
   and debris, 68, 89
   and decentralization, 21, 324, 333, 349
   and destiny, 16
   destructive scale of, 10
   and disaster fiction, 75, 86
   and divisive rhetoric, 66, 92
   economic effects of, 11, 48
   and fatalism, 47, 59
   and fear, 59
   and federal compensation, 67
   and the "Freedom Tower," 48–49, 89–90
   and Giuliani, Rudolph, 62, 88, 90, 339
   and *Ground Zero*, 59, 339
   and heroism, 46, 61, 67
   and history, 46
   and human remains, 60
   and insurance industry, 343
   and Libeskind, Daniel, 48–49, 62, 88–90
   and local businesses, 11
   and looting, 74
   and Lower Manhattan Development Corporation, 62, 88–89
   and market demands, 346
   and mass media, 46, 62, 68
   memorializing of, 16, 47, 55, 58, 61–62, 64, 67, 71, 88–89, 344, 346
   narrative of, 11, 28, 46 47, 61, 341
   and the *New York Times*, 48, 62, 64–65
   and "official memory," 71
   and optimism, 46
   and Pataki, George E., 47
   and patriotism, 90
   and politics, 46, 90, 346
   and the Port Authority, 91
   psychological impact of, 60, 69
   and reconstruction, 16, 48–49, 88–91
   and *Reflecting Absence*, 89
   and rescue efforts, 46
   and resilience, 16, 61, 90
   and Silverstein, Larry, 89
   and social structure, 15, 46, 346
   and Springsteen, Bruce, 47–48
   symbolism of, 11, 59, 62, 320
   and telecommunications, 320–321, 326–327, 350
   and terrorism, 46
   and tourism, 11, 60
   and transportation, 11, 60, 91, 317, 319–320, 349
   and unity, 47, 66
   and urban development, 91
   and the *Washington Post*, 67
   and the working class, 47
World War II, 4, 17, 19, 117–118, 135, 224–225, 227, 229

Yokohama, earthquake of 1923 at
   destructive scale of, 10